KAIRAT ZAKIRYANOV

# UNDER THE WOLF'S NEST.
# A TURKIC RHAPSODY

First published in 2012
by Hertfordshire Press

Suite 125, 43 Bedford Street
Covent Garden, WC2R 9HA, United Kingdom
E-mail: publisher@ocamagazine.com
www.hertfordshirepress.com
© Kairat Zakiryanov

Translators: Dauren Galymjanuly,
Gulbaram Kulakhmetova, Seidanova Assiya
Editor: Alimkhanov Ye.
Proof editor: Robin Thomson
Series editor: Anastacia Lee
Cover & Layout: Victoria Rodionova

British Library Catalogue in Publication Data
A catalogue record for this book is available from the British Library
Library of Congress in Publication Data

ISBN 978-0-9574807-2-8

Printed in Turkey by IMAK OFSET

HERTFORDSHIRE PRESS

# KAIRAT KHAIRULLINOVICH ZAKIRYANOV

Professor Kairat Zakiryanov is an award-winning Kazakh author and academic whose previous books include *The Turkic Saga of Genghis Khan*, and *Secret Legends of the Kazakhs*. He holds doctorates in education, mathematics and physics, and is President of the Kazakh Academy of Sport and Tourism. He was born on the banks of the Irtysh river, in the ancient ancestral lands of the Sumerians, in the Eastern Kazakhstan oblast.

# CONTENTS

*- Alfred Weber: "...world history was created to the accompaniment of the strategic cavalry of the vast mass of nomads..."*

*- To my dear Marziya, the person on whom I can rely, my friend and partner in all my affairs, I dedicate this work.*
*May the spirits of heaven and our ancestors protect her.*

# Under the Wolf's Nest. A Turkic Rhapsody

Who are we, the Kazakhs? Are we the descendants of wild barbarians who could only destroy the fruits of other civilisations, and had no written language or literary or cultural monuments of our own? Or are we rather a nation that nurtured such outstanding figures of the past as Tomyris, Attila, Aristotle, al-Farabi, Genghis Khan, Kүltegin[1] and others?

This book is an attempt to restore historical justice to nomadic civilisations in general, and to the Kazakh nation in particular.

# INSTEAD OF A PREFACE

The rich folk heritage of the Kazakh people has retained the symbolic forms of expression used by our distant ancestors. A 21st-century descendant, reading the lines

*Qyzym Qyrymda, ulym Rumda.*
*Barar zherim Balqn tau.*
*Ol da bizdin vargan tau*

might be puzzled as to the intended meaning. But he or she would gain a strong sense of the vivid imagination that our ancestors had.

In this passage the author speaks of his daughter, who is in the Crimea; of his son, in Rum (then the Byzantine Empire, covering modern Greece and Asia Minor); and of himself, now making his way towards the Balkans, a region he has trodden many times before.

We who read this today are children of the 20th century, brought up in a closed country called the Soviet Union, who never had any possibility of travelling beyond its borders, and who came to believe that this situation had always prevailed, even in the distant past. Moreover, the rigid ideological clichés of the recent era dictated to us unequivocally that our ancestors had been uneducated barbarians without culture or literature, capable of nothing but grazing their countless herds on the vast Eurasian steppes and destroying the fruits of foreign civilizations. On top of that, any reference to national self-sufficiency was remorselessly eradicated from our consciousness.

A glance today at a world encyclopaedia, however, such as that published by Bodo Harenberg, shows that Eurasian steppe nomads known as the Hyksos[2] came to Egypt in the 18th century BC and ruled there for 150 years, while at about the same time, nomads of Shang[3] stock created the first Yin dynasty in China. Meanwhile another body of nomadic groups settled on the Iranian plateau and established, successively, the Achaemenid, Arshahid[4] and other dynasties in that land. Even Babylon was ruled by the Scythians of King Madyas[5] for 28 years.

So, who were these mysterious strangers who succeeded in conquering indigenous settled peoples, and who possessed their own high culture? And who inhabited, at that time, the territory of today's Kazakhstan? Until recently it was believed that the Kazakhs were migrants in their own lands, who came to what is now Kazakhstan only in the fifth century from somewhere to the east, while the laurel wreaths of the conquerors of Iran, Egypt, China, India and elsewhere were awarded to some mythical Indo-European or Indo-Iranian group that was supposedly an autochthonous population of the lands of modern Kazakhstan.

Thanks to the work of an anthropologist of world repute, our fellow-countryman Orazak Ismagulov, we now know that the territory of Kazakhstan has been populated by the same clans and tribes as have lived here down to the present day since at least 2,000 years BC. Accordingly, the mysterious Hyksos, the unknown Parsis and the powerful Shangs, who emanated from the territory of Kazakhstan and established the Hyksos' capital Avaris[6] on the banks of the Nile, great Persia in the Middle East and the Yin civilization in China, were the ancestors of today's Kazakh tribes.

One might now wonder why our ancestors were not satisfied with the unending expanses of the steppe and what they were searching for on those unknown continents. One explanation has been found in the writings of German philosophers and classicists, revived through the selfless labours of the Kazakh scholar Zhumazhan Bayzhumin, in which the notion of the formation of class societies, states and civilisations through an expansionist or conquering impulse had been substantiated back in the 19th century.

Consistent with this idea, our ancestors, nomadic breeders with countless flocks, would from time to time become cramped even on the wide steppe, and as a result of the shortage of pasturing land, stronger tribes would force weaker groups from their lands and create, in the words of the Roman historian Pompeius Trogus,[7] "exules Scytharum" or exiles of the Scythians. In turn, the dispossessed tribes would then conquer new territories for themselves. The weaker among their steppe kinsmen, these tribes were nevertheless far superior to the settled farmers of China, India, Iran and Egypt and the inhabitants of the European forests in strength. With this advantage they formed new state structures and created what are now ancient civilisations in these lands.

There are many examples. In the Middle Ages, all of Spain and not just one of its provinces was known as Andalusia[8]. The Kazakh word *anda* means "out there, far away", and this was the name – Anda Ulys or "distant country" – that our ancestors gave to the state they founded on the faraway Iberian Peninsula. Another state, established in the fifth century BC on the territory of modern Vietnam, was known by the Turks as Aulaq, which also has the meaning of "distant, remote." In modern Turkey, Germany is still called Almania. As is generally known, Kazakhs call their favourite spectacle, a 50-kilometre horse race, the *alaman bayga*.

Examples of the Kazakh ancestors' influence on the wider world can indeed be numbered in the hundreds. My attempt to generalise and synthesise individual observations and examples now forms the basis of the present book.

I would like to express my sincere gratitude to the distinguished Turcologist Marat Uatqan for the many meetings and discussions that gave me much of the impetus to write this book. My heartfelt thanks are also due to the Russian researchers Yu. Drozdov and A. Abrashkin, whose works strengthened my confidence that I was right to pursue this project.

As concerns the opinions of academic historians, the former Dean of the Faculty of History of the Kazakh National University, named Al-Farabi and Doctor of Historical Sciences, Zhaken Taimagambetov, summed the matter up clearly and unequivocally. On reading the book, he commented that not only are my investigations not at variance with common sense, but they also represent areas of some interest for historical research.

# THE MUSEUM OF HISTORY AT THE KAZAKH ACADEMY OF SPORT AND TOURISM; OR, A HISTORY ADVOCATED BY MATHEMATICS

Visitors to our academy are always surprised that my office and conference room look more like a historical museum of the nomadic peoples.

Indeed, a number of paintings by various artists are on display in the Academic Council's conference room at the Kazakh Academy of Sport and Tourism, and I played a part in creating the ideas and subject for these works. The aim was to recreate, in art, something of the rich history that has come down to us from our illustrious ancestors. Significantly, one of the paintings portrays Tomyris,[9] ruler of the Massagetae, while another depicts Attila[10], the outstanding leader of the Huns.

Delving into history can often bring surprises. Suffice it to recall the episode in which Tomyris routed Cyrus II the Great[11], the founder of Great Persia (a state that would not have been foreign for the nomads), who had come, apparently, to increase his holdings in the steppes of Dasht-i-Qypshaq[12]. And Tomyris inflicted a crushing defeat on him, then, before decapitating him, uttered her momentous words: "You dreamed of drinking our blood, so now choke on your own!" Filling a waterskin with blood, she then sank the head of the defeated Cyrus into it. Just think of it: this was the head of the conqueror to whom the mighty powers of Assyria, Media, Palestine, Phoenicia, Lydia, Sogdiana, Bactria and many others had been subjected. Thus, I repeat, one of the pictures is dedicated to Tomyris.

Another canvas depicts the great forefather of the nomads, Attila 'the Hun'. The picture retells the story portrayed so often by Hollywood, and in the works of the painter Raphael, in which Attila comes to Rome and the Pope approaches him to beg him not to harm the Eternal City. While I have added an element of interpretation, essentially the historical version has been artistically recreated and an image of the Pope on his knees, begging Attila to save Rome now exists. This picture is reproduced on the cover of my book, of which I will talk more later. I will not say that this was an easy decision. Putting this image of the begging Pope on the cover of the book caused me a considerable internal struggle, but ultimately the pursuit of historical truth prevailed for both myself and the artist, Zhomart Ibrayev.

When people visit our exhibition  I always tell them that this was the only time in history when the Pope was on his knees not before God but before a man. And this man was our great ancestor. That is who we are - the nation of the Kazakhs!

A further large painting is devoted to Genghis Khan, and it illustrates his traditional practice, before making the most important and far-reaching decisions, of climbing to the top of a mountain in complete solitude and asking the Eternally Blue Sky[13] and its Master Tengri[14] to grant victory to him. Genghis Khan was a great man who could stand on his knees for a whole day, or two days, or a week, waiting for a divine sign from the Great Tengri and attempting no actions until it came. But once he had received the approval of Heaven, Genghis Khan had no match among all the rulers in the world.

A number of other canvases have also been created on my initiative and convey, as it were, a strong educating energy. It has become a tradition here for our first-year students to visit this room, and for me, the rector of the university, to act as a historian and guide, revealing to them the subjects of the paintings and explaining the intricate events of our rich past.

On more than one occasion, I might say, people came to me offering to sell these paintings or to display them in various art galleries, with one such proposal even coming from our young capital, Astana. I cannot part with them, however, for the special reason, in my view, that they serve a significant and very positive educational purpose here.

There are certain representatives of formal historical science who consider my passion for history and the results obtained to be amateurish. My response to this is that time will tell; in due course we will all inevitably be judged and our works put into perspective.

I would like to say that I have succeeded as a mathematician, and cannot pretend not to be proud that Zakiryanov's theorem[15] can be found in encyclopaedias of mathematics. This theorem ranks alongside those of prominent 20th-century American mathematicians such as Bass and Milnor and the renowned French mathematician JP Serra. It is my belief, however, that every person born on this earth has been given many gifts by God. One needs only to "figure out" these talents in oneself and to realise them as much as possible. I could, of course, have gone on to solve another mathematical problem. But destiny decreed differently.

At a certain time an exceptional man who has played a decisive part in the path of my life, Erezhep Alkhairovich Mambetkaziev, then head of the Ust-Kamenogorsk Pedagogical Institute, where I was also working, persuaded me to join his team and to devote myself entirely to the establishment of a university in Eastern Kazakhstan. I made my choice and have never regretted it. Later I became head of this university, and was then given the post of deputy governor of the Eastern Kazakhstan region. After this I worked for the administration of the President of Kazakhstan for three years – alongside a wonderful man who had inherited the best traditions of the rulers of the Great Steppe, Nursultan Abishevich Nazarbayev. Today I regard those years as a time for accumulation of both knowledge and experience – a time of personal self-determination or even, as Pushkin might have said, a time of *samostoyanie* or standing in one's true self . Today I strive to put these valuable gifts to their most effective use in my position as the head of a university of sport.

I think of the Minister of Education of our young country, Krymbek Kusherbayev, with gratitude, for it was talking with him that motivated me to think seriously about the question of who we, the Kazakhs, are and what our place is within the history of civilisations.

Whether one looks at the distant past or more recent history, the Kazakhs were always a great nation. Today it is vital to revive this patriotic feeling, which must convince our nation that not only can and should we become one of the world's 50 most developed countries, as our President keeps saying, but that we are in fact worthy of far more.

The role of sport in this sacred mission cannot, in my opinion, be overestimated. I might also say that it is in many respects thanks to sport that a genetic and ancestral memory has been awoken in me. It might also not be an exaggeration to say that until I was forty I tended to identify myself rather as Russian. The Russian language and Russian culture, literature and traditions were close to me; I had and still have many Russian friends. In this connection, indeed, I would like to offer my own interpretation of the implicit affinity of the Kazakhs to the Russians and our inclination towards and, so to speak, inner acceptance of the Russian language. A number of sources indicate, as it happens, that Turkic elements make up between 30 and 50 per cent of the vocabulary of Russian. Many of the Russian intelligentsia wonder why it is that Russia by no means always reaches an understanding with its neighbours from the former USSR – except with Kazakhstan. Why is Russia so close to Kazakhstan? Why are the Kazakhs the only nation of the former Soviet Union that speaks Russian without a foreign accent? In what follows I will try to give a detailed answer to these complicated questions.

Recently, a number of serious studies have appeared with the hypothesis that Russian history did not begin in the ninth century with Kievan Rus' but rather has far deeper roots, and also that the Sakas of the Scythians, who are now considered to be the ancestors of the Turkic peoples (and of the Kazakhs in particular) are also the ancestors of the Russian people (see for example, A. Abrashkin: *Skifskaia Rus'*, Veche, 2008). In a word, the ancient history of the modern Russians and Kazakhs is a common one, but sadly one that is little studied. It offends me, for example, at international forums and sports contests when Americans and Europeans do not recognise us Kazakhs as an independent nation with its own ancient history. They tend to demand: "Kazakhs? Who are they – Russia or China?" This has evidently also become one of the incentives that made me think more deeply of my nation's past, and these results-orientated searches have led me to unexpected results that I have systematised over several years and then finally released.

Much remains to be done, but I already have evidence showing that our ancestors played a direct part in the formation of the great Chinese Empire and Chinese civilisation; they created Chinese imperial dynasties such as the Yin, Zhou, T'ang, Liao and Yuan.[16] The data I have indicates that the Yin dynasty was created by the Matay Kazakhs[17], the Zhou was ruled by Kete Kazakhs,[18] the Tang by the Argyn[19] and the Liao and Yuan by the Kete and Matay. But then, in order to rule a great country and a great people, it is essential above all that one carries historical greatness in oneself.

Furthermore, I recently discovered that our ancestors could also be found among the Egyptian pharaohs. In the early second millennium BC, for example, people from the Caspian and Black Sea steppes established a powerful state in Asia Minor, Mitanni,[20] that also ruled over Egypt. A little later, Egypt was governed by the Hyksos *siyrshy*,[21] who also hailed from the steppes of Kazakhstan. From the second millennium BC at least, our ancestors lived and created great civilisations in the lands of modern China, Egypt, Turkey, Iran, India, Iraq and Europe: states that included the Shang kingdom, Sumer, Persia, the Roman and Byzantine Empires, the state of the Goths, the Balti and others.

Meanwhile, who were the people that hid under the enigmatic name of the Huns? Who were the "German" tribes that shattered the Eternal City, Rome, in the middle of the fifth century? Who were among the originators of France? And who, by ethnic origin, were Alexander the Great, Jesus Christ, Arthur, king of what would become Great Britain, and Muhammad, the Prophet of all Muslims?

These difficult questions and stupendous facts are what prompted me to engage with history very seriously. This in turn is what influenced the displays in the conference room of the university of sport and the rector's office in which I work.

# AT THE CRADLE
# OF A GREAT NATION

## TURKIC MONGOLIA IN THE 12TH CENTURY

Genghis Khan has been recognised by UNESCO as one of the outstanding men of the second millennium. But what was his lineage? What people were concealed behind the name of the Mongols in the 13th century?

There is a proverb: a picture paints a thousand words. For me the problem concerned the fact that, despite the abundance of historical facts available, it was almost impossible to establish the origin of the Great World Terror, Genghis Khan, clearly and without doubt. An example of this difficulty can be seen in an interesting episode that took place while the Merkit Prince[22], newly married to Oelun[23], Genghis Khan's future mother, was driving her home with him as his lawful wife. It so happened that the future father of Genghis, who was out hunting, saw her by chance after looking under the canopy of her cart, and was struck by her unearthly beauty. Without skipping a beat he rushed to his camp, called for his brothers to help him, and abducted the beautiful woman. A version of the story exists in which Oelun was already pregnant with a child of a Merkit warrior. If this were the case, however, given that today's Merkits are part of the modern Kazakh people and are found among Kazakh Abak-kereys, this episode is not of paramount importance for us, as the descendants, in historical terms.

A later episode involved Genghis Khan himself. When he was already married to Borte, the Merkits, mindful of the long-standing insult, stole her in revenge and gave her to the brother of that Merkit warrior whose wife had been stolen by Genghis Khan's father. The question of who was the father of Genghis Khan's eldest son, Joshi Khan, remains unanswered; nevertheless, after careful research, I was able to give quite convincing arguments in my book *The Turkic Saga of Genghis Khan* in favour of Joshi Khan being the son of Genghis. Uncovering the details of such intimate events that happened 800 years ago is a difficult task, but not impossible.

For me, however, another question was also important. Who, precisely, were the people who lived at the foot of Burhan Khaldun[24] mountain, at the waterhead of the three great rivers Onon, Tuul and Kerulen[25], in the 12th century, the era of Genghis Khan's appearance (which was about 1162)?

Again, it is important in historical terms to be able to ascertain the nationality of the people living in those places. And if it is established that representatives of the modern Kazakh tribes were living in those places at that time, this will provide the final answer to the question I have raised. In my view, the methodological solution to the problem lay in the clarification of this issue. For this reason I had to visit those places personally and finally clarify the question of exactly what people then lived in the lands of what today is Mongolia.

To be sure, before setting off for these places myself I had examined all available historical and archival sources and met and held detailed discussions with the scholars of the Mongolian Academy of Sciences who deal with these questions. In my hands were rare, indeed unique books and materials, such as the results of the 1990 population census of Mongolia. For this, a large group of interviewers had questioned every resident of the country on the subject of their origin and tribal affiliation.

Here, unlike the Mongolian academics, I have drawn attention to the fact that the number of tribes to which the Mongols of the 21st century belong runs into the hundreds – so far 769 tribes have been counted. In the times of Genghis Khan, however, only some 70 tribes lived there. So how did this tenfold increase come about?

I put the direct question to the Doctor of Historical Sciences, Professor Bayar and the Doctor of Philological Science, Professor Dalantay Tseren Sodnom, both of the Mongolian Academy of Sciences, that if one accepts their own data, 40 *tumen* (units of ten thousand soldiers) lived in Mongolia at the time of Genghis Khan. The latter took 34 of these westward with him, leaving only six *tumen* in Mongolia (supposedly of Mongolian soldiers), who started resisting four Oirat *tumen*[26]. And it was these six *tumen* who, losing the fight against the Oirats, called on Manchurian tribes[27] for aid; these came in due course and assisted.

Now the question arises of what happened next to these tribes. In any case, six *tumen* meant a force of 60,000 men, who would have had to face up to a million-strong Manchurian army on the hunt for good lands and rich pastures – and the same army that ruled in umpteenth China!

Naturally, the tribes that remained in Mongolia simply became assimilated into the Tungus[28] Manchurians there. Thinking in my capacity as a mathematician, I have thus derived a formula: one may equate the Kazakhs of the 21st century with the Mongols of Genghis Khan, and can likewise equate the Mongols of modern Mongolia with the Tungus-Manchurian tribes of the 12th century.

And so, to prove to myself the correctness of my hypotheses, I made this journey, which confirmed for me my most daring suppositions. By way of an example, the professor of philology mentioned above, Dr Tseren Sodnom, admitted to me that modern Mongols do not understand the language of *The Secret History of the Mongols*,[29] the most important native source on the history of Genghis Khan, dating from 1240. He further maintains that modern Mongols have lost the language of the Mongols of Genghis Khan. At the same time, however, the historian Kalibek Danyarov, himself a great patriot of the Kazakh nation, claims in his major work *Istoria Chingiskhana* (Almaty, 2001) that that unique historical document contains up to forty per cent of the words used in the modern Kazakh language.

My visit to Mongolia has thus only reinforced my belief that my views are correct and given me additional strength to master a tortuous path through the labyrinths of history and memory.

During my expedition a number of other very interesting discoveries were also made. Some 600 kilometres from Ulaanbaatar, or 25 km from the course of the Kerulen river, is a mineral spring on the spot where Genghis Khan's summer residence once stood. After the collapse of the Soviet Union and once Mongolia had gained its proper sovereignty, a monument was erected here in the form of a gigantic stone dotted with petroglyphs. Looking closely, I realised that the bulk of these characters are the seals or *tamgas*[30] of most of the Kazakh tribes. I counted altogether 45 characters that are still considered today to be the distinguishing attributes and symbols of the Kazakh tribes. When I asked Dr Bayar about these characters he replied that they had been collected from all over Mongolia by an archaeologist friend and carefully transferred to the stone. I then said to Dr Bayar that we, the people of Kazakhstan, should erect a monument in honour of his friend since these petroglyphs were implicit evidence that at least 45 Kazakh tribes had lived in what is now Mongolia and left these stone characters as tokens of their presence there.

Recently I watched a blockbuster film, a Russian-Mongol-US collaboration, on the subject of Genghis Khan in which it was claimed that Kazakh tribes came to Mongolia in the 12th century and suffered defeat. This is a distortion of the historical truth. The territory of modern Mongolia was at that time the ancestral land of many of today's Kazakh tribes. Today I am certain – and my confidence is confirmed by historical facts – that since at least the 4th century BC the Turkic and Kazakh tribes have always lived to the north of the Yellow River. To its south lived the Chinese. This was described, incidentally, by the ancient Greek geographer Ptolemy. The entire territory of Mongolia and northern China has always been, including at the time of the rise of Genghis Khan, the ancestral land of many Kazakh tribes – the Naiman, Kongyrat, Koralas, Zhalayir, Kerey, Merkit[31] and others. In other words, before the Common Era more than half of the present-day Kazakh tribes lived in what is now Mongolia and northern China. Incidentally, the Chinese version of the name of the

Yellow River (Hwang Ho) sounded, in the Turkic and Kazakh languages, like Kyyanki – literally 'wild, unrestrained'. And such is this appearance of this great river of the Turks.

From here the Kazakh tribes mostly went with Genghis Khan to the West. The lands they vacated were quickly filled by Tungus-Manchurian tribes, which absorbed the small number of Kazakh tribes that remained in Mongolia (Kerei, Ongut, Zhalair etc), whom Genghis Khan had intended to conquer Beijing. In number these were not more than four *tumen*.[32] Their assimilation was inevitable, and it was to have a determining effect on the ethnic basis of modern Mongolia.

As for a study of the nature of Tungus-Manchurian tribes themselves, happy coincidence helped me here again. In February, 2009, I visited Harbin[33]. Some 60 kilometres from here is a museum of the Manchurian Jin dynasty, which ruled China before the rise of Genghis Khan.

Concerning the tribes of Tungus-Manchurian origin the following should be noted: the Manchurians, who were previously known as the Dzhurdzhen[34], are today found primarily in the Kazakh ethnos. There is, for example, a large tribal association within the modern Naiman called the Teristamagaly, which in turn has a sub-tribe, the Shursheit. This subgroup is made up of ethnic Dzhurdzhen who were assimilated by the Naiman during the formation of their community. I consider that the Manchurian tribes also had a Turkic basis.

In his book *Kul'tura chzhurdzheney i gosudarstva Tszin'* [The culture of the Chzhurdzhen and the state of Jin] (Moscow, 1997) M.V. Vorobyev notes a large Turkic contribution to the Chzhurdzhen culture, a similarity between the ethnic types of the Turks and Chzhurdzhen, Turkic inscriptions on objects found at Primorye (traditional Chzhurdzhen settlement areas) and even the presence of Turkic words in Chzhurdzhen ethnonyms.

In short, we may propose that Genghis Khan was surrounded by representatives of modern Kazakh tribes, with whom he went to the West. The lands they vacated were occupied subsequently by kindred Manchurian tribes unrelated to the Kazakhs.

Opinions are divided as to the origin of the name of the Mongol ethnos. Kalibek Danyarov suggests that the ethnonym *mongol* is a transformation of *mynkol*, or 'army of a thousand'. Another version is that *mongol* is a corrupted version of *mynkul*, which means 'a thousand slaves', as I recounted in my book *Tiurkskaia saga Chingiskhana. Sokrovennoe skazanie kazakhov* [The Turkic saga of Genghis Khan: the secret history of the Kazakhs] . Tleuberdi Abenai, a researcher into the Turkic ethnos, considers the lexeme *mongol* to derive from mankul – 'nomadic people'. Following the introduction by force of Islam into the lands of today's southern Kazakhstan, those who rejected the new religion (the Mankuls) migrated to other lands and those who remained were called the Sartkuls (Sarts) or settled people.

A number of historians and chroniclers of the past, including Rashid ad-Din, Zhalairi, Abu al-Ghazi and others, have also left interpretations of the *mongol* ethnonym. Of these, Rashid ad-Din held that the Mongols are a part of the Turkic tribes and that, after the rise of Genghis Khan, all Turks began to call themselves Mongols. I am firmly convinced, however, and my position coincides with those of prominent scholars such as R. Bezertinov, H. Kozha-Ahmed and others, of another view in which Genghis Khan announced in 1206, at Kurultai , that there would henceforth be a nation united into a single entity by him, that lived in felt yurts and that would be called *MangiYel* or 'eternal'. Thus was realised the dream of the Turkic Khagans[35] of the people of the 'Eternal Ale', who lived in wealth and prosperity. As a result of a number of transcriptions and transliterations from one language into another, *mangiyel* gradually came to be *mongol*.

The fact that the army-nation established by Genghis Khan called itself *mangiyel*, while other peoples referred to them as Turks, is confirmed by the Arab historian Ibn al-Athir (1160-1233), a contemporary and a direct eyewitness of the Mongols' devastating invasion of the land of the Khorezmshah Muhammad. Here is what the Arab historian wrote about the aliens from the East: "In this year of 617 H. [1221 CE] the Tartars, a huge Turkic tribe, came to the Islamic states (my emphasis, K.Z.); their habitat is in the Tamgadzhi mountains, near China; more than six months' journey lies between them and the Muslim countries. The reason for their appearance is as follows: their king, whom they call Genghis Khan and who is known as Temujin, having left his lands, moved into the lands of Turkestan..." In another part of his record he describes a meeting of the Khorezmshah with the famous lawyer Shihab al-Din al-Khivaki, whom he addressed as follows: "A great thing has happened; we need now to think about it. Give me your view on how we should act. The issue is this: the enemy has moved towards us from the side of the Turks in infinite number ..." (Extract from collected materials relating to the Golden Horde in *Istoria Kazakhstana v arabskikh istochnikakh* [History of Kazakhstan in Arab sources], vol. 1, Almaty: Dyke Press, 2005).

Here is another episode from Ibn al-Athir's writings: "Once they had crossed the Shervan gorge the Tartars moved over these areas, in which were many peoples, including Alans, Lezghins[36] and various Turkic tribes. They robbed and killed many Lezghin, some of whom were Muslims and others were infidels. Bearing down upon the people of the lands they passed through, they came to the Alan, a populous nation, to whom the news about the imminent arrival of the Tartars was already known. They (the Alan) used all resources at their disposal to gather a crowd of Kipchaks around themselves, and fought with them (the Tartars). Neither of the two parties gained the upper hand over the other. Then the Tartars sent a message to the Kipchaks saying: "You and we are kin (my emphasis – K.

Z.), but these Alans are not relations of ours, so there is no benefit for you in helping them; your faith differs from theirs, and we promise that we will not attack you, but will bring you as much money and clothes as you wish; leave us with them ...".

It is superfluous to comment; the Mongols of Genghis Khan and the Kipchak are of one kinship and share the same faith. So why do we, the Kazakhs of the 21st century, persist in denying our great ancestor?

Throughout his long narrative, Ibn al-Athir never referred to the newcomers from the East as Mongols but instead always called them the "Turk Tatar ". This is understandable, however, as Genghis Khan only began to name the people united by him as the *mangiyel* in 1206, and this name was still unknown beyond his *ulus*, whereas the whole world had known the people of the region as Turks since the days of the great Turkic khaganates. In exactly the same way, the Romans previously called the Hellenes of the Peloponnese Greeks and the Celtic nomads Gauls.

Once Genghis Khan's Turks had migrated West, to Kazakhstan, the lands they left behind were taken up by Tungus tribes of Manchurian origin, who, having inherited the Mongol ethnonym, also gained the glory of Genghis Khan's Turks.

This is the flagrant injustice that has triumphed in our world for over 800 years!

It should be noted that for all his undisguised hatred of invading conquerors (he writes: "If somebody should say that since the time that Allah the Mighty and Most High created man up to the present time, the world has never experienced anything of this kind..."), nevertheless Ibn al-Athir pays tribute to the military arts of the enemy: "These Tartars have succeeded in things the like of which have not been witnessed either in past times or in the present. The horde set out from the borders of China; not a year passed but part of them reached the Armenian lands from this side, and another part enters Iraq from Hamadan. " By Allah! – I have no doubt: he who survives after us, at the passing of this era, and sees a description of this happening, will deny it, and consider it to be a fiction, and truth will be on his side. But let him who takes it to be a fiction understand that we and all the compilers of the chronicles of our time wrote at a time when all who witnessed this happening were familiar with it to the same degree – be they scholars or illiterates – because it was common knowledge... From the time that the Prophet appeared – peace be upon him! – to the present day, the Muslims have never been visited by such evil and misfortune as they undergo now ..." The Arab historian writes of the Turks' martial valour and heroism in the words he heard spoken by a marshall from the Georgian troops: "If somebody tells you that the Tartars have fled or been captured, do not believe them, but if they say to you that they have attacked, believe them, because this people never runs away. One day we took one of them prisoner, so he threw himself from his horse and struck his head on a rock so as to die and not to give himself up to captivity alive..."

This was the way in which Genghis Khan made his army and his people, the *mangiyel*, invincible.

## GENGHIS KHAN - A BLOODTHIRSTY CONQUEROR OR A CREATOR OF A NEW WORLD? WHERE IS THE REPOSE OF THE GREAT TERROR OF THE UNIVERSE?

In my book T*he Turkic saga of Genghis Khan* I tried to demonstrate as convincingly as possible to all its readers (though of course it is primarily addressed to the people of Kazakhstan, or if you like, to the Kazakhs) that Genghis Khan is the great ancestor of the Kazakhs. I stand by this view, propagate it and strive in order that as many people are made aware of this as possible.

The fact that the Eurocentrists seek to portray Genghis Khan as a bloodthirsty malefactor is an entirely separate matter. There are, incidentally, a good number among the Kazakh intelligentsia, especially writers and academics invested with academic titles, honorary degrees and other decorations, who claim in all seriousness that the city of Otrar[37], say, was destroyed by Genghis Khan. The barbarian, they maintain, razed to the ground the great library of Otrar, which was comparable with that of Alexandria, and they add that he destroyed, among other things, the Central Asian cities of Khorezm, Merv, Samarkand and Bukhara.

He did of course subordinate and pacify rebellious peoples; no nation has thus far succeeded in waging war without the use of force or even violence. Moreover, modern morals and their purportedly democratic priorities would in no way be applicable to the concepts of morality and virtue prevalent in the 12th and 13th centuries. Yet even European morality is duplicitous and cunning in its readiness to turn a blind eye to any act of cruelty by, say, Caesar, Alexander the Great or Cyrus II the Great; such acts are justified as political expediency, irrespective of how many cities or cultural relics, such as Persepolis[38] or the Acropolis in Athens, they destroyed. And who condemned Napoleon for his treacherous killing of thousands of Egyptians who had thrown themselves upon the mercy of the conqueror? Who even remembers this today? Nobody; rather, for them, the focus of the world's evil has become Genghis Khan. The reasons, I think, are also clear. The Russian writer A. Bushkov, discussing the age of Ivan the Terrible[39] (16th century), writes that when European commanders fought with their neighbours in those times, they burned and devastated whole provinces, since that was the prevailing military doctrine. So what can be said about the era of Genghis Khan (13th century)?

This is why I tried, in my book, to prove with concrete facts that the creative legacy of Genghis Khan was immeasurably larger than that of his destructive actions. Today, for example, the Russia that stems from Rus owes a debt of gratitude to Genghis Khan, as was superbly stated by such outstanding Russian intellects as Prince Trubetskoy, Petr Nikolaevich Savitsky and other representatives of the legendary Eurasian school. They hold to the fundamental idea that had there been no Genghis Khan, there would be no great Russia. Who knows how far the influence of Western Catholicism would have reached, which at that time the Teutonic Knights were seeking to impose on Russia? One cannot but agree with the Eurasians that Catholicism would have "torn out the soul" of Russia, whereas the subjects of Genghis Khan merely paid a ten percent tribute in furs. The taxes we pay the state today are far greater than those people paid in the empire of Genghis Khan.

So you pay taxes – but for what? To cultivate the land, to raise cattle, to feed a family. And all that with the complete guarantee of security, peace and certainty of the future. So consider that in the days of Genghis Khan you could have travelled from the Yellow Sea to the Baltic Sea, and no-one would dare to touch you or to impinge on your rights in any way. The Silk Road was restored, and thus also mutually advantageous trade, the terms of which were entirely satisfactory for the merchants. The role of money grew considerably – a problem that is no less relevant in the present day. It is no coincidence that our President Nursultan Nazarbayev has again raised the question of the introduction of a single currency equivalent, at least in the post-Soviet region and even within Eurasia, since the US dollar has become a spent force. After all, such things have already happened in the history of our land and our peoples.

Let me repeat one more time that it was possible to move, communicate and trade freely from the Pacific to the Atlantic. Consider, for example, China, which had previously consisted of four empires that were constantly at war with each other, and which only gained unity under the rule of Genghis Khan.

The Chinese, incidentally, are grateful to Genghis Khan; they built a gigantic museum in his honour in Beijing, though not without pursuing political goals of their own. They have a state doctrine, according to which wherever the hooves of Genghis Khan's horse trod is Chinese land – and, one way or another, they never lose hope of realising that doctrine.

Suffice it to recall one recent historical episode when the Ambassador of China was invited to the Kazakh Parliament and had to endure the outrage expressed by our elected representatives because geographical maps of China continue to this day to show the territory of Kazakhstan as far as Lake Balkhash as Chinese territory.

Perhaps we have still not fully grasped that we possess one ninth of the land surface area of the world. And due to whom or to what has such wealth has fallen on us, if we say we have no relation to Genghis Khan? How can this be, how is it that we have not fallen easy prey to our  powerful immediate neighbours – China to the south with its population running into billions, or the Muslim East, or vast Russia on our other side? Why do the Uyghurs[40], a people that far exceeds the Kazakhs in numbers, or likewise the Kurds[41], not have their own statehood, while we Kazakhs, a mere ten million of us, have so much?

Surely, then, it is high time for us to acknowledge publicly at the highest level that thanks to Genghis Khan, the Kazakhs are today the owners of a land of immense bounty whose mineral resources include every element. This is a priceless gift left by our great ancestor to his people, and we, the descendants who tend this inheritance, have a debt of gratitude.

One may speak at great length about the Genghis Khan phenomenon. First of all he was a great military leader; there has not been an equal to him and it is unlikely that there will ever be one in future. Over three billion people in more than thirty countries – that is his empire projected onto a modern world map. According to the American scholar Jack Weatherford, author of the excellent *Genghis Khan and the Making of the Modern World* (New York: Random House, 2004), it was Genghis Khan who delineated the architecture of the modern world by his actions, who created the first constitution, *zharlyq* and *bilik*[42] (a code of laws for the military and for civilians), who established freedom of religion and who created a system of governance based on personal qualities and dedication to one's work and leader. By conquering other countries, Genghis Khan developed trade in which, in addition to material goods, ideas and knowledge were also commodities. Master craftsmen from Paris erected fountains on the Great Steppe, while tea, pasta and oriental medicine were brought to Europe from China; mining experts were drawn from Germany, Persian carpets and silk were taken to China and a Chinese method of fingerprint identification was spread to other countries – the examples are numerous.

Eight hundred years later and the world is still excited by the scale of his actions. Hundreds of books have been written and dozens of movies made. Costly American and Japanese expeditions go in search of the final resting place of the Great Terror of the Universe. But all these efforts are in vain; I doubt whether his descendants will ever be able to honour his memory or mourn for him at the site of his burial. The point here is that Genghis Khan was a zealous follower of Tengriism[43] , according to which a person may return to life in this world after death, but only if his remains are kept intact. Warrior nomads therefore sought to keep the burial places of their fellow tribesmen secret so that their enemies could not desecrate them and so prevent the return of the tribesmen to life, while they themselves would readily harm their enemies' burial sites for the same reason. Genghis Khan realized that a warrior of his calibre would attract special attention after his death, and so guarded the secret of his final resting place with his life.

Hope nevertheless seems to spring eternal. Some forty kilometres from Semey[44] (formerly Semipalatinsk) on the river Irtysh, in the homeland of the great poet Abay [45] in the Degelen[46] mountains, which are known popularly as the Genghis Mountains, the geographical centre of Eurasia is situated, as it were its umbilical cord (50° N, 80° E). Shakh-Murat Kuanganov maintains that the Genghis Mountains were previously known as the Kindikkush Mountains, the name Kindikkuh meaning 'umbilical power' or 'point of concentration of the Earth's energy'. It is possible that this place bestowed upon Genghis Khan exceptional strength and energy, and this may be where he is buried. The Mongolist Yevgeny Kychanov writes: "... Genghis Khan, having not taken part in any military campaigns for three years (due to illness), spent the summer of 1224 on the banks of the Irtysh...".

In this connection we also gain a new reading of the toponym 'Hindu Kush', the mountain range that rises in India, Pakistan and Afghanistan. It is probable that as our ancestors roamed from place to place through boundless spaces, they would give familiar names from their former homeland to the mountains and rivers they encountered.

## THE PROPHET NOAH HAD THREE SONS ...
## AND THE KAZAKHS HAD THREE JÜZ

Today the Kazakhs are divided into three territorial divisions or *jüz*[47], while the Mongolian state at the time of Genghis Khan also comprised three wings. Those wings were known as Onkanat (right wing), Solkanat (left wing) and Orta[48] (centre). The central wing was commanded by Genghis Khan's military leader Nye of the Naiman tribe, the left wing was under the command of Mukagali of the Zhalayir, and the right wing was ruled by Borshi of the Argyn. In geographical terms, if one faces South, Orta comprises the steppe of modern Kazakhstan, Onkanat is the Black Sea and Caspian Sea regions and Solkanat includes China and Manchuria.

As mentioned above, the Kazakhs remain divided into jüz even today. Some people regard this as a remnant from the past, though nobody can now say with confidence when it arose. Some attribute the division to Genghis Khan, as I also discuss in my book. Well known, by contrast, is the legend of the prophet Noah, the sole survivor of the flood that God imposed on earth as punishment for the people having forgotten His covenant. Noah had three sons, Shem, Ham and Japheth, and the Bible describes in detail how and where he settled them. The youngest, Japheth, was sent to between the Volga and the Ural rivers, and we, the Kazakhs of the 21st century, are descended from him.

Speaking of the Scythians, Herodotus, the 'Father of History', argued that their ancestor was Targitay, who also had three sons, among whom certain lands were divided up. A similar story is told of the three Kazakh *jüz* – the Akarys, Bekarys and Zhanarys[49]. There are even well-substantiated theories that the division of the Kazakhs into three *jüz* goes back to the time of Noah and thus that his three sons were the founders of the three *jüz*.

The historical analogy is clear. It is however unlikely to be possible to reach a founded and unambiguous interpretation. Clearly, in any case, this division has been necessitated by the sheer scale of the territory itself so that a form of order could be established on it.

# THE TURKIC KHAGANATES: A CAROUSEL OF THE SPEPPE

## NAIMAN'S CHINA

First it should be clarified that by the Turkic khaganates I mean not only those states that were created in the lands of Northern China and Mongolia in the second half of the first millennium AD, but also certain more ancient states that existed in Mesopotamia, Egypt, Persia, India, China and Europe.

In the fifth to eighth centuries the Great Turkic Khaganate was established in what are modern Mongolia and Northern China. The First Turkic Khaganate was formed in 545 and lasted a little over half a century before collapsing under pressure from the Chinese, Yenisei Kyrgyz[50], Tartars[51] and Oghuz tribes of Uighurs. A hundred years later, in the early eighth century, the Second Turkic Khaganate was established; fifty years later this was replaced by the Uighur Khaganate, which in turn was superseded by the Kyrgyz Khaganate. After this the Khitan Liao dynasty appeared in the same land, whose people, as I have proved and as many scholars have agreed, are today fully assimilated into the body of the Kazakh Naiman. Incidentally, the name China was derived from the Naiman Chinese, the Khitan, some of whom are among the Kazakh Kete, of the Alim Uly tribal union of Kazakhs.

In the 12th century Genghis Khan united these territories once again. So what pattern do we see being followed here? It is evident that the Kokturk[52] and Mongol states were created by the ancestors of the Kazakhs!

In *The Turkic Saga of Genghis Khan* I claimed that Naiman tribes, the Mathai and the Sadyr, ruled in this khaganate (on the basis that the seal of the khan of the first khaganate depicted a wolf, while today the tribal *tamga* of only two Kazakh tribes, the Matai and the Sadyr, is likewise a wolf). Moreover, historical data also indicate that these tribes lived in these lands in the fifth century.

In the Second Turkic Khaganate the khan's seal depicted a wild ram. The only modern tribe whose *tamga* is the horns of a wild ram is the Naiman Karakerey[53]. Later the word argali (the common name for the mountain sheep *Ovis ammon*) became the uranium of the present-day Kazakh Tore, who are blood relatives of Genghis Khan. One may therefore assume that the Second Turkic Khaganate was ruled by the Karakerey, some of whom were assimilated into the clan of Genghis Khan.

It can thus be seen that in any case, one of the modern Kazakh tribes, of which there are between 70 and 100 designations in total, was at the head of these Turkic khaganates. In my book I stated that Genghis Khan's empire was again headed by Kazakhs – the Naiman tribes of Baganaly and Matay[54]. The written language of state under Gengis Khan was that of the Naiman and not of the Uighur as is mistakenly assumed by modern scholars, and the seal of the Naiman Khanate became the state seal for Genghis Khan. It is true that Genghis Khan once fought the Naiman, but that battle was for leadership of the Naiman state. Having become their khan, he then had the Naiman Khaganate rule over half the world.

It is generally known that a distant ancestor of Genghis was Borte Chino, which in Mongolian means 'Grey Wolf'. He brought the tribe of the Great Terror of the Universe from the mythical ancestral home of the Turks, Ergenekon[55], to the lands of modern Mongolia. Genghis Khan himself descended from the Borjigin[56] clan, whose ethnonym can be decoded as *bori zhigi*, i.e. part (*zhik*) of the Wolf people. While the whole Turkic world is considered to be the people of the Wolf, among the Kazakh tribes only the Matay and Sadyr have a wolf as their *tamga*.

# HITTITES, KETE, GOTHS AND HUNS
# TURKIC GERMANY

The Turkic Khaganate was preceded by the Huns, and these are without doubt the ancestors of modern Kazakhs. According to the work of the Caucasus historians K. Laypanov and I. Meziyev *O proiskhozhdenii tiurkskikh narodov* [The origin of the Turkic peoples], Cherkessk, 1993, it may be concluded that at the end of the third century BC the Huns were governed by Kazakh Matay, and their leader Mode was also none other than a Matay. Hard consonants in the middle of words were simply dropped or replaced with soft ones by the Chinese, and as a result our Matay became the Chinese Mode-Madi.

The Huns, whose name we associate with the dying days of Roman rule, are described by the fourth-century Roman historian Ammianus Marcellinus thus: "The tribe of the Huns, about whom ancient writers were very little informed, dwell beyond the Maeotic marshes towards the Ice Ocean and their wildness surpasses any measure... They cannot be found even in a shelter covered by reeds. They wander past mountains and forests and are trained to withstand cold, hunger and thirst from the cradle... no-one among them ploughs nor has touched a wooden plough even once. With no fixed abode, without a shelter, law or a stable way of life, they wander like perpetual fugitives with their nomad's tents, in which they spend their lives..."

This is the way in which the enlightened Europeans depicted the lives and ways of our ancestors. Yet by the irony of fate, ours was the nation that became the conqueror and the gravedigger of the great empire.

The Great Hittite Kingdom existed in Asia Minor (Anatolia) in the 18th and 19th centuries BC. It prospered for only for five or six centuries, after which it declined and was then conquered by other nomadic peoples. Later, however, some of the Hittites moved to North-Western China, bringing with them chariots and battle horses, which at that time were still unknown there. They created the Western Zhou state that subsequently conquered the neighbouring states until it ruled all China. In his book *Skifskaya Rus* [Scythian Rus'] (Moscow: Veche, 2008) Anatoly Abrashkin throws some light on events in the 12th and 11th centuries BC: "The Scythians, displacing the Hittites to the East, extended their influence all the way to Northern China. So did the Hittites not give the Chinese the name of their country? In the middle and lower reaches of the Yenisei river in the Krasnoyarsk region lives the Ket people[57], who were previously known as Yenisei Ostyaks. The Ostyaks, however, were simply called the Khanty – a name identical to that of one of the Hittite kings, Hanteli. Also, the ancient capital of the Hittites was the city of Nesa in Anatolia; an association can be made between this and the name of the Yenisei. Another major Hittite city was called Tuvan , which is similar to the name of the Republic of Tuva, also on the Yenisei ..." Before the Hittites arrived in China from Asia Minor there existed the state of Yin, established by Altai nomads from the Shang tribe. I myself have the honour of belonging to this great tribe. Today, descendants of the Shang can be found among the Kazakh Argyn and Naiman[58]. A deep historical continuity also existed between the empire of Genghis Khan and these Zhou and Yin states, as the descendants of the Hittites are, among others, modern-day Kazakh Kete of the Alim Uly tribal union of the Junior *jüz*. In addition, the Ktan-Kete-Kitan-Chinese participated in forming the Naiman union of Kazakh tribes. Nikolay Marr and S.Tolstov have both shown that there are deep links between the Turkic languages and the language of the Hittites.

In the ninth century BC the Hittites established the state of Western Zhou in China, and in about 770 BC, after the start of the Spring and Autumn periods in China, many of the Hittites moved West through Siberia and Kazakhstan to the Caucasus, the Black Sea, the Baltic states and Europe, where they became known as the Goths. Some of the Hittites meanwhile stayed in Siberia and today are considered to be the Kets, while others settled in Western Kazakhstan and took the historical name Kete. In the 10th century AD those Hittites that had remained in China returned to power under the name Ktan-Kitan and established the Liao dynasty, while also giving their name to the Chinese state.

Another group of Hittites apparently remained in Oghuz Lydia, and after the Trojan War some of them went to the Apennine Peninsula and were known as the Etruscans[59]. The Hittites that remained in Lydia[60] after its capture by Cyrus the Great moved towards the Sea of Azov, took the names As (Az, Uz, Guz and Oghuz), then continued to Scandinavia and the Baltic region, where they assumed the name Balti Goths. The king of Lydia, Croesus, was reputed to be a leading expert on the Scythian people, and this is doubtless an indication of the Turkic ethnic composition of the population of Lydia. Jordanes, a sixth-century Roman historian who studied the Goths, claims that the Germanic tribes of Goths were formerly called the Getae. In his work *On the Origin and Deeds of the Getae he writes*: "... Dion, a historian and a diligent scholar of antiquity, who titled his work *Getica* (but these Getae, as mentioned above, are the same as the Goths) ..."

However, Marcellinus (fourth century), Zosimus (fifth-sixth century) and Trajan (eighth century) all attributed the Getae to the Scythians.

The Roman scholar and statesman Pliny the Elder (23-79 CE) wrote more specifically about the origin of the Goths. In his *Naturalis Historia* he wrote: "Beyond the Ister [Danube] live almost only the Scythians, but the banks are inhabited by various peoples: the Getae, whom the Romans call the Dacians, or the Sarmatians (or Sauromats in Greek)... the designation 'Scythian' is often applied to the Sarmatians and Germans..."

Thus the Romans considered the Goths to be Dacians; meanwhile the modern-day descendants of the latter are represented by the Kazakh Aday, and those of the Goths are represented by the Kete. These two modern Kazakh tribes live as neighbours in Western Kazakhstan. We should also note that the Roman historian also believed the Germanic tribes to be Scythians.

In his book *Tiurkoiazychny period yevropeiskoi istorii* [The Turkic-speaking period in European history] (Yaroslavl: Litera, 2011), the Russian historian Yuri Drozdov closely analyses the literary monuments on which the so-called "German" concept of the ethnic origin of the Goths is based and concludes that the written sources he mentions, including as the Codex Argenteus (fifth-sixth centuries), the Codex Carolinus (fifth century) and the seventh-century manuscripts kept in the Biblioteca Ambrosiana in Milan and known as the Codex Ambrosianus "do not by themselves contain any evidence on the basis of which they could be thought to have belonged to the Goths, and on this basis to consider the Goths to be a Germanic-speaking people..." It should be noted that in this context the term 'Germanic' refers to the indigenous people of the lands of what is now Germany, whereas in ethnic terms, the modern

Germans are a symbiosis of the indigenous inhabitants of the German lands, who lived in the forest in Stone Age conditions, and the alien Scythian tribes of Turkic origin who had reached a further stage of civilization. One of the newly arrived peoples was in fact the Hittites (Getae, Goths). Indeed the appearance of the word 'Gott' in the German language, signifying God, is attributable to the Hittites/Goths, who for the wild Germanic tribes were the personification of the unattainable inhabitants of the Eternal Blue Sky. The ethnonym Hittite itself, incidentally, derives in my view from the Turkic (Kazakh) word *katty*, which means 'hard, tough' and thus also 'rigorous, strong' etc.

It should be noted that the Hittites, who arrived in Asia Minor at the beginning of the second millennium BC, there met their kindred Hattites, whose capital was Hattusha. This name can be translated from the Kazakh language as *hatty el* or 'dwelling-place of educated people'. Kuanganov mentions that the royal archive was discovered by archaeologists at Hattusha and was found to contain some 15,000 clay cuneiform tablets. This allows another reading of the Hattite ethnonym – a nation of literate people possessing scripts (Kazakh *khat* – 'letter'). Many linguistic scholars, including Olzhas Suleimenov, associate cuneiform script with the Turkic runes.

Continuing my narrative, Drozdov writes that authors such as Publius Herennius Dexippus, who lived in the third century BC, referred directly in their writings to the Scythian origin of the Goths: "The Scythians, called Goths (my emphasis, K.Z.), after crossing the Ister[61] river under Decius in great numbers, devastated a country that was ruled by the Romans..." This Scythian notion of the origin of the Goths can also be found in the writings of classical authors such as Procopius of Caesarea, Philostorgius, Julius Capitolinus, Titus Flavius Josephus and others.

Many major figures of the past wrote of the Scythian roots of the Germanic tribes. The Greek geographer and historian Strabo, for example, who lived at the end of a bygone era , noted in his *Geographica*: "The areas beyond the Rhine, in the East and lying beyond the territory of the Celts, are inhabited by the Germans. These differ little from the Celtic tribe ... in their build, their customs and way of life they match the description I made of the Celts..." Later we will speak of the Celts as Turkic tribes, and it follows that this is also so for the Germans. Pliny the Elder referred in his *Naturalis Historia*, mentioned above, to all the tribes living North of the Danube as Scythians, including the German and Sarmatian tribes in this umbrella.

The Getae, however, were first mentioned by Herodotus. The historian Viktor Yanovich mentions in *Velikaya Skifia. Istoria dokievskoy Rusi* [Great Scythia:

the history of pre-Kievan Rus] (Moscow: Algoritm, 2008) that the ancestors of the Goths were Hittites from Western Asia, which explains why the remainder of the Oghuz tribe of Hittites (As), leaving Asia in the sixth century BC for the Baltic lands and Scandinavia and who later formed the basis of the German people, became known as the Balti Goths. Incidentally, the ethnonym *ged/ get* is linked to an ancient Indo-European name for large horned cattle. If now one takes into account the sadly familiar term 'ghetto', Yanovich concludes that 'Getae' is an ancient name for a group of settled cattle-breeders who kept their animals in fenced enclosures that in modern language would be called 'ghettoes'.

## KAZAKH ALBANS AND SUANS; CAUCASIAN ALAN AND SVANS. TO WHICH KAZAKH TRIBE DID JESUS CHRIST BELONG?

Following the Trojan War the As Oghuz[65] came to the Black Sea region from Asia Minor through the Armenian highlands that were inhabited by the Wanes of the Urartu group of Venetic tribes. Under the pressure of the As the Wanes migrated to the Caucasus and later established what is now the Svaneti[63]. In my view the Wanes are present-day Suans of the Kazakh Senior *jüz*. My arguments to support this view are as follows. It is known that in the second century BC the Yueh-chih, a Turkic tribe, was expelled from the lands of Western China (Hexi region) by the Mode-Matay Huns. Some authors, in particular Laypanov and Meziyev, consider the Yueh-Chih to be ancestors of the Kazakh Kanly[64]. Marat Barmankulov, referring to the Japanese researcher K. Enoki, writes: "According to my idea, the Yueh-chih of the third century BC were very similar in terms of their territory and power to the Turks of the sixth and seventh centuries."

Thus, having arrived in the Middle East, the Yueh-chih seized the Greco-Bactrian Kingdom and created the Kushan Empire, also known as Tokharistan, in what are today Central Asia, Afghanistan, Pakistan and Northern India. The modern Kazakh Suan has a large independent clan known as the Tokarystan. On this basis, I propose that the Urartu Wanes dwelling on the Armenian highlands included the neighbouring Tocharians of the Kushan Empire, and the residents of present-day Svaneti are themselves descendants of these Tocharians. Another body of the Tocharians, meanwhile, were assimilated into the Kazakh Suan, and this is why the North Caucasian Svan and the Suan of Kazakhstan had common roots and are considered to be kindred peoples. Moreover the Kazakh Suan is related to the

Kazakh Alban, and have always lived side by side. During the period in question the Alban resided on the Western shores of the Caspian Sea and the Suan / Wanes lived on the East coast of the Black Sea; thus they were neighbours. Some of the Suan / Wanes migrated to China along with the Hittites and can now be found among the Naiman Karakerey. The inquisitive reader may consult the ancient Icelandic songs about the As in the Younger Edda and Older Edda series to explore this information.

Once the Huns reached the Caspian and Black Sea steppes, the Alan / Alban moved West, reaching Spain and Britain. Britain is still called 'misty Albion', and according to some scholars the early English and ancient Egyptian languages have up to 3,000 words in common. These common words are derived from the vocabulary of the same people, the Alban, who lived at that time both in Egypt, where they were called the Hyksos, and in Britain. The self-appellation in the fifth century of Shakespeare's homeland, when our ancestors the Saqs came to these islands, sounded like 'Inglend', which in Turkic means 'an obtained country': having won these fertile lands, the Turks established Kent and Calais, which in Kazakh literally mean 'city' and 'fortress' respectively, and the word *saq* transformed into 'Saxon' in the local dialect and formed the basis of a new English nation. Odoacer, the future king of Italy, brought the Saqs to the lands of Albion. His father Edeko was an ambassador to Attila in Constantinople in 448.

In this text, I wrote deliberately about the Alan and the Alban[65] in the sense of related Turkic, or rather Scythian, tribes. In modern academic historiography the view of the Alan as being Iranian is an established axiom; yet some of the Alban are today a part of the Kazakh people and others live in the Balkans. The fourth-century Roman historian Ammianus Marcellinus, recounting Pompey's campaign of 65 BC to the Caucasus and Persia, wrote: "... crossing the lands of the Alban and Massagetae, whom we now call the Alan, he also destroyed this tribe, and saw the Caspian sea..." (*Ammianus Martselian. Rimskaya istoria*, St. Petersburg, 1994).

The only thing that is unclear is whether Marcellinus refers to the Massagetae as Alan or whether he also considers the Alban to be Alan; this confusion arises because, describing the peoples of Eastern Europe elsewhere in his work, he writes: "…alongside these peoples dwell the Massagetae, Alan and Sargetae and many unknown peoples; we do not even know their names, not to mention their customs." In this context the Alan and Massagetae are quite different tribes. Describing the Hun invasion of the Caspian steppe, the Roman historian says: "This mobile and indomitable nation, inflamed by a wild thirst for plunder, moving forward between pillages and killings, went as far as the lands of the Alan, the ancient Massagetae..." Thus Marcellinus again states that in ancient times the Alan were called the Massagetae, and so were definitely Scythian tribes. This thesis is further supported by the same historian's words: "…although they wandered like nomads about the vast spaces at great distances from one another, in the course of time they became united under one name, the Alan, due to the similarity of their customs, their wild way of life, the great similarity of their weapons. They have no huts and none of them has ever ploughed the land; they eat meat and drink milk, live in nomad tents covered with pieces of tree bark bent into the form of an arch and carry them across the endless steppes ... They consider it lucky to die in battle, while those who reach old age and die of natural causes are subjected to brutal mockery..."

In my view, given the statements of Marcellinus here, there is no need for further proof that the ancient Alan is not an Iranian-speaking people.

Titus Flavius Josephus also wrote of the Alan being not Iranian-speaking but rather related to the Scythians in his work T*he War of the Jews* ('*O voyne iudeyskoy'*, *Vestnik drevney istorii*, 1947, No. 4). He describes the terrible invasion of Armenia and Media by the Alan in 72 AD: "We explained earlier that the tribes of the Alan are a part of the Scythians (my emphasis* K. Z.) who live around Tanais and Lake Maeotis."[66] The second-century Greek geographer mentions in his *Geographia*: "Sarmatia is occupied by a great number of tribes:[67] the Veneti throughout the Gulf of Venice; above Dacia, the Peucini and Bastarnae; all along the Maeotis coast, the Iazyges and Roxolani;[68] beyond them, deeper into the country are the Gamaksobians and the Alan Scythians..." From these works of Ptolemy and Marcellinus one may conclude unambiguously that the ethnonym *alan* is a collective name for the nomadic Scythians who lived on the Northern Caucasian steppes, since *alan* translates from the Kazakh as 'open field', 'open space', 'plain' etc. It should also be noted that it was traditional among our ancestors to name a people according to its way of life. Consider, for example, the ancient inhabitants of the Great Steppe that bore the name *kanly* or *kangyly*, which literally means 'vagabonds', 'wanderers'. The name thus imparted to a way of life has since become an ethnoterm. The situation for the Alan is the same.

When speaking of the affinity of the Alban to the historical Alan, what I meant primarily by the Alban were those Alban who lived in the past in what is now Dagestan. It is likely that the Balkan Alban people of our time are relatives of the Caucasian Alban. That the Caucasian Albans are the ancestors of the Kazakh Alban is indirectly confirmed by the Greek historian Strabo. Here is what he wrote in the ninth book of *Geographica*: "The Alban are more inclined to lead a pastoral way of life and are closer to the nomadic type, except that they are not wild, and as a result, are only moderately warlike... the Alban fight using spears and bows, have armour, large shields and helmets made of animal skin... the Alban themselves and their dogs are extremely fond of hunting, not so much for the art of it but because it is a passion... the Alban greatly respect old age; not only that of their parents but also of strangers..."

The might of the Alban state is described by the Roman historian Tacitus. In the Annals he states: "…They had to add a large number of military units, which Nero recruited in Germany, Britain and Illyria and, in preparation for the war against the Albans, sent to the Caspian gorge…" So it can be seen that the entire military power of the Romans was directed to battling with a small but warlike nation of the ancestors of the Kazakh Alban!

It must be admitted that all the qualities of the Alban people mentioned above are inherent to us, the modern Kazakhs. Most probably, when the Huns arrived in the Northern Caucasus around the first century, some of the Alban left for their historical homeland – Kazakhstan – from where they had come to the Caucasus in the eighth century BC, and now became part of the formation of the Kazakh ethnic group. Other groups of Alban settled in the Balkans on their way to Western Europe, and their descendants created what was to become Albania.

Today it is almost impossible to determine what the names were of the various Kazakh tribes three or four millennia ago. In the list of clans that came from Ergenekon in the seventh century BC that later formed the basis of the Turkic people, the Turkologist Rashid-ad-Din enumerates 16 clans, of which only three – the Konyrat, Qoralas and Uysun[69] – have their current names (*Sbornik letopisey*, USSR Academy of Sciences, 1952). In general it is sometimes possible to restore the original ancient names using indirect methods. Let us consider the same Kazakh Alban, who lived in the mountains on the Western shore of the Caspian (and note that what is now Azerbaijan was once called Caucasian Albania). In the third century after the Huns' arrival from the East, some of the Alban travelled far West, to Spain, and created their capital Barcelona in today's Catalonia. As true mountain dwellers the Alban honoured the snow leopard (Kazakh: *bars*) and called themselves the Barseli, or the people of the snow leopard. As an aside I would add that the name of the highest mountain in the Caucasus, Elbrus, is also linked to Kazakh ethnonyms and was originally named Elbars – again in honour of the people of the *bars* or snow leopard, i.e. the Kazakh Alban and Bersh. Translating allegorically, the name catalunya is the 'second Alania', and its capital Barcelona thus means 'city of the people of *bars*', that is, of the Alban, Bersh and other Kazakh tribes. And surely the name of the ancestors of the Kazakh Argyn reminds one of another Spanish city, Aragon, since the Argyn were Huns and lived also in the lands of Spain along with the Alan. What, moreover, for the Basque capital Bilbao? The Kazakhs have a word, *belbau* – a waist belt, a symbol of male honour and courage. By removing this our ancestors became submissive and needed assistance and protection. Let us recall Genghis Khan. Before making crucial decisions he would climb the mountain and take off his belt, asking Tengri to be favourable towards him. The mysterious Barseli can be found today in the literature, but no-one will ever think of identifying them with the well-known Alban, Dulat or Bersh. In *Oktrytie Khazarii* (St Petersburg: Crystal, 2003) Lev Gumilev asserts that the Barsil lived between the Volga and Terek[70] rivers and were Pre-Bulgarian tribes. Certainly, today the Alban and the Dulat (who formed the basis of the Volga Bulgar) belong to the same Kazakh *jüz*, and their *tamga* are almost identical. In addition the Dulat belonged to the Alan union of clans, as testified by the Zelenchug inscription[71] found in the Caucasus and dated to the 10th century.

The text of the inscription reads: "Jesus Christ, the governor of Nicholas, having been called from the house of the Hobs union (Dulo, Batpay, Adwan, Suvan) by Advant Bakatar Beg himself, who separated from their father's country to that of the Alan (steppes, valleys), is striving, tell of the year of the ox." (Laypanov K. and Meziev I.: *O proiskhozhdenii tiurkskikh narodov* [The origin of the Turkic peoples], Cherkessk, 1993). Hence it may be concluded that Jesus Christ belonged ethnically to a union of four Kazakh tribes – the Dulat, Botpay , Alban and Suan. In addition, on the basis of this document, the Kazakh Dulat and Botbay were independent clans; and the fact that today the Botbay are considered to be part of the Dulat has, in my opinion, no historical basis.

Here I would like to touch once more upon the question of the Alan being Iranian-speaking. This view has become common in academic circles because the Ossetians[72],who consider themselves to be descendants of the Alan, are Iranian speakers. But first of all the question of whether or not they are descendants is a complex one, and secondly, as Tayzhan Dosanov shows in his work *Taina runiki* [The secret of the runes], only six out of 70 Ossetian *tamga* can be identified with the Alan. Thus the fact that Alans spoke Turkic and belonged to the ancestors of the Kazakhs is left in no doubt. Modern-day Kazakh Alban, Suan and other tribes are direct descendants of the ancient Alan.

The question in discussion here also relates directly to the problem of Iranian-speaking Scythians. Zhumazhan Bayzhumin also maintains this. He believes that the view of the Scythians as Iranian-speaking in academic historical studies has become established due to an incorrect interpretation of Herodotus or, more likely, incorrect conclusions from Herodotus' own works. Herodotus is known to have said that the Sauromat who lived on the Volga, East of the Black Sea Scythians, spoke almost the same language as the Scythians. Now let us consider the Iranian-speaking Ossetians. It is widely thought that these are descendants of the Alan, who in turn descend from the Sarmatians. So if the Sarmatians and Sauromat were one and the same people, then, the historians conclude, the Scythians were Iranian. Yet both formal logic and common sense would hold that just because a part of a given people speaks a certain language, it does not necessarily follow that the majority of that people speak the same language. In the former USSR Russian was spoken in all the republics, but in 15 of them the local languages were also widely used. In exactly the same way, the fact that the Ossetians are Iranian-speaking and the Alan are their ancestors does not necessarily mean that the

Alan were also Iranian speakers. Moreover – and this is the main point – Bayzhumin demonstrates that the Sauromat were not Sarmatians. The ancestral clan of the Sauromat was the Sabyr or Sapar, which finds representation today in the Naiman and Qonyrat tribes, the Zhapar clan within the Argyn and Qypshak, the Zabir in the Kerey and Qypshak tribes, etc. But the ancestral clan of the Sarmatians was the Sary or Sar, today represented by the Shor of Southern Siberia and by many other Kazakh clans. They can also be found among the Kyrgyz tribes (Sara, Zhora), and of the Khakas[73] (Choro).

Yuri Drozdov also writes about the Sarmatians and Sauromat being different tribes and of Turkic origin. He quotes the unknown author of a major work, *Zemleopisanie* [Description of the Land] in 90 BC: "Asia. On the Tanais, which serves as the Asian border and divides the continent into two parts, live primarily the Sarmatians, who occupy an expanse of space of 2,000 stages. Beyond them, according to the writer Demetrius, there lives a Meotian tribe called Yazamaty, but according to Ephorus they are a tribe of the Sauromat..." (*Vestnik drevney istorii*, 1947, No. 3).

There are thus ample grounds for claiming that the Alan people were Turkic-speaking, and indeed this corrects the serious error among historians of the past who considered the Scythians to be Iranian speakers. Between the sixth and fourth centuries BC the Sarmatians lived between the Don and Tobol rivers, and according to Orak Ismagulov's theory they were ancestors of the Kazakhs and thus Turkic-speaking. So both the Sarmatians and the Sauromat were Turkic-speaking peoples, and therefore if we follow Herodotus, the Scythians are also Turkic-speaking.

The version of the Scythians as Iranian-speaking has been enshrined as an axiom in academic history since Vaso Abayev's work *Osetinsky iazyk i folk'lor* [Ossetian language and folklore] (Moscow and Leningrad, 1949), in which some correspondence was found between Scythian and Ossetian words and on the basis of which it was dogmatically stated that the Scythians were Iranian speakers. Meanwhile, however, other researchers have found many Turkic words in the Scythian language. Additionally, Drozdov remarks: "A vast quantity of historical data from antiquity and the Middle Ages, well known to historians of all generations, contains no information whatsoever about the presence of tribes and peoples in Europe in this period with strongly pronounced Old Persian culture and ethnonyms ..."

Marat Barmankulov, polemicising on a slightly different matter with the Tajik Babajan Gafurov, author of the popular *Tadzhiki*, who develops the idea that the indigenous peoples of Central Asia were the Iranian tribes while the Turks appeared there only in the sixth century from Northern China, wrote indignantly: "And so it is claimed that the Iranian-speaking peoples that appeared in Central Asia in the fifth century BC were the aboriginal people, and the languages of the Turkic family that flourished in India in the sixth millennium BC (the Dravidian people – K.Z.), in Elam in the fourth millennium BC, in Harappa, in the oases of present-day Tajikistan and Turkmenistan, Samarkand and Khiva in the third and second millennium BC, recorded in China in the second millennium BC and in Japan in our own time were not indigenous. So how did they cross over from India to China and Japan? Did they fly?"

The Hungarian Turkologist Geza Kuun demonstrated in his book *Kodeks Kumanikus* (1880) that the Scythians were Turkic-speaking. Other well-known Turkologists such as Meziyev and Laypanov reached the same conclusion, and in a letter of 1523 from the Italian Alberto Campenze to Pope Clement VII he states: "The Scythians, now called the Tartars (my emphasis – K.Z.) are a nomadic people that has been famous since ancient times for their warlike nature" (cited in *Biblioteka inostrannykh pisateley o Rossii*, St Petersburg, 1836, vol I).

No further comment is necessary.

# TROY AND THE CATALAUNIAN PLAINS: TURKS AGAINST TURKS. WHY DID MOSES LEAD THE JEWS INTO THE WILDERNESS FOR 40 YEARS?

Earlier I made reference to the Arab historian Ibn al-Athir, who was a contemporary of the Khorezmshah Mohammed and a direct witness to the latter's defeat by Genghis Khan after he had transgressed the norms of human relations by unceremoniously dispatching the Mongol embassy sent to him. That embassy had arrived offering peace and good neighbourly relations to the Muslim ruler and indeed desired that the Khorezmshah remain master of the West, while Genghis Khan would be the ruler of the East. The words recounted by al-Athir as spoken by the Mongols to the Kipchaks were as follows:[74] "You and we are kin, but these Alans are not relations of ours, so there is no benefit for you in helping them; your faith differs from theirs, and we promise that we will not attack you, but will bring you as much money and clothes as you wish; leave us with them..."

We gave convincing arguments in the previous section that the Alan were not Iranian-speaking but rather Scythian, Turkic tribes. So why did Genghis Khan believe that the Alan were strangers to the Turks, if we are not to question al-Athir's assertion? The point is that since the third millennium BC the Turks had had no match anywhere on earth. From the limitless Eurasian steppe there spilt an immense mass of well-armed and courageous migrants in search of a better life that captured sedentary peoples, who often lived at a simpler level of civilization, and frequently set up new forms of statehood on the captured lands. Zhumazhan Bayzhumin, for example, established that in the middle of the second millennium BC the Achaeans came to the Peloponnese from the steppes of Eurasia, and that their ancestors were the Kazakh Argyn, Naiman and Kanly. Later, in the seventh century BC, the Peloponnese received another tide of nomadic Dorians[75] who worshipped the Old Germanic (read: Old Turkic) god Thor. They called themselves the Donars or Tanars, apparently because they lived in the basin of the river Don or Tan. It was natural that the newly arrived Dorians would have to fight with the nomad Achaeans for the best place in the sun, since the fertile lands had been occupied by tribes that, though ethnically related, were in fact strangers. They had not communicated with one another for centuries!

In the same way, Genghis Khan considered the Alan to be strangers to the Kipchak as the history of the latter began with the Turkic khaganates, from Northern China and what is now Mongolia, whereas the Alan are a different branch of the Turks – one that dwelt in the Northern Caucasus from before the Common Era. Meanwhile some historians, going on this episode in which the Alan people were rejected, began to rank the Alan among the Iranian-speaking peoples. Around the eighth century, moreover, some of the Alan adopted Christianity, while most Turks traditionally adhered to Tengrism. This was the reason for Genghis Khan's reproach of the Alans as to holders of a different religion.

Now let us consider the city of Troy. This was defended by Turkic tribes such as the Thracians, Dorians, Lycians and others. The attackers, meanwhile, were Turkic tribes of the Argivian (Argyn) and Achaean clans. The Turks dominated everywhere – they had nobody to fight except each other. Herodotus wrote that "the Scythians worshipped only the following gods: first Hestia, then Zeus and his wife Hera, and after these, Apollo and Aphrodite, Hercules and Ares..." All the famous characters of the Trojan war – on both sides – were direct descendants of Zeus: Achilles and Hector, Odysseus and Paris. That these Trojan figures were Turks is mentioned by Homer himself when he describes Aeneas, the king of Troy, listing seven generations of his relatives, from Zeus to Hector. The obligation to know seven generations of one's ancestors was a characteristic only of the Turkic peoples.

As is usual in such cases, attractive legends about Paris abducting the beautiful Helen were invented under the Trojan theme, and all subsequent fighting depicted as the revenge of the offended party. Abrashkin however gives quite different, geopolitical reasons for the Trojan War in his *Skifskaia Rus'*: "The Trojan Wars played solely into the hands of the Egyptians and Semites, from whom the menace from the North was thus warded off for over 30 years. Furthermore, it seems that it was during this time that the Jews succeeded in occupying Palestine. To the question of why Moses led the Jews into the wilderness for 40 years we may now answer: he was waiting for the outbreak of the Trojan War."

Next let us look at the battle of Attila and Flavius Aetius on the Catalaunian Plain.[76] Western European historians unanimously maintain that the Huns of Attila were smashed by the united Europeans army under the command of Aetius. But is this true? The Roman historian Jordanes described the battle in his *On the Origin and Deeds of the Getae*: "The right wing was held by Theodoric with the Visigoths and the left wing by Aetius and the Romans; in the centre  Sangiban was placed, whom we mentioned above and who led the Alan..." The point here is the formation of the Huns' enemies before the battle. Who do we see in their ranks but more Alan and Goths? As for the Roman left wing under Aetius, we would note that by that time, three quarters of the Roman armies consisted of Turkic mercenaries, while Aetius himself was an Illyrian Scythian.

So here again we have Turkic peoples fighting Turks! We should point out that for centuries, the only adequate match for the Turkic peoples were the Turkic peoples themselves. The Turkic Kipchak defeated the Turkic Khazars and the Turkic Tartars routed the Turkic Bulgarians. The Emir Timur, ruler of Samarkand, crushed the Golden Horde of Toktamysh Khan[77], the Ottoman sultan Bayezid I and others. As for Attila's defeat in 451, in the same year the Huns, regarded by European historians as defeated, captured and ransacked all of Italy.

# TURKIC THRACE. ARISTOTLE, ALEXANDER THE GREAT AND SPARTACUS

After the end of the Trojan War the As-Oghuz seized the territory of what was to become the state of Thrace[78] in the North-East of the Balkan peninsula (this, incidentally, suggests to me the possibility that the origin of the famous Thracians Spartacus and Alexander the Great was also Oghuz, since Macedonia was then also dominated by nomads and was part of the Thracian state). The second- and third-century Roman historian Marcus Junianus Justinus, who wrote a summary or 'Epitome' of the Philippic History of Pompeius Trogus, writes in his ninth book: "At that time the Scythian king was Athey. When he got into difficulties in the war with the Istrians, he asked, through the Appolonians, for the help of Philip (the father of Alexander the Great – K.Z.) in order to adopt him and create an heir to the Scythian kingdom…"

One might well ask how it is that a Scythian king could choose a person from another tribe as the heir to the throne.

Jordan, a historian of the sixth century, wrote in *On the Origin and Deeds of the Getae*: "…but Philip, father of Alexander the Great, having created a bond of friendship with the Goths, took as his wife Medopa, the daughter of the king Gudila, to strengthen the Macedonian kingdom through such a relationship…"

It can thus be seen that the ancient historians speak unambiguously about the close kinship of the Macedonians with the Scythians and the Goths.

Let me say a few words about the famous philosopher Aristotle, who was the tutor of Alexander the Great. He was also born in Thrace and his name consists of two parts, *arys*, which in the Kazakh language means "frame, support", and *toty* – "tribune, speaker, singer". As the founder of his famous school and having many students, his grateful contemporaries and descendants could honour him as their greatest orator or teacher. Meanwhile, 200 years before Aristotle, Anarys, known to the Greeks as Anacharsis[79], was (in some accounts) one of the Seven Sages of Greece. To the Sumerians, An was the god of Heaven, the judge of all other gods, and the name Anarys can be translated as "the support on earth of the God of Heaven", who, as is widely known, was of Scythian origin.

Herodotus described the Scythians and their worthy son Anacharsis as follows: "We cannot suggest any other nation this side of the Pontus who is endowed with such wisdom, nor any man of such scholarship, as the Scythians and their king

Anacharsis. The Scythian people have invented one of the most important human things, wiser than all peoples that we know, after which I am not surprised by anything…"

The first-century Greek philosopher Plutarch, author of the *Moralia*, wrote of Anacharsis in "The Dinner of the Seven Wise Men" that "At the end of this conversation I asked the men to advise us how we should keep house; after all, few men govern kingdoms and cities, but all of us have hearth and home." Aesop, laughing, responded: "No, not if you include Anacharsis: he has no house, indeed he is proud of having none and of living in a carriage, just as the Sun is believed to travel in a chariot as it visits first one side and then the other of the sky."

"And that", Anacharsis objected, "is why it is one or the only one of the gods, free over all others, self-sufficient and higher than all, subservient to none, governing and ruling. But you have forgotten how superlative in beauty and magnificence is his chariot; otherwise you would not have compared it to ours in jest and for laughs…"

That is how Anacharsis (Anarys), our ancestor, stood before the wise men of Greece and praised his own people, who, like the divine Sun itself, were free and ruled freely over all, and he compared the nomad's dwelling, the yurt, to the Sun's chariot – saying in other words that the shelter and homeland of the nomad, like that of the Sun, is the whole world.

In short, ancient Greece had always had our ancestors as its great sons. This is also true for what is now the greater part of Turkey, known in the middle of the first millennium BCE as Anatolia. The words *ana toli* literally mean "mother's offspring" or, metaphorically, "the young growth of Mother Earth". After all, the territories of Turkey and Greece became a new homeland for nomads who had left the Eurasian steppe.

It is interesting to trace the lexical pair *an-khan*. As already mentioned, in Sumerian, An is the god of Heaven, the judge of all other gods, while the name Han has the meaning for the Turks and people of early Rus of an earthly god or ruler. Yet it is common for loan words taken into the Turkic Kazakh language to acquire a formant, a voiceless consonant "h", during graphic adaptation; this was particularly the case here with the Sumerian *an*. The same can be said for the lexical pair *er-gerr (hur)*. The Kazakh word *er* means a man; in German and Russian, acquiring the formants of the *g* and *h* sounds, results in on case in *herr*, the form of address of a man, and in the other, the term for the male genital organ.

The Thracian state in the Balkans came into being in the first millennium BCE, and according to the Soviet Encyclopaedic Dictionary, was settled by Dacians, Odris and Goths in addition to the Trer-Tour. But the Goths (Getae) are the ancestors of the

Kazakh Kete-Khitan, while the Dacia-Dakhi and others are today also represented by the Kazakh Aday. The modern Kazakh Ydrysh (Idris) clan is the descendant clan of the Odris. Herodotus wrote about the Thracians in the following way: "...They are contemptuous of agriculture. For them the life of a warrior and rogue is considered the most honourable. Rich Thracians are given burial rites as follows. The body of the deceased is put on display for three days. During this time they slaughter all kinds of sacrificial animals, and after the funeral wailing is over they give a funeral feast. After this the body is burned or committed to the earth in some other way, and after filling the *kurgan* (burial barrow), they hold various competitions. The greatest prizes are awarded for single fighting, looking at the importance of the contest. These are the burial rites of the Thracians." In his book *Istoria rozhdenia, zhizni i smerti pastukha Avelia. Ariysky leksikon* (Almaty: Tipografia operativnoy pechati, 2009) Zhumazhan Bayzhumin rightly points out that "The burial customs of the ancient Thracians described by Herodotus almost in no sense differ from the ancient Turkic and more recent Kazakh rites..."

The seventh volume of the *Anthology* compiled in Byzantine times, which makes considerable use of material from Strabo's *Geographica* and minor elements of Ptolemy's *Geographia*, states: "The ancient Hellenes believed the Goths and Missians living along the Ister [Danube] to be Thracians." We have already mentioned that the Goths were Turkic-speakers, so it follows that the Thracians were likewise Turkic-speakers. Plato, who lived in the fifth and fourth centuries BCE (and whose real name was Arystokl, which supports the idea of his Scythian origin), wrote of the Thracians in *The Republic*: "**Do we not have unavoidably to admit – I said – that exactly the same types of moral qualities are present in each of us as are present in the republic? How otherwise would they appear there? It would be absurd to think that a characteristic such as wrath of the spirit** (my emphasis – K.Z.) has developed in some nations not because individuals are carriers of this cause; that is how the matter stands for the inhabitants of Thrace, Scythia, and almost all of the Northern lands..."

Thus, my theory that Alexander the Great and Spartacus had Turkic origins does not seem to be too fanciful. Plutarch wrote that Spartacus more closely resembled an educated Hellene than a barbarian. Hellene (elini) was however the name of the invaders from the Eurasian steppes who are known to have captured the Peloponnese in the middle of the second millennium BCE from the Pelasgians,[80] who worshipped the Slavic deity Bele and from whom their name derives. Later, the Romans called the Greeks Hellenes. Speaking of the ethnicity of Spartacus, Plutarch also testified that he was "a Thracian from the nomadikon tribe", so clearly emphasising his affiliation to nomadic peoples. In his book *Kto vy i otkuda, kolesiashchie?* [Who are you and where are you from, wanderers?] (Almaty, 2004) K. Begalin deciphers the ethnonym *thrace* as "ally" (from the Bulgarian *pirak*). This is indeed how they were known by their neighbours and relatives, the Hittites, who grazed their countless herds of horses on Thracian territory. In addition the Thracians were dependable allies to the Hittites in their war with the Egyptians. Flavius Josephus also wrote of the ancient Thracians that their father was the seventh son of Japheth, sent to live in the land between the Volga and Ural rivers by his father the prophet Noah, whom the Turkic peoples consider to be their progenitor.

In the preface to this book I wrote that from time to time streams of nomads would spill out from the lands of Kazakhstan and the Eurasian steppe like lava from a volcano as space on the steppe became too limited; these "exules Scytharum" then conquered the peoples of the Near, Middle and Far East, Europe and Scandinavia, creating new civilisations there. They came in wave after wave, with different names such as the Cimmerians, Scythians, Sarmatians, Goths, Huns, Turks, Mongols – our ancestors, continually seeking and finding new homelands and making them their own. Bayzhumin, for example, established from Icelandic sagas and Old Scandinavian epics the notion that the old Norsemen consisted of two different peoples: the elite, who wore tall hats with trimmed fox fur, trousers and short caftans, indicating a nomadic origin, and the local population, which lived in Stone Age conditions. The elite were formed of the conquering nomads and forced the local population, who lived mainly in the forests, to breed cattle; later, however, this new binary ethnocultural community of Old Germanic tribes returned to the steppe. In this connection, Bayzhumin writes, it was inevitable that the Germanic tribal leaders should acquire Turkic names, such as Berik, leader of the Guthon, while Hungarian leaders should be called Alim, Karkhan and Soltan and the chief of the Huns would be named Balamber, etc. According to some scholars, the nomads introduced Bronze Age attributes such as patterns similar to those of the Scythian and Sarmatian peoples and the animal style in art and writing into the primitive lifestyles of the Germanic tribes. The French historian Jacques Le Goff writes of the conqueror nomads: "They brought a fine technique of metal working, jewellery and leather craftsmanship, as well as the delightful steppe art with its stylised animal motifs."

So here, yet again, is a comparison of the steppe "barbarians" with the "enlightened" Europeans! This then is why, *pleno jure*, I claim that Aristotle, Alexander the Great and Spartacus belonged to the Turkic, nomadic world, just as they belonged to the elite of their nation, which in turn was formed from the conquering nomads.

# THE HYKSOS OF THE GREAT STEPPE WERE THE PHARAOHS OF EGYPT

Let us now return to the Hittites. The formation of the Hittite state was preceded by the creation of the state of Mitanni in Northern Asia Minor, on the Southern shores of the Black Sea, in the early second millennium BCE. Mitanni was ruled by ethnic Matay Meot, who gave their name to the Meotian (or Matay) Sea or Lake, today the Sea of Azov. This state gifted some of the Pharaohs of the Egyptian dynasties to the world.

The Hyksos were also Pharaohs in Egypt. They invaded the land of the Pyramids in the 18th century BCE and came to Asia Minor from the Eurasian steppes of Kazakhstan before the Hittites. They created the 15th dynasty of the Hyksos pharaohs. One of the first kings of the Hyksos was Hiyan or Qiyan. You may remember that the large tribal union from which Genghis Khan himself originated was called Qiyat or Qiyan, and the city of Biruni on the Amu-Darya river once also bore the name Qiyat. Given that the Hyksos named their capital Avaris (Abaris), we may assume that the Hyksos were also related to historical nation of the Avar.

My hypothesis is obliquely confirmed by Herodotus, who, discussing the Hyperboreans who lived far to the North of the Scythians, wrote in the fourth book of his *Histories*: "So, enough said about the Hyperboreans. For I do not want to mention the legend of Abaris, who was also said to be a Hyperborean: he wandered all over the earth with an arrow in his hand…" Modern commentators on Herodotus (for example see *Istoria Kazakhstana v proizvedeniakh antichnykh avtorov*, Almaty: Foliant, 2005, vol. 1, p.96) also associate the name Abaris with the Avar ethnonym – an ancient nomadic tribe of the Altai. Indeed, the name of the capital of the Hyksos is reminiscent of the ethnonym of the rulers of Northern China and Mongolia before the creation of the first Turkic khaganate, the Zhuzhan Avar, who, having been forced by pressure of the Turks to leave their familiar lands in the sixth century, formed the powerful Avar Khaganate in Europe. It may also be that the word *avar* is far more ancient, and in the 18th century BCE was the name of the Hyksos, who later, in the 12th century BCE, migrated with the Hittites to China, where they later became known as the Zhuzhan.

The philosopher Iamblichus, a contemporary of Constantine the Great, writes in *De vita pythagorica* (On the Pythagorean way of life): "When the Scythian Abaris came from the Hyperborean country, unfamiliar with Hellenic scholarship, not acquainted with it and in his later years, Pythagoras introduced him to the course of this knowledge…and in a very short time explained to him his work about nature and another about the gods…" Thus, thanks to Herodotus and Iamblichus we have learned that Abaris the Hyperborean was a Scythian and, it follows, if the Hyksos, having migrated from the far North (known to the Greeks as Hyperborea) in the eighth century BCE to Egypt, called the capital of their new home Abaris, then the Scythian roots of the Hyksos are also undeniable.

The Avars in Europe became powerful Bavarians who together with the Hittites, Goths, Saxon Saq and Toringi formed the basis of the modern German nation. The Turkic, Aryan roots of the ancestors and descendants of the composers Bach and Beethoven, the philosophers Nietzsche, Kant and Hegel, the mathematician Carl Friedrich Gause, the poet Heinrich Heine, the writers Bertolt Brecht and Remarque, the statesmen Bismarck and Hitler, are thus obvious. As we will demonstrate later, in prehistoric times the Kazakhs' ancestors were of a purely Caucasoid racial type, and for this reason, counting the great figures of the past and present among the Turkic world should not cause any feelings of rejection.

After the Hyksos had ruled in Egypt for 150 years they migrated towards Syria and founded the new city of Jerusalem, which later became the capital of Judaea. Do today's Israelis realise to whom they are indebted for their beautiful city in the Promised Land?

If we recall that Beybarys,[81] a Kazakh of the Bersh clan, ruled Egypt in the 13th century BCE, and a snow leopard (*bars*) was depicted in his seal, we may assume that the Bersh formed part of the Hyksos, since *bars* and *abaris* are closely consonant. Thus, Beybarys became the ruler of lands that had formerly been ruled by his ancestors. Many researchers infer from the ethnonym *hyksos* the word *giksaq*, or "royal Saq". Royal Scythian Saqs lived at the headwaters of the Volga and Dnieper rivers, occupied traditionally by Kazakhs of the Junior *jüz*, which allows me to suggest the following: the Alshin (Kete, Aday, Bersh, Cherkesha[82] et al) were among the Hyksos, as also were the Matay, Sadyr and Karakerey[83], because later, after the Hyksos had left Egypt in 1535 BCE, it was these Kazakh tribes that created the Alshe-Alzi states and that of the Hittites in Mesopotamia and Asia Minor. In *The Turkic Saga of Genghis Khan* I proposed that the Hyksos, arrivals from Central Asia and the Caspian steppe, were the Koksesi – a group of tribes and clans that had proved their might over other clans and that worshipped Eternal Blue Sky.

In other words, these were the Royal Scythians. The Kazakh utterance *ses korsetti* literally means a person who strikes fear into those around him due to his menacing look. In addition the Chinese call the Kazakhs 'Hassaq', which translates from Chinese as 'real Saq'. Therefore I consider that the ethnonyms *giksak* (Hyksos) and *hassak* are different versions of one nation's name – that of the Kazakhs. Bayzhumin links the origin of the *hyksos* ethnonym with the name of the Kazakh clan Kokshe[84] that is found among the present-day Argyn and Ysty[85]. The once numerous and powerful Kokshe tribe roamed the steppes of Northern Kazakhstan and gave its name to the Kokshetau mountains; the modern capital of the Akmola region of Kazakhstan is now called Kokshetau. Contrary to the widely held view among academics that the Hyksos were tribes from the Arabian peninsula, Bayzhumin makes the justifiable point that the horse – the basis of the Hyksos army – was not brought to the peninsula until 2,000 years after the Hyksos invasion. At the time of the Hyksos, the Arabians used camels; they began to rear horses only at the start of the new era. Strabo visited Arabia in the first century BCE as a member of the Roman delegation and found no signs of the presence of horses, never mind of their use for military purposes.

# THE ANCIENT ALTAY, BIRTHPLACE OF KING ARTHUR AND SCOTCH WHISKY: TURKIC GREAT BRITAIN

The popularity in England of the King Arthur legends can be judged from the statement of Queen Elizabeth I's secretary in 1568 that "these books often oust the Bible from the chambers of monarchs…" British scholars agree that the historical Arthur lived in the early sixth century and was the leader of the Celtic tribe of Britons. The Celts are known to originate from the Central Asian steppes. The first invasion of the Celts to the British Isles occurred in the early second millennium BCE, the second wave is dated to 750 BCE and the third to the first century BCE. While in England in March, 2011, I had occasion to meet the administration of Coventry University. When I posed a question as to the origin of the current Queen, Elizabeth, the dean of the faculty of tourism, Professor John Beech, answered that she was from the Celts, and that the Celts in turn were immigrants from Central Asia!

As Orazak Ismagulov demonstrates (*Etnicheskaia antropologia Kazakhstana*, Almaty, 1982), Central Asia and Kazakhstan were at that time inhabited by Turkic and Kazakh tribes. According to written sources, the Celts occupied the vast territory from Germany to Asia Minor and from Holland to Spain and Italy. Celtic settlements can be found close to Ankara that date back to 270 BCE. In Central Asia an archaeological expedition led by S. Tolstov has discovered the Neolithic culture of the Aral region, called Celtic on the basis of the name of the village Kelteminar. Later, as a result of drought in Central Asia, the Celts migrated to the Dnieper, the Carpathians and the Lower and Middle Danube, from where they attempted a number of incursions into the British Isles as mentioned above. Nikolay Kikeshev writes in his book *Metaistoria. Otkuda my rodom? Mify, gipotezy, fakty* (Niola, 2010): "Rolling into Europe in the fourth millennium BCE, wave after wave of the ancestors of the Celts, Saqs and Illyrians' ancestors settled the peninsula and the areas protected by mountains, forests and wetlands from the storms that raged so often in the vast lowland of Turan, and they shaped the modern world of Europe."

Scholars note that "the Celtic languages have a number of features that link them with the dead 'Tokharian' languages of Turkestan and the ancient languages of the Hittites. This indicates the ethnic affinity of the Hittites and the Celts." In previous chapters we discussed the Hittites as Turkic tribes whose descendants were the German Getae (Goths) and the Kazakh Kete. The fact that the Goths were a Turanian tribe was mentioned as early as in the sixth century by Procopius of Caesarea: "In former times the Goths were called the Sauromat". The fifth-century Byzantine historian Priscus of Panium identified the languages of the Huns and Goths, and the Russian scholars Yuri Petukhov and I.N. Vasileva suggest that: "It is clear that the Gothic language that was common to all the barbarians that descended on Rome had no relation to the modern German group. Nor could the language of the Goth-Sauromat belong to the Iranian group either: for in Europe, subjected to repeated waves of invasions, no traces of the Iranian Aryan remain." So, who are the Goths, if they are not Germans and Iranians? There is only one answer: they are Turkic tribes!

Returning to the words of Queen Elizabeth's secretary, I would like to say that we, the Kazakhs, are grateful to our ancestor, the legendary King Arthur of Britain, if only for the fact that the monarchs of the early medieval era preferred to read the stories about the exploits of this knight of the Great Steppe in their chambers over reading the Bible.

I think we have made sufficient argument in favour of the Turkic origin of the Celts of Britain, from whom King Arthur of the Britons descended.

Let me add just a little information from Plutarch's *Parallel Lives* (see eg I*storia Kazakhstana v proizvedeniakh antichnykh avtorov,* vol. 1, p. 289), where he points out in the chapter on the Roman general Gaius Marius: "Some say that the Celticum, due to the width and size of the country from the outer sea and Northern latitudes turns East at the Maeotis[86] and adjoins Pontic Scythia, and that the mixing of the peoples occurred there. Having arisen out of there, though not immediately and not continuously, but annually at a convenient time moving ever forward, they fought their way through the entire mainland. **That is why, regardless of their numerous private names, they commonly gave their hordes the common name Celto-Scythians"** (my emphasis – K.Z.). So we see from Plutarch that the Celts considered themselves to belong to the Scythian people.

Now let us look at the origin of the Celtic tribe of the Britons in more detail. The Anglo-Saxon Chronicle testifies to the fact of the Britons being the first inhabitants of the islands of 'misty Albion'. Nennius, the Herodotus of British history, recorded the oral history of the Britons in the ninth century: "I will try, following the legends of our ancestors, to discover what is known about the British island. The island of Britain was named in honour of Britton, son of Isiocon, who was the son of Alan of the clan of Japheth" (*Nenniy. Istoria brittonov. Formy istorichestogo soznania ot pozdney antichnosti do epochi Vozrozhdenia*. Ivanovo, 2000). But we know that Japheth, son of Noah, became the father of the whole Turkic family, and that the Alan/Alban belong to the Oghuz wing of the Turks. Other tribes of the Scots and Picts, who were also among the first inhabitants of the British Isles, were also Turkic-speaking, as Nennius wrote: "But when the Brittons began to be disturbed by the barbarian tribes, namely the Scots and Picts, they asked the Romans for assistance." At that time the warlike nomads of the Eurasian steppes were called barbarians. Yuri Drozdov, analysing the ethnonyms of the seven kingdoms that had been created in the British Isles by the end of the sixth century, concludes that the names of four of them – Anglia, Mercia, Northumbria and Kent – have Turkic roots. For example, the name *anglia* is derived from the ethnonym *angly*, which can be interpreted as 'intelligent', 'wise', 'clever', etc. The Turkic sonorant sound [ӈ] is transcribed into the Latin alphabet by the diphthong [ng], and the hard sound [ы] is replaced by the soft sound [i].

Drozdov further proves names familiar to British ears such as Stonehenge, and the suffix 'shire', that designates many of the counties of the UK, such as Yorkshire, Staffordshire, Shropshire, Nottinghamshire, etc, to also have Turkic roots. Other words such as 'parliament', 'lord', 'king', 'baron', 'squire', etc, also belong to this category. Drozdov concludes: "...since ancient times Britain was populated by Turkic tribes...", so that the entire ethnonymy of British names is also Turkic-based. Now let us go back a little further, to the first centuries of the Common Era.

According to authoritative sources, in the middle of the second century BCE the Sarmatian Iazyges crossed the Danube and attacked the Roman Empire, so beginning what were known as the Marcomannic Wars. The Iazyges were supported by the Lombard and the Alan, who, as we have shown and will show again, also originated on the Kazakh steppe. Rome was forced to sign a peace treaty with these allies, under which the Iazyges were obliged to deliver to Rome 8,000 cavalry soldiers annually to provide a service for the protection of Roman possessions. Some of these Iazyg mercenaries served in the Roman British legion. Bayzhumin writes that "this is how Sarmatian knights appeared in the lands of Britain; and scholars associate that cultural environment with the origin of the King Arthur legends."

According to the European historian H. Nikel, "At the heart of the Arthurian cycle is the pre-feudal, heroic epos that prevailed among the Sarmatians and Alan who found themselves in France and England as part of the Roman army at the time of the Great Migration..."

The French comparative philologist Georges Dumezil also wrote of the possible Sarmatian origin of King Arthur.

We are thus entitled to suppose that King Arthur's direct ancestor, who originated from the Sarmatian tribe of the Iazyges, arrived in the British Isles as a member of the Roman imperial army under the peace treaty between the Sarmatians and the Romans. It remains only to add that the Naiman clan Qarauyl Zhasaq is the ancestral clan of the Iazyges, who now inhabit Eastern Kazakhstan. The Kazakh word *zhasaq*, meaning 'band of men, army', was eventually transformed into the name Iazyg, a tribe of Sarmatians. The etymology of the name Arthur also hints at Turkic roots.

In Kazakh, *ar* means 'honour', 'holiness', 'conscience'; *tur* and *oghuz* are one and the same concept and refer to the Oghuz, the largest Turkic tribe, who worshipped the moon, the night-time companion of Eternal Blue Sky. *Oghuz* itself means 'bull', and so the name Arthur could mean 'sacred bull'. In addition the Iazyg Zhasaqs belong to the Oghuz wing of the Turkic nation.

Commenting on Strabo's *Geographica*, the editorial board of *Istoria Kazakhstana v antichnykh istochnikakh* notes that the Sarmatian Iazyges lived on the coast of Lake Maeotis (Matay) at the start of the Common Era. Among today's Kazakh tribes, the pedigree Iazyg Zhasaqs belong to the Naiman Matay, which is thus a further argument in favour of the historical Meot and today's Matay being the same peoples.

Now a few words about the origin of Scotch whisky. I would like to quote some passages from M. Adzhi's book *Bez vechnogo sinego neba* (Moscow: Astrel, 2010). Let us take a simple question: where, apart from whisky production, is barley used? This crop is a basic fodder for horses, you will say, and you will be absolutely right. We now have evidence at our disposal from researchers at the University of Oxford that the wild horse was first domesticated in the fourth millennium BCE on the Kazakh steppes, and archaeological findings near the town of Botay in Northern Kazakhstan strongly support this. It was at that time, four millennia BCE, that our Kazakh ancestors learned to cultivate barley as the primary fodder for tamed horses. The Oxford researchers also showed, from the analysis of the internal composition of drinking vessels of that period, that *kumys* – a drink made from mare's milk that intoxicated the body and soul of the steppe warrior – was invented at this time. Our meticulous ancestors noticed that boiled mare's milk does not intoxicate, while the unboiled milk does so.

They thus concluded that the intoxication is lost in the steam when boiled. From this the first distillation equipment appeared for collecting the precious moisture from the vapour, and they gave it the name Al Kǝk Ol, which literally means 'take the heavenly moisture'. Since, however, it was not possible to obtain kumys all year round (as the milk is only available when a mare foals), a substitute was devised in which barley was milled into flour for use in a home brew. As Adzhi writes, alcohol is as sound a cultural symbol of our ancestors as were iron, bridles, thick felt, bricks and the other 'birthmarks' of the Altai.

In the eighth century BCE, long before the Great Migration mentioned above, the ancestors of the Kazakh Alban arrived on the Caspian steppe from the Altai; there they founded Caucasian Albania and propagated their faith in Tengri, the God of Heaven, among the conquered peoples. Subsequently, some of them moved to the area between the Tigris and Euphrates rivers and established Persia under the leadership of the Achaemenid dynasty. The creator of this royal dynasty was Kurush, who later became known as Cyrus II (the Great). In Kazakh, *qurysh* has a figurative meaning of 'steel', thus implying 'strong', 'powerful', and that was how the ancestor of the Kazakh Alban must have looked. *Bars/Pars* became the totem and *tamga* of a foreign people. Caucasian Albania was once known as Arran, which in Turkic means 'sacred'. The fact that Great Persia was created by alien nomads from the Altai is confirmed by the British explorer Mary Boyce in her book *The Zoroastrians: beliefs and practices* (Moscow, 1987) where, writing about the proto-Iranians, she says that in ancient times they "ranched cattle in the Southern Russian steppes and produced weapons Eastward of the Volga, in the mountains that fringed the Central Asian steppes, particularly in the Altai..."

The impatient reader may wonder how all this is connected to Scotland and its whisky. The point is that once the Huns arrived on the Caspian steppe from the East at the start of the Common Era, the ancestors of the Kazakh Alban went West. In what is now Spain the Alban – the people of Bars – founded Barcelona (Bars Eli). Having crossed the English Channel they named their new home Albion, and ultimately the newly arrived monks, ministers and disseminators of the Tengrian faith settled on the island, in what became Scotland, and to remind them of their lost home on the Caspian, gave the island of Arran its name (Caucasian Albania). This then became the cradle of whisky. Archaeologists in our own times have discovered inscriptions in Turkic runes on cave walls on Arran, and nearby burial sites with a horse, created according to the Altai ritual, and much else that make the early masters of the island recognisable.

The writings of the Arab historian Ibn al-Athir further indicate that there was a state named Arran in the previous homeland of the Northern Caucasus. In his 'Collected materials relating to the Golden Horde' (*Istoria Kazakhstana v arabskikh istochnikakh*, Almaty: Dyke Press, 2005, vol. 1) he describes the following episode concerning the Mongol invasion of Transoxiana in the summer of 1221: "After dealing with it [the city of Baylakan], they devastated and ravaged its surroundings completely. Then they set off for the city of Ganju, the mother city of Arran. But having learnt of the number of its inhabitants and of their bravery, as evidenced by the many battles with the Georgians, and of the extent of the city's fortifications, they did not even approach it, but rather sent messengers to its citizens asking for money and clothing..."

Anyone who has visited the museum of Shakespeare  in England may have been curious about the exhibit of a baby's cradle named Besik. To the question of how a Kazakh cradle may have arrived on the misty island of Albion, however, I hope I have given an adequately comprehensive answer.

# THE MAEOTIANS, MITANNI AND MEDIA.
# THE GOSPEL OF MATAY

In *The Turkic saga of Genghis Khan* I suggested, on the basis of certain documentary data, that the ancient Maeotians who lived on the Maeotian coast are represented today by the Kazakh Matay. I will continue to substantiate my hypothesis with further data. Eustathius of Thessalonica wrote a commentary on the description of the world by the Greek Dionysus Periegetes (see e.g. *Skify*, Moscow: Vysshaia shkola, 1992) in which I found the following passage: "The Maeotian lake lies to the north of the Euxine. The Scythians surround it and it sets the limits on their lands, ... but also the Maeotians, who are also a Scythian people, large in number and strength, who are engaged in agriculture and war. The Maeotian lake is called the mother of the Pontus, and this is why, according to some sources, it was named 'mata', in the sense of a 'wet nurse'."

The waters of lake Maeotis feeds into the Black Sea through the Kerch Strait, formerly known as the Cimmerian Bosporus. For this reason the lake was named Maeotian, or 'nursing'. Accordingly, the Scythians living near the lake were named the Matay (mata – 'mother', 'nurse') or the Maeotians. The Sanskrit Vedas contain a saying, attributed to the ancient Aryans, 'Dyaur me Pita, Mata Prthivi iyam' – 'Father of mine is the Sky, Mother is the Earth'. Here the word 'Mata' (in Greek transcription mata) is understood as 'mother-nurse'. In Egyptian mythology MAAT is the goddess of truth and justice and is the daughter of Ra, the Sun God. She is the nurse of all matter and all that pertains to the earth. According to legend, those who passed into the next world fell into the hands of Osiris, the god of the Underworld, and had to undergo certain trials, the results of which enabled Osiris to decide whether to let the deceased pass on to heaven or to enter the purgatory of hell. The deceased person's heart was placed on a balance with a depiction of the goddess of justice, Maat. If the heart was lighter than the goddess's image, the deceased would go to heaven. Hence perhaps the expression 'to live with a light heart', that is, without spiritual discord.

We can see that Eustathius ascribed the Maeotians to the Scythians. Strabo, however, a Greek living in the first century BC, attributed them to the Sauromat. In the second book of his *Geographica* he writes: "These countries are occupied in the first place by the Maeotians [Sauromat] and the tribes living between the Hyrcanian [Caspian] Sea and the Pontus as far as the Caucasus, the Iberians and Alban, namely the Sauromat, the Scythians and the Achaeans." It is not important, ultimately, whether the ancestors of the Kazakh Maeotian Matay were in fact Scythians or Sauromat, since either way they belonged to the Turkic people. There is however another fact that is of fundamental importance. Modern historians believe that the vanished Scythians were replaced by the Sauromat, even though Strabo, an eyewitness to the event, continues to assert that "...to their south and above the Maeotis live the Sauromat and the Scythians as far as the place of dwelling of the eastern Scythians..."

The past of the Kazakh Matay is inextricably linked with the history of Mesopotamia, the first highly developed culture in the history of mankind. Here I make reference to *Neue Chronik der Weltgeschichte*, an overview of world history by the German scholars Brigitte Beier, Uwe Birnstein, Beatrix Gehlhoff and Ernst Christian Schütt (Gütersloh: Chronik Verlag, 2005). We learn that the first migration of nomadic Sumerians from Central Asia to Mesopotamia occurred in the fourth millennium BC. It was they who built the first towns and created a written language and a developed culture. Then in about 2340 BC the state of Akkad was founded in Central Mesopotamia that 200 years later was conquered by a warlike nomadic people, the Gutians, who held power over the conquered lands for 130 years.

Later a nomadic tribe of Elamites known in the Bible as the Amorites began to dominate in the region. In his book *Tiurkskaia vselennaia* Marat Barmankulov suggests that an alphabet was created more than three millennia before Christ that gave rise to the various agglutinative Turkic languages. So who were the inhabitants of this ancient state by descent, if not Turkic? Today the descendants of the Elamites are represented by Kazakhs of the Junior *jüz* from the Alim Uly tribal union.

In 1531 BC the Babylonian kingdom of southern Mesopotamia was seized by the

Hittites, who came to Asia Minor from the Caspian steppes around 1900 BC. The Hittites did not rule in Babylon for long, however. Soon another even larger group of nomads, the Kassites[87], took the capital of the kingdom of the 'four corners of the earth' and ruled for nearly 400 years. After this the Kassitian kingdom was captured by nomads again – the Elamites. Parallel to this, and at almost the same time as the formation of the Hittite state, the state of Mitanni was established in Mesopotamia that vied with the Hittites for the palm of victory in the Middle East and south-eastern Asia Minor. At the turn of 1500-1000 BC waves of other nomadic groups were arriving on the Plateau of Iran; these created Media and then Persia, which was established by Cyrus II the Great of Persia in 550 BC.

Then in 250 BC another group of nomads led by Arsaces[88] founded the Arsacid dynasty, which ruled in Iran until 224 AD. In the eighth century BC the Scythians displaced a kindred group of nomads, the Cimmerians, from the northern Black Sea. These, now also 'exules Scytharum', found refuge in Lydia in Asia Minor and participated along with Media in the destruction of Assyria (625 BC).

Further examples may also be cited from this source that draw pictures of Eurasian nomadic tribes invading the lands of Egypt, Mesopotamia and Persia. There is no better description of the horrors of the Scythian invasions than in the Old Testament book of Jeremiah: "Behold, I am bringing against you a nation from afar, O house of Israel, declares the Lord. It is an enduring nation; it is an ancient nation, a nation whose language you do not know, nor can you understand what they say. Their quiver is like an open tomb; they are all mighty warriors. They shall eat up your harvest and your food; they shall eat up your sons and your daughters; they shall eat up your flocks and your herds; they shall eat up your vines and your fig trees; your fortified cities in which you trust they shall beat down with the sword" (Jeremiah 5: 15-17 ESV).

According to the Ismagulov-Bayzhumin theory, during these two thousand years the Eurasian nomads who were displaced from their lands by more powerful clans were forced to find new territory by conquering sedentary peoples in the Middle East and in south-east Asia. The Gutian Hittites are found today among the Kazakh Naiman and Alshin clans (of China and the Kete), while the Elamites are represented by the Alim Uly union of Kazakhs of the Junior *jüz*. In the view of some scholars the Kassites later gave the Kazakhs their ethnic name. In about 1750 BC the Kassites came across the northern Caucasus to Mesopotamia from the steppes, which at that time were inhabited by Turkic, Kazakh tribes. Under the leadership of Qandash they captured Babylon. The Kazakh name *it*, denoting 'wolf' or 'dog', is *saq* in Persian, and thus the lexemes *kassit* and *kassaq* contain the same semantic load. Aleksandr Bernshtam believed that the union of two As tribes, the Kas and the Saq ('Wolf People') under the common name Kassak led to the name of the Kazakhs. It should also be remembered that the Chinese called the Kazakhs' ancestors the Hassak. Later I will return to this question when discussing the legend of the origin of the Kazakhs from the union of a swan (*kaz*) and a wolf (*saq*).

In *Skifskaia Rus* Abrashkin makes a compelling case for the Mitannians and Medes being none other than descendants of the Maeotians, who, as we have shown, are today represented by the Matay.

Indirect arguments that Media was at that time inhabited by Turkic tribes were given in the second century BC in the Greek historian Polybius' *The Histories* (see e.g. I*storia Kazakhstana v proizvedeniakh antichnykh avtorov,* Almaty: Foliant, 2005, vol. 1). In book ten of the *Histories* we find: "Media is a wonderful state in Asia, in terms both of its extent and of the size of its population, and equally for the outstanding quality of its horses. Media supplies nearly the whole of Asia with horses, as even royal herds are entrusted to the Medes for their fertile Indian pastures…" It is known also that the ancestors of the Kazakhs, the nomads of the Great Steppe, were renowned and unrivalled in the rearing of horses.

The ten-volume *Vsemirnaia istoria* (Moscow, 1956, vols. 1 and 2) tells us that the tribes of the Medes were known from the ninth century BC and came to the Near East from the northern Caucasus and Central Asia. Researchers suggest that they were the ancestors of the Scythian Matay who lived by the Maeotian Sea and comprised the bulk of the Sarmatian people. Subsequently the Medes united the kindred groups of the *Gutians and the Kassites* to themselves and created a powerful state that covered what is now Iran, the Armenian highlands, northern Mesopotamia and Asia Minor. The Medes were related to the Persians, spoke the same language and shared their customs and religion. In the following chapters we will argue that the founders of Persia were of Scythian origin. Among the principal cities of Media, Ecbatana (in Kazakh, *Kokbata*) and Gazak may be drawn out.

In this book I have repeatedly spoken of the Turkic roots of the Sumerians. The source used by the authors of *Neue Chronik der Weltgeschichte* concerning the expulsion of the Cimmerians by the Scythians and their persecution in Asia Minor in the eighth century BC is Herodotus; but, as Abrashkin writes, Herodotus contradicts himself. The 'Father of History' said that the Cimmerians were moving towards Asia Minor along the eastern shore of the Black Sea, but the Scythians supposedly pursuing them he places on the coast of the Caspian. These routes thus hardly suggest fleeing on one part and pursuing on the other. In fact, as Abrashkin correctly concludes, the Scythians and Cimmerians, being related, were devising a common objective for establishing control over Mesopotamia and Asia Minor. In the same way, in the twelfth century BC the Hittites, who had dominion over Asia Minor, travelled to western China to aid related tribes in establishing control over the Celestial Empire. This was how the Western Zhou dynasty came into being.

Many Kazakh tribes considered the *bars* (snow leopard) to be their totem, so it is no coincidence that the *bars* has become a symbol of Kazakh rebirth and power, while Kazakhstan's southern capital Almaty has the *bars* on its coat of arms.

As for the ancient state of Mitanni, some believe that it was inhabited by the Hurrians, who are ancestors of the Kurds. Yet our study has shown that the indigenous inhabitants of China, Persia, Egypt and Europe were ruled by our ancestors for centuries. It is therefore possible that the Kurdish Hurrians of Mitanni were also ruled by our ancestors. Yet the majority of the multinational state was made up of Aryans who had migrated from the Eurasian steppes, that is, they were ancestors of today's Kazakh tribes. In addition, the military guards of the kings of Mitanni were composed of Marian Amorites – and again, as will be shown later, the Marians were ancestors of Turkic nomads. We have already said that the Amorites are referred to in the Bible as Elamites, and their descendants today are the Kazakhs of the Alimuly tribe.

The ancestral lands of the Maeotians/Matay in the Black Sea steppes were occupied later (in the fourth to seventh centuries AD) by related tribes – the Bulgars, who created Great Bulgaria. It is known that after the death of the Bulgarian khan Kubrat, his three sons departed under pressure applied by the ascendant Turkic Khazars and went their separate ways to other lands: the eldest, Asparuh, went to the Danube, where, together with the indigenous tribes of the Danube, he founded modern Bulgaria; the second son, Qotyrak, established the state of Volga Bulgaria on the Qama River, and the youngest, Botbay, moved to the south of Kazakhstan and founded a large Kazakh tribe. The Botbay Bulgarians lived in the Azov steppes with their capital at Phanagoria (now Taman). Besides the Botbay the Bulgarian khaganate also included a number of other Kazakh tribes, primarily of the Junior *jüz* and in particular the Tama clan, which gave its name to the Taman Peninsula.

For their name the Bulgarians or Bulgarians were indebted to the Balgaly tribe of Kazakhs, who today belong to the tribal union of the Kazakh Zhalair. It was this tribe that chose the Volga floodplain for pasturing their countless herds; they named the river Balga or Volga.

The greatness of the Kazakh Botbay tribe is depicted in our national folklore: "If you are Uysin then be a Botbay, if you are Alshyn then be an Aday, if you are Argyn then become an Altai, if you are Naiman then be a Matay." All these clans and tribes are Kazakh.

A discovery by the anthropologist Orazak Ismagulov has been a great support to me. He demonstrated that two thousand years before the time of Christ, Kazakhstan, including the Caspian and the Black Sea steppes, was populated by tribes and clans whose descendants still live there today. They may now have other ethnic names, but the fact remains that our ancestors have lived on this very land since ancient times. Tribal unions have changed their names, alliances have been created and broken, but as indivisible atoms the Kazakh clans have always existed. It is simply that, to solve political questions at various points in their history, they formed alliances and other forms of relationship and contact that then mutated or broke down over time, but the kinship always remained. The Kazakh clans created the unions of the Saqs, Sarmatians, Huns, Turks and Mongols; these unions eventually disappeared, but the Kazakh clans always remained. And when, today, it is stated in world encyclopaedias that nomads came at some time or other from Central Asia or other fringes of the Eurasian steppe to countries such as Egypt, Persia or China and established one or another civilisation, then these nomads were, for certain, the ancestors to the Kazakhs; this is the main thrust of Ismagulov's theory.

Let me remind us that in the middle of the second millennium BC the Alshin, represented today by Kazakhs of the Junior *jüz*, created the state of Alzi in Upper Mesopotamia, and from this are derived the Halizones, Alshins and others. It is generally accepted that the Dahi mentioned in the Avesta, whom Strabo called the 'Dai' who lived in the middle of the second millennium BC on the eastern shore of the Caspian and in what is now southern Turkmenistan are today the Kazakh Aday. Murad Adji also believes that the Iranian tribes at the time of the Achaemenids and Arsacids included the Dahi. The encyclopaedia *Vsemirnaia istoria* (Moscow: Eksmo, 2003) describes the Getae (Goths) as the northern group of the Thracian tribes, kindred with the Dahi-Dai who lived in what are now Romania and Bulgaria in the fifth century BC. When the Persians under Darius I (513 BC) rose against the Scythians, the Getae and Dahi supported them. This is understandable, since they were kin to the Scythian, Turkic tribes. They also fought in close union against Alexander the Great.

Let us however return to the Hittites. Today the Kete clan, under the name of the Kitay, is part of the Tolegentai association of the Naiman tribal union, while a small part of it is an independent clan within the Alimuly of the Kazakh Junior *jüz*. In ancient times it is likely that the Hittites-Kete-Kitay and the Matay were blood relatives. It is known, for instance, that in 15 AD the Roman general Germanicus, recruited by the Romans from the German tribes of Turkic origin, during a confrontation with the German Chatti tribes (see e.g. *Chronik der Menschheit*, pub. Bodo Harenberg, 1999) took their capital Mattium. It may be assumed or even asserted that the Chatti-Hittites-Kete, who formed the basis of the German people, named their capital by the name of their people, the Matay. Incidentally, in the Bible the grandson of Noah, the son of Japheth, was Madai, while some Finnish editions of the Gospel of Matthew title it the 'Gospel of Matay'. Titus Flavius Josephus writes in *Antiquities of the Jews* that the Madey, called the Mede by the Greeks, are descendants of Japheth's son Mada. Some sources maintain that the Apostle Matthew/Matay was buried in accordance with his wishes in a monastery beside Lake Issyk-Kul. Incidentally, the brothers of the Madai, as indicated in the Bible and in the *Shajare* of Abu al-Ghazi Bahadur were Turk, Khazar, Oguz, Kimar, Rus, Chin and others.

I believe that the modern Russians take their roots from Rus', the Cimmerians originated from Kimar and the Northern Chinese from Chin, and the situation was the same for the Oghuz, Turks and Khazars. It should however be noted that the Naiman tribal union stands apart. In addition to the ancient Matay tribe, which was formed at the same time as the birth of the Turkic peoples, this also includes the Manchurian Chzhurdzhen (the Shursheit clan of the Teristamgaly tribal association). In addition to these, this union also includes descendants of the Hittite-Kete and many of the Khitan who established the Liao dynasty in northern China in the tenth century. Recently I took a DNA test (I belong to the Matay clan); an American laboratory issued me a certificate stating that my maternal ancestors lived in Germany, Spain, Italy and the Middle East.***

As we have seen, what are now the Matay and Kete could long ago have entered into friendly and familial relationships. The same could be said of the Argyn and Naiman. Discussing the kingdom of the Cimmerian Bosporus beside the Azov and Black Seas during the first millennium BC, Shakh-Murat Kuanganov links the Sindi people,[89] with their capital Sinda (present-day Anapa), with the large Argyn clan, the Suiyndyk (*Ariy-gunn skvoz' veka i prostranstvo: svidetel'stva, toponimy.* Astana: Foliant, 2001). I would point out that all rulers of the Bosporan Kingdom bore[90] the title of 'Archon and Basileus of all the Sindi and Maeot'; an example is Spartok II, son of Levkon I, Archon of the Bosporus and Theodosia, Basileus of all the Sindi and Maeot (reigned 349-344 BC).

At that time the Sindi tribes were part of the Maeotian (Matay) tribal alliance. But let us also consider the Matay and Botpay. The first of these can be found among the Kazakhs of the Middle *jüz* and the second among the Senior *jüz*. Today these clans live in different regions, and on top of this the Matay belong to the Naiman tribal alliance whereas the Botbay are part of the Dulat union. Earlier, while discussing the Zelenchug inscription, I mentioned that the membership of the Botbay in the Dulat union is artificial. In fact, however, I will try to show that the Matay and Botbay were in fact also closely related.

The Kazakhs had various words for a wolf: *kaskyr, sakkulak, kokzhal, itkus, bori, baskurt*, etc. Accordingly, the Wolf clans (the Matay and Sadyr) gave different names to the territories, mountains and rivers by which they lived. The Volga, for example, was once known as the Itil (*itel* – wolf peoples) in honour of the Matay and Sadyr who then lived in its basin. In classical antiquity the Dnieper was named the Borysthenes; in my view this literally means Boriozen, the 'river of the Wolf clan'. I have substantiated the thesis that the Volga was later known by the name of the Balgaly clan of the tribe of Zhalair, who once wandered in the Volga basin. There was thus a linguistic shift Balga – Bolga – Volga. Meanwhile the Baltic Sea was in turn named after the other major clan, the Kazakh Baltaly, who lived on its coast from about the fifth or sixth century BC. This view is supported by Yuri Drozdov: "The ancient European nations usually named their territories not for their landscape features but for the ethnonym of the tribe that dominated there (but not vice versa)."

The etymology of the Aspar river in the Zhambyl region of Kazakhstan is also of some interest. According to Kalihan Iskakov this name, and also that of Asparuh, founder of the Bulgarian khanate on the Danube, are distortions of *ash bori*, literally 'hungry wolf'. Thus the river is named after the 'hungry wolf' Aspar, while Asparuh is in fact Asparhan or Ash Borihan, khan of the Wolf nation. It turns out that Botbay was one of the sons of Khan Kubrat of Old Great Bulgaria, the capital of which was located in Phanagoria, close to Lake Maeotis in the ancestral land of the Maeotians or Matay, and was the brother of Asparuh and related to the Matay tribal union. According to the modern Shezhire (Kazakh genealogy), the Botbay clan is part of the Dulat tribal union, but this is doubtful, since according to the tenth-century Zelenchug inscription the Botbay and Dulat were independent Kazakh tribes of equal standing. The fact that the Maeotians/Matay and Volga Bulgars, particularly the Botbay, shared the same territory in the Azov region is also not unimportant. This is what lends plausibility to the notion that the Volga Bulgars belong among the Wolf peoples, and hence to the modern Kazakh Matay and Sadyr. By extension, a kindred relationship between the Matay and Botbay is also possible, although the modern Shezhire places them in different *jüz* groups. This version is also supported by an ancient legend shared widely among the Kazakh Naiman.

According to this, our ancestor Naima was left without a male heir as a result of constant warfare. His daughter-in-law (*kelin*) was an intelligent woman from the Dulat clan, who was also worried that Naiman clan would die out. Early one morning she inadvertently witnessed her father-in-law relieving himself. The froth and the deep channels left on the ground where the man had urinated convinced her that despite his 85 years he was still capable of offspring. She set off for her Dulat relatives, and told the council of *aqsakal* (elders) of her concern about the potential disappearance of the Naiman. With the support of her relatives, she created a match of her cousin as a wife to her Naiman father-in-law. She bore him two sons, Sujinshi and Sugirshi. When Sujinshi reached 14 she married him, gave birth to many children, and thus saved the Naiman from extinction. As a sidenote, Kalihan Iskakov also decoded another ethnonym contained in texts of the Orkhon-Yenisei monuments to Turkic writing. A stone dedicated to Kultegin and containing inscriptions warning Turkic warriors of the temptation to live in luxury in the conquered cities after their seizure from the Chinese, includes the following lines: "O Turkic nation, if you settle in that land [China], you may die. But if you are at the place of Otuken and send caravans for gifts and tributes, you will have no grief. If you dwell among the rabble of the Otuken, you can live and support your eternal state…"

The 'place of Otuken', today called Karakorym, was the headquarters of the Turkic khagans. Its etymology is *oty ken*, literally 'spacious, vast hearth or shelter', or in other words, 'native land, ancestral land'. In my view, the translation 'rabble of the Otuken' is also lame. The fact is that the Kazakh word *kara* ('black') has multiple meanings. While the primary meaning is 'black', it can also mean 'multiple', 'great', 'powerful', etc. In this instance it would thus be better to refer to the 'great, mighty Otuken' rather than referring to it as a rabble.

## THE ETRUSCANS AND BASQUES, ROME AND ITELI

What can be said about the mysterious Etruscans? It is known that their ancestors were called Tirsen, Tauri and Tur ('Tirsen' literally means 'children of Tur' and the Greek 'Tauri' also means 'Tur'; all of them are Oghuz) and that they moved from the Caspian steppe to Asia Minor in the second millennium BC, settling in the state of Lydia. According to the findings of Orazak Ismagulov, then, they were our ancestors.

Let us develop our idea. Before the start of the Trojan War (Troy, incidentally, means the city of the sacred bull, Oghuz, Tur) Ital (Iteli), the ruler of Sicily, moved from Asia Minor to the Apennine Peninsula.

As a consequence, his name became the ethnonym for Italy. Then after the Trojan War (1260 BC), the Tirsen tribes migrated from Lydia to the Apennines and established the state of Etruria. It is possible that there were seven tribes (Oghuz and Seir) and that they called themselves Zhetyru. Something similar is thought to have occurred in Kazakhstan in the 18th century when seven small clans, closely related to that of Genghis Khan, were united by Tauke Khan into the large Zhetyru tribe. According to one version, this then is the origin of the ethnonym 'Etruscan'. The Etruscans built twelve cities in what later became Italy.

In his book *Skifskaia Rus'* Abrashkin provides another possible origin for the ethnonym 'Etruscan'. In this version, there existed in the Mediterranean two millennia BC the state of Rusen, situated between Egypt and the Great Hittite state. Drawing on the sources used in the works of the Russian historians Nikolai Karamzin and Vasily Tatishchev, he argues convincingly that Russiain history began not with Rurik and Kievan Rus, but far earlier.

The author by the statue of a she-wolf who reared Romulus and Ram, exhibited in the Capitol Museum in Rome.

The Etruscan sarcophagus of spouses from the Banditaccia Necropolis. Polychrome terracotta, 6th century BC. Villa Giulia Museum, Rome.

Thus, after the end of the Trojan War, the Rusen and some of the Hittites left for the Apennine peninsula under the name Hetrucian. Just as with the analysis of the lexical pairs *al-khan* and *er-hur*, we may suggest that the ethnonym *hetruscan* was transformed in Italy to 'Etruscan'.

Drozdov writes in similar vein about the origin of the Etruscans, saying that they called themselves 'Rasen'. Using his method of breaking words into their constituent parts, he concludes that *rasen* is derived from the Turkic language as 'clan of men of the As', and thus that the Rasen are As people, and so part of the Turkic group.

The Romans in turn called the Etruscans the Tusci, whence the name of the province in which the newcomers initially settled: Tuscany. They themselves, however, called their hospitable new homeland Apa Ene, which in Kazakh means 'nursing mother', and Kuanganov suggests that this is the origin of the name of the Apennine peninsula.

By the eighth century BC the Etruscans founded Rome and erected a symbolic monument of the she-wolf said to have suckled Romulus and Ram, the city's founders. The tale of a wolf becoming the ancestor of the Turks has however become overly familiar. Apart from the Etruscans, the peninsula was also inhabited by the Gauls, who also formed the indigenous population of modern France. In his *Commentaries on the Gallic War*, Julius Caesar claimed that the Gauls were given this name by the Romans, whereas their self-name was 'Celts' and that they were Turkic-speaking, as we established earlier.

The ethnonym 'Italy' is itself nothing other than *iteli*, which means, again, 'people of the Wolf', while the only Kazakh clans that are considered to be wolf clans are the Sadyr and the Matay. The original ethnonym of a wolf (before its domestication) was the word *itkus*. The wolf was master of the steppe and the *bars* (snow leopard) was master of the mountains, and this is why our ancestors the Matay and Alban put them on their totems. The most direct reference to the arrival of the Wolf peoples on the Apennine peninsula is an inscription on the Gollini tomb that has been deciphered by the Kazakh writer and poet Olzhas Suleimenov. The fresco, carved above the sarcophagus, depicts horses harnessed to a chariot with a charioteer and carries the inscription *zatl ad aidas*, which may be read as *zhatyr at aidaushy*, or 'here lies a horse drover'. The inscription dates to the eighth century BC.

Murad Adji interprets the 'Italy' toponym somewhat differently. He considers that the name of the Apennine peninsula state is connected with the last Roman emperor, Romulus Augustus, who was the son of Attila's confessor and who was removed from the throne by Odoacer, mentioned earlier, who was the Hun king of the new Italy. The word *ytala* in Turkic means 'rejecting', and it came to be associated with the country that had refused the legacy of the Roman Empire. The new name has come to replace the older names, such as that of the Roman state, Hesperia, etc.

Here is another version, also linked with the toponym of a wolf people. It is interesting to note that some of the Etruscans departed for the Iberian Peninsula and created the Basque Country in Spain with its capital Bilbao. According to the just observations of some scholars, if Italy was brought up in the cradle of Etruscans, then Spain was raised in the cradle of the Basque. The Basques also inhabited the area of Gascony in southwest France. And who knows, maybe our Kazakh blood flowed in the veins of the famous Gascon, the Comte d'Artagnan, or those of his double. Linguists have noted a similarity between the Basque language and that of the Mexican Athabaskans. In *The Turkic saga of Genghis Khan* I analysed in detail the kinship of the North American Indians to modern Kazakh clans. The parallels between the Basques and the Athabaskans ethnonyms also speak volumes. The Athabaskan are a senior, main clan and the Basques are a branch of it.

It has become an axiom in today's society that the Romans were the teachers of Europe. We may therefore claim that the teachers of Rome, in turn, were the Etruscans, ancestors of the Kazakhs.

# ALBAN PERSIA AND ADAY PARTHIA
# KULTEGIN AND TOMYRIS
# HERODOTUS ON THE SCYTHIANS

Let me make a few more remarks about today's Alban, Matay, Aday and other Kazakh clans. For one thing, it is widely known – and discussed by Murad Adji – that Persia, founded in 550 BC by Cyrus the Great, owes its greatness to the nomadic Turkic tribes that came to the Iranian lands in the 10th-15th centuries BC from various parts of Eurasia and comprising the Parsi, Dahi, Medes and other groups. The Parsi, as scholars agree, is an ethnonym for *bars* clans, represented today, as we have said, by the Bersh, Alban and other modern Kazakh clans. The Dahi are unquestionably the Kazakh Aday, whom Strobo described in the first century BC as the principal Scythian tribe. The Medes, as we mentioned in earlier chapters, are descendants of the Scythian Maeotians/Matay. And as is widely recognised, in 612 BC Media, in south-western Asia Minor, was conquered once again by the army of the Scythian king Madiy of the Kazakh Matay clan. Later a part of Media became part of Azerbaijan, and it is quite possible that the Medes are Turkic Oghuz, among whom plenty of Kazakh tribes, particularly the Matay, can be found today.

The Greek historian Xenophon, who lived in the fifth and fourth centuries BC, wrote in his *Cyropaedia* ('*The Education of Cyrus*') that: "Cyrus was so superior to other kings, who received their power by right of succession or acquired it by themselves, **that while a Scythian** (my emphasis, K.Z.), although the Scythians were great in number, he could not subdue any other tribe, but was satisfied to rule, if only over his own tribe, whereas Cyrus, on the other hand, ruled over many peoples."

It is not possible to assert indubitably from this passage of Xenophon that Cyrus II's origins were Scythian, but there is indirect evidence. Indeed the Roman historian Quintus Curtius Rufus testified to his origin as Scythian in the first century. In his *Historiae Alexandri Magni* (see e.g. *Istoria Kazakhstana v proizvedeniakh antichnykh avtorov*, Astana: Foliant, 2006, vol. 2) he describes the opening of Cyrus' tomb at the order of Alexander: apart from Cyrus' shield, almost reduced to dust, only two Scythian bows and an akinak were found; nothing else. Ammianus Marcellinus wrote more specifically about the ethnic origin of the Persians of Cyrus II in his history of the Roman empire, saying: "Therefore the Persians are of Scythian origin ..." (*Istoria Kazakhstana v proizvedeniakh antichnykh avtorov*, Astana: Foliant, 2006, vol. 2, p. 242).

According to the World Encyclopaedia published by Bodo Harenberg, in 250 BC a second tide of Eurasian nomads came to the north-western area of the Iranian plateau. From part of the earlier Persia they created the no less great Parthia, which existed until 224 AD. Parthia was founded by Arsaces I, whose name in Kazakh means 'Saq endowed with honour' (the particle ar means honour or conscience). A seal left behind from the Achaemenid (Cyrus II) and Arsacid dynasties indicate their Turkic Kazakh origin. This seal is exhibited in the State Museum of Iran together with the image of the Turkic runes and also writings based again on Turkic runes.

In the sixth century, Jordanes describes (in *On the Origin and Deeds of the Getae*) the battle between the Goths under the leadership of their king Tanauzis against the Egyptian king Vesozis, where the Goths defeated the Egyptians and chased them up to the Nile: "Pompeius Trogus says that it was from their name and kin [the Goths – K.Z.] that the Parthian generation originated. That is why, to this day, they are known in Scythian as fugitives, i.e. Parthians…" And this is correct; forced from the Eurasian steppes by their more successful kinsmen and in turn becoming 'exules Scytharum', they established a new home in what is now Iran and called it Parthia.

According to some data, Arsaces I was the leader of the Dahi tribe, who were ancestors of the Kazakh Aday. This idea is supported by Tacitus, who writes in the *Annals*: "And so they called for Artabanus, Arsacid by blood, who grew up among the Dags ; defeated in the first battle, he gathered new strength and captured the Parthian kingdom." Elsewhere he writes: "This was greeted with joy by all who cursed the cruelty of Artabanus, who was raised in Scythia… after delaying not longer than was necessary to appeal to the Scythians for help…" And, finally, Justinus' *Epitome* of *Pompeius Trogus'* Philippic History, referred to the Scythians as follows: "They themselves founded the Parthian and Bactrian kingdoms… were the ancestors of the Parthians and Bactrians…" (*Skify*, Moscow: Vysshaia shkola, 1992, pp. 249-251).

I think that we have now argued sufficiently that it was the ancestors of the Kazakhs who played the most direct part in establishing and ruling the states of south-western Asia. Persia was established by descendants of the Alban, the Medes by the Matay and the Parthians by the Aday. The Kazakhs have every right to ascribe Cyrus II the Great, king of Persia, Cyaxares, king of the Medes and Arzak, king of Parthia, to the pantheon of our illustrious ancestors.

The greatness of the Parthian state, which rivalled Rome, is described in Plutarch's *Parallel Lives*, in the chapter on the Roman general and orator Pompey: "…to please the latter, Pompeius wanted to address the Parthian king in the return letter by the aggrandising title 'King of Kings', as did all others…"

And now for something different.

According to the famous legend, Oghuz Khan distributed the *tamgas* among the Turkic clans. In *Taina runiki* Tayzhan Dosanov justly assumes that the base table he discovered, which contained all *tamgas* of Turkic tribes, and also the symbols (runes) of the Turkic alphabet, should also contain the *tamga* of Oghuz Khan, and eventually he finds it.

He deciphers the character  for 'Kək' or 'blue sky' as Oghuz – "sheltered river" (og in Turkic means 'shelter' and 'uz' means 'river'). However, the character is the *tamga* for the modern Kazakh Aday clan. Analysing the legends of the births of Aday and Oghuz Khan, Dosanov concludes that the two are in fact one person. Oghuz, as we know, was the grandson of Noah, the son of Japheth, and so his clan is large. For example, at the time of the Turkic khanate the Ade and Adye clans, along with the Baegu-Baiuly, belonged to the Toguz-Oguz who set up the Uyghur khaganate after the collapse of the Second Turkic khaganate. Modern-day Uyghur do not have a link to the Uyghur khaganate, claims Dosanov, as they are not divided into clans and do not have *tamgas* or clan signs. This conclusion was additionally confirmed by Barmankulov, far earlier than Dosanov, in *Tiurkskaia vselennaia* cited earlier; here he notes that the Ancient Uyghur language does not form a basis for the modern Uyghur language, and so the modern Uyghurs are related only indirectly to those Uighurs who became the heirs to the Second Turkic khaganate and who were called by the Chinese the Hoihu or Huihe.

The Kazakhs are contemptuous of such people, calling them 'Sarts' and asserting that if the Turkic nation was conceived from the sperm of a wolf, the Sarts originated from its urine. Referring to works by Nikita Bichurin, Dosanov claims that Great Turkic khagans Kultegin and Mogilyan were from the Aday. The Soviet orientalist Vasili Vaslievich Struve in his study of on the history of the northern Black Sea, the Caucasus and Central Asia, published in 1968, concluded that the Dahi, Dai, Massaget, Caspians, Alans and Aday were one and the same tribe, and with reference to the writings of the Babylonian priest Marduk Berosus, that the Persian king Cyrus II the Great met his death in the valley of the Dai. From this it follows, concludes Dosanov, that Queen Tomyris of the Saq-Massaget, who defeated Cyrus II the Great, came from the Aday clan. Her brave feat is portrayed in the Behistun Inscription on a stele from near the modern Iranian city of Hamedan, established by order of the Persian king Darius the Great. The eastern coast of the Caspian was populated mostly by the Aday, and these had different names: the Dai, Parthians, Alan and Caspians.

As a result of internal strife, some of the Aday migrated westwards under the name Alan, while others headed south to the Iranian Plateau, as mentioned earlier, under the name of the Parthians and formed the famous Parthian state. The Dai left for the Balkans and founded Dacia, a rival to the Roman Empire. Those who headed for what is now Turkmenistan were known as the Oghuz and those who remained in what is modern Kazakhstan retained their ethnic name, the Aday.

Herodotus noted very precisely the main character traits of our ancestors. Here is what he wrote in book 4 of the *Histories*: "…Among all other peoples known to us, only the Scythians have mastered one art, but one that is of greatest importance for human life. This consists in the fact they do not allow any enemy who has attacked their country to escape; and no one can catch them, so long as they do not allow it. The Scythians have no cities or fortifications, so they carry their dwellings with them. All of them are mounted archers, and they live not by farming but by cattle-breeding; their shelters are their tents. How could such a nation be anything but invincible and unassailable?"

This then is the heroic ode is dedicated by the famous citizen of Greece of the fifth century BC to the ancestors of the Kazakhs. Later, at the transition from the first century BC to the first century AC, Pompeius Trogus spoke of the morals of the Scythian steppe nomads: "Their concept of justice is instilled in them by their own reason and not by laws. Their most serious crime is stealing: after all, for a people that does not take refuge under a roof, and who keep herds and flocks, what would remain for them in the forest if theft were permitted? They do not feel passion for gold and silver as do other mortals... This forbearance has shaped the justice of their morals, that is, the lack of passion for other people's possessions... Oh, if only other mortals had such abstention and forbearance from the property of their fellow men! It is astonishing that nature herself gifts them that which the Greeks cannot achieve even by the deep wisdom of its sages and the teachings of its philosophers, and that uneducated barbarism turns out to be higher when compared to highly educated manners: insofar as ignorance of vices is more useful for the former than is knowledge of virtues for the latter..."

Pompeius Trogus also wrote of the military prowess of the Scythians: "The Scythians have tried to achieve dominance over Asia three times; yet they themselves have remained untouched and unbeaten by foreign domination at all times. They drove Darius of Persia unceremoniously out of Scythia; Cyrus and his army were slaughtered; Zopirion, a commander of Alexander's the Great army, was killed along with his army in the same way... They themselves founded the Parthian and Bactrian kingdoms." (*Skify*, Moscow: Vysshaia shkola, 1992, pp. 250-1).

The author was familiar with the episode connected with the signing of the treaty delegitimising the borders between Kazakhstan and Turkmenistan. When all the necessary procedures had been completed, the now deceased Turkmenbashi addressed our President, saying that he was giving ancestral Oghuz lands to their neighbours the Kazakhs. The Kazakh president replied with words to the following effect: "Thanks to the indomitable military spirit of the Kazakh Adays' ancestors, the border between our two countries has its present shape, but it could extend south of Ashgabat." For myself I would add that if our nation had not had its brave Aday, there would also have been no basis for the power and prosperity of the Kazakh state in the form of Caspian oil.

In any case we may state unequivocally that there were no losers in this situation. The Oghuz Turks displaced from what is now the Mangistau region of Kazakhstan in the early eleventh century went on to conquer most of Persia, Azerbaijan, Kurdistan, Iraq,

Armenia, Georgia and Asia Minor, creating the royal house of the Seljuks. Later, their descendants created the Ottoman Empire that extended its influence to countries in Asia and Europe.

# The Argyn and Argentina.
# Who oversaw the origin of France?

A few words about the Bura clan of the Yergenekti Naiman of the Kazakh Middle *jüz*. In his book *Tiurki i mir. Sokrovennaia istoria* (Moscow: Khranitel', 2004) Murad Adji writes that in 411 Constantius, commander of the Roman army, a Danube Kipchak and the future Roman emperor, attracted a group of Burgundians from the Altai to the West and allowed them to settle in what later became France. In my view the ethnonym of French Burgundy owes its origin to the Hun clan Bura, who today belong to the Kazakh Yergenekti Naiman. Nikolay Kikeshev provides an interpretation of ethnonyms with the root *bur* with reference to the work of the Soviet archaeologist Alexei Pavlovich Okladnikov. In Sumerian, *bur* means 'water', 'pool'. In Siberia and the Altai there are settlements of groups named Bur, Buruhan, Burhan, Burhal and Buran situated on rivers called Bureya, Burunda, Burkala and others. In antiquity the Euphrates was called the Buratta. Constantine VII (Porphyrogennetos), the 10th-century Byzantine emperor of the Macedonian dynasty, named the Danube Bulgar the Burgar, and in the 20th century Tsar Simeon II of Bulgaria held the title of King of Saxe-Coburg-Gotha. The following conclusion thus naturally suggests itself: if the Burgundians came from the Altai, then the Burgun are Huns who lived near rivers, in this case the major Siberian rivers Irtysh, Ob and Yenisey, whereas the Burgoth is a Gothic tribe that also lived near water. In short, in antiquity French Burgundy was populated by our ancestors, who gave it the name of their clans.

It is worth pointing out that the Scythian Burgundians left a distinctive mark in the history of the Great Steppe. The Kazakh epic *Alankay batyr* describes the events that took place in the North Caucasus around the beginning of the Common Era: "Mighty like a dragon, he was thrown from his horse. Having expelled the Burgundians, he freed his horse. In the Sea of Azov the soldiers watered their horses…" Following Attila's death the Burgundian tribe split into two, one part of which settled in France and the other returned to its Altai homeland.

Today many of us chuckle at the idea that the ethnonym of Argentina could be connected with the illustrious Kazakh clan of the Argyn, yet the example of the French Burgundians might convince us to the contrary. We now have access to serious studies that confirm the similarity of the languages of the South American nations and the Turkic peoples (see for example the works of Otto Rerig, A. Ahmetov, Ebrar (Abrar) Karimullin, etc), and who knows – maybe the Argyn indeed left their traces even in faraway Argentina. Even Xenophon wrote in the fifth century BCE that there were islands in the Aegean known as the Arginuuz. With the arrival of the Huns in Europe in the first millennium ethnonyms such as Argen, Argim, Argentin and others appeared on the old continent. The Turkic Lombard tribe came to power during Attila's reign in the fifth century, leaving the *Codex Argenteus*[91] by way of a literary monument, and there are reasons to believe that the ancestors of the Kazakh Argyn lived in Northern Italy, in the Lombardy region with its capital Milan (which, incidentally, was Attila's capital). Toponyms of this clan can be found elsewhere: from the Argun river that flows to the Pacific in the Far East to the Aragon valley in the Pyrenees in Western Eurasia. Moreover, 22,000 years BCE the Bering Strait and the Panama Canal did not exist, and nomads could move freely across the steppe of Eurasia and into North and South America without interruption.

In February 2010 a group from the Kazakh Academy of Sport and Tourism climbed Aconcagua in Argentina, the highest peak in the Western Hemisphere. As Kazakhs we were pleased to discover a real cult of meat among the people of this country. Cattle-breeding in Argentina, local people told us, has an ancient tradition that was developed by the local population, who came to South America long ago, long before Columbus, from the territory of the Eurasian steppes.

According to our data, the Turkic Lombards came to Europe together with the Huns. They included not only the ancestors of the Argyn but also other Kazakh clans. It is known that a *bars* (snow leopard) adorned their banners, a symbol we associate with the Bersh, Alban and other modern Kazakh kinships. Additionally, the Lombards belonged to the Germanic tribes that lived in the Po river basin and repeatedly besieged Rome during the time of its prosperity. The Germanic tribes were primarily Goths (Getae, Kete), i.e. the kinships of the present-day Naiman, and representatives of the Alimuly tribes. Interestingly, the Lombards, having become Italians, scorned the native inhabitants of Italy and called them their slaves. This is reflected in their Code of Laws of 643. Murad Adji discusses this. The following historical fact also reveals the power of the Lombards. In 774 Charlemagne, the founder of France, was crowned with the Lombard crown. Incidentally, the title *king* itself has roots in the name Charles. Referring to Adji, K.K. Tompiev, author of *O tiurkskikh plemenakh i narodakh Azii i Yevropy* considers that the French king originated from the Turkic Balt and was named Sharlamaq, which means 'a devotee of wandering and journeys'. Incidentally, the Duke of Burgundy at that time was also called Temir, and later became known as Charles the Bold. Today the Balt belong to the Naiman Baltaly clan and probably belonged to the Lombards. Bayzhumin asserts that the Russian philologist and connoisseur of Western European manuscripts Alexey Shakhmatov concluded that Charlemagne's roots were from the Turkic Bulgarian nomads, and his grandchildren were thus the first kings of France, Italy and Germany.

There is thus also another hypothesis concerning the origin of the founder of the Carolingian dynasty as being from the Kazakh Botbay, since Botbay was a brother of Asparuh, who founded Bulgaria. The truthfulness of the Bayzhumin-Tompiev-Adji hypotheses is confirmed by Sergey Baimukhametov in his book *Prizraki istorii* (Moscow: AST, 2008), claiming that during the eighth century one of the Mauritanian emirs of Spain, which at that time was dominated by Turkic Muslims in the war against the emir of Zaragoza, appealed to Charlemagne, king of the Franks, for assistance. The question is: why should the French emperor have helped the Turkic ruler of the Spanish province unless they were bound by ties of kinship? It would follow that not only French Burgundy but all of France was ruled by our ancestors in the eighth century. But later, at the instigation of the Jesuits, this campaign of Charlemagne's was predictably designated a war for Christ against the wicked.

## ALEXANDER 'THE TWO-HORNED ONE' AND THE ALTAI. THE SWORDS OF ATTILA AND ARTHUR AND THE SACRED STAFF OF PIR BEKET. SCYTHIAN ROOTS FOR HYPERBOREA AND APOLLO.

As is well known, the indigenous inhabitants of North America, thanks to Columbus, were called Indians. This was due to a great error on the part of the famous explorer, who thought until the end of his life that he had sailed to India and not discovered a new continent. A delusion on a similar scale, by a historical person of similar fame, Alexander the Great, is reported by Nikolay Kikeshev. Making reference to the Greek historian Arrian of Nicomedia, author of *Anabasis Alexandri* [The Campaigns of Alexander] written 500 years after the death of 'two-horned Alexander', and also to Eratosthenes, he comes to the sensational conclusion that Alexander did not reach India, but rather arrived at the Irtysh and then the Ob rivers across the territory of Kazakhstan, then returned home across central Kazakhstan.

Just think how many memorable places exist in Kazakhstan that are related to this great man! A real Mecca for tourism! Quintus Curtius Rufus, who lived in the first century BCE and wrote *Historiae Alexandri Magni*, describes the commander addressing his men on his Indian campaign thus: "Oh soldiers, I know well that the inhabitants of India are telling you things that might intimidate you, but these empty lies were not unforeseen by us. In just the same way, the Persians brought fear on us near the Cilician Gates and before the expanses of Mesopotamia, the Tigris and the Euphrates... But what are you most afraid of – a crowd of animals or of enemies? As regards elephants, we have a recent example: they crushed more of their own masters than us... We are standing on the threshold of our deeds and works, we have almost reached the end. Soon we will come to the rising of the sun and the ocean. Just do not yield to cowardice. From there, once we have conquered the edge of the world, we will return home the victors... Do not tear the palm branch out of my hands that will equate me to Hercules and Liber Pater if jealousy does not intervene... Whom do I address? What do I want from you? I want to save your greatness and glory. Where are those whose power I have seen recently, who hurried to retrieve the body of their wounded king? **I will find one who will go with me, whom you rejected; the Scythians and the Bactrians**[92] **will be with me** (my emphasis – K.Z.). The commander would rather die than become a beggar... Go home! Go, celebrate, abandoning your king! I will find a place here for a victory that you do not believe in, or for an honourable death!"

The commander's words to his exhausted soldiers took place in Bactria, in northern Afghanistan, near what was later Balkh. India was far away...

The Roman historian did not mention whether the soldiers obeyed their king or not, but Arrian was probably right: Alexander did not reach India.

A prominent public figure of Kazakhstan, O. Baygeldi, told me an interesting story of a sword that fell from the sky, destined by the Almighty for Attila. So who was this man, referred to as the Scourge of God by scholars and writers of the European countries? The Byzantine historian Priscus of Panium wrote of Attila: "The Romans obeyed his every demand, each of his coercions was regarded as the sovereign's order."

It all began like this. Attila was had reached the Irtysh, presumably near the Kaznakov crossing by the village of Samarskoe in Eastern Kazakhstan, and, having crossed to the right bank, was preparing to punish Northern China, whose ruling Wei dynasty had refused to pay tribute, when an enormous sword fell from the sky. Attempts by Attila's soldiers to pull it out of the ground were in vain; it yielded only to the leader of the Huns himself, and on its glistening blade was the inscription 'Eskini endir', which translates literally from the Kazakh as a command from the sky to restore the old and good traditions in the world that had been desecrated by earthly kings (*eski* – 'old', 'decrepit'; *endir* – 'introduce', '*let in*', 'initiate').

In short, he received a divine order to restore the norms of human morality that had been violated by the rulers of Rome, mired as they were in sin and debauchery. As he stood deep in thought, holding in his hands this message from heaven, Chinese ambassadors appeared at the pass bearing precious gifts and asking forgiveness for their disobedience. Sighing with relief that he needed no longer to worry about the lands to the rear, he set off to the West to fulfil his divine mission.

The etymology of the name Iskender/Alexander is also associated with *eskini endir* and now, with new data indicating that Alexander the Great also visited the Irtysh river, it is unclear whether the Alexander Pass in Eastern Kazakhstan is associated with Attila or with Alexander.

As a parenthetical note, the story of a sword falling from heaven, or other tales in which a sword is involved, are found in the folklore of many nations, yet they remain connected, one way or another, with the actions of the Turkic peoples. We may recall the Arthurian version of this legend roughly as follows. Uther Pendragon, King of Britain, falls in love with the wife of the Duke of Tintagel, the beautiful Igraine. He asks the magician Merlin to give him the appearance of the old duke in order to be able to sleep with Igraine in the matrimonial bed. The magician fulfils the king's request, but on the condition that he give him the child born of their union. Soon Uther dies, and the country is plunged into the chaos of internecine war owing to the lack of an heir. By the time Arthur reaches 20, however, the Archbishop of Canterbury and Merlin propose a test for the knights they have gathered: to pull a sword out from the stone in which it is stuck fast. Whoever succeeds would gain the throne. Only Arthur is able to pull the sword from the stone, at which Merlin reveals the secret of Arthur's birth to the assembled knights and proclaims him king of all England. Later this sword, granted by God like that of Attila, will make King Arthur invincible. Not all of the knights, however, recognised Arthur as their king. A cruel struggle began, and only with the help of relatives, Sarmatians from continental Europe, was Arthur able to gain his foothold as king.

In the modern era the legend of the divine predestination of a sacred sword has become transformed into the legend of the sacred staff, the *asa tayak*, the owner of which receives spiritual authority over the world and people. A well-respected Sufi spiritual leader, Beket ata, whose monument is situated in the Mangystau region of South-Western Kazakhstan, was given possession of Kok Asa – which made him a sheikh of his Sufi order and gave him magical powers. According to the legend, the asa tayak was intended by divine will for a selected person and only the one marked by God's seal could find it, pull it from the earth or a rock, and use it for their spiritual purposes. Towards the end of his life the owner of this divine sign would throw it up to the heavenly height, and only a worthy successor would be able to find the *asa tayak* and become the new spiritual leader. After Beket ata the Kok Asa passed to a man by the name of Shekty Bay, whose great-great-grandson is Tursyngali

Nakesh, now the director of the memorial complex of Koblandy batyr in Hobdin region, Aqtobe oblast, who today possesses this precious sign from heaven. The grandfather of my wife Marzia, Ilyas ata, who was given the second name Aukyn (Akyn) for his poetic talent, also held Asa Tayak in his hands, but knowing the immense responsibility of its owner, chose to pass the sacred relic to another man, whose descendant, the heir of the holder of the sacred Asa Tayak, was invited by Krymbek Kusherbayev, the Akim (mayor) of Mangistau region, to live in Aktau. Today, I believe, the huge success in terms of social and economic development of this oil-rich region has been made possible thanks in part to the favour of the heavens.

For Kazakhs and the wider Muslim world, the Oglandy escarpment in the Ustyurt plateau, where the remains of Beket ata lie, is a place of pilgrimage, as the following poetic lines illustrate: "In Mecca-Medina is Mohammed, in Turkestan is Khoja Ahmed, in Mangistau is Pir Beket." Among the Aday clan of Kazakhs, whenever misfortune or a difficult situation befalls a person, they call for help from *ar-ruh*, the spirit world, by naming Beket ata; in battle with the enemy in times past, and in modern times when making difficult and important decisions, the cry Beket ata! helps them reach their goal. Among the Muslims many legends passed concerning this holy man. Like Jesus Christ, he cured the sick, restored justice and stood up for the poor and needy. But there is one particular legend I would like to discuss. While a student at the *madrasa* in the town of Urgench, Beket's classmates decided to play a trick on him. One of them put on a shroud, and pretended to be dead, while the others called for Beket and asked him to pray for the peace of the deceased soul. After fulfilling this request, the young Beket said: "The High God has called him to himself." The prank turned out to be disastrous, resulting in the death of the *madrasa* student.

Returning to the Indians of North America, in *The Turkic Saga of Genghis Khan* I substantiated the thesis of the kinship between the North American Indians and the Kazakhs. The explanation is simple. After the Great Flood, caused by the collision of the Earth with an asteroid, the population of Hyperborea abandoned their land. Only part of this group migrated to the Eastern hemisphere, the steppes of Eurasia; the remainder preferred the Western hemisphere, the territory of what is now the United States. Thus a single people was dispersed to the far corners of the earth.

This version is supported by Mayan dictionaries from the Yucatan Peninsula. The Tatar linguist Aribzhanov, having acquainted himself with the manuscript of the Spanish archbishop Diego de Landa, who visited tribes of the Maya in Mexico in 1562, proposed a genetic affinity between the languages of the Turkic peoples and those of the Maya. The studies of the Kazakh scholar A. Akhmetov also indicates this. Here are some words and phrases in Yucatan Maya with their Kazakh equivalents in brackets.

Tash (tas - stone), yash chilan (zhas zhylan - young snake), tsibinche (shybyn - fly), tule (toly - stout), kalak mul (kalak mol - spoonful), ak (ak - white, clean) chamo (shama - possibility), ich (ish - abdomen), iki (yeki - two), bacalar (bakalar - frogs), tun (tun - clean), etc. Some toponyms are also preserved on the Yucatan peninsula: Tsilan (zhylan - snake), Yachil (zhasyl - green), Soyyl (soyyl - stick), Bacalar (frogs) Bay, etc. It is also known that the ruler of the large Mayan city of Calakmul was called Han (Kan).

The civilisation created by the Mayan Indians is worthy of admiration. Previously I mentioned their 19-digit number system, which was subsequently used in the seventh century on the Arabian Peninsula by the Quraysh in writing down the Qur'an.[93] The reasoning for our decimal system is straightforward – we have ten fingers – but why was the number 19 sacred to our ancestor Indians of North America? What supernatural knowledge moved them? I found the answer in Nikolay Kikeshev's book: Apollo, the sun god born in Hyperborea, visited his distant ancestral home every 19 years, since this is the exact period in which the stars complete their transit across the sky and return to their former positions; moreover, lunar and solar calendars coincide at this interval, which enables us to calculate the times and locations of eclipses.

That was the knowledge our ancestors possessed even in prehistoric times! And the fact that the Qur'an is based in certain respects on the number 19 (for example, if we consider the date of its revelation to be 568, then $5 + 6 + 8 = 19$; the text of the Qur'an consists of 114 *sura* and 634 *ayat*, both of which numbers are divisible by 19; the number of times the names *rahman* and *rahim* are mentioned are also divisible by 19, etc.) confirms again my hypothesis that our ancestors were directly involved in the creation of the sacred book of Islam. We will discuss this again.

Let us note another important point. The ancient Greeks believed that the mythological Hyperborea was the home of the Sarmatian Scythians, **thus Apollo, born in Hyperborea** (this is confirmed by the sixth-century BCE Greek poet Pindar) **was Scythian by origin**. He was revered by the Gauls and other Celts, and modern scholars believe that the cult of Apollo was indeed formed in ancient Greece, but among immigrants from the Eurasian steppes, the Dorian tribes. As we mentioned earlier, ancient Greece was ruled by a sequence of Eurasian nomads – the Pelasgians, Achaeans, Dorians, Ionians, etc. They created myths and legends that were later considered to be Greek. In *Tiurkskaia vselennaia* (p. 158) Marat Barmankulov maintains that coins were minted in Central Asia at the time of Alexander the Great carrying images of Apollo and Artemis, Aphrodite and Hercules and Zeus and Poseidon, but "…it was long ago, when the (Ancient Greek – K.Z.) Gods were not Christian but pagan (i.e. Turkic – K.Z.)."

# ADAM AND EVE ARE FROM ALMATY.
# WHAT LANGUAGE DID THE ALMIGHTY SPEAK?

Now let us turn to the origins of the time of the creation of the universe and the Garden of Eden. Here we have found some interesting coincidences, and it seems unlikely that they are by accident. Consider the name Adam; this word in Kazakh means 'man'. Meanwhile *alma* (as in the city of Alma-ata or Almaty) translates in two ways: 'apple' and the prohibition 'do not take it'. In the Biblical story of Eden, then, God warns Adam and Eve not to touch (*alma*) the forbidden fruit of the apple (*alma*) tree. So, is it coincidental that the word *alma* should be used for an apple?

British scientists have established that the apple originated in the vicinity of Kazakstan's Southern capital, Almaty. It would clearly follow from this that the story of the expulsion of the first humans must be associated with the surroundings of Almaty. If this is so, is it not time for us to restore the historical name of our beautiful city, a name that has been honoured over the centuries, Alma-ata?

In connection with the above, let me recall the history of the appearance of the word 'kangaroo'. When the colonialists set foot in Australia and saw this strange animal for the first time, they asked the natives what kind of animal it was and what its name was. The reply they heard was *kangaroo*. Yet in the local language this word simply means 'I don't know', 'I don't understand', as they could not understand the language of the strangers. The latter, however, took this sound and fixed it as the name for the unfamiliar creature.

What happened with the word alma was the same, and the name of Eve's partner Adam has become used in Kazakh as the ordinary designation of a human being ('man', 'person'), whereas the name Eve was a transformation of the Kazakh names 'Ana', 'Ene'. If the Kazakhs retained the name of the first man as the definition in their language of a human being in general, then it is most likely that the original name of the world's favourite fruit was the Kazakh word *alma*. Is this then not evidence that God first spoke Kazakh when he uttered the command 'Alma!' ('do not touch!')? In the Biblical account the world was created in seven days, so, if it is established that apples were first grown on Kazakh territory, then the first people, Adam and Eve, appeared here too, walking about these heavenly apple trees – and during the same week of creation as the apples. According to formal logic, it follows that the homeland of the first person was our Kazakh land, and so God would have spoken our Kazakh language.

# A STRONGHOLD OF TENGRIISM: THE OGHUZ AND SEIR

The whole Turkic world of Tengri worshippers may be divided into two groups: the sun-worshippers, the Seir, who later became known as the Kipchak and have left a significant mark on history, and worshippers of the night guardian, the moon, known as the Oghuz. And today the problem can be worked on in separate parts as to which Kazakh and Turkic clans adhered to which of these groups.

The clan signs of the Oghuz feature a crescent moon, and the Yergenekti Naiman and the Shapyrashty and Alasha clans can be clearly assigned to this group. It is likely that the Oghuz also include the Matay, Sadyr, Karakerey and Tortuuly, since they came to China in the 12th century BCE under the Hittites from Asia Minor, then in the eighth century BCE they reached Kazakhstan and in the third century BCE they came to the Black Sea territories and Western Europe under the name of the Iazyges, the Roxolani and the Alans, all of whom are Oghuz tribes. We have discussed the Sarmatian tribe of the Iazyges above. Their ancestral clan today is the Kazakh Qarauyl-Zhasaq tribe of the Naiman clan union. As for the Alans, if we add the previous chapters, we may comment that Chinese sources from the time of the Han dynasty (206 BCE) show that the Oghuz As then used the name *a-lan*-a, i.e. Alan. According to my data the Kazakh Aday and Alban are related to these Alans. As for the Roxolani, this word translates from German to give an ethnonym 'royal Alans'. Having firmly established themselves in Europe, they formed the basis of the Germanic tribes. The present-day Turks, Turkmen, Azerbaijanis, etc, can also be ascribed to the Oghuz. The Kyrgyz, for example, are *kyrykazy* (Az, Uz, Guz, Oghuz), i.e. the union of 40 Oghuz clans, whereas the modern Uygurs are Togyz Oghuz: the union of nine Oghuz clans. Eight Oghuz clans formed the major part of the Kazakh Naiman. According to my information, the crescent moon on the green banner of Islam also came into being due to the Oghuz, who captured the citadel of the Muslim world, Baghdad, at the start of the second millennium, and so the rise of Islam as the religion of the Muslim world is also due to the Turkic peoples.

The Seir include the vast majority of the Kazakh tribes, whose clan sign features the sun. These include the Argyn, Kanly, Siqym, Zhanys, Botbay, Shymyr, Ysyk, Aday, Baybakty and others. It should be said that after the collapse of the First Turkic Khanate, the basis of which was primarily Seir, they changed their collective name and began to be known as the Qypshaq or Kipchak, and the huge area in which they lived – from the Irtysh to the Danube – was named the land of Desht-i-Qypshaq, i.e. the Steppe State of the Qypshaq. The Kazakhs have a special attitude towards cows as the holy protectress of the Seir. They affectionately refer to her as Zengi Baba, although the relict ancestor protector of the horse was known as Qambar Ata and the ancestor of sheep was Shopan Ata. The reader will agree that the terms 'Baba' and 'Ata' (both terms of respect and affection for old men) are in different categories of importance. In honour of the Seir, a constellation in the Northern hemisphere is named Seirshy .

The naming of the worshippers of the crescent moon as Oghuz has a certain logic, since *oghuz* in Kazakh means a bull, and the crescent shape is identifiable with bull horns. Moreover, for the Sumerians the god of the moon was called As, from which come the names As, Uz and Oghuz. But why are the sun's worshippers called the Seir? It turns out that Egyptian and Sumerian sun god was called Horus, and his wife was called Hatgor and portrayed as a cow. What an unexpected connection! In mythology the sun and moon were Horus's eyes. By this image the Turkic peoples, the Oghuz and the Seir, are the eye of heaven on the earth. They are the ones who are watching!

The Seir began to be called Qypshaq after the fall of the First Turkic Khaganate in the early seventh century. Before this they had been known as the Kuns or Huns (*kun* in Kazakh is the sun). The largest of the Argyn clan has two circles in its *tamga*, OO, and is indebted to the Huns for this etymology. They rank themselves as the elite among the Hun community, since ar means 'honour', 'dignity'.

## Russian Samara, Kazakh Samarka and Mesopotamian Samarra.
## The Altai: the ancient homeland of the Sumerians

The same Seir were sometimes known as the Mar. In Kazakh, *maral* means 'doe'. Another derivation is an animal's first offspring, for example, *marqa buzau* is a calf. The Sumerians who created the earliest civilisation in Mesopotamia were in my view the Shumar, i.e. Mar people who came to the Tigris and Euphrates from the basins of the Shu (Chu) river in the lands of Kyrgyzstan and Southern Kazakhstan. The Czech linguist Bendrich Hrozny considered that the Sumerians came to Mesopotamia from the Irtysh basin and the Kazakh steppes, having lived for a time in the Chu valley; then, passing the Southern end of the Caspian, they reached the Tigris and Euphrates. We may note that the ethnonym of the ancient Sumerians is wholly preserved to this day in the Samarskoe district in Eastern Kazakhstan. Many of the local inhabitants mistakenly assume that the district was established by immigrants from the Russian province of Samara during the Stolypin reforms of the early 20th century. In fact, however, the ethnonym *samar* is very old and evokes only a sense of regret that, as a result of administrative divisions of the territory, the name of the region was lost from the map of the country. While ignorance of their roots and real history is typical today not only of government officials, the question is: where were the educated people at that time? Who asked them for help? On a map drawn by the Italian mapmaker Giacomo Cantelli in 1683, the lands of 'Samara' stretch across what are today the Altai oblast of Russia and parts of Eastern Kazakhstan. There was a town Samarra on the banks of the Tigris 4,000 years BCE, although researchers agree that this Mesopotamian usage is secondary in comparison with the Altaic. In any case the Sumerians came to Mesopotamia with a culture and literature already formed. Sumerian cuneiform and Turkic runes are related to one another. Referring to Pompeius Trogus, the Byzantine emperor Justinian argued that cuneiform was invented by the Turanians before they reached the kingdom of Urartu (Northern Mesopotamia). Phonetic equivalents of the ethnonym *sumer* include Sumer, Shumar, Suvar, Samar, Sabir, etc.

Let us say a little more about the Seir who were also known as the Mar. The Cimmerians, who lived in Eastern Europe, the Northern Black Sea region and along the Dnieper between the 15th and seventh centuries BCE, have a genealogy as follows. When the Hyksos left Egypt in the middle of the 16th century BCE, most of them returned to their traditional homeland and became known as the Cimmerians. I have several etymological explanations of this ethnonym. Living in deltas of rivers such as the Dnieper and the Danube and having a reputation as skilled boatmen, they used poles or sticks (*kii*) to guide their boats. Thus was the origin *kii-mar*, or Mar people with sticks. Another possibility is based on the Kazakh word *kieli*, meaning 'holy' or 'under the protection of a good spirit'. Then the root *kimar* would be a truncation of *kielimar*, which would designate the Mar under the protection of the spirits of their ancestors, or if you like, of Tengri himself. Close to this interpretation of the 'Cimmerian' ethnonym is another that relates to the name of the Indo-European goddess Ki, associated with epithets such as 'great' or 'divine'; in this case the Cimmerians are 'the great and divine Mar'. Similarly, the ethnonym of the Samarians can be interpreted as a shortened version of *sakmar*, i.e. 'the Mar of the Saq clan union', as suggested in Sarqytbek Shora: *Zengi Baba* (Almaty: Alash, 2000). Some descendants of the Mar live, for example, in Russia. These are the Mari, formerly known as the Cheremis, or, say, the Mordvin. All of them belong to the Turkic-speaking Finno-Ugric tribes.

The situation with the Oghuz is the same as for the Seir. The same Oghuz nation is sometimes referred to as the Tur, while some history books refer to the nomadic tribes of Eastern Iran as the Tur. This root has given rise to words such as Turan, Turkistan, Turkey, Turku, Turin, Turukhansk etc. Today the name 'Oghuz' is widely used to designate a Tur bull or to an ethnic appurtenance of certain Turkic peoples, notably of the Turkmen.

# SIRE, SIR AND ER SERI, THE GREAT KNIGHT OF THE STEPPE

A different fate awaited the ethnonym *sir – seir*. As mentioned above, the Seir formed the basis of the First Turkic Khanate, but changed their name after its collapse to the Qypshaq. Nevertheless, the word *seir* or *sir* did not disappear from the speech of many peoples but rather acquired different shades of meaning. As an example, I believe that the European Serbs are direct descendants of the Turkic Seir. Ptolemy refers in his *Geographia* to Serbs who lived to the West of the Volga, "…between the Keravn mountains and the Ra river - Orin, Walas and Serbs.:.". And Pliny mentions the Serbs as the Serni, a part of the Maeotian tribes. We know that it was the Maeotians/Matay who ruled during the First Turkic Khanate, and the Orkhon-Yenisei monuments dedicated to Tonykok, an advisor to four Turkic khans, mention a Turkic people known as Sir several times.

In the same way as the Alan/Albans of Transcaucasia moved West under the pressure of the Huns and established Catalonia, the Sir or Serbs of Transcaucasia eventually created Serbia in Europe.

As was said earlier, the Turks left a significant mark on the culture of European nations, and also on their languages. Everyone knows the French word 'sire' and the English 'sir', used respectively when addressing royalty and the nobility. The Turkic root *sir* or *seir* forms the basis of this lexeme.

As a result of several transcriptions this word has been altered, for example, to the word 'tsar' in Russian, to 'caesar' in Italy and to 'Kaiser' in Germany. Modern Kazakh has a word 'erseri', which is used to address a man with the status of a popular idol or a knight, or who has the character of a dandy or a smart dresser.

It can thus be seen that language reflected the extent of the historical and political influence of our ancestors very accurately. The Seir subdued almost all of Asia, Eastern and Western Europe and the Caspian and Black Sea regions.

No less bright a fate befell the word that came to designate the Turkic peoples themselves, as we shall see. Having become the appellative name, it came to be at the root of the designations in the principal European countries for their rulers (sire, caesar, Kaiser, tsar etc.) and their aristocracies, notably in the usage in Britain of 'sir'.

In addition, in carrying in itself the spirit of the warrior inherent to the Sir or Seir, the word influenced the primary military orders of the Middle Ages in Europe: the chevaliers or knights, in whose name lies the highest military rank of the steppe warriors, the Seri, a name awarded to only the best of the best – a small number of individuals. By contrast, the title of, say, batyr, borne by many sons of many Kazakh clans, is much lower on the 'Table of Ranks' of the steppe; the rare occurrence of a Seri, on the other hand, was awarded the highest of glory, honour and nobility. In my view, the need has become apparent for establishing an authoritative public body in our country that would confer the title of 'Er Seri' or Great Knight of the Steppe on outstanding national individuals for their contribution to the revival of the greatness of the Kazakh state.

It should be noted that a knight was a standard of reference not only for battle but also for gallantry. The model of chivalry was the French Marshal de Boucicault who, it is said, when accused of accidentally bowing to two prostitutes in the street, replied that it would be better for him to bow to ten street women than to neglect even one woman of honourable virtue. It is thanks to the knights, the *erseri*, that women gained the same place in society that the Turks gave to their goddess Umai. [94]

Throughout this book, I have reasoned and stated positions that leave no stone unturned of long-standing stereotypes or situations that seem implausible, but they are the results of the latest research. It should be said in general that, in the unanimous view of the historians, of all that happened in the world from the Sumerian civilisation to the early Iron Age, no unequivocal interpretation is available today owing to the lack of the necessary source base. We can only make our guesses and assumptions, which arc impossible to either prove or disprove. Pilgrims to Mecca, for example, are shown a stone that was supposedly fixed in the place where Adam and Eve met after God banished them to this world for their sin. But where does this information come from? What is the factual basis? The pilgrims are required merely to believe, as there is no scientific proof. It is impossible to say where this will lead. Johann Wolfgang von Goethe suggested that blind faith is not the beginning but rather the end of wisdom. The Russian poet and diplomat Fyodor Tyutchev wrote the famous line

| | |
|---|---|
| Umom Rossiu ne ponyat', | Russia cannot be contained by the mind |
| Arshinom obshchim ne izmerit'. | Nor measured by the ordinary yard. |
| U ney osobennaia stat' – | She has her own particular path – |
| V Rossiu mozhno tol'ko verit'. | You can only know Russia by believing. |

According to Karl Popper's principle, a theory is first created and then attempts are made to disprove it with facts. I therefore invite academic specialists to come with facts to hand to disprove my theory of the greatness of our ancestors, who once created the civilisations of China, India, Mesopotamia, Egypt and their *alma mater*, Eurasia. In doing so, of course, we will also look for new arguments in favour of our theory. To verify the kinship of Kazakh Albans and Spanish Catalans, for example, it is sufficient simply to compare their DNA. This is an accessible and inexpensive procedure.

# THE TURKS: CREATORS
# OF ANCIENT CIVILISATIONS

## THE SUMER, HELLAS, ELAM. INSTEAD OF A PREFACE, TURKIC ETHNONYMS: THE PARTICULARITIES OF THEIR FORMATION

In his exhaustive work *Tiurkoiazychny period yevropeyskoi istorii* (Moscow: Litera, 2011) Yuri Drozdov proposes that "the ancient or original ethnolinguistic affiliation of a nation (tribe) can be determined sufficiently reliably by its ancient self-appellation..." The question is then in what form the self-named auto-ethnonym of a given nation has survived to the present from the time of its 'original' state. In this respect we, the Turkic-speakers, are in a more advantageous position than are the European nations whose languages have become known in the academic community, for whatever obscure reason, as Indo-European, although Drozdov again maintains that there is no source from antiquity that records the presence of the ancestors of Indian people in Europe.

World languages are classified into two groups: the inflected and the agglutinative. In inflected languages, word structures undergo significant changes over time, and after centuries of development such languages often have a very different phonetic structure. It can thus be problematic for speakers of inflected languages to access the ethnic roots buried in the language. Most European nations have languages of this type.

For the agglutinative languages, which include the Turkic, the situation is quite different. Here the roots have remained practically unchanged over millennia and the phonetic system is likewise little altered. It is therefore possible today to discover the phonetic structure of ethnonyms and other words contained in ancient written sources. V.N. Budanova claims that "... ethnonyms as names are conservative in nature and have immense longevity. They are kept sacrosanct by members of their corresponding ethnic group and passed down from generation to generation" (*Etnonimia plemen Zapadnoy Yevropy: rubezh antichnosti i srednevekov'ia*. Moscow, 1991). This view is particularly characteristic of Turkic ethnonyms. The data available enabled Drozdov to conclude: "The phonetic sustainability of Turkic lexical items is also the unique feature that enables us to determine, on the basis of isolated terms relating to the remote past, and in particular of ethnonyms, the fact of a given tribe or nation being Turkic-speaking." Drawing on the study by Mirfatyh Zakiev, *Proiskhozhdenie tiurkov i tatar* (Moscow, 2003), he provides rules for the formation of Turkic ethnonyms. These rules consist in the merging of simple words into complex ones and the joining of individual words with ethno-forming affixes: "…in the first case, the initial component of a compound word serves to define the following one, which is a determinative word… Various parts of speech, such as adjectives, numerals or roots of verbs are used for the defining function. For the determinative, however, nouns are generally used. There is a large group of ethnonyms for which several of the same words are used as the determinative, but with a different set of definitions. These as it were typical determinatives provide a fairly reliable ethnic marker for Turkic ethnonyms. Common examples of such words include: *ir* (er) – 'husband', 'man', with phonetic variants *ar, er, ur* and *or*; min – 'I', with variants men, man, ban; *bai* – 'rich', 'owner', 'master', with variants *bi, bei, mei, pi, bik, bek*; as – 'bottom', 'of low rank', with variants *as, az, uz, us*. … Sometimes the determinative word may take the position of the first element."

We may illustrate these rules using the ancient name of the Uyghur, the Toghyzoghyz, i.e. the Union of nine Oghuz clans, the ethnonyms of the Karakerey, part of the large Kazakh Naiman, and the names Qonyrat, Qonyr Borik and Qyzyl Borik, the largest clans of the Alban. Here the words *qara* (or *kara*), *qonyr* and *qyzyl* mean the colours black, brown and red respectively. The following Kazakh tribal ethnonyms can also be read in this way: *besnayza* ('five arrows'), *saryzhomart* (*sary* - yellow), *tortqara* (*tort* - four) and *zhetyru* (*zhety* - seven). We have previously discussed, and will later analyse, the ethnonyms 'Hellene', 'Italy', 'Barcelona', Albion' and others by these rules.

Drozdov himself deciphers the island of Osel or Esel in the Baltic Sea, the land inhabited by the Rus at the start of the first millennium AD, as 'Asll' or 'AsEl', i.e. 'the land of the As people', and these were also Turkic tribes. In a different case, applying his technique of interpretation to the word 'Catalonia', he suggests that the first component of this lexeme, *cat*, is translatable from ancient Turkic to mean 'sturdy', 'strong'; the second element, *alon*, suggests the ethnonym 'Alan'. The third component *ia* means 'farm(land)', 'territory', 'country'. In total, then, the name of the territory 'Catalonia' can be literally translated as 'the land of the strong Alan'.

It is worth noting that a similar word in Kazakh, 'ie', means 'master', 'owner'. Another Kazakh word, 'uya', means 'nest', 'home hearth', and so a Kazakh interpretation of 'Catalonia' could be 'the house (nest) of the strong Alan'.

As for the forming of Turkic ethnonyms with the aid of ethno-forming suffixes, the most characteristic of these are *-ly/-dy* or *-lyk/-dyk* with a large number of phonetic invariants, such as l*ek, luk, lok; dik, dek, tyk, tek; nek; li, ny, dy, zy, t, ty*. These can be found, for example, as the suffixes of many tribal ethnonyms: Tobyk*ty*, Shapyrash*ty*, Oshaq*ty*; Qan*ly,* Balga*ly*, Balta*ly*, Bagana*ly*, Qanzhyga*ly*, Shanyshqy*ly*; Shek*ti*; Sirge*li*; Quan*dyq*, Suyin*dik*, Begen*dik* and Syrma*naq*, Shuma*naq*; Moldys*tyq*, Zheldys*tyq*; Baiu*ly*, Alimu*ly*, etc.

\*\*\*Reference is sometimes made in the literature to a 'great division of labour' – the point at which humans began to be divided into two areas of activity – sedentary farming and nomadic animal breeding. By some estimates this was in the late Neolithic period, by others it was in the fourth and third millennia BCE. Antagonism between the two groups is discussed by the historian Arnold Toynbee, who saw the root of their conflict in their different spiritual outlooks. In the 19th century a number of eminent German thinkers including Franz Oppenheimer, Friedrich Ratzel, Omelijan Pritsak and Ludwig Gumplowicz put forward concepts of the 'aggressive' formation of states, class societies and civilisations in general. They demonstrated plausibly that these processes are directly linked to the movements of cattle-breeding tribes from the Eurasian steppes.

In his brilliant work *Istoria rozhdenia, zhizni i smerti pastukha Avelia. Ariysky leksikon* the young Zhumazhan Bayzhumin shows convincingly, using the example of specific Kazakh and other Turkic clans, how over the millennia Turkic clans who were driven from the Eurasian steppe by stronger groups captured the settled peoples of China, India, Mesopotamia, Asia Minor, Egypt and Eastern and Western Europe and created new forms of states, cities and civilisations. The extensive method of farming used by the cattle-breeding communities required ever more grazing land for ever-growing livestock populations, and this was the motivation by which, as Pompeius Trogus put it, the stronger Kazakh tribes pushed out those that were less powerful and made these into "exules Scytharum" or exiles from Scythia. Leaving the steppe behind, the latter in turn conquered the agricultural and settled peoples they encountered. The necessities of life itself forced the arriving nomads to settle carefully and stay together (they were after all the minority), and as a result the preconditions were formed in which new cities, states and civilisations could arise; since in order for the nomads to govern the people they had captured, they needed institutions of coercion such as a form of police, taxation authorities, courts of law and the like. Earlier I mentioned how the Oghuz, displaced from the Eastern Caspian by stronger tribes in the early 11th century, took the agricultural civilisations of Armenia, Georgia, Iraq, Persia and Asia Minor and established the Seljuk state.

As Alfred Weber, the German economist and theoretician who lived from the late 19th to the mid-20th century, noted: "World history was created to the accompaniment of the tramping of great masses of the strategic cavalry of the nomads." This was the case in Mesopotamia, where in the fourth millennium BCE our ancestors founded the Sumerian civilisation between the Tigris and the Euphrates; the Turkologist Altai Sarsenuly Amanzholov, the poet and thinker Olzhas Omaruly Suleimenov and other scholars believe that this people was Turkic-speaking.

What do we know about the great Sumerian state today? Possibly we realise that its people worshiped the supreme deity Tengri (the river Tigris is in fact Dengir Tengri). Later we learned that the Sumerians were brilliant inventors and brought the world writing, the wheel, the sexagesimal counting system (by which minutes, seconds and degrees are measured) and some of the secrets of ironworking – things without which life in the 21st century would be scarcely conceivable.

The English archaeologist Leonard Woolley wrote: "We grew up at a time in which the beginning of all beginnings in art was considered to be Greece, when it was thought that Greece, like Pallas Athena, simply emerged from the head of Zeus the Olympian. But we later realised that Greece itself drew its vitality from the cultures of the Lydians, the Hittites, the Phoenicians, the Cretans, the Babylonians and the Egyptians – Greece is indebted to all of them in no small way for its flourishing. Its roots go back still deeper through the centuries; before all of these peoples stand the Sumerians." Shakh-Murat Kuanganov proposes that the people of the Sumerian city-state of Uruk (which in Turkic and Kazakh means 'seed', thus, figuratively, 'the beginning of all beginnings') honoured three gods: Inanna, the goddess of fertility and sexual love (*ilanu* in Turkic/Kazakh: 'faith', 'submission'), Ana ('mother') and her brother Utu, the sun god (*ot*: 'hearth', 'fire'). Olzhas Suleimenov defends the view that the earliest inhabitants of Mesopotamia were not mythical proto-Turkic people but rather speakers of already established dialects of the Oghuz, Kipchak and Bulgarian languages. In both Sumerian and Turkic languages, for example, *yer* means 'earth', *ush* means the number three and *tengri* or *dengri* means 'God'.

The nomadic tribes came in wave after wave to the ancient Mesopotamian lands, superseding those who had gone before them. In the 17th century BCE Kandash, leader of the Kassites, took Babylon and became king of the four cardinal points. The Kassites ruled this ancient land for some four centuries; as we have previously mentioned, their ethnonym later became the name 'Kazakh'.

From the middle of the second millennium BCE tribes of Aryan cattle-breeders, Eurasian steppe nomads, began to penetrate India and by the first millennium BCE the subcontinent was firmly under the rule of the Eastern Scythian tribe of the Saq. With their arrival, a new religion, Buddhism, appeared; the Buddha himself, Siddharta Gautama, was believed in some accounts to be of the Shaq clan, whose descendants today are found in the Kazakh Argyn and Naiman. They are also present in the modern Aday, Zhalair, Suan, Uaq and Qypshaq.

According to the Japanese historian Namio Egami the first state to be formed on the Japanese islands, which occurred in the third century BCE and was called Yamoto, was created by nomads from the Altai, who, having conquered Eastern Manchuria and Korea, then crossed to the Japanese archipelago. The first Japanese emperor had a Turkic name, Maiman. Before this, during the Bronze Age, the Sacki tribes, whose ancestors remained in the Kyrgyz Sayak clan and in the Kazakh Zhaiyk among the Shapyrashty and Aday, Shuaq and Sayiq and the modern Tam and Zhalair, created the Yaen bronze culture in Japan.

As for Korea, its name dates back to the ancient Turkic invaders from the Qara clan who came to the Korean peninsula in the early first millennium, and founded there the states of Baekje, Goguryeo and Silla. Today's descendants of the Qara are found among the Argyn, Naiman, Qonyrat, Dulat, Ysty, Baybaqty and Uaq, and also in some Turkmen tribes. At a reception by the President of South Korea of the President of Kazakhstan, the guest was presented with a sword found during excavations on Korean territory that had been made by Kazakh craftsmen at the dawn of the ages.

At the scholarly forum Altai: Golden Cradle of the Turkic World, held in August, 2011, in Ust-Kamenogorsk in the Eastern Kazakhstan region, the Japanese historian Mariko Harada said that Japanese and South Korean ethnologists support the theory of their peoples coming from the Altai region and, accordingly, of their languages belonging to the Turkic group of the Altaic languages.

Much of what has been said can be drawn from the work of Zhumazhan Bayzhumin mentioned above. One may learn, for example, that the Greek Achaeans who conquered Troy in the 13th century BCE are represented by Akay clans in the Naiman and Argyn tribes and the Agay clan in the Qanly tribe, and that they first reached the Peloponnese from the Eurasian steppes. Let us note again that the Greeks call themselves the Hellenes; I would repeat that the Hellenes are none other than the *Elini* (younger brothers of the main continental nation). That is to say, the nomads who left the Eurasian steppe for the Peloponnese regarded themselves as the younger brothers of the main body of the Turks who remained in Eurasia. Yet by the 20th century, scholars regarded the events of the distant past quite differently. Bayzhumin gives a classic example of academic blindness in the peculiar way in which the Soviet academician Daniil Avdusin interpreted the dramatic changes that had taken place in the Belogrudov culture at the headwaters of the Bug, whose carriers were Thracian tribes. Up to the eighth century BCE, he suggested, "…agriculture, supplemented by domestic cattle-breeding, dominated the household…

Their herds include many pigs and are found in their herds, which is inconsistent with nomadic cattle-breeding. Accordingly, the basis of this culture is entirely dissimilar to that of the Scythians." At the same time, he goes on, "From the eighth century BC the Black Forest Belogrudov tribes became more war-like. Weapons started to appear frequently in graves and took the form of those of the Scythians…" Avdusin is puzzled as to why these peaceful tribes of farmers should suddenly start to resemble the nomadic Scythians. Yet the conquest theory of the origin of civilisations explains this phenomenon easily and puts everything in its place. In the eighth century BCE agricultural tribes in Southern Europe were captured by nomadic Scythians, who also introduced elements of the nomadic cattle-breeders' way of life into that of the settled population. These invaders, later called the

Thracians and Illyrians, came in fact from the Eurasian steppes because they had been forced out by other, more powerful tribes of our ancestors. These Thracian and Illyrian tribes, just like the Greek Dorian, Achaean and Ionian tribes, consisted of conquered tribes of local farmers together with their conquerors from the nomadic cattle-breeders of the Eurasian steppes. The Greeks were called Greeks by the Romans; they called themselves the Hellenes or Denyens, so emphasising that they came from the Don (Tana) river basin, home of the Kazakh ancestors of the same name. Hellene, as mentioned above, means the Elini, and so by this name they emphasised their real kinship and affiliation to their continental conquering nation.

Both Toynbee and Weber pointed out that because of their conservative nature, neither sedentary nor agricultural cultures, taken alone, are capable of creating a civilised society. According to the canons of Tengriism, however, the sky is considered to represent the masculine principle and the earth the feminine. The nomadic way of life is linked to the former and that of the farmer relates to the latter. Life, or what amounts to the same thing, civilisation, can therefore only be born as a result of the 'insemination' or conquest of the sedentary people by the nomadic way of life.

We have thus ascertained that the extensive method of farming adopted in nomadic societies created economic conditions in which, to increase livestock numbers (as the primary indicator of wealth) some tribes seized the pastures of others inferior to them in strength. The latter were forced to leave their habitual lands and become "exules Scytharum", whereupon they found new territories, subdued the settled peoples they encountered and created new state formations. In these states the incoming nomadic tribes took the positions of lords and rulers with a primarily managerial function. The local agricultural populations, by contrast, found themselves in the position of the exploited and took a subservient role. With time, the upper class of the binary societies thus formed acquired a mixed ethnic physiognomy, and when they returned to their historical homelands on the Eurasian steppes, sometimes after a period of several centuries, they introduced new ethnic elements into their native ethnos. This would explain the rich ethnic diversity among the populations of the Great Steppe. Today's Kazakh Qypshaq, for example, are divided into the Quba (fair) Qypshaq, the Tori (dark) Qypshaq and so on.

Let us now ask why the nomads had such overwhelming superiority over the settled populations. We, the nomads, were first to domesticate the horse and make as it were a breakthrough in the development of communications. It was us, the nomads, who were first in our lands to learn how to smelt bronze and iron and thus gain superiority in weapons. But why were the nomads higher in spirit than the others? Where did this unprecedented strength, courage and self-sacrifice come from? Answers to these questions must be sought out in the particulars of our ancestors' faith and in the harsh conditions for survival in the severe climate and environment of the steppe. The root of all religions that propose a return to this world after death is Tengriism, and accordingly, the nomads took a philosophical approach to the frailties and transitory nature of earthly life. For them, death was not the end of life but the beginning of a new one. As for the harsh living conditions of the steppe, this contributed to the fighting spirit of the steppe warriors and also led to the formation of the polygamous family of the nomadic cattle-breeders.

## POLYGAMY: THE BASIS OF POWER OF THE KAZAKH ANCESTORS

Over the centuries the Kazakhs created their families in the form of communities based on blood relations, and this necessarily entailed polygamy. Survival in conditions with a temperature variation of some 80 degrees, from -40° to +40°, was immensely difficult. There was no irrigated land, and sometimes the grazing land would be coated with a layer of ice, resulting in massive losses of livestock. The need to migrate constantly to new pastures and the requirement for many working hands to rework the implements of cattle-breeding and to protect the herd from wild animals and from *barymty*, the violent theft of livestock by neighbours – all these demands could not be satisfied by a nuclear family of husband, wife and five or six children. A polygamous family, by contrast, bound by the ties of kinship, functions purposefully and effectively to achieve its specific goals. Abiding by the 'rules of play' of this large family, based on the respect of the young for the old, the honouring of parents and adults and genetic purity achieved through knowledge of the 'Zhety ata', their ancestry to the seventh generation, enabled our ancestors to avoid incest, to cope with the harsh steppe conditions and to produce raw materials for clothing and food, to keep herds of horses and camels and to produce and work goods in metal, including weapons in bronze and later in iron. All this attracted merchants to the steppe from all over the world, and thus the Silk Road emerged.

Polygamy, however, led to another problem, the solution of which brought still further strength to our ancestors, improving the demographic situation on the steppe such that it was occupied from the Danube to the Yellow River – a situation that cannot be claimed of present-day Kazakhstan, where the 'Chinese question' has become acute. A direct consequence of polygamy, for all its successes, was the phenomenon of gender tensions in society: supposing that one of seven brothers takes seven wives, the other six are left without a partner, unable to satisfy their physiological needs. This, moreover, in a situation in which, thanks to genetic purity, protein-rich nutrition and a healthy way of life in an ecologically pristine environment, young men would be physically strong and would feel keenly the urge to regularly satisfy their instinct for procreation. There was help, however, in long handed-down traditions, whereby all the elder brothers (the *shanyraq iesi*) were forced to leave home, leaving only the youngest (the *kenzhe bala*) behind with their parents. And where would a young man go in search of a soulmate if he has a good horse beneath him, a sword in his hands, a taut bow on his back and a hot, fearless heart beating in his breast? The neighbours, other friendly Kazakh tribes, were in the same situation and so the men formed into bands and rode together to China, India, Persia, Egypt and Europe, where they would gain several attractive women each, who became their wives and performed the duties of caring for the livestock and preparing meat and wool.

The question of what was the original cause for our ancestors to have built up such a presence among other, non-related peoples deserves further investigation. Perhaps the reason was economic in nature: the impossibility of further development at home due to lack of pasture for increasing head of cattle and the consequent displacement of neighbouring, related tribes from their habitual place in order to take possession of their grazing lands; the displaced tribes thus became 'exiles from Scythia' and went on to subjugate neighbouring settled peoples. Alternatively, the reason consists in the instinct for procreation, a purely physiological consideration that was studied in depth by Sigmund Freud. I would tend to prefer the second version.

***These aspects of our ancestors' lives were described by the classics of Kazakh literature, and this subject continues to concern modern Kazakhs today. Among these is Nurkasim Abuyev, a metallurgical equipment engineer who wrote to me; the main aspects of his letter are also issues I have considered in my work.

Let us mention the phenomenon of the 'Axial Age', the period in which the focal points of the great religions arose and strides were made by spiritual thinkers, apparently simultaneously, in lands as far-flung as China, India, Mesopotamia, Egypt and Greece. Alfred Weber's search for the causes of this event led to his significant theory that this period of blossoming happened at the time that the Eurasian nomadic peoples were invading the settled regions. Does this not point to the dominant role of our ancestors in those distant historical times? In my opinion it is convincing enough.

## THE THEORY OF PASSIONARITY. WAS GUMILEV RIGHT?

The Russian Eurasianist Lev Gumilev coined the term 'passionarity', which he understood as an excess of biochemical energy in a person or people that instilled in them an irrepressible desire to undertake certain acts – be they constructive or destructive.

A surplus of this energy occurs as a result of a passionate impulse from space in the form of heightened solar activity or the explosions of supernovae. For a certain time and in a certain region one ethnicity or another will reap the fruit of this impulse of passion and as a result will emerge into the international arena and make itself known to the world. This is the explanation and driving force, Gumilev proposes, for the deeds of Rome, for the success of the Arab conquests and those of the Mongols. But is it true? It is certainly appealing, and it has brought Gumilev fame as a 'great Eurasian'. Yet while it is helpful in explaining many historical events, the Gumilev hypothesis seems to me not to apply to the rise of the nomads on the Eurasian steppe from the second millennium BCE.

The reasons, nevertheless, arise from nature.

Summing up the ideas and facts given in this book, we can say that our ancestors were the first to tame the wild horse and the first to discover the secrets of producing artefacts in metal. Consequently, as warriors they became unstoppable. Their character was forged in the harsh conditions of the steppe, while the steppe economy of nomadic cattle-breeding precipitated the phenomenon of the 'exules Scytharum', their 'forced' conquests of new homelands and subjugation of settled farmers and forest dwellers and their creation of new states and civilisations in the conquered lands.

# THE FLOOD AND THE DISTANT ANCESTRAL HOME OF THE WOLF PEOPLES

Earlier I mentioned that the Aryans, ancestors of the Kazakhs, came to their present lands from 'Hyperborea', the North, where civilisation was blossoming more than 20,000 years ago. So what happened? Why were they forced to leave? Today scholars are more or less in agreement with the view that some 22,000 years ago a large asteroid impacted the Kamchatka region (in what is today Russia's Far East), resulting in a major shift in the Earth's axis. Previously the axis passed through Western Europe; now it was displaced by 23.5 degrees to its present position through the poles. Nikolay Kikeshev comments that the formerly tropical climate at the North Pole suddenly changed to ice cold, and there is evidence for this in the well-preserved carcass of a mammoth uncovered during a French excavation on the Taymyr Peninsula in the far North of Siberia in 2001. Scientists say that it was 22,000 years ago that permafrost came to Siberia. Glaciologists also say that Western Europe was freed from permafrost only 9,000 years ago; the first humans came to the Baltic region only 5,000 years BCE.

The Great Flood appears in the mythology of 140 nations. In the Bible it is sent by God as punishment for the sin into which the world has fallen. Science, however, explains the phenomenon as a result of the Earth colliding with an asteroid, resulting in a break in the crust and causing the waters of the Pacific to breach the Bering Gap, inundating the North Pole and forming the Arctic Ocean. Of course, the inhabitants of this previously favourable region were forced to leave, and this included our ancestors. Kikeshev compared the toponyms and hydronyms of the far

North with those of regions inhabited today and came to a startling conclusion. He found, for example, that the hydronyms of the Arkhangelsk and Vologda regions of Northern Russia show a similarity of 90% to those of Iran, Afghanistan, India and Pakistan. Yet this is not difficult to explain, since people who migrate to new lands tend to name the rivers and other bodies of water after those of their former homelands.

The situation in Kazakhstan is similar. The Tana clan of the Baiuly tribal union, for example, once lived in the Southern Russian steppes, in the Don basin. The name 'Don' is in fact a transformation of the clan name Tana. Now, in the far North (of what is now Norway) is the bay of Tana Fjord on the Barents Sea, and this is the mouth of the river Tanaelv; a tributary to this is the Anar Yokka, on which stands the settlement of Ishkuras. For the Sumerians, ancestors of the Kazakhs, Ishkur was the god of thunder, while the common Kazakh name Anar means a pomegranate. This is evidence, then, that our ancestors left Hyperborea after the catastrophe and brought their old, familiar names to their new homelands.

The possibility that over 20,000 years ago other ancestors of the Turks lived in what is now the USA was confirmed by a group of researchers led by Dr Theodore Shurr, who analysed the findings at the Diring-Yuryakh site in Siberia, some 40km from the famous Lena Pillars. Discovered in 1982 and attributed to the late Neolithic period, Shurr concluded on the basis of molecular genetics that the ancestors of the Native American Iroquois and Mohicans originated in the Altai mountains, the ancestral home of the Turkic peoples (*Komsomolskaya Pravda*, 2-9 February 2012).

The homeland of the Aryan was described as follows by Ptolemy: "Beyond the Sarmatian [Baltic] waters there lies a great island called Scandia or Erythius. And this is the legendary land of our ancestors the Hyperboreans, the crucible of peoples, the forge of the peoples of the world. Great rivers flow from the Rithius mountains, and along them are glorious meadows with countless herds of cattle. There are fertile fields among great forests there, and nowhere does the earth yield greater harvests. It was from here that the skills for working the land and forging metal first spread."

**This is the distant homeland of the Kazakhs!**

It is my view that after the Great Flood our ancestors settled permanently in their present territories, and it was from there that they set out, as previously mentioned, to conquer the agricultural lands of China, Japan, Egypt, Iran and India.

The name 'Hyperborea' can be interpreted in Turkic as 'huge wolf'. From his runic concept of the god Tengri, Tayzhan Dosanov concludes that the outlines of the constellations Ursa Major and Ursa Minor depict two wolves, and the Aryans of Hyperborea are thought to be settlers from those stars. All this is correct; the Turks, descendants of the Aryan, take their progenitor to be a wolf. Dosanov interprets the ethnonym *kazakh* as *qazsaq*, suggesting that the primogenitors of the Kazakhs were a wolf and a swan. The second syllable, *saq*, is understood as a variation of the name for a wolf. Sometimes the variant *saqqulaq* is used to name the wolf, meaning 'sensitive ear'. Findings by M. Tanyshpaev at Zhetysu, near the village of Qaratal, support the notion that the mythical ancestors of the Kazakhs were a wolf and a swan.

This image, discovered at Zhetysu, was made on stone and depicts a creature with the body of a wolf and the head of a goose. In a word, this is the *itqus*, another name used by the Kazakhs for a wolf. It happens that the *tamga* of the Matay clan features a wolf with a curved neck and a swan-like head. According to legend, the whole Turkic world was originally thought to be the people of the wolf, the *borieli*, but later the name began to be applied to only limited groups and today only the Matay and Sadyr have the honour of belonging to the 'people of the Wolf'. A similar reduction occurred for the *qypshaq* ethnonym, which was initially used of a vast population of Eurasian Turks from the Yellow River to the Danube, but later it became restricted to particular tribes of the Kazakh Middle *jüz*.

In the British Museum in London is a bronze pot for water heating that dates to between the sixth and third centuries BCE. Dosanov cites an interesting comment by A. Mekteptegi, who considered that the handle of the pot is a stylized figure of a wolf, chained by its lower jaw to the metal post, and depicts the Pole Star, known by the people as Temirqazyq. The pot's handle symbolizes Ursa Major. The spout of the pot shows a swan, the mother of the Kazakhs, and beside the lid lies a wolf cub in the shape of Ursa Minor that represents the offspring of the wolf and the swan, i.e. the sons of the

Kazakhs. If we recall the arrangement in the Northern sky of the Seirshy and the two Ursa constellations, Mekteptegi's interpretation is not without a basis.

A curious legend on the origin of the Kazakhs is cited by I.I. Kraft (*Sbornik uzakoneniy o kirgizakh stepnykh oblastey*) as follows: "A miracle has happened! As if hearing the prayers of a dying man in the waterless Kalcha-Qadyr desert, the sky opened up and the White Goose, a kind peri with life-giving water on its wings, descended and saved him from inevitable death… They married and their descendants began to bear the name Kazak or Kaisaq."

This is the kind of labyrinth we may encounter when seeking out the roots of our people!

# MADIUS, KING OF THE SCYTHIANS AND SHAN YU MOED OF THE HUNS, OR HOW THE KAZAKH CLANS WERE FORMED

I have long pondered why it is the Kazakhs' way to know seven generations and why it was forbidden to intermarry within those seven generations, and other such questions. It turns out that seven generations were what it took to form an independent Kazakh clan. Simple mathematical calculation has shown that under favourable conditions (no war, natural disasters or epidemics, etc) the number of inhabitants would reach several hundred thousand people wit hin seven generations. This group of people would then form a clan, name it after their ancestor and assume an autonomous existence. After a further seven generations each offspring could, in principle, then found another new clan. This explains why clan names were lost over the centuries, as there were many of them. Only the names of powerful clans have survived, those that were created by extraordinary people who were in some way superior to their fellow tribesmen. You may ask why this was so. The reason is that if a clan had a strong individual who gave his name to the clan, then seven generations later, with the forming of new clans, one of these offspring would be given the name of that outstanding person in order to preserve the name in the new clan.

For example, in 209 BCE the Huns were led by Mode (or Maodun) Matay, who was later marked by historians as an outstanding individual who created a state equal to that of Han China. But the name of the founder of the Hun state was merely a repetition of the name of the Scythian leader Madius Matay, who had conquered Asia Minor in the mid-seventh century BCE and had ruled Babylon for 28 years. The Scythian king had another name, Ishpaqay, and was an ancestor of the famous Queen Tomyris of the Saq-Massagetae. The name of the Kazakh clan Matay has been preserved for posterity as a group among the Naiman because such prominent figures as the king of the Huns, Mode and the king of the Scythians, Madius, belonged to this clan. The first descendants of the Matay chose, seven generations later, not to change the name of their clan; they cherished the name of their illustrious ancestor.

The story of the rise of the Hun Mode-Matay is interesting and instructive. His father, Shan Yu Tuman, capitulated to the will of his overlord the Emperor of China by marrying a Chinese woman who was the daughter of the ruler of the Han. It was the intention of the Chinese that the heir to the throne of the Huns should become the grandson of the ruler of the Celestial Empire; the grandson would then never aspire to equal rights with his grandfather, so the Huns would be servants of the Han without any war being waged. With this purpose, at the demand of the Chinese he sent his eldest son Matay as *amanat* (hostage) to the quarters of the enemy, the leader of the Yueh-chih, with whom they had just concluded a truce. Knowing for certain that his son would be killed if the conditions were violated, he intentionally and perfidiously attacked the Yueh-chih. His son, showing miraculous courage, managed to escape. His father was forced to put him in charge of an army of 10,000. Matay became renowned for the methods he used to gain the dedication and readiness to act of his subjects, ordering them to follow his actions blindly. When he released an arrow into his favourite horse, for example, he ordered the execution of all who did not follow and do likewise. The same applied when he dispatched his favourite concubine, and when one day he was out hunting and took aim at his treacherous father, nobody missed.

Later, the Han Emperor put the young ruler of the Huns to a test of strength. He asked Matay to give him the best argamak from among his horses, and Matay did so, believing that the request of a neighbour should be honoured; likewise, when requested, he gave the emperor his favourite concubine, despite the protests of his attendants. To the now excessive appetite of his neighbour, who had allowed himself to believe that the young Shan Yu would always follow his directives, and to his next request, namely that he give to him his empty and abandoned lands, however, Matay replied: "By the will of the almighty Tengri, the land belongs to the people. While there is land there will be a state with a thriving population. A people without land of its own is doomed to humiliating dependence and a gradual death." At the earliest opportunity after gathering the necessary troops, Mode-Matay inflicted a crushing defeat on imperial China and made it his vassal.

Whoever said that history could not be both instructive and illuminating?

My seventh-generation ancestor was called Shang. In Chinese history, the first Yin dynasty existed in the middle of the second millennium BCE and was ruled by the nomadic Shang tribe. Bearing in mind that China was ruled by dynasties of Turkic nomads at various stages of its history, I fully concede that my ancestors gave the name Shang to a descendant at each seventh generation in order to keep the name of their forefather who ruled the Celestial Empire for centuries to come. Interestingly, the name Shang is associated with the title of the ruler of the Huns, Shan Yu, which can be literally translated from Kazakh as 'house of the sky' or 'state of the sky', as the word *shang* relates to 'dust', 'air' and 'sky'. There is a Kazakh expression *shang tim-es*, which is used of the Tulpar, the winged horse that does not run but literally flies through the air. The English explorer Edward Harper Parker, who wrote interestingly about our Tatar ancestors (*Tartars: The History of a Great Nation*), believes that the title *shanyu* literally means 'son of heaven'. I suspect he is not far from the truth, as the state of the Turks was always under the protection of the Sky, Tengri.

# FROM THE EUROPEAN FAMILY TO THE ASIATIC; OR HOW THE KAZAKHS LOST THEIR CAUCASOID LOOK

One explanation of the anthropological peculiarities of the Kazakhs' physical appearance, which combines Caucasoid and Mongoloid features, is given by Orazak Ismagulov and other authors in *Etnicheskaia dermatoglifika kazakhov* (Almaty, 2007). First, I mentioned earlier that according to the latest data, the same races of people have inhabited the territory of Kazakhstan for 40 centuries. They created what has been called the Andronov culture, the tribes of which had in anthropological terms the physiological features of the ancient Caucasoid race. The indigenous population of Kazakhstan was thus a purely Caucasoid race. Later, however, the following took place. Being the first to tame the horse around 4,000 BCE, our ancestors acquired the greatest mobility, and later they mastered the secrets of making weapons in bronze and iron. Steppe warriors by spirit, they then began to make incursions into both neighbouring and distant countries, eventually reaching the Arabian Peninsula, Egypt, the Ganges and the Yellow River. Thus Ismagulov concluded from studies of paleoanthropological materials and craniological data that in the fifth century BCE Mongoloid elements began to penetrate the general racial composition of Kazakhstan's ancient inhabitants, and this proportion reached 10%. Why did this happen? As we saw earlier, by this time our ancestors had begun to live in Asia Minor, and then in the eighth century BCE the Hittites (Kete) migrated to China and subsequently returned to their homeland, having absorbed elements of the Chinese race. They, together with other groups returning from Asia Minor, introduced the 10% of Mongoloid elements to our Caucasoid type.

During the Usun period (third century BCE to fourth century CE) the relative proportion of Mongoloid features of our people reached 25%. We saw, indeed, that a large proportion of our ancestors (the Uysun and Qanly), under pressure from the Huns, left the lands of Mongolia and China and came to what is now Kazakhstan. But their long residency among the Mongoloid Chinese had 'corrected' their Caucasoid appearance, and this resulted in 25% 'yellow' in their features. Then came the period of the pre-Mongol invasions (fifth to eighth centuries CE). During this time the Turkic khanates rose and fell in Mongolia and Northern China, and under Chinese pressure the Turks moved West towards Kazakhstan. At the same time, many of the ancestors in Asia Minor began to return to their historical homeland to flee the growing influence of Islam. Between them they added a further 25% of Mongoloid traits to our native Caucasoid type. By the 15th century the ethnic mixing in Kazakhstan had settled to final proportions of 70% Mongoloid and 30% Caucasoid features.

These proportions remain today. I would explain the addition of a further 20% of Mongoloid features primarily by the fact that the Naiman, Kerey, Qonyrat, Zhalair and other Kazakh clans, who had lived long beside the Chinese and Manchurian Tungus tribes and acquired clear Mongoloid features, returned to their historical homeland with Genghis Khan. Today the racial type of the Kazakhs is sometimes called the 'Kazakhstan type' of the Turanid race. This 'race' comprises three 'types': Kazakhstan, which includes the Kazakhs; the Tien-Shan, which includes the Kyrgyz; and the Altai-Sayan, which includes the Khakas, and each has different proportions of Caucasoid features. In these terms the Kazakhs have the most obvious Caucasoid features, followed by the Kyrgyz and finally the Khakas. It should be noted also that these metisational processes occurred only within the lands of Kazakhstan, since there was no mass settlement of foreign tribes from neighbouring states here and we have never been an occupied nation. So it was we, the Kazakhs, who 'spoiled' our Caucasoid appearance by conquering neighbouring countries and peoples of the Mongoloid race, and the long periods spent by Kazakhs among other nations inevitably brought changes in our ancestors' natural, lineal appearance, since they bore children in those places too. This has however been discussed previously.

# UNDER THE SIGN OF THE CROSS

## CHRISTIANITY AMONG THE NAIMAN AND KEREY. WHY IS KAZAKH NOT SPOKEN IN THE MOSQUES?

Most of Kazakhstan's indigenous population professes Islam. The ways in which Islam is developing today are known to us and we watch them with some concern. Its foundations have been undermined by the antagonism between the Sunni and Shiite principles, and there is also a growth in Wahhabi tendencies. Our famous countryman Shoqan Walikhanov wrote that prior to allegiance with Russia, the Kazakhs were Muslim only formally, but that the Russian government later introduced Islamic canons as a means of controlling a recalcitrant people.

From the middle of the 18th century Islam continued to gain ground in Kazakhstan, though I would admit that its roots are not strong among the Kazakhs. The reason, I suspect, is that the people have been prevented from addressing God in their own language, a language understandable to them. The Muslim rites are performed without people understanding the words or meanings being invoked. The Arabic language thus becomes an intermediary – or an obstacle – between the believer and his God that makes it difficult for him to really address his weaknesses and ablute himself of the impurities of the everyday, or in short, to achieve spiritual peace and balance. The faith does not deliver the desired results.

I would add, how much trouble have we gone to just to let the Kazakhs speak Kazakh? If the Spiritual Directorate of Muslims gains the right for us to speak with the almighty in Kazakh, though, I am certain that every Kazakh will start to use their mother tongue to address God, which is a need we all have. Moreover the belief that God understands Kazakh will become a powerful incentive for people to learn it. Apologists for Islam forbid that the rites be performed in the language of the local population, as they argue that the Qur'an was revealed to humanity in Arabic. But is this true? We will discuss this later. But it is not entirely the truth.

Recently opinions have become more frequent that the most damaging factor in the collapse of the Golden Horde was the introduction by force of Islam to our ancestors. This view would seem not to be groundless. Firstly, it is well known that the world's oldest religion was Tengriism, such as was widespread among our nomad ancestors. When these conquered other countries, they adapted their faith to the beliefs of the indigenous peoples of those places. Earlier I mentioned Persian Zoroastrianism; its prophet Zoroaster (who incidentally came from what is now Uralsk in Kazakhstan) introduced Tengriism to Persia's indigenous inhabitants, the Arameans, and the result was a new world religion. Christianity was also introduced to the West by our ancestors, but under a different name. In the fourth century this religion was accepted by both East and West, and monotheism was brought to the Western world by us, the nomads.

It is well known that Rome, destroyed by nomads in the fifth century, was not converted to Christianity. The Romans worshiped Mars, Jupiter and other gods; Jesus Christ was revealed to that world only later. Over time the form of Tengriism that had become adapted to the Western mentality was eradicated from European consciousness by the Jesuits, guardians of the Pope and soon the West had completely forgotten about the Turkic roots of its new religion. Murad Adji challenges us to think again on the origin of Christianity: suppose its roots are not in Judaism? Is Palestine really the home of Christianity? Here let us address the curious question about how Christianity was prevalent among the Naiman and Kerey at the time of Genghis Khan. Our ancestors practiced Christianity in its Nestorian form. Nestorius, at one point the Archbishop of Constantinople and thus the highest priest of the Byzantine Empire, became estranged from the established Church because of his view that Christ could not be simultaneously God and man and tended towards his being a man, a prophet, which is consistent with the Tengriist view. Varieties of the Nestorian doctrine appeared in Achaemenid Persia in the sixth century BCE as Persianised forms of Tengriism. Thus although Nestorius's teachings were condemned by the Council of Ephesus in 431 CE, they found support among certain Kazakh tribes, particularly those that had lived in Northern China and Mongolia for centuries. So in its early phases, Christianity was perceived by our ancestors as their own doctrine, and it follows that the 'Christian' Naiman or Kerey at the time of Genghis Khan was in fact followers of pure Tengriism. The Christian symbol, a cross, was also a symbol of

Tengri and was the tamga of many Kazakh tribes, particularly of the Kerey. The genealogy of this ancient sign attracts considerable interest. Murad Adji believes, for example, that the direct equilateral cross, the sign of Tengri, is not merely the intersection of two lines; on the contrary, the cross that appeared in the Altai three or four thousand years ago has a quite different sense. Four rays extend from the centre to the cardinal points, while at the centre is the sun, whose divine grace warms all the matter created by Tengri.

## THE SIGN OF TENGRI, THE KAZAKH YURT AND THE RUSSIAN FLAG

To me the equilateral cross seems to mean something different. First, the history of the Kazakh nomad's tent or yurt, topped with the *shanyraq*, forms the basis not only of the nomads' domestic life but also of their spiritual orientation. The *shanyraq*[95] on the vault of the yurt depicts the vault of heaven, in which the band stretching from East to West is the path of the sun, which the nomads associate with their spiritual sun, Tengri. For millennia, the sun has indicated the main direction of our ancestors' encampments, from East to West and then from West to East.

The other arm of the cross represents the Milky Way, passing in a wide channel from North to South. For centuries this signified the path of migratory birds, the sky-inhabitants of Tengri's dwelling place, with whom the nomads always associated their independence and freedom.

From these two perpendicular axes arose the shape of the cross, which has become a sacred symbol of Tengri.

In the context of the above the following observation arises. Our ancestors' ancient religion was based on two basic principles: the masculine, associated with heaven (spirit and the soul) and his master Tengri, and the feminine, the carnal, earthly principle. Umay, the goddess of earth and fertility, was the embodiment of the flesh of life.

Accordingly, the routes of the nomads as they roamed from East to West, protected by the goddess Umay of the earth, intersecting with the path traced by Tengri of the migratory birds from North to South and fertilising all matter, symbolised the birth of life on earth, whose parental sources are Tengri and Umay. The cross, then, is for us the main symbol and sense of our being. It is not by chance that in Christianity it is sometimes called the life-giving cross.

Here it is appropriate to consider the etymology of the hordes of Genghis Khan's empire. Its Eastern part, including what are now Western Siberia and Eastern Kazakhstan, was called the Blue Horde; the central section (the Sary-Arka steppe) was the White Horde, and in the West was the Golden Horde.

Such names have obvious analogies. The rising sun in the East colours the sky a deep blue; on reaching its zenith or centre, the sky is white, and when it sets, the sky turns gold and red. Now let us recall the national flag of Russia. It is a tricolour of blue, white and red. Does this not tell of a tradition from the depths of Turkic culture? And is not this tricolour a form of evidence that Mother Russia in fact has Turkic roots?

We have already discussed the various aspects of both the historical convergence and also the linguistic affinity of the Turks and Slavs, particularly at the level of lexis. Here, however, let us talk of more general attributes that unite the two ethnic groups, Russian and Kazakh, at the level of the ancestral memory that has determined the uniqueness of the symbols of state.

For many centuries, history kept us apart. Having tamed the horse and thus come to subjugate space, the Kazakhs spread their influence over vast territories, and as they settled in, not only did they assimilate the indigenous inhabitants but also became themselves assimilated into these countries, and this had a significant resultant effect on their physical appearance.

Europe and Asia lay like a cross over the nation's very genotype. This explains the very different appearance of modern nomads. It is as though the whole universe is reflected in it.

Let us make a few more observations concerning the Kazakh yurt. It is known that its right-hand half is the female side: this is where utensils and dishes are stored, where food is prepared, etc. The left side is the male half – it contains hunting gear, guns and the like. The centre is where guests are received – the *tor*. Until recently I had been unable to solve the mystery of the ethnonym of my native river Irtysh (*yertis*), which flows north through China, Kazakhstan and Russia. Then, however, Nurbergen Balgimbayev, a connoisseur of Kazakh folk art, customs and ceremonies, told me that if one looks down from the heights of the Altai mountains – the ancestral homeland of the Turks – to the North, the river Ob flows on the central axis, the Irtysh is to the left and the Yenisei to the right. So if we mentally place the dome of a Kazakh yurt over the lands from the Irtysh in the West to the Yenisei in the East, we have, by analogy, the Ob flowing along the central axis (*tor*) (note also that in the Altai peoples, ob means the axis). To the left of the Ob is the Irtysh (Ertis-Ertus). Being on the left, it is a male (*er*) element of the yurt (and the first syllable of *ertus*), while the other half, tus, means a figure or a side. In this case we have a male side. And to the right of the Ob is the Yenisei (in Kazakh, Enesay), the female womb, or the yurt's right-hand, female side. Kazakhs speak of a girl who has been left on the shelf (unable to marry) with a saying: *bagy ashylmady, on zhakta qaldy,* which literally means 'stayed too long in the right-hand half'.

Previously I said that the cross was a symbol of Tengri and that this had a close relationship to the *shanyraq* of the Kazakh yurt. Also related to the nomad's dwelling is another ancient Turkic symbol, the eight-pointed star. The entrance (*bosaga*) to a Kazakh yurt faces strictly South-East, to where the sun rises at the summer solstice. In accordance with the Turkic calendar, 'East' is understood as a sector of 90 degrees of the compass, from North-East to South-East. The sun rises at different points in this sector throughout the year. Bearing this in mind, we can visualise that two lines intersecting over the *shanyraq* form the outline of an eight-pointed star. Our laws stated that people should sleep in a yurt with their head to the North-West, whereas the deceased were laid with the head to the North-East and the face turned to the East. The road from the South to the North was considered to be the birds' road; the departure of the soul of the deceased was associated with this road. It is interesting that in Russian chronicles the Milky Way, stretching from South to North, was sometimes called the 'path of Batyi Khan' (a Mongol khan particularly dreaded by the Russians), thus also associating it with the end of their lives. In this sense, the cross in the sky symbolises the intersection of the road of life (from East to West) with the road of death (from North to South).

So, the celestial cross is defined by the road of the sun, stretching from East to West, which intersects with the Milky Way, the road of the stars, running from North to South. This cross embodies Tengri, the Sky. He in turn is reflected in the earth as the symbol of the earth goddess Umay, where the road of the nomads from East to West crosses that of the birds, from North to South.

These signs of eternity are reflected symbolically in the cross formed by the *shanyraq* of a Kazakh yurt.

The other cross, offset by 45 degrees, is formed from South-East to North-West and becomes a symbol of short-term earthly existence, where two lines intersect, those of life and death. These are reflected in the patterns and manners of life in a Kazakh yurt.

The superposition of these two signs – the crosses of heaven and earth – forms the eight-pointed star as a majestic symbol of the unity of the two principles, Tengri and Umay, masculine and feminine, heaven and earth, life and death.

Another note on the philosophy of Tengriism. For the ancient Turkic people the divinity, Tengri and the sky designated the same reality, like a unity of two elements – the material and the world of the imagination. Tengri is the creator of all matter, including the sky. In turn the sky symbolises the upper world; earth, home to earthly beings, is the middle world. The lower world is not the world of the dead but, like the upper world, has a quite different meaning. If a person lived righteously on earth and did good works, and so realised himself as a person, then after death his soul would pass to the upper world and the presence of Tengri. Known then as an *aruah*, he could then be called down to the middle world to help his tribesmen when they encountered difficulties. As for the souls of the sinful who had wasted their possibilities in this world, their souls passed after death to the lower world where Yerlik reigned. From time to time Yerlik would send souls of sinners back to the middle world to tempt people to unrighteous acts. It was believed that the inhabitants of the upper world wore a kind of tie around their necks, those of the middle world wore a belt, and dwellers of the lower world had chains on their feet since they were not masters of their own destinies. The same happens in ordinary life: a man wearing a tie is perceived by society as an intelligent, independent person, but a weak-willed person who lacks initiative is spoken of as wayward or dissolute.

# ROUND THE QUR'AN. NIZAMI ON THE TURKIC ORIGIN OF THE PROPHET MUHAMMAD AND ALEXANDER THE GREAT

Now let us consider the origins of Islam. At the beginning of the Common Era a major part of the Arab peninsula belonged to the Parthian state founded by our ancestors, who continued to live there until more recent times. In *The Turkic Saga of Genghis Khan* I recounted how our ancestors, having united into an independent unit of the Quram , also participated in creating the new religion of Islam, again by adapting Tengriism to the outlook of the local population, which only began to be known as Arab in the 10th century.

The 12th-century Persian poet Nizami Ganjavi wrote of the Prophet the following lines:

"Praise to you, son of the Turkic nation! You led the seven tribes. From the seas to the skies, you are glorified in all the world". After the death of Muhammad, his son-in-law Ali and his followers, the founders of the Shia branch of Islam, abandoned many of the tenets of Tengriism, just as Jews, Greeks, and Egyptians had done before with Christianity by adding new elements that were distant from Tengriism. Incidentally, when Islam was introduced to Central Asia, it was brought by ethnic Turks from the Arabian Peninsula known as the Quraish. The word *quraish* can be translated from the Kazakh as 'sheep's hat'. Today their clan has a different name, Qozha. This was a wise step, as the adherents of Tengriism on the steppe would never have accepted a new religion from the mouths and hands of strangers. The time at which Islam was introduced to what is now Kazakhstan coincided with the rule on the Arabian Peninsula of the Abbasid dynasty of the Quraish tribe, which had determined the path of development of Islam for 200 years from 750 to 945 CE. The indigenous inhabitants of the Arabian peninsula are today called Bedouins, whereas their ancestors were called the Akmar, i.e. fair-haired Mar. As we saw earlier, the Mar are in fact the Turkic Seir.

In *Tiurki i mir. Sokrovennaia istoria* Murad Adji gives an interesting view on the origins of Islam. He claims that the Qur'an was originally written in a language that had been developed in Persia during the times of the Arsacid dynasty (third century BCE to third century CE). Thus the language of Islam at the time of the Prophet Muhammad was Turkic and not Arabic. The original Turkic text, written in the 10th century, he maintains, is kept at the Hermitage . Arabic was only adopted for Islam after a certain 'Book of Corrections' by Abu Mansur Muhammad ibn al-Azhar al-Azhari appeared in the 10th century. By now the Turkic version of the Qur'an had existed for 300 years. A well-known Turkologist of our time has said that "...Soviet scholars know that period of history well, and are aware that the formation of the culture known as 'Arab' involved a number of peoples, particularly the Turks..." It would not be out of place to mention here that, according to the Ukrainian scholar Ahatanhel Krymsky, many of the primary historical sources considered to have been written in Arabic are in fact translations from Turkic. This is the case, for example, for the *Thousand and One Nights*. Unfortunately, the Qur'an also did not escape this fate. Murad Adji claims that the original Qur'an included the following lines, spoken by God: "I have an army that I call the Turks, whom I have settled in the East; when I am angry with a certain nation, I give power over these people to my army!"

The late professor Marat Barmankulov suggests in *Tiurkskaia vselennaia* that Nizami Ganjavi, the Persian poet and philosopher mentioned above, saw in a Turk not only his national characteristics but also an embodiment of the qualities of kindness, justice and humanity. The reader will recall that we have discussed the Scythian roots of Alexander the Great. Here Barmankulov quotes Nizami's words about the great commander: "How else could a Turkic man from Rum have seized the Indian throne and the crown of China?"

People often accuse me of artificially seeking 'Kazakh' traces in historical events. But just look at how Nizami, in the 12th century, considered Alexander the Great and the Prophet Muhammad to be of Turkic stock and stature. Perhaps Nizami was himself a Turk; after all, we have found many deep Turkic roots in the Persian, Parthian and Iranian states of which he was a son.

✦

## Бер Тәңір, қолда Тәңір
## THE ORIGINS OF RUSSIAN ORTHODOXY.
## THE TENGRIIST VIEW OF LIFE AFTER DEATH

As we have seen, for thousands of years the Kazakhs' ancestors had their own faith, Tengriism, and despite the fact that the warriors of Islam introduced their religion on pain of death by means of blood and the sword, they remained faithful to their Tengriist faith. And this is astonishing!

In Kazakh the word *tan* means 'dawn', *inir* is translated as 'twilight', 'sunset', and so Tanir, or Tengri, gradually came to mean the master of the Eternal Blue Heaven and of all matter from dawn to dusk.

For fourteen centuries our fathers and grandfathers kept Tengri in their hearts and souls. My own late parents would always say: "Бер Тәңір, қолда Тәңір". So perhaps everything is not lost and the Kazakhs can still return to their ancestral faith.

How then does Islam relate to this? And I do not mean Mecca and Medina so much as our Spiritual Directorate and the Muslims in our country.

Today all religions agree on at least one thing, which is that God is One and God is the Unique. I would say that Allah and Tengri are one and the same, without contradiction – the two names are simply historical variations on the naming of the same reality. And yet, why should the world view of a Kazakh, his ideology, his interior world and his distinctive identity be identical to those of an Arab? Surely we are all created differently. The followers of the Prophet taught their countrymen to live under particular spiritual laws, but we are Kazakhs and not Arabs. Our mentality is completely different. Our God may therefore be one, but His prophets may be different, and this is a perfectly acceptable situation. It is said that a prophet is not recognised in his own land. But we have prophets, and these include Qorqyt Ata, Beket Ata, Bukhar Zhyrau, Abai Qunanbayuli, Mustafa Shokay, Alikhan Bukeikhanov and many other worthy sons of our homeland. Yet I could not add, say, Khoja Ahmed Yasawi to this list, because this brilliant man, seeking to reconcile Tengriism with Islam in Kazakhstan, instigated a form of Sufism. The result of this was a loss of identity and civilisation, since each civilisation rests on three pillars: language, literature and religion. In essence we were left with only the first of these, language, and have had to resort to extraordinary measures for the Kazakhs to revive their identity and preserve themselves as a nation.

The British historian Edward Gibbon famously praised Genghis Khan's religious beliefs: "But it is the religion of Zingis that best deserves our wonder and praise. The Catholic inquisitors of Europe, who defended nonsense by cruelty, might have been confounded by the example of a barbarian, who anticipated the lessons of philosophy and established by his laws a system of pure theism and perfect toleration. His first and only article of faith was the existence of one God, the author of all good; who fills by his presence the heavens and earth, which he has created by his power" [my emphasis]. The Yasa, Genghis Khan's code of law, states: "I order all of you to believe in one God, creator of heaven and earth, the only giver of wealth and poverty, life and death, who possesses omnipotence in all things".

In other words, Genghis Khan instilled a faith in one god, Tengri, in all his subjects, while leaving the choice of prophets up to individual groups of believers. He considered Jesus, Mohammad and Buddha to be prophets of the one and only creator Tengri. It is not irrelevant to cite the example of Ivan the Terrible, who, in a visionary step announced at the Stoglavy Synod (of Russian bishops) in 1551 that Tengriism would now be the official religion of Muscovy, so turning Moscow into the spiritual centre of the population of the former Golden Horde, while declaring himself Genghis Khan's successor. With this far-reaching act of genius that laid the foundation for the future greatness of the Russian Empire, he forced all the population of Dasht-i-Qypshaq to recognise the state he headed; after all, after the collapse of the Golden Horde, our ancestors who had remained in the Kazakh, Kazan, Crimean and Astrakhan khanates and the princedom of Moscow were basically opposed to Islam, which became the official religion of these countries, having by now displaced the ancient Tengriism of the nomads.

At the Moscow Synod of 1667 the decisions made at the earlier Stoglavy were hushed up and their mention forbidden by Patriarch Nikon. He classified the writings as heretical, and they remained in archives until almost the nineteenth century. This may also be understandable in that the state religion of Rus' had been Greek Christianity since the reign of Boris Godunov. Rus' became Christian not in the tenth century but exactly 600 years after the official date of the baptism of Rus'. In 1586 Boris Godunov had invited Jokim, Patriarch of Antioch to Moscow to discuss the conditions for the establishment of a branch of the Greek Church in Russia, and a year later the Greek Patriarch Jeremiah came to Moscow himself. And thus the Russian Orthodox Church was established.

It is interesting to observe that it was from the moment of adoption of Christianity in Russia that the modern Russian nation began to form. In Novgorod, for example, the Varangians – including Scandinavians, Wends, Veps, Finns and Karelians – became Russian, though they each had a language of their own. The Finno-Ugric peoples of the Komi, Mari and Mordvinians also became Russians. The Mari and Krivichi, the Vyatichi and the Murom, not to mention many Turkic peoples – they all became Russian. This is perhaps not so surprising, however, as with the rise of Islam, the Arab nation had formed in a similar way some five hundred years earlier. The Egyptians and Syrians, Lebanese and Turks all become Arabs, although each spoke their own languages and had their distinctive culture.

So here we have an illustration of how religions can shape peoples and nations. I would venture to add the unexpected idea that the various Turkic peoples, though they are first mentioned only in the fifth century BC, probably formed a historical community much earlier, and the focal point of that community would have been Tengriism. Even the ethnonym *türk* shows a phonetic similarity with *tengri* and associated words, and one version of the origin of the Turks is based on this relationship.

As for the Russians and Kazakhs of the present day, it is my belief that these are two ethnically identical nations that are separated by religion.

Today, environmental issues are on everybody's lips, yet in essence Tengriism is the ecology of the soul, mind and body. One of the reasons man turns to God is his fear of dying. Generally, the religious powers of this world regulate man's behaviour and indeed his life through religion by threatening hell after death. By contrast, the basic postulate of Tengriism is that the human being is a child of nature and his life has a cyclical basis, just as a tree lets fall its leaves in the autumn and is covered again with fresh green the following spring. Followers of Tengri believe that after death a person passes into another world, the world of their ancestors. Later, in accordance with a given cyclical pattern, that person returns to earthly life as a human being – in my case as

Kairat Zakiryanov – and not as a spider, a snake or a horse, or, as some religions would have it, as a soul in paradise, hell or nirvana. Many people today are still fascinated by the idea of re-incarnation, which is often in response to the *déjà vu* ('already seen') effect formalised by the French psychologist Emile Boirac. It is believed that over 90% of people experience an action or situation at least once in their lives that they sense as being familiar from the past, even though they have no recollection of anything like this having happened to them before. Leo Tolstoy, for example, described an incident that occurred while hunting in which one of his horse's hoofs fell into a hole and he was flung from the saddle and fell hard; at that instant he recalled that something similar had happened to him two hundred years before. Some people have attempted to explain the *déjà vu* effect, for example by means of 'quantum psychology', while a group of scientists led by Nobel laureate Susumu Tonegawa discovered the area of the brain responsible for the déjà vu effect. The effect is considered by many to be a genetic memory of a past life. Vedic psychology proposes that a person experiences an imprint, known in Sanskrit as *samskara*, that is 'written' into the subtle body and linked to the senses. When a person dies, the subtle body is separated from the physical body and after a certain time is incarnated in another physical body. Thus, when a person finds himself in a place or situation that he experienced in the previous life, one or more *samskara* is signalled from the subtle body and the person feels that he or she has experienced the situation before, even though there is no recollection of it in their own life. These are, then, echoes from a previous life.

Tengriism is the only faith that regards human life as renewable, along with the phenomena of nature. It thus holds no real concept of death or fear of death, but rather encourages the believer to do everything necessary in this life for self-realisation. If there is not sufficient time or opportunity to accomplish that in this life, then what remains unfinished can be completed in the next, which will invariably come. The pain of losing loved ones and relatives also becomes less like inconsolable grief and can be accepted philosophically, since the believer knows he or she will soon be reunited with them.

This is perhaps why it was not possible to eradicate the faith in Tengri from the hearts of our ancestors in fourteen centuries!

The next episode associated with Genghis Khan is well known. After his conquest of Bukhara, Genghis Khan came to the mosque and met with the imams. These told him the basic canons of Islam and the principles of their faith. After listening to them, Genghis Khan responded that Islam is peaceful, compassionate and worthy of all respect. But he asked them why they made all believers love and worship only the homeland and family of the Prophet (as the daily prayer, prayed five times each day, sets out: "May the blessings of God be upon the Prophet Muhammad and all his family and companions"). But who, I ask, would ask for mercy on their own family, their own nation and their own native land? The Russian Orthodox Church obtained approval from Byzantium to address God in Russian. Why then should our Muslim Spiritual Directorate do the same? This would, as I said before, bring Islam closer to many of its followers. And as was noted earlier, the original text of the Qur'an is thought to have been written in a Turkic language and the first rituals carried out in that language.

After listening to the imams of Bukhara92 Genghis Khan replied that the only land sacred to any person is that place where his first drops of blood fell when the umbilical cord was cut. One of the vital tenets of Tengriism is to love one's homeland and one's nation and to serve them wholeheartedly.

The Turks have always guarded their faith. Let us recall the year 711, when Tonykok, counsellor to four Turkic khagans, was marching at full speed from northern China to the Black Sea to prevent the penetration of Islam into the native Turkic lands. Likewise, no matter how Genghis Khan was famed for religious toleration, some key situations called for resolution and a definite position. One of the reasons for undertaking the western campaign was to halt the further spread of Islam among the Turkic peoples. By now the Khorezmshah Muhammad had achieved the position of the deputy to the Caliph in Baghdad, had people under him and converted many Asian peoples to Islam. Much earlier, meanwhile, Herodotus had described the episode when King Skil was executed by the Scythians for apostasy from their ancestors' faith.

# THE GREAT TRAGEDY OF RUS' AND THE STEPPE.
# THE QYPCHAQ: THE COLOUR OF THE RUSSIAN NOBILITY

The Kazakh writer and thinker Aqseleu Seydimbek spoke of the millions of lives lost when the Arabs introduced Islam by fire and sword in what is now southern Kazakhstan. Sadly, those events of the seventh century found continuation in fierce fighting for the throne of the Golden Horde, and those who laid claim to this were not averse to opportunity, including the money of wealthy Arab merchants. Let us recall 1312, when Uzbek Khan made Islam the official religion of the Golden Horde by way of repaying Arab loans.

He invited the most famous descendants of Genghis Khan and then had them cunningly killed, since they defended the Yasa of Genghis Khan that forbade that the old religion of the Turks, Tengriism, should be replaced. This resulted in a division in the Steppe, in which the worthiest and highest-born abandoned the Horde and moved to the princedom of Moscow, where they became the foundation and the adornment of the Russian nobility. By the start of the fifteenth century, 95% of all noble Russian families included descendants of the Horde, direct descendants of Genghis Khan. Nikolay Aleksandrovich Baskakov gives a long name of Russian surnames with Turkic roots: Saburov, Mansurov, Godunov, Glinsky, Kurakin, Ermolov, Cherkassky, Ushakov, Suvorov, Apraksin, Yusupov , Arakcheyev, Urusov, Aksakov, Musin-Pushkin, Golenischev-Kutuzov, Akhmatov, Berdyayev, Turgenev, Kornilov, Sheremetyev and others (*Russkie familii dvorianskogo proiskhozhdenie*, Moscow, 1979). Lev Gumilev adds more equally eminent surnames: Alyabyev, Arsenyev, Babichev, Balashov, Baranov, Basmanov, Baturin, Beketov, Bibikov, Bilbasov, Bichurin, Boborykin, Bulgakov, Bunin, Burtsev, Buturlin, Bukharin, Velyaminov, Gogol, Gorchakov , Gorshkov, Derzhavin, Yepanchin, Yermolayev, Izmailov, Kantemirov, Karamazov, Karamzin, Kireevsky, Korsakov, Kochubei, Kropotkin, Kurbatov, Milyukov, Michurin, Rachmaninov, Saltykov, Stroganov, Tagantsev, Talyzin, Taneyev, Tatishchev, Timashev, Timiryazev, Tretyakov , Turchaninov, Tyutchev, Uvarov, Khanykov, Chaadayev, Shahovsky and Shishkov.

For the sake of fairness we should note that when the Catholic faith was introduced into the principality of Lithuania, which in the Middle Ages extended from the Baltic to the Black Sea and included some Turkic groups, there was another outflow of devotees of Tengriism to Moscow. So when Ivan the Terrible later adopted Tengriism as the official religion of Muscovy, this was prompted by the descendants of the elite clans from the Golden Horde and from Lithuania. Again when a century later, Russia under Patriarch Nikon abandoned Tengriism in favour of Greek Christianity, a split occurred between the church and state that resulted in the so-called Old Believers. In my view, the cause of this violent division in Russian society was not the question of how to cross oneself, whether using two fingers or three, but more fundamentally that of the choice between the religion of one's ancestors or the new, alien religion of Christianity.

Sergey Baimukhametov cites the political scientist Si Frumkin in stating that a total of just three Nobel Prizes for scientific achievement have been awarded to a population of 1.4 billion Muslims. There is little to add to this. According to Rafael Bezertinov, 2000 mosques were built in Kazan, Tatarstan, for which they were given a grant of one billion US dollars by Saudi Arabia. Yet when a group of Tatar noblemen travelled to the Arabian Peninsula they were stunned by the rejection they received from the Arabs, who told them flatly that they were not Muslims because they believe in the *aruakh* (the spirits of their ancestors), worship their holy shrines and do many other things that are incompatible with Islam.

So, Kazakh Muslims, let us remain ourselves, continue as in olden days to honour our elders and our shrines, to ask for help and advice from the *aruakh* of our ancestors and to keep and respect our sacred land, watered with the first drop of blood from our umbilical cord!

# SCYTHIAN RUS'. WHO CAME FIRST: THE KAZAKH ORYS OR THE SLAVIC RUS'?

**Russia is not only in Europe, but also in Asia: the Russian is not only a European, but also an Asiatic. Moreover, in Asia, perhaps, we have even greater expectation than in Europe. Moreover, in our future destinies, perhaps Asia is our main outlet... F.M. Dostoevsky, Diary**

Many of the facts at our disposal support one or another view that the Kazakhs and the Russians are relatives by history and by descent and that the modern Russians have a Scythian origin. Researchers have recently examined this question on a number of occasions, and there are deep and compelling observations by both Kazakh and Russian scholars. Examples include: Kazken Kalievich Tompiev (*O tiurkskikh plemenakh i narodakh Azii i Yevropy*. Almaty: Kazakparat, 2009); Akhmet Murzabulatov, Kalibek Daniyarov (Amanat, 2005, № 5, pp. 121-146); Valerii Demin, Yevgenii Lazarev and Nikolay Slatin (*Drevnee drevnosti*. Moscow, 2004, from the series *"Rus'mnogolikaia"*); Anatoliy Abrashkin (*Skifskaia Rus'*. Moscow, 2009) and others.

I would like to return at this stage to the Hyperborean theory, which goes back to Herodotus and is being developed intensively by modern scholars, including Russians. According to this concept, which is covered in detail in *The Turkic Saga of Genghis Khan*, there dwelt the thriving civilisation of the Hyperboreans at least thirty thousand years BC in the vast territories that are now lapped by the cold waters of the Arctic. After the Earth's suspected collision with an asteroid about 22,000 years ago and the resultant shift of its axis, the Flood took place and this civilisation began to move south. Part of it ended up on the North American continent and part in Eurasia. The genetic similarity between North American Indians and Altaic Turks (including the Kazakhs) established by modern scholars supports this hypothesis.

Some five or six thousand years BC the descendants of these Hyperboreans came to the territories of Eurasia and settled along major rivers such as the Rhine, Oder, Vistula, Danube, Volga, Ural, Irtysh, etc., and became known as the Aryans.

Modern evidence suggests that after the Flood there existed a single cascading water chain that covered what are now the Black, Caspian and Aral seas. As the land dried out again the present layout of the region emerged, notably including the path of the Volga, and this resulted in a natural division of the Eurasian Aryans (as they would later be called) into those who lived to its west and those to its east. From this moment the single ethnos was divided into two, who would later become the Kazakhs and the Russians. Then, as we noted earlier, the Aryans began to occupy Asia Minor, Mesopotamia and the Middle East. Historians have pointed out the ancient states that were created by the Aryans in the fourth and third millennia BC – Rusen (Arzava), Mitanni, the Hattite State, Sumer, Akkad and others.

In the second millennium BC, especially after the end of the Trojan War, there was a mass return of the Aryans to their historical origin. Referring to the work of Orazak Ismagulov I have shown convincingly, in my view, that the ancestors of the Kazakhs in the fifth century BC belonged to the same ethnic formation. All that happened is that the ancestors of the Russians tended to remain west of the Volga and assimilated with other Slavic peoples, thus retaining their Caucasoid appearance, whereas the ancestors of the Kazakhs went through an intensive period of assimilation from the first millennium BC to the middle of the second millennium AD with the 'yellow' races – today's Iranians, Indians, Chinese and Mongols, etc.

Thus what was once a unified ethnic group has acquired a diversity of physical types owing to extended contact with other peoples and civilisations. Modern Russians are a mixture of the Rus', Turkic-speaking, Finno-Ugric and Slavic tribes that arrived over the centuries on what has become Russian territory, while the racial appearance of the Kazakhs consists of 30% residual Caucasoid and 70% Mongoloid features.

In *Skifskaia Rus'* Abrashkin comments that "...one must be firmly aware that the names 'Russian' and 'Slav' began to be treated as synonymous only after the tenth century.

Previously, these two ethnic groups differed one from the other. And this makes sense, since the Slavs were newcomers to the Russian plain, whereas the Russians were its native inhabitants."

The Soviet historian Boris Aleksandrovich Rybakov, making reference to Constantine Porphyrogenitus, wrote in his major work *Mir istorii* (Moscow, 1984): "Such is the severe winter way of life of these very Rus'. When November comes, their princes go out at once from Kiev with all their Rus' and set out on the *poliudie*, i.e. a circular tour of precisely the Slavic lands: the Varvians, Dzhruguvits, Kriveteins, Severians and the other Slavs who pay tribute to the Rus' …". No more need be said.

According to known data, in 852 the Khan of Baqarah came to power in Bulgaria, who later became known as Boris I. He was a descendant of Khan Asparuh, brother of the Kazakh Botbay whose descendants can be found today among the Kazakh Dulat. Under the influence of the Greeks he reformed the Bulgarian khanate and made all his subjects equal under the common name of the Slavs. Thus a Slavic Christian power was formed from a Hunno-Turkic khanate. Under the aegis of the Bulgarians, neighbouring tribes including the Serbs, Bosnians, Bohemians, Moravians, Croats, Czechs, Poles and others also began to become known as Slavic peoples. Prior to the formation of the Slavic language, communication had naturally been in Turkic, which was considered the language for communication between tribes. Before Boris there was not one tribal association considered to be Slavic.

The word slavi, in the Latin sense of a 'slave', was first used by Jordanes in the sixth century. The moniker slavi was first applied to the Wends, who lived in central Europe and were forest-dwelling hunters. They were frequently captured by Norsemen and sold into slavery. Slavdom thus began with slavery. However, the word 'Slav' did not refer to ethnos. A similar state under the Mamluks was founded in Egypt by Sultan Beybars of the Kazakh Bersh clan. Since 852 the Bulgarian tribal union has historically been called the Slavs. In 864-65 Boris imposed Christianity on his subjects. Baptism gave him the possibility of reigning supreme over the united Slavic tribes, including the Turkic tribes that had become Slav. The Russian poet Maksimilian Voloshin expressed his respect for his fellow Slavs, which I share:

Grasp the great purpose
By Slavdom's smouldering fire:
There glimmers the sun of tomorrow,
And its cross is service to the world.
Its destiny is to take a double road –
Whose very name has two heads:

So SCLAVUS is a slave, but Slava is GLORY
The aureole of victory crowning the slave! (from *Europe*, 1918)

Next into the historical arena come the Varangians. St Nestor 'the Chronicler' wrote: "Certain brave conquerors, called the Varangians in our chronicles, have come from the Baltic Sea and laid tribute on the Chud, the Ilmen Slavs, the Krivichi and the Meria. In 862(?) the Slavs, exhausted by internal discord, summoned three Varangian brothers of the Rus' tribe, who became the first rulers of our country and because of whom our country became known as Rus'." I have mentioned elsewhere that the newcomers, the Varangians, were directly related to the ancestors of the Kazakhs. The place from which they came was called Gotland, i.e. the land of the Goths or Balts. According to one hypothesis, Rurik was Danish, and Denmark was founded by Danes who came to northern Europe from the banks of the Don and who at that time bore the name of the Kazakh Tana clan and roamed the banks of the Don.

Russian chroniclers, and particularly Nestor, identified the Varangians clearly with the 'Rus" nation. Anatoly Petrovich Novosel'tsev cites the conclusion of the Arab historian al-Hanafi: **"Description of the country of the Rus'. They are a large nation from among the Turks. Their country borders on the lands of the Slavs… The people of this land are fair-skinned, dark blond and tall. Of all the creations of Allah the Great they have the blackest disposition, and their language is unknown."** (*"Vostochnie istochniki o vostochnykh slavianakh i Rusi VI-IX vv."*, in Drevnerusskoe gosudarvstvo i iyego mezhdunarodnoe znachenie. Moscow, 1965). Here then is further proof of the Varangians being Turkic-speaking.

In the Annals of St Bertin, on the other hand, the governor of Rus' is recorded as bearing the title of khagan, which was peculiar to Turkic rulers. The circle is closed! On visiting Kiev the Arab geographer al-Gharnati described the country of the Slavs as having "…thousands of Maghrebians, with the appearance of Turks, speaking a Turkic language and shooting arrows like Turks…" (*Puteshestvie abu Khamida al-Garnati v Vostocnhuiu i Tsentral'nuiu Yevropu*, 1131-1153 gg. Moscow, 1971). His impressions are easy to explain. Following the Russification of Kiev by the Turks, the language of the latter naturally dominated there. Kazken Tompiev notes in *Ochevidnoe i veroiatnoe* (Almaty, 2011) that there is a stone inscription in a cave at Salzburg, Austria that reads: "The Year of our Lord 447, Odoacer, leader of the Ruthenians (my emphasis), Gepids, Goths, Ungarians and Heruli, raging against the Holy Church, threw from a cliff the blessed Maxim and his fifty companions who were hiding in this cave because of their faith". It turns out that the Ruthenians were a part of the Huns. This is unsurprising, since the Huns came to Europe from the east. The eleventh-century Muslim scholar of Turkic languages, Mahmud al-Kashgari wrote that the ethnicity of the ancient Rus' originated in the Altai. They came to Europe among the troops of the Huns and later established the state of Rus' on its eastern fringes. In his book *Kitayskie izvestia o narodakh Yuzhnoy Sibiri, Tsentral'noy Azii i Dal'nego Vostoka* (Moscow, 1961) N.V. Kuner states that "The Russians are the immigrants of the Uysyn tribe. This can be demonstrated precisely." He clarifies that the Uysyn state was located between Dunhuang and Tsilyan, and its inhabitants were called the Olos. Given that the Chinese tend to change hard consonants in the middle of a word into soft consonants, it is likely that Oros or Orys changed into Olos.

In his work *Usun'i etnogenez kazakhskogo naroda* (Almaty: Nash Mir, 2006) B. Irmakhanov analyses a variety of historical sources to conclude that "...without a great risk of error, we may state that ethnically the Uysyn are of Caucasian origin...".

To sum up the ethnogenesis of the Russian people, it may thus be assumed that the ancestors of the Rus' came to the Semirech'ie (Seven Rivers) region of Kazakhstan from the Ganzu Province of China around 120 BC; then at about the start of the Common Era they went to Europe with the Huns, where some of them reached the island of Osel in the Baltic. From there, under the name of the Varangians, they played their part in the formation of the Russian state. In Europe the Rus' were still known as the Scythians. A Georgian source from 1042, referring to the siege of Constantinople by the Avars and other groups in 626, mentions "The siege and storming of the great and holy city of Constantinople by the Scythians, who are the Rus'..."

In the 9th century there emerged the 'European Slavs' with their lexis and dialects of the Turkic language. Their early ethnic roots are not clearly established. It is known in chronological terms, however ,that Europe was dominated from ancient times by Turkic tribes including the Cimmerians, Scythians, Sarmatians, Alan and Huns including the Avars, and tribes related to them including the Rus', Getae, Goths, Germans and others. The Black Sea region was inhabited by the Polans (Anty), the Pechenegs, the Cumans or Polovtsians (Qypshaq,) the Kosogs (Cherkesh), the Alan and other Turkic tribes. It was the Varangian Rus', of Turkic origin, who founded Kievan Rus' in 882, and not the 'Slavs'. From time immemorial through to the eighth or ninth century the territory of the Dnieper, i.e. Kievan Rus, was inhabited by tribes such as the Cimmerians, Scythians, Sarmatians, Rus' and their descendants. The Varangians of Scandinavia are related to these tribes, some of whom, as far as we know, moved to northern Europe at the start of the first millennium and ruled there; this is why the ancestors of the Russians and Kazakhs called on them to rule in their territory also.

The Varangians ruled for over 60 years, from 882 to 944, and their descendants remained in power for many centuries thereafter. Curiously, in the ancient chronicles the Rus' are portrayed as friends with the Varangians, enemies of the Slavs and the vassals of the Khazars. It turns out that the Rus' had close relations with the Turkic tribes. An intensive period of miscegnation took place between the Rus' and Slavs in the tenth century, resulting in the mixed East Slavic ethnic group and the Slavic language. The Rus' retained their Tengriist faith, and perhaps this is why they were called 'khohols' (from the Turkic 'Kokul', 'son of heaven').

Later, following the conversion of Rus' to Christianity during the reign of Boris Godunov in the late sixteenth century, unions with Turkic and Finno-Ugric tribes, the Viatichi, Muroma, etc., resulted in their acquisition of the modern Russian appearance. I have already described the genesis of the eastern Aryans, the ancestors of today's Kazakhs, who acquired largely Mongoloid features.

As for language, which is the most conservative part of the culture, then if one were to remove the Persian, Arabic, Chinese and Manchurian borrowings from the Kazakh language, while also removing Western European borrowings from Russian, the two – Kazakh and Russian – will be almost identical. Thus language, as the main custodian of ancestral memory, has preserved the features of kinship between the two fraternally related quite clearly. making reference to Murad Adji, Tompiev claims that Rubrukvis wrote in 1253: "The language of the Ruthenians, Poles, Bohemians and Slavs is the same with that of the Turk Vandals..." A papal legate sent to Russia to study the issue of the adoption of Catholicism by the Rus' reported to the Pope that the Rus' population spoke a Slavic dialect of a Turkic language.

A dictionary of Turkisms in the Russian language (Slovar' tiurkizmov v russkom iazyke) prepared by the Academy of Sciences of the Kazakh SSR demonstrates that the following words, in everyday use by Slavs, have Turkic roots: *stakan* ('drinking glass'), *slovo* ('word'), *syn* ('son'), *tovar* ('product', 'commodity'), *karman* ('pocket'), *karandash* ('pencil'), *divan* ('sofa'), *dengi* ('money'), *vlaga* (moisture), *boyarin* ('noble', 'boyar'), *knyaz'* ('prince'), *bogatyr* ('hero' of Russian epics), *Bog* ('God'), *gospod'* ('lord', 'Lord God'), *ambar* ('barn', 'storehouse'), *neft'* ('oil'), *kocherga* ('poker'). The same is shown for proper names such as Matvey, Aleksandr, Yermolai, Arseny, Gleb, Boris, Dasha, Darya and many others.

Murad Adji supplements this list with hydronyms and toponyms. These include the Don, Volga, Oka, Ural, Irtysh, Ob, Yenisei and Amur rivers and the towns Orel, Tula, Tambov, Saratov, Chelyabinsk, Tyumen and many others. Also interesting are items of clothing: *shtany* ('trousers'), *karman* ('pocket'), *shapka* ('cap'), *kolpak* ('cap'), *kaftan* ('caftan'), *bashmak* (type of shoe), *sapog* ('boot'), *kabluk* ('heel'), *shuba* ('fur coat'), *tulup* ('sheepskin coat'), etc. The question of the origin of the ethnonym 'Rus" and 'Russian' remains unanswered. The

Turkic-speaking peoples of the former USSR referred to the Russians as the Orys. It may be that the ethnonym orys or urys originally related to the name of the Russians. In his *Ariy-gunn skvoz' veka i prostranstvo* Shakh-Murat Kuanganov discusses the question roughly as follows. It is known that the Polans formed a significant proportion of the tribal union of the Rus'. Boris Rybakov cites a famous phrase of the chronicler: *"Polianie iazhe nyne zavomaia Rus'"* – 'the Polans who are now called the Rus'.' 'Polan' is not an ethnonym; it was the name given to Scythians who lived in the fields or on the steppe. Meanwhile in Kazakh the words 'field', 'plain' or 'pasture' are called oris. Accordingly, the steppe and plain dwellers referred to themselves as the Oris or Orys, and over time the pronunciation of this word mutated to sound more like rus', whence 'Russian'. Let us add that the Arab traveller and geographer Muhammad al-Idrisi, who was then living in Palermo in what is now Italy, expressed his confidence that the Rus' were a Turkic tribe and that their ethnonym was derived from the Turkic word orys.

In other words we are confirming the Biblical account, according to which the Rus' and the Turk were both sons of Japeth, one of the sons of Noah.

# TAMGA FAMILIES OF THE TURKIC-RUSSIAN ELITE

As we noted earlier, up to the fifth century BC there lived on the territories of what are now Russia and Kazakhstan a single ethnic group that assumed a variety of names: Cimmerians, Scythians, Sarmatians, Goths, Balts, Huns, Turks, etc. Moreover, according to Orazak Ismagulov, only since the fifth century BC did Mongoloid elements of the 'yellow race' begin to penetrate the Caucasoid surface of the ancestors of the Kazakhs, and gradually, at no particular time, the single ethnic group began to acquire the features of the present-day Russians and Kazakhs. A fundamental turning point was reached in 1312 when Uzbek Khan betrayed Tengriism and imposed Islam by force on the Golden Horde as its state religion. The best of the Turkic nobility departed for Muscovy and created the modern Russian nobility.

Ultimately, the process of moving away from Scythian *Rus'* and of gradual transformation into what is now Russia was completed in the seventeenth century, after the Time of Troubles was over and the Romanov dynasty was in power. *In Bez vechnogo sinego neba* (Moscow: Astrel, 2010) Murad Adji suggests that a Slavic dialect of Turkic was created by the pen of Lavrentia Zizania, a member of a Jesuit order, and later, in 1618, this was anchored in a textbook on grammar by Meletius Smotritsky, also a Jesuit. In the Kremlin, boyars were replaced by noblemen; the Turkic roots of Rus' were ruthlessly destroyed, and at the same time a new ideology was being propagated through made-up Slavic myths. Let me reiterate that in Scythian Rus' the ancestors of the Kazakhs and the Russians belonged to one and the same people and ethnic community. When Russian historians such as Vasily Tatischev, Mikhail Lomonosov or Aleksandr Chertkov substantiated the ethnocultural affinity of the Slavic Rus' and the ancient peoples of the Mediterranean – the Pelasgians (fourth to second millennia BC), the Thracian tribes of the Balkan peninsula and the Etruscans of the Apennine peninsula – they probably had no idea that these peoples were directly related to the Kyrgyz Kaysaks of the steppe, as the Kazakhs were called in Tsarist Russia. We have already discussed in previous chapters the Turkic roots of the Thracians and Etruscans; let us now turn to the Pelasgians, who are thought to be an indigenous population of ancient Greece. One of the most respected Greek historians, Thucydides, who lived in the fifth century BC, wrote of the Pelasgians as an Asian tribe that captured Peloponnesus in the third millennium BC and gave it their name. We mentioned previously that after them the Balkan Peninsula was visited by the Achaeans, Dorians and Ionians in turn, who had also arrived there from the Eurasian steppes. It can be seen, then, that the ancestors of the Russians and Kazakhs were jointly involved in developing the fertile land of the continent.

But let us return to Ancient Rus' and the Polovtsian field. Among the large number of Russian princes who had Turkic genes there were many outstanding leaders. One of these was the famous Prince Igor. According to Vadim Kozhinov, Prince Igor was three quarters or half Cumanian. In addition, the famous Russian prince was married to the daughter of Konchak (Kunshuak), a Cumanian[93] khan. It was natural that relations between Konchak and Igor would be friendly, since Igor's grandmother, the wife of his grandfather Oleg Sviatoslavich, was the daughter of the Cumanian khan Osuluk (Asyluyk); Cumanian blood thus flowed in Igor's veins, as also in those of many other Russian princes, and the daughter of another khan, Aepa (Aip), was the first wife of his father Sviatoslav Olegovich, and Igor himself maintained good relations with her Polovtsian relatives.

Prince Andrey Yurevich was another prominent member of the Turkic-Russian elite. He was the son and heir to Yuri Dolgoruky, the founder of Moscow, and to the daughter of the Cumanian khan Aepa. In the twentieth century the anthropologist and sculptor Mikhail Gerasimov restored the likely appearance of Andrey Yurevich on the basis of his remains. In this sculptural portrait of the prince, classical features of the Cumanian, Kazakh type are clearly visible. Prince Andrey left a significant imprint on history and was canonised by the Russian Orthodox Church.

One of Prince Andrey's cousins was the well-known Vsevolod III Yurievich ('the Big Nest'). He, like Andrey, was half Cumanian and was the grandson of Khan Aepa. He was the progenitor of many famous princely families, including those of Suzdal, Vladimir, Starodub, Yaroslavl, Rostov, Tver and Nizhny Novgorod, and the Rurik dynasty; the epithet 'Big Nest' stems from the number of his children, at least fourteen.

One of Vsevolod's descendants was Prince Alexander Yaroslavovich. It was said that this young Prince achieved a brilliant victory over the Swedes on the Neva, from which he then became known as Alexander Nevsky. Subsequently another sole victory was ascribed to him over the formidable opponent of the Teutonic Order. Alexander Nevsky was one quarter Qypshaq and these Turkic genes contributed to his friendship with Sartaq, son of the great Batu Khan. The future tsar Sartaq and the prince Alexander Nevsky became *anda* or named brothers. It should be remembered that the laws of the Golden Horde forbade Russian princes from having military resources of their own, and so Alexander Nevsky's brilliant victories were in fact victories of Sartak's forces.

The friendship between Sartaq and Alexander Nevsky formed the foundation of the military and political power of the most important empire of the Middle Ages – the Golden Horde. Thanks to its alliance with the Golden Horde, Turkic Russia became its successor and subsequently a leading world power.

The tradition of marriage between khans of the Golden Horde and Russian rulers continued in later times. Thus Tsar Ivan III gave his daughter Eudoxia to the prince Kudai Kul of Kazan. The Urusov princes, who were descendants by the maternal line of Orys Khan of the Golden Horde, became related to the Russian ruling dynasty. Note the similarity of the ethnonyms Orys, Urus and Rus'! Peter Urusov was married to the daughter of the boyar Vasily IV of Russia of the Shuysky royal dynasty. Simon Urusov was married to the cousin of the first Russian tsar Mikhail Romanov, while their children were second cousins of Tsar Alexey Mikhailovich, father of the first Russian Emperor, Peter the Great.

One result of the marriages between the Turkic aristocracy and the Russian nobility was the emergence of a superb Turko-Russian elite that was of the cream of European nobility and a glory for Russia.

Ivan IV ('the Terrible'), who created the Russian Empire, had a Turkic origin by both paternal and maternal lines. On his father's side he was the thirteenth-degree descendant of the Cumanian Aepa. Gerasimov's reconstruction of him clearly reveals Turkic genetic features. The portraits of Ivan IV and Andrey Yurevich display typical Cumanian features characteristic of the northern Kazakhs.

Ivan IV's Turkic inheritance found expression in his relationship with the Tatar nobility. He wed his eldest son Feodor to Irina Godunov. The noble clan of the Godunovs descended from the Tartar prince Sheta, as also did the Saburov family. It was because of Ivan's Turkic genes that his sons were married to Tatars. Some sources suggest that the Tartar clan Sheta and the Kazakh Shekty tribe of the Junior *jüz* have a common root.

Irina Fedorovna's brother Boris Godunov, of the Tartar clan Sheta, also gained great influence at court, and when he was chosen by the Zemsky Sobor for the throne he did much for the people and also colonised the east and the south. It was by Boris's efforts that towns such as Saratov, Samara, Tsaritsyn, Voronezh, Belgorod, Oskol, Tyumen, Tobolsk, Surgut and Narym were established and the towns of Yam, Oreshek and Ivangorod, previously forfeited, were restored.m When the Romanov dynasty came to power. Its second representative, Tsar Alexey Mikhailovich, was married to Natalia Naryshkin, whose noble family descended from the Turkic nobleman Narysh. The son of Natalia and Tsar Alexei Mikhailovich was Peter the Great.

The Emperor Peter the Great had an enormous impact on the course of world history. His achievements marked the beginning of the Golden Age in Russia. His brilliant organisational skills and talent for military leadership made Russia a leading world power. The Emperor's noted military victories turned Russia, heiress to the Golden Horde, into the hegemon of Europe. Much of the brilliance and glory she gained are linked to the Turkic heredity of Peter the Great. Peter's Turkic genes formed the basis of his friendship with the Turkic elite. One of his friends and associates was Feodor Apraksin, whose palatine clan genus originated from the Turkic nobleman Salihmir. Tsar Peter Alekseevich was also strongly attached to his Tartar relatives; during his European voyages he entrusted control of Russia to his uncle Lev Kirillovich Naryshkin.

As we have seen, three great Russian tsars, who made substantial contributions to Russian power, have Turkic origins. Ivan IV, 'the Terrible', was a descendant of Emir Mamai who famously took part in the Battle of Kulikovo, and of the Polovtsian khan Aepa. Boris Godunov was a descendant of the Tatar prince Sheta. Peter the Great was the offspring of the Tatar princes Narysh and Abatur. Three great Russian tsars – a grand and magnificent symbol that embodies the centuries-old friendship of the Kazakh and Russian peoples. There remains only to add that, as I examined in The Turkic saga of Genghis Khan, in ethnic terms the Tatars of Kazan, Crimea, Astrakhan and Lithuania consist of basically the same clans as do the modern Kazakhs. Also, there is no point in pretending that Russia is not striving to become a part of European life; yet Europe does not recognise Russia as a European power, not because she is unworthy of this, but because she simply has her own, special place. As the poet Tyutchev said: "She has her own particular path – You can only know Russia by believing". Russia is an Asiatic country. And Asia, as we know, has a much older history, and the contribution made by the Asian Turkic peoples and the Russians to the treasury of world civilisation is far greater than those of the other nations of the world.

# OUR NATIONAL IDEA

## THE WILD HORSE: THE BASIS OF THE NOMAD'S POWER

Throughout this book I have maintained that our ancestors made a great contribution to the achievements of the world civilisations of Egypt, Mesopotamia, Persia, China and Europe. There is already a significant number of academic studies that are analysing this phenomenon of such a large contribution to the treasury of world knowledge by nomad groups.

Speaking of the unique identity of the Kazakhs and about what made our ancestors great, I would like to mention one particular event of global significance, equal in importance, I believe, to the invention of the wheel.

There are many monuments around the world that depict great warriors on beautiful horses. Yet the main thing is lacking – why is there not, in the magnificent sculptural ensembles of Almaty, Astana and other historical locations, a depiction of the wild horse itself – which was the source of greatness for our ancestors? The presence of centaurs in ancient Greek mythology was not by chance; they were cast in the type of our nomadic horsemen, who had grown up as it were in the saddle and so gained mastery of the situation in any land where their faithful companion let fall their hoof. Having tamed the wild horse in around 4000 BC on their own territory (e.g. the excavated settlement of Botay in northern Kazakhstan), our ancestor came to possess a vehicle of the greatest mobility, and then, having learned how to smelt bronze (first in the Altai, Zhezkazgan and Arkaim) and then iron, our ancestors made a number of victorious marches, reaching the Tigris and Euphrates in the fourth millennium BC, the Arabian Peninsula and the Nile in the second millennium BC, and later the Yellow River and the Ganges and the settlements of Albion and the Basque country. Incidentally, our ancestors were also the first to domesticate the sheep; wild sheep can still be seen in the Mangistau region of western Kazakhstan, and these are ancestors of the Edilbay sheep strain.

A monument was erected in Greece to the runner who, in 490 BC, announced the long-awaited news of the Greek victory over the Persians to the Athenians. One is tempted to ask why, if the Greeks were by now using horses in their wars, was a horse not used to deliver the good news, fast and efficiently, rather than sacrificing a human life? The monument, after all, was created to honour the man who ran 42 kilometres in debilitating heat to gladden his countrymen with the good news – and fell down dead on the spot.

# THE INTELLECTUAL ELITE: THE BRAND AND BASIS OF POWER IN THE FUTURE OF KAZAKHSTAN

The Aryans, Seir, Oghuz and the otherwise named Mary, Shumar, Kimar, Samar, Tur, Taur, and then the Scythians, Saqs, Huns, Sarmatians, Turks and Mongols defined the shape of the civilisation that we were destined to have. Regrettably, however, world history keeps deep silence about the great deeds of our ancestors. How many talented graduates of the excellent Bolashak[96] programme, established by our President, do we already have? Why do they keep 'proud' silence? Either they were not taught to speak out, or else they have forgotten the taste of the motherland that nursed their mothers and gave them power?

As regards a national idea for the Kazakhs of the twenty-first century, this complex issue continues to occupy the minds of all who are not indifferent to the destiny of their homeland. I remember that one of Boris Yeltsin's first decrees as Russian president was to charge the Russian Academy of Sciences with posing this problem before the Russian people and state. But as far as I am aware, this question has not so far been resolved.

Yet other countries have set themselves goals and followed them through. In America everybody was thrilled when, after the Great Depression, Franklin D. Roosevelt proposed the goal of making every American richer than the people in other countries. Japan revived after its humiliation in World War II thanks to the idea that goods made in Japan had the best quality and were thus also competitive. Moreover, Japan's impressive progress was based to a large extent on its declaring that loyalty to one's company or business took priority over the interests of family and state. As for Kazakhstan, our president Nursultan Nazarbayev has spoken more than once on this subject, offering a national idea in the sense of ensuring the welfare of every Kazakhstani citizen and promoting unity in Kazakh society. All this is crucial for the development of any country. Yet in my opinion our President's persistent and coherent search for a global idea capable of rallying the community and draw it out in world leaders has been successful.

**Nurturing our national intellectual elite is our state's most important task!**

Our ancestors, who conquered many states in the course of thousands of years and assimilated them, have created a powerful genetic potential for their descendants. Look at our young people, who today are not only world and Olympic champions in sport but who are winning first place at the International Mathematical Olympiad and top prizes at all kinds of international festivals and competitions, while graduates of the Bolashak programme are taking up leading positions as specialists in many foreign companies.

While declining to have his name given to cities and villages, our president has agreed to the creation of 'Nazarbeyev schools' and universities, 'Nazarbaev' research centres and the like. If every Kazakh oligarch, or indeed every moderately successful entrepreneur or company – and we have tens of thousands of them – allocated just one per cent of their income to seek out a child in the remote Kazakh hinterlands with a gift for mathematics, the arts, science or sport and develop his talents in the Nazarbayev schools and universities, then there would be no country in the world equal to us! We would become a great nation again – but not due to the strength of our arms or ability to fight but due our intellect.

**Here is a national idea for all citizens of Kazakhstan!**

The realisation of such a national idea should be imbued with the creation of Kazakhstan 'brand products'. One such brand product might be the Nazarbayev universities. Another brand would be the Nobel Prize winners (who must necessarily appear) schooled at these universities. Indeed, a Nobel Prize winner is the pride, dignity and, if you will, the brand of the country that has reared and nurtured him or her. Consider the states of the Persian Gulf: when a citizen is born a sum of money is immediately transferred to his or her personal account. As a result there is no desire for a good education, as a place under the sun is destined from birth. Can anybody name a citizen of the Emirates who is a Nobel laureate or Olympic champion? There are none! Yet Kazakhstan, which is also an oil power, should have its own Einsteins and Shakespeares, the mere mention of whom should trigger associations with the limitless steppe of Sary-Arka[97], the canyons of Mangistau or the Altai mountains. Who knows little Macedonia, somewhere in the Balkans? Yet everybody knows Alexander the Great, whom some also call Alexander the Macedonian. In terms of industrial output we may never reach the levels of Britain, Russia or China, but Kazakhstan should have its own Newtons, Pushkins, Rockefellers and Confucius. That is how I would determine the issue of the national idea for the diverse and multi-ethnic peoples of Kazakhstan.

\*\*\*

After this book went to press it was reported from France (*Argumenty nedeli*, Moscow, 22-29 February 2012) that a study of DNA samples of Charles Napoleon, a descendant of the famous general's brother, reveals that Napoleon Bonaparte is of Caucasian origin. Earlier research based on a lock of his hair had indicated a Middle Eastern origin. Throughout this book, however, we have given ample evidence of the overwhelming presence of Turkic Scythian clans across the Middle East and the Caucasus territories. French geneticists now seek to exhume the body of Napoleon in order to "dot the i".

I have repeatedly raised the issue of studying the remains of Zhoshy Khan, the eldest son of Genghis Khan, to determine the origin of the Great Terror of the Universe.
All of this, I hope, will become the subject of our next investigation.

# GLOSSARY

1. Kyltegin – Kul Tigin – a general of the Second Turkic Khaganate. He was the second son of Ilterish Shad and the younger brother of Bilge Kagan.

2. Hyksos or Hycsos – an Asiatic people that took over the eastern Nile delta, ending the thirteenth dynasty and initiating the Second Intermediate Period in ancient Egypt.

3. Shang or Yin Dynasty. According to traditional historiography, ruled in the Yellow River valley in the second millennium BC, succeeding the Xia Dynasty and followed by the Zhou Dynasty.

4. Arshahid – the Arsacid or Arshakuni dynasty – a branch of the Iranian Parthian Arsacids.

5. Madyas, king of the Scythians – Madius or Madyas was a Scythian king. He conquered and ruled the Median Empire c.633-625 BC.

6. Avaris – the Hyksos first appeared in Egypt around 1800 BC during the eleventh dynasty; they began their climb to power in the thirteenth dynasty, and emerged from the second intermediate period in control of Avaris and the Nile delta.

7. Pompeius Trogus or Gnaeus Pompēius Trōgus, also known as Pompey Trogue, was a Roman historian of the Celtic tribe of the Vocontii in Gallia Narbonensis in the first century BC, who was at the height of his powers during the age of Augustus, roughly contemporary with Livy.

8. Andalusia is the most populous and the second largest in area of the autonomous communities in Spain. The Andalusian community is officially recognised as a nationality of Spain.

9. Tomyris – queen of the Massagetae, a pastoral-nomadic Iranic people of Central Asia east of the Caspian, at about 530 BC.

10. Attila - frequently referred to as Attila the Hun, was ruler of the Huns from 434 until his death in 453. He was leader of the Hunnic Empire, which stretched from the Ural river to the Rhine and from the Danube to the Baltic.

11. Cyrus II the Great or Cyrus II of Persia was the founder of the Achaemenid Empire. Cyrus the Great is also well recognised for his achievements in human rights, politics and military strategy and for his influence on both Eastern and Western civilisations.

12. Dasht-i-Qypshaq - the name Cumania originated as the Latin exonym for the Cuman-Kipchak confederation, a state in the western part of the Eurasian steppe between the tenth and thirteenth centuries. The confederation was dominated by two nomadic Turkic tribes: the Cuman (also known as the Polovtsians or Folban) and the Qypshaq or Kipchak. Cumania was known in Islamic sources as 'Desht-i Qipchaq', which means 'steppe of the Kipchak' or 'foreign land sheltering the Kipchak' in Turkic. Some Russian sources refer to Cumania as the Polovtsian Steppe or the Polovtsian Plain.

13. Eternal Blue Sky - Khukh and Tengri literally mean 'blue' and 'sky' in Mongolian and modern Mongols still pray to Munkh Khukh Tengri ('Eternal Blue Sky'). Therefore Mongolia is sometimes poetically referred to by the Mongols as Munkh Khukh Tengriin Oron ('Land of Eternal Blue Sky').

14. Tengri - one of the names for the chief deity in the religion of the early Turkic (Xiongnu, Hunnic, Bulgar) and Mongolic (Xianbei) peoples. Worship of Tengri is sometimes known as Tengriism. The core beings in Tengriism are the Sky Father (Tengri/Tenger Etseg) and Mother Earth (Eje/Gazar Eje).

15. Zakiryanov's theorem – the theory for symplethctic liner goups

16. Yuan - the first foreign dynasty to rule all of China

17. Matay Kazakhs are among the Kazakh's middle juz

18. Kete Kazakhs are among the Kazakh's youngest juz

19. Argyn are among the Kazakh's middle juz

20. Mitanny - the country which was in the north of Mesopotamia

21. Hyksos sirshy - the group of nomadic tribes from Western Asia

22. Merkit or Mergid – one of the five major tribal confederations (khanlig) on the Mongolian plateau in the twelfth century. The Mergids lived in the Selenge and lower Orkhon river basins.

23. Oelun or Hoelun was the mother of Genghis Khan and the wife of his father Yesügei, the chief of the Khamag Mongol confederation.

24. Burhan Khaldun is a peak in the Khentii Mountains in the Khentii province of Mongolia. The mountain itself or its proximity are rumoured to be the birthplace of Genghis Khan, as well as the purported location of his tomb.

25. Onon, Tuul and Kerulen rivers - the Onon is a river in Mongolia and Russia with a length of 818 km and a watershed area of 94,010 km². The Tuul is a river in central and northern Mongolia that the Mongols consider sacred. The Kherlen river is 1,254 km long and flows through Mongolia and China. It originates on the south slopes of the Khentii mountains, near the Burkhan Khaldun mountain some 180 km north-east of Ulaanbaatar. This area is the watershed between the Arctic (Tuul) and Pacific (Kherlen and Onon) basins and is known as 'Three River Basins'.

26. Oirat tumen - the westernmost group of the Mongols, who unified several tribes that originated in the Altai region of western Mongolia. A tumen (unit of 10,000 warriors) was a part of the decimal system used by the Turks and Mongols to organise their armies.

27. Manchurian tribes consist mainly of the northern side of the funnel-shaped North China Craton,

28. Tungus Manchurians – Manchuria is a historical name given to a large geographic region in north-east Asia and today in north-eastern China. This region is the traditional homeland of the Xianbei, Khitan and Jurchen peoples, who established several states in the course of their history. The region is also the home of the Manchus, after whom Manchuria is named.

29. The Secret History of the Mongols is the oldest surviving literary work in the Mongolian language. It was written for the Mongol royal family some time after Genghis Khan's death in AD 1227.

30. Tamga – an abstract seal or stamp used by eastern Eurasian nomads and by cultures influenced by them. The tamga was normally the emblem of a particular tribe, clan or family. They were common among Eurasian nomads (including the Alan, Mongols, Sarmatians, Scythians and Turks) throughout classical antiquity and the Middle Ages.

31. Naiman, Konyrat, Koralas, Zhalair, Kerey and Merkit – tribes among Kazakh jüzes

32. Tumen – an army unit of 10,000 soldiers.

33. Harbin is the capital and largest city of Heilongjiang Province in north-eastern China, as well as the tenth most populated city in the People's Republic of China.

34. Dzhurdzhen or Jurchen – a Tungusic people that inhabited the region of Manchuria (now in north-eastern China) up to the seventeenth century, when they adopted the name Manchu. They established the Jin Dynasty (1115–1234).

35. Turkic Khagans – a title of imperial rank in the Mongolian and Turkic languages equal to the status of emperor or someone who rules a khaganate (empire). The words 'khagan' and 'khan' are distinct today, though historically they were regarded as the same.

36. Lezghin – an ethnic group living predominantly in southern Dagestan and north-eastern Azerbaijan who speak the Lezgian language.

37. Otrar was a Silk Road city in Kazakhstan. It played an important role in Central Asian history and was at the border with settled agricultural civilisations. It was the centre of a major oasis and administrative district, commanding a key point that connected Kazakhstan to China, Europe, the Near and Middle East, Siberia and the Urals.

38. Persepolis was the ceremonial capital of the Achaemenid Empire. To the ancient Persians the city was known as Pārsa, which means 'City of the Persians'.

39. Ivan the Terrible – Grand Prince of Moscow from 1533 until his death. His long reign saw the conquest of the khanates of Kazan, Astrakhan and Siberia, transforming Russia into a multi-ethnic, multi-confessional state that extended over a million and a half square miles. Ivan oversaw many changes during the progression from a medieval state to an empire and emerging regional power, and was the first ruler to be crowned Tsar of all Russia.

40. Uyghur – a Turkic ethnic group living in eastern and central Asia. Today the Uyghurs live primarily in the Xinjiang Uyghur Autonomous Region in the People's Republic of China. An estimated 80% of Xinjiang's Uyghurs live in the southwestern portion of the region, the Tarim Basin.

41. Kurds - are an Iranic people native to western Asia and mostly inhabit a region known as Kurdistan, which includes parts of Iran, Iraq, Syria and Turkey. They speak the Kurdish language, which is a member of the Iranian branch of the Indo-European languages

42. Zharlyq and Bilik – codes of laws for the military and for civilians

43. Tengriism is a modern term for a Central Asian religion characterised by features of shamanism, animism, totemism, polytheism and ancestor worship. Historically, it was the mainstream religion of the Turks, Mongols, Hungarians and Bulgars. It was the state religion of ancient Turkic khaganates such as the Göktürks, Avars, the Western Turkic Khaganate, the Avars, Old Great Bulgaria, the Bulgarian Empipre and eastern Tourkia. In modern Turkey, Tengriism is also known as Göktanrı dini, 'the religion of the Sky God'; the Turkish gök (sky) and Tanrı (God) correspond to the Mongolian khukh (blue) and Tengri (sky).

44. Semey or Semipalatinsk – a city in north-eastern Kazakhstan.

45. Abay Qunanbayuli was a Kazakh poet, composer and philosopher. He was also a cultural reformer whose basis was an enlightened form of Islam.

46. Degelen mountain is near Semipalatinsk, Kazakhstan.

47. Jüz – one of the three main territorial divisions in the Kypchak Plain that covers much of contemporary Kazakhstan. A jüz is believed to be a confederation or alliance of Kazakh nomads. Kazakh legends tell that ancestry of the three main Kazakh jüz derived from three brothers: the Great jüz, the Middle jüz and the Junior jüz.

48. Onkanat, Solkanat and Orta – the right, left and centre 'wings' of the Mongolian state at the time of Genghis Khan.

49. Akarys, Bekarys and Zhanarys – the three Kazakh jüz, the Senior, Middle and Junior respectively.
50. Yenisei Kyrgyz, also known as the Khyagas or Khakas, lived along the upper Yenisei in the southern section of theMinusinsk Depression from the third century BC to the thirteenth century AD.

51. Tartars are an indigenous Turkic people in Russia, numbering around 7 million. The Tatars originated with the Tatar confederation in the north-eastern Gobi desert in the fifth century. After subjugation by the Khitans in the ninth century, they migrated southward. In the Mongol Empire of the 13th century they were subjugated by Genghis Khan and reassigned particularly by his son Jochi.

52. Kokturks – The Göktürks or Kök Türks ('Celestial Turks') were a nomadic confederation of Turkic peoples in medieval inner Asia. Under the leadership of Bumin Qaghan (d. 552) and his sons they succeeded the Rouran khaganate as the main power in the region and took hold of the lucrative Silk Road trade. Gök means 'sky' in modern Turkish.

53. Naiman Karakerey – the Middle jüz.

54. Baganaly and Matay – are among the naiman tribe of midlle juz

55. Ergenekon – the valley of legend in which the Turks were said to have been trapped for four centuries until a blacksmith melted the rock and opened a gate, which enabled the grey wolf Börteçine to lead them out.

56. Borzhigin – the imperial clan of Genghis Khan and his successors.
Matay and Sadyr – the Middle jüz.

57. Ket– a Siberian people who speak the Ket language. In Imperial Russia they were called the Ostyak, without differentiating them from several other Siberian peoples. Later they became known as the Yenisey ostyak because they lived in the middle and lower basin of the Krasnoyarsk region of Russia.

58. Argyn and Naiman – the Middle jüz.

59. Hetrusc or Etruscan civilisation – Etruscan is the modern English name given to a civilisation settled in what are now roughly Tuscany, western Umbria and northern Latium in Italy. The ancient Romans called them the Tusci or Etrusci. This Roman name is the origin of the term Tuscany, their heartland, and also Etruria, which can refer to the wider region.

60. Lydia was an Iron Age kingdom in western Asia Minor, located generally east of ancient Ionia in the modern Turkish provinces of Manisa and inland Izmir. Its population spoke an Anatolian language known as Lydian.

61. Istre – a river in Moscow region, Russia.

62. Oghuz – the Turkmen, also known as the Oghuz (a term that distinguishes the Western

Turkic or Oghuz languages from the Oghur languages) were a Turkic tribal confederation of the Oghuz Yabgu State in Central Asia in the early medieval period. The word oghuz is a Common Turkic word for 'tribe'.

63. Svaneti –a historic province in north-western Georgia. It is inhabited by the Svans, a geographic subgroup of the Georgians.

64. Kanly – Senior jüz.

65. Alan or Alani and Alban (Senior jüz), occasionally termed Alauni or Halani, were a group of nomadic Sarmatian tribes in the first millennium AD. They spoke an Eastern Iranian language derived from Scytho-Sarmatian and which in turn evolved into modern Ossetian.

66. Tanais and Lake Maeotis. Tanais was the ancient name for the Don river in Russia. Strabo (Geographica 11.1) regarded it as the boundary between Europe and Asia. In antiquity, Tanais was also the name of a city in the Don river delta (the Maeotian marshes) that reaches into the north-eastern extremity of the Sea of Azov, which the Greeks called Lake Maeotis. The site of ancient Tanais is about 30 km west of modern Rostov on Don.

67. Sarmatia – The Iron Age Sarmatians were an Iranian people of classical antiquity who flourished between roughly the fifth century BC and the fourth century AD.

68. Iazyges and Roxolani – The Iazyges were a nomadic Sarmatian tribe that formed a tribal alliance and in the second century BC settled in the region around the northern shore of the Sea of Azov. Later the Iazyges' clan structure began to disintegrate and a class society emerged. Together with the Roxolani, the Iazyges warred against the Roman Empire. In the winter of A.D. 69 they invaded Moesia.

69. Konyrat, Qoralas and Uysun – Kazakh tribes

70. Volga – the largest river in Europe in terms of length, discharge and watershed. It flows through central Russia and is widely viewed as the national river of Russia.

71. Zelenchug inscription – a gravestone inscription in Greek letters dated to the tenth century, found by the archeologist D. Strukov in 1988 on the right bank of the Zelenchug river in the Caucasus. It is considered to the best-known monument of the

Alan language or an ancient monument of the Ossetian language

72. Ossetians – an Iranic ethnic group from the Caucasus Mountains, indigenous to the region known as Ossetia. They speak Ossetic, an Iranian language of the Eastern branch of the Indo-European languages family, with most also fluent in Russian as a second language.

73. Khakas (Choro) – the Republic of Khakassia is a republic in southern central Siberia, Russia, with its capital Abakan.

74. Qypchak or Kipchak were a Turkic tribal confederation. Originating in the Kimek Khanate, they conquered large parts of the Eurasian steppe during the Turkic expansion of the 11th to 12th centuries, together with the Cumans, and were in turn conquered by the Mongol invasions of the early 13th century. With the Cumans, the Kipchaks formed the Cuman-Kipchak confederation, also known as Desht-i Qipchaq ('Steppe of the Kipchaks') or Cumania, which lasted until its defeat by Mongol forces in 1241.

75. Dorian – one of the four major Greek ethnē into which the classical Hellenes considered themselves divided (along with the Aeolians, Achaeans and Ionians). The term ethnos has the sense of 'ethnic group'.

76. Catalaunian plains – The Battle of the Catalaunian Plains took place in AD 451 between a coalition led by the Roman general Flavius Aëtius and the Visigothic king Theodoric I against the Huns and their allies, commanded by Attila.

77. Golden Horde – a Mongol and later Turkic khanate that was established in the 13th century and formed the north-western sector of the Mongol Empire.The khanate is also known as the Kipchak Khanate or as the Ulus of Jochi. Descendants of the Golden Horde include the Nogai.

78. Thrace is a historical and geographic area in southeast Europe. As a geographical concept, Thrace designates a region bounded by the Balkan Mountains on the north, Rhodope Mountains and the Aegean Sea on the south, and by the Black Sea and the Sea of Marmara on the east. The areas it comprises are southeastern Bulgaria (Northern Thrace), northeastern Greece (Western Thrace), and the European part of Turkey (Eastern Thrace). The biggest part of Thrace is part of present-day Bulgaria. In Turkey, it is also called Rumelia. The name comes from the Thracians, an ancient Indo-European people inhabiting Southeastern Europe.

79. Anacharsis - was a Scythian philosopher who travelled from his homeland on the northern shores of the Black Sea to Athens in the early 6th century BC and made a great impression as a forthright, outspoken "barbarian", apparently a forerunner of the Cynics, though none of his works have survived.

80. Pelasgians - the name Pelasgians was used by some ancient Greek writers to refer to populations that either were the ancestors of the Greeks or preceded the Greeks in Greece, "a hold-all term for any ancient, primitive and presumably indigenous people in the Greek world." In general, "Pelasgian" has come to mean more broadly all the indigenous inhabitants of the Aegean Sea region and their cultures before the advent of the Greek language.

81. Beybarys - nicknamed Abu l-Futuh was a Mamluk Sultan of Egypt. Born in the Crimea, Baibars was a Kipchak people/CumanTurkic.

82. Kete, Adays, Bershs, Cherkesha – they are among the Kazakh juzes

83. Matays, Sadyrs, Karakereys - they are among the Kazakh juzes

84. Kokshe - among the Kazakh juz

85. Argyn and Ysty - among the Kazakh juz

86. Maeotis – the name of the Azov sea (by Greek and Romans), may be connected with the tribe of Meotis lived there.

87. Kassites - were an ancient Near Eastern people who gained control of Babylonia after the fall of the Old Babylonian Empire after ca. 1531 BC to ca. 1155 BC (short chronology). The Kassite language is thought to have been related to Hurrian, and not Indo-European or Semitic although the evidence for its genetic affiliation is meager due to the scarcity of extant texts. However, several Kassite leaders bore Indo-European names, and they might have had an Indo-European elite similliar to the Mitanni.

88. Arsaces - was the founder of the Arsacid dynasty, and after whom all 30+ monarchs of the Arsacid empire officially named themselves. A celebrated descent from antiquity (the Bagratid "line") begins with Arsaces.Arsaces or Ashk has also given name to the city of Ashkabad.

89. Sindi people - were an ancient people in the Taman Peninsula and the adjacent coast of the Pontus Euxinus (Black Sea), in the district called Sindica, which spread between the modern towns of Temryuk and Novorossiysk.

90. Bosporan kingdom - (also known as the Kingdom of the Cimmerian Bosporus) was an ancient state located in eastern Crimea and the Taman Peninsula, on the shores of the Cimmerian Bosporus (now known as the Strait of Kerch).

91. "Codex Argenteus" - The Codex Argenteus, "Silver Book", is a 6th century manuscript, originally containing bishop Ulfilas's 4th century translation of the Bible into the Gothic language. Of the original 336 folios, 188—including the Speyer fragment discovered in 1970—have been preserved, containing the translation of the greater part of the four gospels. A part of it is on permanent display at the Carolina Rediviva library in Uppsala, Sweden

92. Bactrians - Bactria, the territory of which Bactra was the capital, originally consisted of the area south of the Āmū Daryā with its string of agricultural oases dependent on water taken from the rivers of Balk̲ (Bactra), Tashkurgan, Kondūz, Sar-e Pol, and Šīrīn Tagāō. This region played a major role in Central Asian history. At certain times the political limits of Bactria stretched far beyond the geographic frame of the Bactrian plain.

93. Qoran - is the central religious text of Islam, which Muslims consider the verbatim word of God. It is regarded widely as the finest piece of literature in the Arabic language.
94. Umai - is the goddess of fertility and virginity in Turkic mythology and Tengriism and as such related to women, mothers and children. Umay resembles earth-mother goddesses found in various other world religions. Literally in the Mongolian language, "eje", "ece" or "eej" means "mother." In Mongolian "Umai" means womb or uterus. The earth was considered a "mother" symbolically.

95. Shanyraq –the circular top in the Turkic yurt.

96. Bolashak - Association of Kazakhstan President's Bolashak International Scholarship Fellows

97. Sary-Arka    - Saryarka — Steppe and Lakes of Northern Kazakhstan is a part of the Kazakh Uplands (known in Kazakh as saryarka, or "yellow range") which has been designated a world heritage site by UNESCO

# REVIEWS

In historical Eurasian development there are many renowned figures who played a significant role not only in their own epoch, but also for successive generations in terms of ethno-cultural development. In this regard, in particular we can focus on the historical role of Genghis Khan. Amid an inactive, disconnected and largely unknown medieval Eurasia, he for the first time brought about colossal social and economic changes and development. The consequences of these innovations in civilisation are still among us 800 years later.

So it is not unusual that there has been through time a wide range of researches, from mathematicians to literary scholars, that have shown a profound and multidimensional interest in the Genghis Khan phenomenon. An example is the work of the Doctor of Sciences, Professor of Mathematics and President of the Kazakh Academy of Sport and Tourism, Kairat Zakiryanov: Under the wolf's nest. A Turkic Rhapsody, published in Almaty, in 2012.

Professor Zakiryanov has made use of a huge stratum of historical sources, with many familiar points of reference providing supporting detail for the first time on this theme. He also makes a number of personal observations on the main historical places connected with Genghis Khan. As a result the book presents a wide range of historical, ethnic, linguistic and religious connections between different nations and the ancient Turkic world, and about their genesis; and also some interesting interpretations of the historical image and ethnic origin of Genghis Khan. But in our opinion, not everything said by the author on this subject is certain. However, the author's key concept of the antiquity of the Kazakh people and their cultural origins has the right to take its place in the historiography of Kazakhstan.

The main informative value of this book for the reader is that its argument is primarily represented by unusual historical judgments, and ideas related to the Genghis Khan phenomenon which are not found in other historical research papers.

This book rightly points out that the outstanding activity of Genghis Khan was at the same time when East and West were in a medieval stage of passive development. Therefore, for the contemporary intellectual world, readers can consider afresh various aspects of a reformist ideology for Genghis Khan, which to an extent can be compared with modern globalisation, now that the development of nations is even closer and more interconnected than ever before.

In general, the descriptions in this book of historical events, ethnic relationships, and Genghis Khan's role in public and state activities during the middle ages is of some interest in terms of developing knowledge of his real ethnic roots within Eurasia. Despite some bold interpretations of anthropological research, we should note the undeniable value of this book: it is written in lively and understandable language, excites the imagination and emotions, but most importantly makes the reader think, to look deeper and beyond, to try and get to historical truths from other points of view that are not always unambiguous or even go beyond the academic frame of knowledge.

It should be noted that to the study of the Genghis Khan phenomenon Professor Zakiryanov devoted a separate book, The Turkic Saga of Genghis Khan. In Under the wolf's nest. A Turkic Rhapsody, the author creates a concept of ancient world history based on the works of the 19th-century German school of philosophy. This is substantiated as the 'conquest concept', in accordance with which only after the conquest of the settled and semi-settled inhabitants of Central Asia and other countries by nomads appeared the great civilizations of Eastern and European countries.

As a result, in these countries binary ethnic societies appeared in which the alien nomads occupied the dominant positions, and local autochthonous peoples were to some extent under their influence - therefore, we may assume that prominent figures from these civilisations could belong to the descendants of migrants from Central Asia.

And it is reasonable that Professor Zakiryanov refers to the works of ancient authors, in accordance with modern scientific methodology, and analyses the Turkic roots of such great figures of the past, as Genghis Khan, Cyrus II the Great, and others.

Overall, Professor Zakiryanov has created a historical concept uniting the most disparate data into a single theory, from which we can see the Turkic peoples' crucial role in the creation by Eurasian steppe nomads of many foundations of European civilisation. The renowned German scientist Alfred Weber said that world history was created to the accompaniment of nomad cavalry, and Professor Zakiryanov in his book again and again proves the historical roots of this process. I believe that this book will find many sympathetic readers and admirers among a wide range of people that are interested in understanding socio-cultural Turkic history, as well as the phenomenon of Genghis Khan, who in the modern civilised world has been recognised as the man of the second millennium.

**Professor Orazak Ismagulov**
**Chief scientific worker in**
**Department of Ethnology and Anthropology**
**Institute of History and Ethnology**
**Ministry of Education and Sciences of Kazakhstan;**
**Academician of the National Academy of Science of**
**the Republic of Kazakhstan; corresponding member of**
**the Bologna Academy of Sciences; Doctor of Historical**
**Sciences Returning to the point of origin**

The ancient land of our ancestors which, for centuries, has been shrouded in silence has in recent decades awakened from its deep sleep to give us astonishingly enigmatic historical facts, endlessly enriching our understanding with Turkic events from history that more and more are capturing the imagination.

As it is written in the Holy Qur'an: "I have created you differently, divided you into separate races, and given you different languages for you to discover each other." It would have been easier to know each other if all mankind was of one race and spoke in a single, common language. But, therefore, there would be so little for us to work together to discover.

It is time to ask who the world shakers were, who created great empires, a unique civilisation, the history of which nowadays evokes such profound interest.

The amazing Turkic world – nomads, fearless warriors for whom there were no borders, nor distances too great, including death. While reading Professor Kairat Zakiryanov's works The Turkic Saga of Genghis Khan, and Under the wolf's nest. A Turkic Rhapsody, I sense the smoke of fires, hear the roar of hooves and steeds, the ringing of equipment, the guttural Turkic language, and I see the white yurts.

They are our distant ancestors, playing with death over enormous distances, conquering other worlds, leaving an indelible mark on foreign lands. The Turkic people esteemed military honour as higher than death.

The author's vision is not a simple fantasy or cheap jingoism, but the result of deep, relentless research, an unquenchable thirst for recognition of the roots of these people, which is confirmed by renowned historians both past and present. What emerges is the greatness of the Turkic empire, so much so that the author's arguments can seem at times almost fantastical.

But it can be difficult to balance what, throughout the centuries, has been removed from the pages of the history of the Turkic world, with what was retained. The Turkic people, again and again, have had their history rewritten by others to favour certain key individuals. According to certain evidences, the early adherents of Buddhism, and even the creators of early Chinese hieroglyphs, were Slavs. Pseudo-scientists never tire of uncovering new proof that Attila was the first Russian prince, that the nomadic peoples could not have created anything of lasting importance, and that the Huns are also a Slavic or Russian people. Fortunately, today we have more than enough evidence through historical researches to disprove this obscuring of science.

"Defense is a sign of fear. Brave is the one who strikes. Vengeance is the great gift of nature. We go to win…Who is at rest is already buried," said the great warrior Attila. The Turkic people led by Attila twice conquered the Byzantines. The Greeks recognised their defeat when they went to the North Balkans. The borders of Desht-i Qipchaq were closed to the Mediterranean and Constantinople. No single nation was conquered by the Turkic people in the history of the Great Migration, and no single country was captured. They simply settled new lands, and there built their cities.

The Kazakh ethnos which consisted of many tribes and nations played an important role in the history of the Eurasian steppe, as one of the ancient Eurasian peoples. Central Asia is the connecting link between East and West, North and South. It was the place where the religions of Christianity, Islam and Buddhism all met. It was a highway for nomadic migration, as well as for trade routes of transcontinental significance. From the territory of Kazakhstan and Central Asia the nomads made conquests in every direction. The ethno-cultural process of this region played an extremely important role in the ethno-genesis of all continents, and in the creation of many ancient, medieval and modern Eurasian nations' languages.

Interest in the amazing Turkic world first appeared in Europe; in France, the Turguere movement which was established several years ago demonstrated a huge interest in Turkic culture. Turkic peoples' craftworks and artworks began to be acquired for private collections, and exhibited at international events.

European scientists' archeological findings and historical researches about the ancient Turkic, Hun, and Mongol peoples proved that they are very old, occupying massive spaces, creating great nations, and in different historical periods have been highly influential in the development of world history. Thus was born the study of Turkology.

Revisiting historical memory, rebirthing languages, and religious values, was therefore a preservation of the soul, character and spirit of a people in an era of intense cultural intermixing and modern materialism.

The peoples of the world are interesting to one another because of their uniqueness and diversity, languages and cultures, religions and beliefs. We now come to appreciate the old Kazakh ancestral ways of spirit, optimism, kinship, and preservation of cultural heritage.

Relentless time moves on. We do not forget about the years of Soviet ideology, the ways in which the best sons and daughters of our nation were ultimately fashioned into a slave mentality. So, we try and restore our national vision, without embellishment or exaggeration. Reading the work of Professor Zakiryanov, you become part of a huge and vibrant Turkic universe, which played a key role in forming the history of all mankind. You have to catch your breath at its immensity.

To do this it is necessary that historians and scientists from all over the world work together. What Professor Zakiryanov has achieved is an immense feat, as a true son of Desht-i Qipchaq. It is not a false patriotism to return a true sense of historical memory and sense of civic responsibility to a land, to its history; it can encourage in each of us deeds and actions in the name of a life, and worthy of the title – a MAN.

**Rollan Seissenbayev**
**Writer, and President of the International Abai House**

Professor Kairat Khairullinovich Zakiryanov leads one of the country's largest educational academies, and in recent years he has become known as the author of books dedicated to the history of his people. That this eminent Kazakh academic, whose expertise is connected with professional studies, should address the themes of the nation's history should be regarded as entirely legitimate. This interest in the ancestral history of the Eurasian steppe nomads is rooted at a very deep genetic level. As stated in one of the early Chinese annals about the people of the Turanian steppe, who founded the ancient state of Botszy on the Korean Peninsula: "...they are most fond of shooting on horseback and dealing with ancient history..."

However, the relatively recent establishment of Kazakhstan as an independent state has set
before its intellectual elite a number of very complex tasks. First of all, a reappraisal of national history due to its previous tendency to be dictated in the political interests of the Russian and Soviet empires, with a correspondingly Eurocentric worldview. An accurate and true history of the people is an essential and necessary ideological condition for all further successful development of the Kazakh state.

It should be noted that in recent years prominent individuals from certain fields have emerged as academia begins to deal with solving this common national issue, of the humanistic and historical character. With their analytical ways of thinking and processing data, a number of experts in mathematics and physics have combined their researches with a love of their people and a deep interest in ancient history.

Among them we can name our former compatriot and one of the leading nuclear scientists, Dmitriy Madigozhin; nuclear physicist Smatay Ayazbaev, who published as co-author with Madigozhin the research work The Logic of Heavenly Law: Kok Torah; and Samat Nabiyev, the published author of many mathematical papers.

An impressive example in this direction is the newly published fundamental historical and linguistic research of a technical sciences' candidate from Moscow, Yuri Drozdov. This talented scholar has researched extensively in ancient and modern Turkic languages, approaching conclusions individual from previously established world history. Based on a thorough analysis of ethnic names in Europe since antiquity and the early middle ages, he has posited that the development on the continent was determined by the movement of pastoral tribes from the steppes of Central Asia, and these tribes were Turkic-lingual.

Professor Zakiryanov takes a special place among this group of researchers, by focusing attention on the linguistic analysis of Eurasian ethnonyms, and by dealing with the one of the key issues of Turkic history: the origin of Genghis Khan's Mongols. This matter is extremely important and revealing, particularly in the context of rethinking the character of historical development on the continent in ancient and medieval times. However, Genghis Khan and his successors are found to be the creators of some of the largest and most well-known empires of the middle ages, the existence of which is firmly connected with the history of many Asian and Eastern European countries.

Professor Zakiryanov's deep interest in this theme is perhaps due to his originating from the Kazakh Naimans. The Naimans were powerful Central Asian nomads, who at first were the formidable opponents of Genghis Khan, and later became a most important strategic element of troops within the empire he created. This indicates the key role of the ancient steppe tradition of tribal union in Genghis Khan's empire. According to which, during the funeral of the great world-shaker, on the right of his white horse stood a Naiman roan horse. Naimans were also the main military support of the powerful Ilkhan state that was established by Chinggisids in the Muslim East, one of the four tribal groups of nomads who participated in the conquest by the Golden Horde of ancient Rus kingdoms.

The detailed researches by Professor Zakiryanov into the ethnicity of Genghis Khan's Mongols, and his scientific expeditions within Mongolia as well as meetings with leading Mongolian historians, brought him to a firm conclusion about the Turkic origin of the great middle ages empire creators. Recognition for Professor Zakiryanov's research has come in acclaim from the World Genghis Khan Academy, established in Ulan Bator, awarding him the title of Academician.

Another achievement is his study of the historical place of the steppe Turanians' ancient monotheistic faith, Tengriism. Along with Murad Adji and other researchers, based on extensive data Professor Zakiryanov has come to the lasting conclusion that Tengriism became the primary source, or the initial cultural and historical basis, of major world religions ostensibly of Middle Eastern origin such as Judaism, Christianity and Islam.

The most important result of Professor Zakiryanov's research is that along with the other members of this growing group of like-minded individuals from Kazakhstan and Russia, an understanding of key developmental patterns on the continent in ancient and medieval times has been reached, along with our ancestors' fundamental role of lasting scientific and historical significance.

**Zhumazhan Baizhumin**
**Historian, author of The History of the Birth, Life and Death of Abel: An Aryan Lexicon**

Until recently, history was dominated by a Eurocentric view. Peoples of the Great Steppe were assigned to the role of destructors living only for the sake of plunder, and were far away from the beginnings of civilisation. It was considered that they had no written language nor philosophy, and, ultimately, they were unable to create anything of lasting importance.

Unfortunately, today among us we still meet adherents of these kinds of views, however, the latest archeological findings and historical discoveries now assert evidence of their absolute fallacy. On the basis of analyses made by Dutch scientists, the genomes of Saka kings from the Shilikti mound, in the Eastern Kazakhstan region, show that the Altai Saka were the forefathers of many Eurasian nations. In this regard, the work of Professor Kairat Zakiryanov evokes profound interest, relying on different sources as well as his own historical vision, estimates and interpretations of social, political, and ethnic processes in Eurasia; he also makes special reference to the key role of the Scythians, Huns and Turkic peoples. The history of the Great Steppe is filled not only with heroic spirit, which abounds in the popular legends and ancient written sources of the East and the West. It is also, primarily, a history of the intermixing of cultures, worldviews and philosophies. During three millennia the tribes of the steppe constantly journeyed from Central Asia to the West and to the East. The author's point of view on this historical process compels the reader to reconsider that well-known Eurocentric view of history. From when mankind first domesticated horses, the Great Steppe continued to be a great influence on all neighbouring peoples, and has also left an indelible place in the ethnic and cultural history of all Eurasia In the ancient world the early riders - nomads - were portrayed in Greek mythology by the image of a centaur. This was due to the astonishment experienced by others when first seeing these nomadic riders on horses. Interestingly, in this mythology the centaurs were the mentors and teachers of future kings and heroes. From this time the images of Saka-Scythian warriors appear in early Greek paintings on ceramics, and in ancient sources appear references to Scythian philosophies and kings, their way of life and traditions. The steppe-influenced everyday life and military affairs of the nomads began to be adopted by other peoples: for example, the appearance of the round table, a symbol of the 'steppe democracy' in the court of King Arthur. Therefore it is not unusual to find in many traditions and customs the steppe relics of pre-Islamic beliefs. Professor Zakirianov does not make these conclusions on the basis of unsubstantiated opinions, he presents strong evidence from written sources and toponymies, and with logical conclusions.

The steppe tribes of Saka, the Huns and the Turkic peoples, in addition to their advanced military technology, also gave to posterity their worldview: Tengriism, and the concept of monotheism. The legacy of these tribes therefore extends beyond the steppe's vast expanses that stretch several thousand kilometres. Steppe, desert, woodlands, lowlands and high alpine meadows: all this can be found under the one sacred sky – Tengri.

Another remarkable proposition in this book is that those peoples and states which were in contact with the steppe tribes began to develop and advance to the next level of civilisation.

To some readers, these conclusions may seem a historical mythologisation. But amid detailed analysis it can be seen that after the arrival of the Huns the slave system collapsed, and in Europe new feudal states appeared. There is also the shift of the Slavic tribes from the Rhine to the Balkans and the Southern Russian steppe. After the Golden Horde we did not see a feudal disunity, but instead the unique central Rus. What now emerges is an understanding that the progress of world history would be incomplete without the Saka, the Huns, and the Turkic peoples.

The important role of the steppe tribes can be found on the pages of ancient manuscripts and chronicles referred to in this book. Professor Zakiryanov rediscovers these truths, drawing them to the attention of historians and of all those engaged in finding out what lies hidden in the blank spots of history.

At present, the historians of England, Germany and other European countries have turned their gaze on the East and are showing interest in the ancient history of Kazakhstan and of Central Asia. This is not an occasional diversion, but an attempt to trace links between antiquity, their ancestors and the vast Great Steppe.

This book is of interest not only to historians, but also for those interested in seeing the restoration of truth.

**Professor Zhaken Taimagambetov**
**Dean of the History, Archeology and Ethnology Faculty**
**of Al-Farabi Kazakh National University**
**Ch. Valikhanov prize-winner**
**Doctor of Historical Sciences**

*Queen Tomiris's Revenge.*
*Artistic composition's author Kairat Zakiryanov, painter Zh. Ibrayev*
*Томирис патшайымның өші. Көркем композицияның авторы*
*Қ. Закирьянов, суретшісі Ж. Ибраев*

*Governor of Great Persia*
*Ұлы Персияның Әміршісі*

*The ceremony of presenting credentials to the Hun's King Attila. Artistic composition's author Kairat Zakiryanov, painter Zh. Ibrayev*
*Сенім грамотасының ғұнның патшасы Атиллаға салтанатпен тапсырылуы.*
*Көркем композицияның авторы Қ. Закирьянов, суретшісі Ж. Ибраев*

*Governor (Khagan) of the 2nd Turkic Khaganate*
*Екінші Түркі Қағанатының Әміршісі (Қағаны)*

*Genghis Khan. Last blessing of Tengri. Artistic composition's
author Kairat Zakiryanov, painter Zh. Ibrayev*
Шыңғысхан. Тәңірдің батасы. Көркем композицияның авторы
Қ. Закирьянов, суретшісі Ж. Ибраев

*Tamerlane XIV century*
*Әмір Темір XIV ғасыр*

*President of the Republic of Kazakhstan N.A. Nazarbayev, Artistic composition*
*author  Kairat Zakiryanov,  painter Isabaev I.N.*

Қазақстан Республикасының Президенті Н.Ә. Назарбаев,
Көркем композицияның авторы Қ. Закирьянов, суретшісі Исабаев И.Н.

КАЙРАТ ЗАКИРЬЯНОВ

# Көкжал белгісімен. Түркі рапсодиясы

# МАЗМҰНЫ

*- Альфред Вебер: "...Әлемдік тарих көшпенділердің сансыз топырлаған тұлпарларының тұяғы дүбірінің аккомпанементі арқылы жасалынды.."*

*- Осы еңбегімді өмірімнің тірегі досым және барша істерімнің серіктесі менің қымбатты Мәрзияма арнаймын. Тәңір мен аруақ қолдап жүрсін.*

# АЛҒЫ СӨЗДІҢ ОРНЫНА

Қазақ халқының бай мұрасы фольклорде көне дәуірлердегі бабамыздың аты аңызға айналған символдық сөздерін сақталып қалған:

> ...Қызым Қырымда, ұлым Рұмда,
> Барар жерім Балқан тау.
> Ол да біздің барған тау.

XXI ғасырдың ұрпағы ата-бабадан қалған бұл жырды оқи отырып, қайран қалады: бабаларымыздың қиялы мен ғажап ойының ұшы қиыры жоқ қой шамасы.

Мұнда оның қызы-Қырымда, ұлы-Рұмда (қазіргі Греция мен Кіші Азия аймағы, сол дәуірлердегі Византия империясы) жүргендігі туралы емес, көшпендінің өзі талай рет барып қайтқан Балқан тауға бет алғандығы жайында мәселе қозғалып отыр.

Біз- XX ғасырдың балалары – КСРО сынды дүние жүзінен бойын аулақ ұстап, жабық тұрғыда, жеке дара өмір сүрген алып мемлекетте өсіп жетілдік. Бұл елдің шекарасынан аттап өтуге мүмкіндігіміз болмады, өйткені сол кезеңдерде бұл әбден қалыптасқан қағида іспеттес еді, осы дәстүр бағзы замандардан бері келе жатқандай көрінді. Оның үстіне қатаң тұрғыдағы идеологиялық тұжырымдар біздің санамызда ата-бабамыздың жазуы-сызуы, мәдениеті жоқ білімсіз жабайы варварлар болғандығы, ұшы-қиыры жоқ Еуразияның кең даласында тобыр-тобыр малдарын бағып, өзге өркениеттерді талқандаумен айналысқан деген қатаң пікірлерін қалыптастыруға барша күшін салды. Сондай-ақ ұлттың қадір-қасиетін көрсетуге бағытталған кез келген еркін пікір сол сәтте адамның санасынан алынып, аяусыз түрде қудалауға түсетін.

Бүгінгі таңдағы бүкіләлемдік энциклопедияларға, мәселен Бодо Харенбергке жүгінсек, келесідей мәліметтерге көз жеткізесің: мысалы, Еуразия алқабының көшпенділері б.з.д. XYIII ғасырда Мысыр еліне гиксостар ретінде келіп, 150 жыл бойы осы елді билеп төстеді делік, ал тура осы кезеңде Шаң руынан шыққан көшпенділер Қытайда алғашқы Инь әулетін құрады.

Ал көшпенділердің тағы бір бірлестігі Иранның таулы аймақтарына келіп, кезек-кезегімен бұл өлкеде Ахеменид, Аршахид және тағы басқа әулеттердің негізін қалыптастырады. Тіпті Вавилонның өзін 28 жыл бойы Мәди патшаның скифтері басқарып келді.

Ең жоғары мәдениетке ие, жергілікті отырықшы көшпенді халықтарды бағындырған бұл жұмбақ көшпенділер кім болды екен сонда? Қазіргі Қазақстанның аймағын сол кезеңдері кім мекендеді? Біраз уақытқа дейін тарихта қазақтар Қазақстан жеріне шығыс аймақтан Ү ғасырда көшіп келген келімсек халықтар деген пікір белең алып келді. Ал Иран, Мысыр, Қытай, Үндістанды жаулаған халық деп қайдағы бір ойдан құрастырылған индоевропалықтар мен индоирандықтар деп жарияланды? Олар шамасы қазіргі Қазақстанның автохонды жергілікті тұрғындары болса керек.

Бірақ аты әлемге, дүниежүзі мойындаған, көрнекті ғалым-антрополог Оразақ Исмагуловтың зерттеу еңбектері нәтижесінде, қазіргі Қазақстан аймағында б.з.д. кем дегенде 2000 жыл ішінде қазіргі мекендеп жатқан рулардың ата-бабалары өмір сүргендігі бізге мәлім болды. Яғни, Қазақстан аймағынан келіп, Қытайда-Инь, Орта Шығыста – Ұлы Парсы, ал Ніл жағалауында-гиксостардың елордасы - Аваристі құрған белгісіз, жұмбақ гиксостар, парсылар мен құдіретті шандардың арғы тегі қазіргі қазақтардың ата бабасы екендігі сөзсіз. Ата-бабаларымыздың еуразияның ұшы-қиыры жоқ шексіз кең алқаптарға қанағаттанбай, белгісіз құрлықтарға жылжуына не себеп болғандығын қазақстандық зерттеуші ғалым Жұмажан Байжуминнің ерен еңбектерінің арқасында білдік, ол немістің классикалық философтарының еңбектеріне талдау жасаған, неміс данышпандарының түсініктемесі бойынша, 19 ғасырда таптық қоғам және мемлекет пен өркениеттердің қалыптасуының "жаулаушылық негізі" болған деген тұжырымдама пайда болды.

Сансыз көп малды иеленген біздің көшпенді малшы бабаларымыз уақыт өте келе жер тапшылығына тап болып, Еуразияның кең алқабына сыймай, өнімді жайылымдарға зәру болды, оның үстіне күш қуаты жағынан басым түсетін рулар жер тапшылығына байланысты соғыс ашып, әлсіз руларды жерлерінен қуып тынды. Антикалық көне дәуір тарихшысы Помпей Троганың айтуына қарағанда, олар "Скифиядан қуғындалғандар", яғни әлсіз рулар өз жерлерінен кетуге мәжбүр болып, өмір сүруге лайықты жаңа жерлерді жауалап алады. Еуразиялық көшпенділер руластарының ішінде әлсіз болғанмен, әйтседе Қытай, Үндістан, Иран, Мысырдың отырықшы егіншілері Еуропа ормандарының тұрғындарынан күш қуат жағынан әлдеқайда басым түсетін. Олардың жаңа жерлерге келуі нәтижесінде жаңа мемлекеттік құрылымдар мен өркениеттерді қалыптасты.

Мәселен, Орта ғасырда бүкіл Испания мемлекеті және оның барша провинциялық аймақтары Андалусия деп аталғандығын көпшілік біле бермейді. Бұл қазақ сөзінің бірінші "анда" бөлігі – ана алыс жақта дегенді білдіреді, осылайша бабаларымыз алыстағы Пиреней түбегіндегі "Анда Ұлыс" –яғни алыстағы мемлекет деп атаған. Ал біздің заманымызға дейінгі Ү ғасырда Вьетнам аймағында құрылған мемлекетті көне түркілер "Аулақ" деп атаған. Бұл да "алыстағы, қашықтағы ел" - деген ұғымды білдіреді. Мәселен Түркияда Германияны әлі күнге дейін "Алмания" деп атап келеді. Белгілі деректерге сәйкес қазақтар өздерінің сүйікті 50 шақырымнан артық ат жарысын - "Аламан" бәйге деп атайды.

Мұндай жүздеген мысалдарды келтіре беруге болады. Жекелеген тұжырымдарды және осыған іспеттес мысалдарды талдау үлгілерін біріктіру әрекеті - оқырманға ұсынылып отырған кітаптың негізгі тірегіне айналды.

Көрнекті түрколог Марат Уатқанға алғысым шексіз. Әйгілі ғалыммен сөйлескен әңгімелерім мен сұхбаттарым осы кітапты жазуыма кеңінен ықпалын тигізді. Ресейлік зерттеуші ғалымдар Ю.Дроздов пен А.Абрашкинге де алғысымды білдіремін, олардың еңбектері ойларым мен тұжырымдарымның дұрыстығына сенімімді арттыра түсті.

Ал, тарихшы ғалымдардың пікіріне келсек, Әл-Фараби атындағы ҚазҰУ-дың тарих факультетінің бұрынғы деканы, тарих ғылымдарының докторы Жакен Таймағамбетов өзінің нақты және жүйелі тұрғыдағы ой пікірін білдірді. Ол мен жазған кітапқа түсініктеме бере отырып, мынадай қорытындыға келді: яғни менің ой ұстанымдарым мен тұжырымдарым ақылға қонымды, сонымен бірге ресми түрдегі тарих ғылымы үшін оте маңызды және құнды зерттеу болып табылады.

# ҚАЗАҚСТАННЫҢ СПОРТ АКАДЕМИЯСЫНДАҒЫ ТАРИХ МҰРАЖАЙЫ НЕМЕСЕ МАТЕМАТИКА НЕГІЗДЕГЕН ТАРИХИ АҚИҚАТ

Академияның қонақтарын менің жұмыс бөлмем мен мәжіліс залының тарих мұражайына ұқсайтындығы үнемі таңқалдырады.

Шынымен-ақ, Қазақтың спорт және туризм академиясыпда бірпеше сурет туындылары сақталуда, бұл көркемшығармаларды менің тапсырысым бойынша бірнеше суретші дүниеге әкелді.

Туындыларды өмірге әкелудегі негізгі мақсат – біздің ұлы ата-бабаларымыз мұра етіп қалдырып кеткен ұлы тарихымызды көркемдік тұрғыда қайта жаңғырту. Көркем туындылардың бірінде сақ массагеттердің патшайымы-Тұмардың бейнесі, ал келесі бір суретте ғұндардың патшасы –Аттілініц бейнесі сомдалған.

Тарих беттеріне мұқият зер салсаң, таңданбасқа амал қалмайды. Көшпенділердің ата мекені болып табылатын, Дешті Қыпшақ алқабына өз мемлекетінің жер аумағын ұлғайту мақсатында келген, Парсы елін құрған ұлы ІІ Кир патшаны Тұмар ханшайымның қалай жеңгенін еске алсақ жетіп жатыр. Ол Тұмар ханшайымнан ащы жеңілістің дәмін татып, мынадай сөздерді естігені аян: "Сен қанға тоймай, қан ішуді аңсадың, ал енді өз қаныңды тойып іш", деген сөздерді айтып, басын шауып тастайды, сонан кейін қаптың ішін қанға толтырып, жеңілген ІІ Кирдің басын қанға толы қапқа салады. Ал Кир патша Ассирия, Мидия, Палестина, Финикия, Лидия, Согдиана, Бактрия және тағы басқа ұлы мемлекеттерді бағындырған даңқты қолбасшы болатын. Сондықтан да осы көркем туындылардың бірі Тұмар патшайымға арналғанын қайталап өтейін.

Ал келесі бір көркем туындыда көшпенділердің ұлы бабасы Аттілінің бейнесі айшықталған. Бұл сурет Голливудта талай рет қойылған көркем туындылар сюжеті мен атақты Рафаэльдің шығармашылығында сан мәрте бейнеленген: Аттілі Римге келген кездегі, Римнің әулие әкесінің Аттіліне қалаға тиіспеуін өтініп, аяғына жығылған сәтті кескіндеп бейнелейді. Бірақ мен бұл сюжетті өз көзқарасым бойынша сәл ғана өзгерттім, ал енді нақты айтқанда, бұл көркем туындының тарихи айғағы толық айшықталды, -деп есептеймін. Аттілінің аяғының астында жатып, Римге тиіспеу туралы әулие әкейдің жалынышты бейнесі салынған көркем туындының өмірде болуы заңдылық. Бұл көркем туындының репродукциясы менің кітабымның мұқабасына салынды, енді осы мәселе жайында әңгіме қозғайық. Бұны оңай шешім деп айтуға дәтім бармайды. Ғұндардың патшасына тағзым етіп жатқан әулие әкейді бейнелейтін кезде, тұла бойымда екі жақты күрес орын алды, бірақ тарихи ақиқатты бейнелеу мақсаты жеңіп, суретші Жомарт Ибраев екеуіміз тарихи шындыққа жол бердік.

Біздің тарихи мұражайымызды тамашалап келетін қонақтарға айтарым: "Тарихта бір рет болса да, Рұмның әулие әкейі, Құдайдың алдында емес, адамға тағзым етті, ал бұл адам-біздің ұлы бабамыз. Міне, қазақтар- біз осындай ұлтпыз!". Тағы бір көркем туынды Шыңғысханға арнап салынды. Бұл сюжет Шыңғысханның халықтардың тағдырына қатысты өте қиын шешімдерді қабылдау алдында, жалғыз өзі таудың басына көтеріліп, Көк Тәңірінен және оның иесі Тәңірден өзіне жеңіс тартуын сұрап, ғибадат екен.

Ұлы Шыңғысхан тағзым етіп, бір, екі, тіпті бар апта бойы қозғалмай тұра алатын, Ол Тәңірден белгі кемлмейінше ешқандай амал әрекеттер жасамайтын. Ал Тәңірден белгі берілген кезде, жер бетіндегі билеушілердің ішінде Шыңғысханның мерейі артып, оның қаһары басқалардан басым түсетін.

Жер жаһанды дүр сілкіндірген Шыңғысхан. Тәңірдің соңғы рет бата беруі. Идея авторы Қайрат Закирьянов, суретші Жомарт Ибраев.

Менің ұсынысым бойынша өмірге бірнеше көркем туынды әкелінді. Бұл суреттердің тәрбиелік-ағартушылық маңызы зор. Қалыптасқан дәстүрге сәйкес, бірінші курсқа түскен студенттер осы мұражаймен танысуға келеді. Ал мен өз басым, ректор тарихи экскурсоводқа айналып, жастарға көркем туындылар туралы әңгімелеп, көне замандардың құпиялары мен жұмбақтары жайында сыр шертемін.

Несіне жасырайын, маған осы туындыларды сату немесе оларды әртүрлі көркем сурет галеряларына орналастыру туралы бірнеше ұсыныстар жасалды. Тіпті елордамыздан да ұсыныстар келіп түсті. Бірақ мен бұл суреттерге әуес болғандықтан, ұсыныстардан бас тарттым. Өйткені бұл туындылардың жағымды тұрғыдағы дидактикалық мәні ерекше маңызды екендігі сөзсіз.

Менің тарихқа деген құмарлығымды және зерттеу еңбектерімнің нәтижелерін ресми тарихшылар әуесқойлық деп санайды. Бірақ Уақыт бәрін өз орнына қойып, ақиқатты айғақтайтыны аян.

Ал ғалым математик рстінде жеткен табыстарым айтарлықтай. Өте үлкен табысты нәтижелерге қол жеткіздім. Қуанышпен және мақтанышпен айтатыным: математикалық энциклопедияларда, Закирьяновтың да теоремасын көре аласыз, Қайрат Закирьяновтың теоремасы американдық ірі ғалымдар: Басс, Милнор және аты аңызға айналған француз математигі Ж.П.Серрдің теоремаларымен қатар тұр. Өз басым жер бетіне келген әр адамға Жаратушы дарынды аямай-ақ тарту еткен. Осы дарынды дер кезінде байқап қалып, шама жеткенше оларды дамытуға әрекет жасап, жүзеге асыруға күш салу керек. Әрине, тағы бір математикалық жұмбақты шешуге болатын-ақ еді. Бірақ тағдырдың жазуымен басқа бағытқа бет бұрдым.

Кезінде Ережеп Альхаирович Мәмбетқазиев сынды айтулы тұлға, тағдырымның өзгеруіне айтарлықтай үлес қосқан адам, өзім қызмет атқаратын педагогикалық институттың басшылығына келіп, мені өзінің командасына тартып, Қазақстанның шығысында университет құруға көмектесуім қажет екендігін түсіндірді.

Таңдауымды дұрыс жасадым, бұған өкінішім жоқ. Кейінірек бұл университетті басқарып кеттім, ал содан соң, Шығыс Қазақстан облысы губернаторының орынбасары қызметіне ауыстым, кейінірек үш жыл бойы Қазақстан Президентінің әкімшілігінде Ұлы Даланың барша қадір қасиетін, салт дәстүрін бойында жинақтай білген, таңғажайып адам Нұрсұлтан Әбішұлы Назарбаевтың жанында қызмет атқардым. Осы жылдарды білім мен тәжірибе жинау жылдары, өз-өзіңді тапу кезеңі деп атаймын. Пушкин сөзімен айтқанда "өзіндік қалыптасу" кезеңі. Ал енді бүгінгі таңда бұл жинаған құнды тәжірибе білігімді спорт академиясының ректоры ретінде барынша пайдалы тұрғыда жүзеге асырып келемін.

Мен біздің жас мемлекетіміздің Білім министрі Қырымбек Көшербаевты құрметпен еске аламын. Осы тұлғамен сұхбаттасу барысында: біз, қазақтар - кімбіз осы, өркениеттер тарихында алатын орнымыз қандай?- деген сұрақтары мені жиі мазалайтын болды.

Қазақтар - көне дәуірлердегі және кейінгі кезеңдердегі тарихқа үңіліп айтар болсақ – біз әрқашан ұлы халық болғанбыз! Бүгінгі таңда бұл отансүйгіштік қасиетті қайта жаңғырту ерекше маңызды мәселе болып отыр. Отансүйгіштік қасиет арқылы біз ұлтымыздың дамыған 50 елдің қатарына кіріп, олармен тереземіз тең тұратынына халықтың сенімін күшейтуіміз қажет. Бұл жайында Елбасымыз жиі айтады, ал біздің бұдан да биік мақсаттарға жететініміз кәміл.

Сондықтан да мақсатқа жету барысындағы спорттың қосатын үлесі өте зор. Осы спорттың арқасында менің бойымда генетикалық тектік рулық сана жадым оянғандығын айта кеткім келеді. Бастапқы қырық жыл ішінде менің түсінігім орыс ұлтына жақын болғандығын жасырмаймын, Менің орыс достарым көп, қазір де баршылық. Тіл мәселесіне байланысты орыстар мен қазақ ұлтының бір - біріне жақын екендігін айта кеткім келеді. Біздің орыс тіліне деген құмарлығымыздың ерекше себебі бар. Әртүрлі мәліметтерге сәйкес, орыс тілінің сөздік қорында 30-50 пайызға жуық түркі тілінен енген сөздер бар екен. Орыс зиялыларының көпшілігі таңданып, мынадай сауал қояды: Ресейдің Қазақстаннан басқа, бұрынғы КСРО-дағы өзге көршілерімен кейде тіл табыса алмайтыны неліктен? Ресейдің Қазақстанға жақындығын немен түсіндіруге болады? КСРО аймағындағы бұрынғы КСРО елдерінің ішінде неге қазақтар ғана орыс тілінде ежіктемей, таза сөйлейтінін қалай түсінеміз? Ал енді осы күрделі сұрақтарға біртіндеп жауап беруге талпыныс жасайын.

Соңғы уақытта Русьтің тарихы IX ғасырдағы Киевтік Русьтен бастап емес, бұның тамыры өте тереңде – сақтар мен скифтер дәуірінде басталғандығы туралы зерттеулер жасалуда, осы пікірлерге сәйкес, қазақ халқының ата-бабасы түркілер, орыстардың да арғы тегі екендігін әлемдік тарих мойындауда (А.Абрашкиннің "Скифская Русь" "Вече" баспа үйі, 2008, кітабын қараңыз). Яғни қазіргі ресейліктер мен қазақтардың шығу тегі бір, ортақ тарихы бар, бірақ өкініштісі, бұл тұжырымдарға қатысты зерттеулер аздау болып тұр. Мәселен, әртүрлі халықаралық форумдарда немесе жарыстарда бізді-қазақтарды американдықтар мен еуропалықтар көне тарихы бар жеке дербес ұлт ретінде қабылдамайтыны ашуымды келтіреді. Олар әдеттегідей, келесідей сұрақтарды жаудырады: Қазақтар, кімсіңдер: Раша немесе Чайна? (орыссың ба, қытайсың ба?) Осы жайттың өзі елімнің өткен тарихы туралы тереңінен ойлануыма себін тигізген себептердің бірі болар. Мақсатқа сәйкес жүргізген зерттеулерімнің нәтижесінде таңқаларлық нәтижелерге қол жеткіздім: бірнеше жыл ішінде бұл зерттеулерімді жүйеге келтіріп, қалың бұқараға жария еттім.

Әрине, жасайтын қыруар жұмыс жетіліп артылады, бірақ қазіргі кездің өзінде-ақ ұлы Қытай империясын, қытай халқының өркениетін қалыптастыруда біздің ата-бабаларымыздың тікелей түрде қатысқандығы туралы дәйекті айғақтар мен дәлелдер қолымда баршылық. Ата-бабаларымыз аспанасты еліндегі Инь, Чжоу, Тан, Ляо, Юань қытайлық императорлық әулеттерін құрған. Қолымдағы мәліметтерге сәйкес, Инь әулетін қазақтың Матай руы, Чжоу әулетін - қазақтың Кете руы, Тан-әулетін – қазақтың Арғын руы, Ляо мен Юань әулетін –Кете мен Матайлар басқарған. Бірақ ұлы елді және ұлы халықты басқару үшін билік жүргізуші халықтың өзіндік ұлы тарихы мен өткені болу керек қой.

Сонымен бірге жақында Мысыр перғауындарының арасында біздің ұлы бабаларымыз бар екендігі жайында мәліметтердің анық-қанығына қол жеткізудің сәті түсті. Мәселен, Каспий және Қара теңізі маңы алқабынан шыққан тайпалар мен рулар б.з.д. екі мыңыншы жылдықтың басында Кіші Азияда Митанния атты қуатты мемлекетті құрған, бұл мемлекеттің қарамағына Мысыр да кірген. Ал кейінірек, Мысырды Қазақстан даласынан келген гиксостар-сиыршылар руы басқарған. Б.з.д. 2 мыңыншы жылдықтан бастап, қазіргі Қытай, Мысыр, Түркия, Үндістан, Иран, Ирак, Еуропа аймағында Шаң, Шумер, Парсы, Рим империясы, Византия империясы, готтар мен балттардың мемлекетін және тағы басқа өркениеттерді біздің арғы тегіміз: қазақтардың ата-бабалары құрған. Ал, Мәңгілік Римді У ғасырдың ортасында ойран еткен ғұндар мен герман тайпалары деген жұмбақ атаудың ар жағында қандай халық бар деп ойлайсыз? Ұлы Францияның қайнар басында кім тұрды? Александр Македонский, (Ескендір Зұлқарнайын) Иисус Христос (Иса Мәсіх), болашақ ұлы Британияның королі Артур, бүкіл мұсылман жамағатының пайғамбары Мұхаммедтің (с.ғ.с) этникалық тұрғыдағы шығу тегі қандай? Бұл адамды ойландыратын сұрақтар мен таңқаларлық айғақтар менің тарихқа назар аударып, зерттеулер жасауыма ықпал етті. Осының нәтижесінде біздің мәжіліс залымыз бен менің жұмыс бөлмем де тарихи жәдігерлерге толы безендіріліп, өзгеріп құлпырып шыға келді.

# ҰЛТ ҰЛЫЛЫҒЫ БАСТАМАСЫНЫҢ ҚАЙНАР КӨЗІНДЕ

## XII ҒАСЫРДАҒЫ ТҮРКІЛІК МОҢҒОЛИЯ

Бүкіләлемдік ЮНЕСКО ұйымы Шыңғысханды ІІ мыңыншы жылдықтың адамы деп мойындады. Бірақ ол шығу тегі жағынан кім екен сонда? XIII ғасырда моңғол деген атпен қай халық құпия қалды?

Мынадай мақал бар: "Жүз рет естігенше, бір-ақ рет көргеннен жақсы". Мен үшін мәселе келесідей жолмен туындайды: Тарихи айғақтардың тым көптігіне қарамастан, барша әлемді дүр сілкіндірген Шыңғысханның нақты және бірегей түрдегі шығу тегін анықтау қиын болып шықты. Мәселен, Шыңғысханның болашақ анасы Әуелімге Меркіт ханзадасы үйленіп, заңды тұрғыдағы әйелі ретінде шаңырағына апару үшін жол тартады. Ал аң аулауға шыққан Шыңғысханның әкесі кездейсоқта арбаның ішіне үңіліп, Әуелімнің жүзін көріп қалып, оның ғажайып сұлулығына ғашық болып қалады. Ол кідірместен ордасына қарай жол тартып, бауырларын көмекке шақырып, сұлу қызды тартып алады. Меркіттің жауынгерінен Әуелімнің аяғы ауыр болып қалды деген жорамал да бар. Бірақ дегенмен де, қазіргі заман Меркіттері –қазіргі қазақ ұлтының бір бөлігі, олар- Абақ-Керейлердің бір бұтағы болып табылатынын ескерсек, тарихи тұрғыда біз үшін бұл онша маңызды емес.

Шыңғысханның өзіне байланысты тағы бір дерек бар. Ол Бөртеге үйленген кезде, Меркіттер бұрынғы кектерін алу мақсатында, Шыңғысханның әйелін ұрлап, Бөртені, Шыңғысханның әкесі Есікей ұрлаған Меркіт жауынгерінің бауырына тарту етеді. Шыңғысханның тұңғышы Жошы ханның әкесі туралы мәселе құпия қалды. Әйтседе, "Шыңғысханның түркілік ғұмырнамасы" ("Тюркская сага Чингисхана" Современное сказание казахов "Жібек Жолы" баспасы, 2008) кітабымдағы күрделі және тыңғылықты зерттеулер арқылы Жошы хан Шыңғысханның ұлы екендігін дәлелдейтін нақты айғақтар келтірдім. 800 жыл бұрын орын алған өте құпия түрдегі сезімге байланысты оқиғаның анық-қанығын анықтау - қиямет - қайым дүние, дегенмен, бұл мәселенің де ара жігін анықтауға болады.

Бірақ мен үшін басқа мәселе маңыздырақ: 12 ғасырда, Шыңғысхан дүниеге келер кезеңде (бұл шамасы б.з. 1162 жыл), Бурхан Халдун тауының етегінде, Өнен, Керулен, Толы өзендерінің суы бір-біріне келіп құятын мекенде қандай халық өмір сүрген?

Тарихи тұрғыда осы аймақта тұрған халықтың тарихи болмысын анықтау өте маңызды екендігін атап өтейін. Егер, осы кезеңде, бұл аймақта қазіргі қазақ халқының ата-бабалары тұрғаны анықталса, онда қойылған сұрақтың жауабы табылды дей беріңіз. Осы сұраққа жауап тауып, бір шешімге келу үшін, бұл мәселені методологиялық-әдістемелік жолмен шешуді ұйғардым. Сондықтан да маған сол аймаққа барып, қазіргі Моңғолия жерінде қандай халық өмір сүргендігін біржола анықтау қажеттілігі туындады.

Әрине үлкен жолға шықпастан бұрын барша тарихи-мұрағаттар көзін зерделеп, зерттедім. Осы мәселемен айналысатын Моңғол академиясының ғалымдарымен жүйелі тұрғыдағы келіссөздер де жүргізілді. Өте сирек кездесетін, таптырмайтын құжаттар мен деректер қолыма тиді. Мәселен, Моңғолияның 1990 жылғы адам санағын өткізудің нәтижелері. Санақ жүргізушілердің көп бөлігі Моңғолия тұрғындарынан шығу тегі мен қай руға жататындығы туралы сұраған.

Мұнда мен моңғол ғалымдарының көзқарасынан тыс, XXI ғасырдағы моңғол халқының руларының санына ерекше ден қойдым: Рулардың саны жүздеп басталады – 769 ру болып шықты. Ал Шыңғысхан дәуірінде бұл аймақта небәрі 70 ру ғана өмір сүрген. Сонда бұл рулар қалайша он есе артып, көбейіп кетті?!

Осы сұрақты Моңғол Академиясының ғалымдарына, тарих ғылымдарының докторы, профессор Баярға, филология ғылымдарының докторы, профессор Долантай Церен Содномға тікесінен қойдым. "Егер сіздердің мәліметке сүйенсек, Шыңғысхан дәуірінде Моңғолия аймағында 40 ру өмір сүрген, ал Шыңғысхан батысқа 34 түменді қосып әкетті, Моңғолияда 6 түмен (моңғол болса керек, шамасы) қалып қойды, олар ойраттың 4 түменімен бітіспейтін шайқасқа түсті. Осы алты түмен ойраттарға жеңіліп қала берген соң, көмекке маньчжур тайпаларын шақырды. Олар осы 6 тайпаға қолын созып, көмек көрсетті.

Ал, сонан кейін осы тайпалардың тағдыры қалай болды? – деген сұрақ туындайды. 6 түмен – 60 мың адам. Олар енді саны миллионнан асып жығылатын, жайлы жер мен қолайлы алқаптар іздеген маньчжур әскеріне төтеп беруі тиіс еді. Осы кезде математик ретінде мынадай формуланы шығардым: 21 ғасырдағы қазақтар мен 12 ғасырдағы Шыңғысханның моңғолдары арасындағы тепе-теңдік белгісін қоюға болады, сондай-ақ қазіргі заман моңғолдары мен 12 ғасырдағы тунгус-маньчжур тайпалары арасында да тепе-теңдік белгісі бар екендігі сөзсіз.

Сондықтан да ғылыми жорамалдарымының анықтығына көз жеткізу үшін, менің ең батыл ойларым мен жорамалдарымды айғақтайтын сапарға аттандым.

Мәселен, жоғарыда аталып өткен, профессор Далантай Церен Содном маған: "қазіргі заман моңғолдарының Шыңғысхан тарихы бойынша 1240 жылғы дерек көзі болып табылатын "Моңғолдардың құпия тарихының" тілін білмейтіндігін" айтып жеткізді. Сонымен бірге, оның айтуынша, қазіргі заман моңғолдары Шыңғысхан дәуіріндегі моңғолдардың тілін біржола ұмытқан болса керек. Осыған сәйкес, қазақ ұлтының отансүйгіш азаматы, Қалибек Данияров өзінің "Шыңғысханның тарихы" (Алматы, 2001) атты мазмұнды еңбегінде осы құнды тарихи шығарманың мәтінінен қазіргі қазақ тілінде қолданылатын қырық пайызға дейінгі сөздер қорын табады.

Осылайша, Моңғолияға саяхат жасау арқылы өз ойымның дұрыс екендігіне сенімім арта түсіп, тарихи құпиялар мен жұмбақтарды шешудегі қиындықтардың алдын алып, тарихи ақиқатқа қол жеткізуде жаңа серпін мен жаңа күш берді.

Сонымен бірге, аталмыш сапар барысында басқа да табыстарға қол жеткіздім. Ұлан-Батордан 600 шақырымдай жерде, Керулен өзеннің ағысынан 25 шақырымдай аймақта кезінде Шыңғысханның жазғы ордасы орналасқан минералды су бұлағының қайнар көзі табылды.

КСРО құлап, Моңғолия шынайы егемендікке қол жеткізген соң, бұл жерде ескерткіш орнатылды: петроглифтерге толы үлкен тас. Осы ескерткішті мұқият зерттеп шыққан кезімде, белгілердің көпшілігі қазақ руларының тамғалары екендігіне толық көз жеткіздім. Қазіргі күнде қазақ руларының жеке тамға белгісі болып табылатын 45 белгіні санап шықтым. Доктор Баярдан аталмыш белгілер жайында сұрағанымда, бұл белгілерді оның археолог ғалым досы бүкіл Моңғолиядан жинап, осы тасқа сол күйінде қашағандығын айтты. Баярға былай дедім: "Біз Қазақстанда сіздің досыңызға ескерткіш қоюымыз керек, өйткені бұл петроглифтер кем дегенде 45 қазақ руының Моңғолия жерінде өмір сүріп, осында өздерінің тұрғандығының белгісін тасқа қашап қалдырып кеткен". Жуырда Шыңғысханға арналған ресейлік, американдық және моңғолдар бірігіп түсірген блокбастерді көрдім. Бұл фильмде қазақ рулары 12 ғасырда Моңғолия жеріне жаулау мақсатында келіп, жеңіліп қалады. Бұл тарихи ақиқатты бұрмалау әрекеті болып табылады. Қазіргі Моңғолияның жері қазіргі біздің көптеген қазақ руларының ата қонысы болып табылғандығы аян. Бүгінгі таңда осыған сенімім мол және болжамдарым көптеген тарихи айғақтар арқылы дәлелденді. Б.з.д. кем дегенде 4 ғасырдан бері Хуанхе өзенінен солтүстік жақта әрқашан түркі қазақ тайпалары көшіп қоныстанған. Жалпы бұл жайында көне грек тарихшысы Птоломей де жазып кетеді. Моңғолияның барша аймағы мен Солтүстік Қытайдың аумағы (Шыңғысханның билік құрған дәуірінде де) Найман, Қоңырат, Қоралас, Жалайыр, Керей, Меркіт және тағы басқа қазақ руларының мекені болған. Басқа сөзбен айтқанда, қазақ руларының жартысы б.з.д Моңғолия мен Солтүстік Қытайды мекендеген. Хуанхэ өзенінің қытайша үлгісі де көне түркі, қазақ тілінде "қияңқы" деген ұғымды білдіреді. Ұлы түркілердің өзені атауының тарихы осындай.

Қазақ рулары Шыңғысханмен бірге батысқа бет алады, ал босап қалған жерге тунгус-маньчжур тайпалары қаптап кетеді, олар осы Моңғолия жерінде Шыңғысханның ұйғарымы бойынша Бежінді бағындыру үшін қалған аздаған қазақ тайпаларын (Керей, Оңғыт, Жалайыр және тағы басқалары) өздеріне сіңіріп алады. Олардың саны небәрі төрт-ақ түмен еді.

Ассимиляция орын алып, осының негізінде қазіргі Моңғолияның этникалық негізі қалыптасты.

Ал енді тунгус-маньчжур тайпаларының табиғи болмысын зерттеуге келсек, маған осы шарада сәттілік көмекке келді: 2009 жылдың ақпан айында Харбинге жол түсті, ал Харбиннен 60 шақырым жерде, Шыңғысхан билікке келгенге дейінгі Қытайды билеген маньчжурлық Цзинь әулетінің мұражайы орналасқан. Шығу тегі тунгус-маньжурлық тайпалары туралы айтатыным: осыған дейін шүршіттер (джурджени) деп аталатын маньчжурлар қазіргі кезеңде қазақ руларының құрамына енген. Мәселен, қазіргі заманғы Найман тайпасының ішінде Шүршіт атты бұтағы бар Терістамғалы руы өмір сүреді. Міне осы этникалық шүршіттер Наймандар тайпасының құрылымы құрылған кезде, осы елдің құрамына сіңіп кеткен. Меніңше, манчжур тапаларының да түркілік негізі бар екендігі сөзсіз.

М.В.Воробьев өзінің: "Культура чжурдженей и государства Цзинь" (Мәскеу, 1997) атты кітабында шүршіттер мәдениетіне түркілердің қосқан үлкен үлесі және түркілер мен шүршіттердің этникалық тұрғыда ұқсастығын, шүршіт тайпаларының қоныстанатын жері Приморьеде табылған заттардағы түркі жазбалары мен шүршіттердің этнонимдерінде түркі создерінің коп кездесетінін атап отеді.

Бір сөзбен айтқанда, Шыңғысханның маңына қазіргі қазақ руларының өкілдері шоғырланды, оларды ертіп Шыңғысхан батысқа бет алады. Ал бос қалған жерге қазақ руларына еш қатысы жоқ маньчжурлардың туыстас тайпалары келіп қоныстанды.

Ал моңғол нәсілінің атауына келсек, бұл жерде пікір қайшылығы әркелкі. Кейде ерекше пікірлер де айтылып жүр. Мәселен, Қалибек Данияров моңғол этнонимі "мыңқол" –жүз мың әскер деген сөзден шыққан деген пікір айтады. Басқа болжам бойынша, моңғол сөзі- "мың құл" деген ұғымды білдіреді. Бұл пікір туралы "Шыңғысханның түркілік ғұмырнамасы. Қазақтардың киелі сөзі" атты кітабымда нақты айтып өттім. Түркі этносын зерттеуші Тілеуберді Әбенайдың пікірі бойынша, "моңғол" лексемасы "маңқұл"-көшпенді халық деген ұғымды білдіреді. Қазақстанның оңтүстігінде ислам діні күштеп тұрып енгізілген кезде, жаңа дінмен келіспеген халықтар басқа жерлерге көшіп кетсе (маңқұл), ал қалып қойғандары "сартқұл" - жергілікті, отырықшы халық деп аталып кетті.

Моңғол этнонимін түсіндіруде өткен дәуірлердегі көрнекті ғалым тарихшы-жылнамашылар: Рашид-ад Дин, Жалайыри, Әбілғазы Баһадүр өз пікірлерін қалдырды.

Рашид-ад Дин мәселен моңғолдарды түркі тайпасының бір бөлігі деп санайтын және Шыңғысхан билікке келген соң, барша түркілер өздерін моңғолдар деп атап кетеді. Ал мен осы мәселеге қатысты өз көзқарасымның атақты ғалымдар: Р.Безертинов, Х.Қожа Ахмет және тағы басқа ғалымдармен сәйкес келетіндігіне толық сенімдімін. Яғни осы пікір бойынша Шыңғысхан 1206 жылғы құрылтайда "өзінің қоластындағы киіз үйлерде тұратын халық бұдан былай "Мәңгі ел деп аталады"-деп жариялайды. Осы ойы арқылы Шыңғысхан түркі қағандарының байлық пен салтанат құрып өмір кешкен "Мәңгілік ел" жөніндегі армандарын жүзеге асырды. Бір тілден бір тілге транскрипция және транслитерация тәсілі арқылы, уақыт өте келе "мәңгі ел" сөзі "моңғол" сөзіне айналып кетеді.

Шыңғысхан басын қосқан халықтың аты "мәңгі ел-моңғол" болғандығын атының өзі-ақ айтып тұр, ал басқа халықтар оларды түркілер деп атаған. Бұған араб тарихшысы Ибн әл-Әсиридің (1160-1233) сөзі дәлел болады. Ол моңғолдардың хорезмшах Мұхаммед жеріне жасаған жойқын жорығын өз көзімен көрген куәгер. Шығыстан келген халықтар жайында араб тарихшысы былай деп жазады: "Осы 617 жылы (1221 жыл) ислам елдерінен үлкен түркі тайпасы Татарлар келді. (Өзім бөліп көрсеттім-Қ.З.). Олардың тұрғылықты жері Қытай маңындағы Тамғадж таулары, олар мен мұсылман елдері арасындағы ара-қашықтық алты айлық уақытты құрайды. Олардың келу себебі мынадай: Теміршін деген атпен белгілі олардың ханы Шыңғысхан атамекенінен кетіп, Түркістан елдеріне қарай бет алды..." Өзінің жылнамасының басқа бір бөлігінде ол Хорезмшахтың әйгілі құқықтанушы Шихаб Хиуалықпен кездескендігі туралы жазады. Хорезмшах оған былай деген екен: "Үлкен іс болды. Ойланбаса болмас. Мәселе мынада: Түркілер елінен бізге қарсы сансыз көп әскер бет алды..." ("Алтын Ордаға қатысты деректер жинағы" "История Казахстана в арабских источниках" 1 том, "Дайк пресс баспасы",Алматы, 2005 кітабынан).

Қарастырылып отырған жазбадан тағы бір көрініс келтірейік: "Шерван шатқалы арқылы өтіп, Татарлар осы облыстар арқылы жүрді, олардың ішінде Алан, Лезгин және басқа түркі тайпалары да бар. Олар лезгиндерге шабуыл жасап, тонап, көбін қырып жойды, олардың жартысы мұсылман болса, жартысы кәпір еді. Осы елдің тұрғындарына шабуыл жасап, саны жағынан көп өздері туралы естіген Аландарға келіп жетті. Аландар бар күшін жинап, Өздеріне Қыпшақтарды қосып, Татарларға қарсы соғыс ашты. Бірақ екі жақ бір-бірін ала алмады. Сол кезде Татарлар Қыпшақтарға былай деді: "Біз сендермен туыс халықпыз (Өзім бөліп көрсеттім-Қ.З.). Ал мына Аландар сендерге жат халық. Оларға көмектесіп қайтесіңдер. Сендердің діндерің оларға ұқсамайды, сендерге шабуыл жасамаймыз-деп уәде береміз. Қаласағандарыңша ақша мен сыйлар тарту етеміз. Бізді олармен жеке қалдырыңдар".

Түсіндірудің қажеті шамалы... Шыңғысханның моңғолдары мен Қыпшақтардың діні бір болып шықты. Ал ендеше XXI ғасырдың қазақтары біз неге ұлы ата-бабамыз-Шыңғысханнан қасарысып, бас тартып отырмыз?!

Өзінің ұзақ жазған жылнамасында араб тарихшысы бірде бір рет Шығыстан келген әскерді моңғол деп атаған жоқ. Ол өз жазбасында түркі-татар этнонимін жиі қолданады. Бұл түсінікті жайт, тек 1206 жылы Шыңғысхан өзінің қоластындағы халықты "мәңгі ел" – моңғол деп атайды, бұл атау дүниені дүр сілкіндірген қағанның ұлысынан шығып, басқа халықтарға тарап үлгермеді, бар әлем осы аймқтың тұрғындарын түркі қағанаттарышап бері көне түркілер ретінде танитын. Римдіктер Пелопонесстің эллиндерін – грек, ал кельт көшпенділерді - галл деп атайтын. Шыңғысханның түркілері батысқа -Қазақстанға бет алған соң, бос қалған жерге тегі маньчжурлық тунгус тайпалары келіп жайғасты. Олар мұрагерлік жолымен моңғолдардың этнонимін сақтап, сонымен бірге Шыңғысхан түркілерінің атақ даңқын иеленіп қалды.

Міне, 800 жылдан бері жер бетінде осындай ақылға сыймайтын әділетсіздік орын алып келеді!

Өз жерін жаулауға келген келімсек жауынгерлерді қаншалықты жек көріп тұрса да (мәселен: Егер әлдекім Құдіретті және Жаратушы Аллаһ Тағала адамды жараттты деп айтса, онда шамасы мұндай адамдарды ешкім әлі күнге дейіне көрмеген болар), Ибн әл-Асир жауларының әскери өнеріне лайықты тұрғыдағы бағасын берген: "Бұл татарлар бұрын соңды көне және жаңа заманда болмаған жеңістерге қол жеткізді. Қытай жақтан бір топ көшпенді тобыры шығып, бір жыл өтпей жатып, бір бөлігі Арменияға келіп жетті, ал басқа бір бөлігі Хамадан аймағынан Иракқа басып кірді. "Алланың атымен ант етейін! Бізден кейін аман қалған адамдар, осы ғасыр өткен соң, осы жайттың сипаттамасын оқып көріп, жоққа шығара бастайды, әйтседе шындық оның жағында болады. Бірақ бұны жоққа шығармай, мұқият зерделесе, бұл оқиғаларды сол заманның жылнамашылары біздің жазып кеткенімізді ескерсін, осы оқиғаларды көзімен көрген көзі ашық және оқымаған адамдар да бірдей дәрежеде басынан өткізді.. Пайғамбарымыз Мұхаммед (с.ғ.с.) дүниеге келгеннен бері қазіргі кезде қиямет қайымды басынан кешіріп отырған мұсылмандарға мұндай қатер қауіп төнбейтін еді..."

Түркілердің жауынгерлік рухы мен олардың батыл жігері туралы араб тарихшысы грузин әскері қолбасшыларышың бірінен естіген сөздерін баян етеді: "Егер сендерге біреулер Татарлар қашып кетті, немесе тұтқынға түсті десе, оларға сенбеңдер, егер күйретті деп жарияласа, онда айтарым: бұл халық жаудан қорқып, соғыс алаңынан ешқашан қашпайды. Жуырда олардың бірін қолға түсіргеніміз сол еді: ол аттан құлап, басымен тасқа соғылып, тіл қатпай кетті. Оны тірідей қолға түсіре алмадық..."

Міне осылайша Шыңғысхан өз әскерін жеңімпаз етіп, елін мәңгі жасайтын "Мәңгі Елге" айналдырды.

# ШЫҢҒЫСХАН ҚАНҚҰЙЛЫ ЖАУЛАУШЫ МА НЕМЕСЕ ЖАҢА ӘЛЕМДІ ӨМІРГЕ ӘКЕЛГЕН ЖАҢАШЫЛ ӘМІРШІ МЕ? ДҮНИЕНІ ДҮР СІЛКІНДІРГЕН ҚАҒАННЫҢ МҮРДЕСІ ҚАЙДА ЖАТЫР?

"Шыңғысханның түркілік ғұмырнамасы. Қазақтардың киелі шежіресі" (Алматы, 2008 жыл) атты кітабымда барша оқырмандарға (ең алдымен, бұл кітап қазақстандықтарға, соның ішінде қазақтарға арналып отыр) Шыңғысханның қазақтардың ұлы бабасы екендігін дәлелдеуге күш салдым. Осы көзқарасты ұстанамын, барша жұртқа паш етемін, осы жайында адамдардың көпшілігінің білгенін қалаймын.

Еуропацентристік бағытты ұстанушылар Шыңғысханды қатігез жаулаушы ретінде сипаттап көрсеткісі келетіні басқа мәселе. Оның үстіне қазақ зиялыларының ішінде, жазушылар ортасынан шыққан, ғылыми атақтар мен даңқтарға бөленіп, "Шыңғысхан Отырарды талқандаған, жабайы Шыңғысхан осы шаһардағы атақты Александриялық кітапханамен теңелетін кітапхананың күл талқанын шығарған. Бүкіл Орта азиялық қалалар: Хорезм, Мерв, Самарқан, Бұқара және тағы басқа қалларды жер бетінен жойып жіберген" –дегендей жалған пікірлерді айтып жүргендер көп.

Әлбетте, бағынғысы келмеген халықтар күштеп бағындырылды, Әскери күш қуатты қолданбай, зорлық зомбылық көрсетпей басқару әлі ешкімнің қолынан келген емес. Сонымен қоса, демократиялыққа негізделген қазіргі заман ұстанымы мен тұжырымдары 12-13 ғасырдағы өмірдің салт-дәстүріне мүлде қайшы және керағар. Екіжүзділікке негізделген еуропалық дәстүр көзді тарс жұмып, Цезарь, Александр Македонский (Ескендір Зұлқарнайын), Ұлы Екінші Кирдің кез келген қатігездігін ойланбастан саяси қажеттілік тұрғысында түсіндіруге дайын. Осының барысында олар бұл билеушілердің қанша қаланы қиратқанын, Персеполь немесе Афиндік Акрополь сынды қаншама мәдени ошақтарды ойрандағанын есіне алғысы да, айтқысы да келмейді. Жеңімпаздың құрметіне тағзым етіп етіп, басын иген он мыңдаған Мысырлықты қасақана жер жастандырған Наполеонның зұлымдығын кім әшкерлеп отыр?! Бүгінгі таңда бұны ешкім есіне де алғысы келетін емес. Олар үшін зұлымдықтың бейнесі болып Шыңғысхан танылды. Себептері де түсінікті деп ойлаймын. Орыс жазушысы А.Бушков қаһарлы Иван заманын (XYІ ғ.) зерттей отырып, бұл кезеңдерде суропалық қолбасшылар көршілермен соғысып, біртұтас губернияларды түгелдей өртеп жібергендігін жазған. Өйткені сол кезеңнің соғыс тәртібі қатал еді. Ал ендеше XIII ғасырдағы Шыңғысхан дәуіріндегі қатігездік туралы не айтуға болады?

Сол себепті өз кітабымда нақты түрдегі тарихи дәйектер мен дәлелдерге сүйене отырып, Шыңғысханның адамзаттың дамуына қосқан үлесі, оның қатігездігінен әлдеқайда басым екендігін айтуға бар күшімді салдым. Мәселен, бүгінгі таңда Ресей-Русь Шыңғысханға алғыс айтып, құрметін білдіруге тиіс. Бұл жайында орыстың ақыл ойының қайнар көзі, атақты ойшылдар: князь Трубецкой, Савицкий және аты аңызға айналған еуразиялық мектептің басқа да өкілдері айтып кеткен болатын. "Олар Шыңғысхан болмаса, Ресей де өмір сүрмес еді" деген негізгі пікірдің иелері. Сол кезеңдерде Тевтон орденінің көмегімен Русьті католик дініне уағыздауға бет бұрған Батыс католицизмінің ықпалы қаншалықты жоғарылай түсетінін кім білсін? Шынымен де, еуразиялық ойшылдармен келіспесе болмас, католицизм ресей тұрғындарының жанын иеленсе, ал Шыңғысханның қоластындағы жұрт бар жоғы он пайыздық ясак салықты ғана төлеумен шектелді. Біз қазір мемлекетке салықты Шыңғысханның дәуірімен салыстырғанда әлдеқайда өте көп мөлшерде төлеп келеміз.

Ал, салықты не үшін төлейсің? Жер игеріп, мал бағып, отбасыңды асырағаның үшін салықтан құтыла алмайсың. Бұл салық төлеу ісі толық қауіпсіздік қамтамасыз етіліп, ертеңгі күнге деген сенім арта түскен кезде жүзеге асырылды. Шыңғысхан дәуірінде Сары теңізден Балтық теңізіне дейін сапар шексең саған ешкім тиіспейтін, ешкім құқықтарыңа қол салып, мазаңды алмайтын. Ұлы Жібек жолы қалпына келтірілді, өзара екіжақты сауда өркендеп, бұл сауданың шарттарына көпестердің көңілі көтерілді. Ақшаның құны арта түсті. Бұл мәселе қазіргі күннің өзінде өзектігін жоғалтпай отыр. Елбасымыз Нұрсұлтан Әбішұлы Назарбаевтың бұрынғы кеңестік мемлекеттер шеңберінде, тіпті Еуразиядан тыс жерде бірегей ортақ ақша баламасын (эквивалентін) енгізу туралы ұсынысын бірнеше мәрте қайта көтергендігі кездейсоқ емес. Өйткені американдық доллардың күні қараң, оның дәуірі келмеске кетті. Ал мұндай тарихи оқиғалар бұрынғы замандарда жеріміз бен халықтарымыздың тарихында орын алған екендігі сөзсіз.

Тағы бір қайталап өтейін: Тынық мұхиттан Атлант мұхитына дейін емін еркін жүріп, саяхат жасап, саудамен айналысуға жағдай жасалды. Шыңғысханға дейін тек төрт империядан құрылған, ұдайы өзара қырқысып, шайқасумеп күнін өткізген, тек Шыңғысханның қоластына өткен соң ғана бірлікке қол жеткізген Қытайды мысал ретінде алайық. Қытайлықтардың Шыңғысханға ризалығы шексіз. Олар Бежінде оған арнап үлкен мұражай тұрғызды, дегенмен осы арқылы өздерінің белгілі бір саяси мақсаттарын көздеді. Олардың саяси ілім тәртібіне сәйкес, Шыңғысханның тұлпарларының тұяғы тиген жер – қытайдың жері болып табылады. Бұл ілімді кейін олар жүзеге асыруды ойластыруда.

Жуырда орын алған тарихи сәтті еске алсақ жетіп жатыр: ҚР парламентіне ҚХР елшісі шақырылып, халық қалаулыларының "әлі күнге дейін Қытайдың жағрафиялық карталарында Қазақстанның Балқаш көліне дейінгі жерлер қытайдың аймағы деп көрсетіледі"- деген наразылыққа толы сөздерін мен ескертулерін тыңдауына тура келді.

Біз бәлкім әлі күнге дейін әлемде көлемі жағынан тоғызыншы орынды алатын жерге ие екендігімізге мән бермей келеміз. Егер біздің Шыңғысханға еш қатысымыз болмаса, онда мұншама байлық қазақтың басына қайдан келді? Бір бүйірімізде айдаһардай миллиардтаған қытай» жатса, келесі бүйірде Мұсылмандық Шығыс елі орналасса, келесі бір жақта аюдай Ресей империясы ақырып тұрса, мұншама байлық пен игілік бізге қайдан келді? Саны жағынан қазақтардан әлдеқайда басым түсетін ұйғыр халқы мен күрт халқының осы күнге дейін жері жоқ, ал біздің – небәрі 10 миллион ғана қазақ халқының мұншама бай жерді иеленуі неліктен?!

Міне, сондықтан да ең жоғары деңгейде тек Шыңғысханның арқасында ғана бүгінгі қазақ халқының өзіне тиесілі жер қойнауларында Менделеев элементтерінің барша кестесін сақтап жатқандығын мойындағанымыз жөн. Осы мұраны көздің қиыршығындай сақтап отырған ұрпақтарға разы болуымыз керек.

Шыңғысханның ғажайып тұлғасы жайында ұзағынан сыр шертуге болады. Біріншіден, ол ұлы қолбасшы. Әскери өнер жағынан оған тең келетін қолбасшы кемде кем. Мұндай қолбасшының енді өмірге келуі екіталай. Отыздай мемлекетте өмір сүретін үш миллиондаған адам – қазіргі заман картасындағы Шыңғысхан құрған алып империяның бейнесі осы. "Чингисхан и рождение современного мира" (издательство "Аст", Москва, 2005 жыл ) атты кітаптың авторы американдық ғалым және жазушы Джек Уэзерфордтың айтуынша, тек қана Шыңғысхан өзінің әрекеттері арқылы қазіргі заманның сәулеттік бейнесін салып кетті, ол алғашқы Конституцияны құрып, Жарлық пен Билік заңдарын әскери және азамат тұлғаларға арнап шығарды. Дін таңдау еркіндігін бекітіп, іске сенімділік пен көшбасшылықа және жеке қасиеттерге негізделген басқару жүйесін қалыптастырды. Басқа елдерді жаулай отырып, Шыңғысхан сауданы дамытты, ол заттар мен мал мүліктен тыс, идеялар мен білімнің өркендеуіне үлес қосты. Париждік шеберлер Ұлы Далада фонтандар (субұрқақтар) орнатса, ал шай мен спагетти және шығыс медицинасы Қытайдан Еуропаға жеткізілді. Тау кен шеберлері –Германиядан, парсы жібегі мен кілемдері – Қытайға, осы елдегі дактилоскопия әдісі басқа елдерге ауысты.

800 жылдай уақыт өтсе де, барша әлемді Шыңғысханның әрекеттері тағы бір рет дүр сілкіндіруде. Жүздеген кітап жазылып, ондаған кинофильм түсірілді. Әлемді дүр сілкіндірген әміршінің сүйегін табу үшін американдықтар мен жапондықтар өте қымбат экспедицияларды жасақтауда. Бірақ бәрі бекер! Оның ұрпақтарының Шыңғысханға тағзым етіп, жатқан жерінде ас беруі екіталай. Өйткені Шыңғысхан Тәңір дініне жан тәнімен берілген тұлға болатын. Ал Тәңір діні бойынша, егер мәйіт бүлінбей сақталса ғана, онда о дүниелік жан иесі бұл жалғанға қайта оралатын көрінеді. Неліктен көшпенді бабаларымыз соғысқа аттанып, қанды қырғыннан соң, өз руластары мен тайпаластарының жерленген зираттарын құпия сақтап қалуға тырысуы неліктен? Өйткені, бұл шара жаулардың өз руластараның зираттарын бүлдіріп, өмірге қайта келуіне кедергі жасамас үшін жүзеге асыратын. Шыңғысхан өзіндей жауынгер тұлғаға о дүниеге кеткен соң, үлкен нзар аударылатынын түсініп, тірі кезінде өзінң жерленетін орнын құпия сақтап қалуға бар күшін салды. Бірақ "үміт үзілмсйді"- деген сөз бар. Семей қаласынан 200 шақырымдай жерде, Ұлы Абайдың туған жері – Жидебай қыстау маңындағы халық арасында Шыңғыстау атты тауда Хантау деген жер бар. Еуразияның жағрафиялық орталығы орналасқан. Оның кіндігі 50° солтүстік ендік, 80° шығыстық ұзақтықты құрайды. Ш.Қуанғановтың айтуына қарағанда, Шыңғыстау бұрын "Кіндіккүш" тауы деп аталған. Яғни кіндіктің күші – жер күшінің жиналған нүктесі деген ұғымды білдірген. Шамасы тек осы жер ғана Шыңғысханды еш адамда жоқ күш қуатқа бөлеп, оның мәңгілік сапарға аттанған орны болса керек. Әйгілі моңғолтанушы Е.Кычанов: "1224 жылдың жазын міне үшінші жыл қатарынан жаулаушылық жорықтарға қатыспаған Шыңғысхан (науқастануына байланысты) Ертіс жағалауында өткізді" – деп жазады.

Осыған байланысты біз Үндістан, Пәкістан мен Ауғанстан аймағында орналасқан "Гиндукуш" топонимі- таудың атының жаңа мәніне көз жеткіздік. Ата-бабаларымыз шексіз кең далада көшіп қоныстанып жүріп, тоқтай қалған жерлеріндегі таулар мен өзендерге бұрынғы атамекендерінің құлаққа жағымды естілетін атауларын қойып отырған.

# НҰХ ПАЙҒАМБАРДЫҢ ҮШ ҰЛЫ БАР ЕДІ... ЖӘНЕ ҚАЗАҚТЫҢ ҮШ ЖҮЗІ

Қазіргі кезеңде қазақтар үш жүзге бөлініп өмір сүруде. Шыңғысхан дәуіріндегі моңғолдар да үш қанатқа бөлінетін. Оңқанат, Солқанат және Орта. Әскердің орта бөлігін Шыңғысханның Найман руынан шыққан қолбасшысы Най, ал сол қанатты –Жалайыр руынан шыққан- Мұқалы, ал оң қанатты – тегі Арғын Бөрші басқарды. Бет жүзімізді оңтүстікке қарай түзесек, Орта бөлік – бұл қазіргі Қазақстанның кең даласы, Оңқанат – Қара теңіз және Каспий теңізі аймағы, сол қанат –Қытай мен Маньчжурия.

Қазақтардың жүзге бөлінуі қазіргі кезде де сақталып қалды. Біреу бұны ескінің қалдығы дегенмен, бұл бөліністің қашан шыққандығын нақты тұрғыда айтып бере алмайды. Кейбіреулер бұл бөліністі Шыңғысханмен байланыстырады. Мен өз кітабымда да бұл жайлы ойланып толғандым. Дүниежүзілік топан су апатынан кейін аман қалған, бірақ Құдайға берген өсиеттерді ұмытқан жер тұрғындары дәуіріндегі Нұх пайғамбар жайлы аңыз баршаға мәлім. Осы Нұх пайғамбардың үш ұлы бар болатын – Сим, Хам және Яфет. Інжілде оның өз ұлдарын қайда орналастырғаны туралы егжей -тегжейлі баяндалған. Ал кенжесі Яфетті ол Еділ (Волга) өзені мен Орал өзені жағалауын мекендеуге аттандырған, осы заман- яғни XXI ғасырдың қазақтары біз Яфеттен тараған ұрпақпыз.

Тарихтың атасы Геродот? Скифтер туралы сыр шертіп, скифтердің негізін қалаған тұлға Тарғытай екенін айтқан. Оның да үш ұлы бар еді, олар белгілі бір өздерінің үлесіне тиген жер аймақтарын өзара бөлісіп алады. Дәл осындай аңыз қазақтың Ақарыс, Бекарыс және Жанарыс рулары туралы да айтылады. Бұл негізделген ақылға қонымды болжамдар, бұл болжамдар қазақтардың үш жүзге бөлінуі Нұх пайғамбар және оның үш ұлы дәуірінен бері келе жатқандығын айғақтайды. Яғни пайғамбардың үш ұлы қазақтың үш жүзінің негізін салған.

Осылайша тарихи ұқсастықтар арасында байланыстар бар екендігі айқындалды. Бірақ оларды бір жақты талқылау және сараптау әсте мүмкін емес. Шамасы бұл бөліну белгілі бір бөлініске салынған жер аймағында өмір сүру дәстүрін бір ретке келтіру мақсатында өмір және заман талабына сәйкес негізделген де шығар.

168

# Түркі қағанаттары.
# Ұлы даладағы оқиғалар
# желісінің ізімен

## Наймандық Қытай

Бірден айтайын дегенім: Түркі қағанаттары дегенімде, б.з.д. бірінші мыңжылдығының алғашқы жартысында Солтүстік Қытай мен Моңғолия аймағында құрылған мемлекеттер ғана емес, сонымен бірге Месопотамия, Мысыр, Парсы елі, Үндістан, Қытай, Еуропада өмір сүрген көне мемлекеттер жайында сөз қозғағым келеді.

5-8 ғасырларда қазіргі Моңғолия мен Солтүстік Қытай аймағында Ұлы Түркі қағанаты құрылады. Бірінші Түркі қағанатының негізі 545 жылы қаланса, бұл құрылым жарты ғасырдай уақыт өмір сүріп, қытайлықтар, енесай қырғыздары мен татар, оғыз, ұйғыр тайпаларының ықпалының әсерінен өмірін тоқтатты. 100 жыл өткен соң, 8 ғасырдың басында екінші Түркі қағанаты бой көтереді. Тағы бір елу жыл өткен соң, оның орнын Ұйғыр қағанаты басты. Тағы бір ғасыр өткен соң, Қырғыз қағанаты құрылды. Кейінірек осы өлкеде қытандық Ляо әулеті пайда болды, осы әулеттің халқы өзім дәлелдеп және басқа ғалымдар пікірімді қолдап, келіскендіктен, толық құрамымен қазіргі кезеңдердегі қазақ халқының ішіндегі Найман тайпасының құрамына еніп кеткен. Сондай-ақ Қытай өз атауын Наймандық Қытайлар-Қытандардан алған болатын. Осы рулардың бір бөлігі Кете руы қазіргі кезеңде қазақтардың Әлімұлы атты тайпалық одағының құрамына кіреді.

12 ғасырда Шыңғысхан осы аймақтарды кезекті тұрғыда тағы бір рет біріктіреді. Яғни мұнда қандай заңдылық болғаны? Өйткені бұл көк түркілер мен моңғолдардың мемлекеттерін қазақтардың ата-бабалары өмірге әкелген еді!

Өзімнің "Шыңғысханның түркілік ғұмырнамасы.Қазақтардың киелі шежіресі" атты кітабымда нақты тұрғыда айтарым: (Бірінші Түркі қағанатында қағанның мөрінде қасқырдың бейнесі белгіленді. Ал бүгінгі таңда бөрінің белгісін тамға ретінде ұстанатын қазақтың екі руы Садыр мен Матай ғана) бұл қағанатта Найманның Садыр мен Матай рулары билік құрды. Тіпті тарихи мәліметтердің өзі де, 5 ғасырда аталмыш рулардың осы аймақтарда өмір сүргендігін айғақтайды.

Екінші Түркі қағанатында қағандардың мөрінде арқардың бейнесі бенйеленді. Оның тамғасында арқардың мүйізі салынған – бұл Найманның Қаракерей руы. Ал кейінірек, "арқар" сөзі Шыңғысханның қандас бауырлары, қазақ төрелерінің ұранына айналды. Екінші Түркі қағанатын да Қаракерейлер басқарды деп болжам жасауға болады, олардың бір бөлігі Шыңғысхан руының құрамына еніп кетті.

Яғни, қазіргі қазақ руларының бірі – саны 70-100 атаудан тұратын бірлестіктер, осы Түркі қағанаттарындағы биліктің басында тұрған. Өз кітабымда Шыңғысхан империясының төбесінде Қазақтың Найман тайпасындағы Бағаналы және Матай рулары тұрғандығы туралы пікірімді айттым. Шыңғысхан мемлекетінің жазба тілі Найман жазуына негізделді, қазіргі ғалымдар бұл жазуды қателесіп, ұйғыр жазуы деп жүр. Ал Шыңғысханның мемлекеттік мөрі ретінде Найман хандығының мөрі қолданылды. Иә, Шыңғысхан Наймандармен соғысқан, бірақ бұл соғыс Найман хандығындағы билікке талас тартыс түрінде өрбіді. Ең алдымен, Найман хандығының тағына мінген соң, кейінірек барша Найман хандығын әлемнің жартысында орналасқан елдердің билік басына қондырды.

Шыңғысханның алыс арғы тегі Бөрте Чино болғаны мәлім. Моңғол тілінен аударғанда көк бөрі деген ұғымды білдіреді. Бұл руды Шыңғысханның бабалары қазіргі Моңғолия жеріне түркілердің аты аңызға айналған атамекені Эргенекуннен алып келген. Шыңғысханның өзі боржігін руынан тарайды. Бұл сөздің этнонимін бөрі жігі деп түсіндіреміз. Яғни көк бөрі халқы. Бірақ қазақ руларының ішінде тек Матай және Садырларда ғана көк бөрі белгісі тамға ретінде қолданылады.

# ХЕТТЕР, КЕТЕ, ГОТТАР ЖӘНЕ ҒҰНДАР. ТҮРКІЛІК ГЕРМАНИЯ

Түркі қағанатынан кейін оның жалғасы ретінде Ғұндар мемлекеті өмірге келді. Олардың қазақтың ата-бабалары екендігі сөзсіз. Кавказдың ірі ғалымдары Лайпанов пен Мезиевтің еңбектерінің негізінде ("О происхождении тюркских народов" изд-о ПАО "ПУЛ" Черкесск, 1993) мынадай қорытынды жасауға болады: б.з.д. III ғасырдың аяғында ғұндардың басында қазіргі заманғы қазақтың Матайлары билік құрған, ал олардың қолбасшысы Модэ – Нақ Матайдың өзі. Жуан дауыссыздарды қытайлар сөздің ортасында айтпай, немесе жіңішке дауыссыздарға алмастыратын, осының салдарынан біздің Матайымыз қытайдың Модэ-Мадиі болып шыға келген.

Ұлы Римнің құлдырау дәуірін байланыстыратын Ғұндар тайпасы жайында көне антикалық заман тарихшысы Аммиан Марцелиан (IY ғ.) былай деп жазады: "Көне заман жазушылары біле бермейтін Ғұндар тайпасы Меотиялық саз балшықты аймақтың ар жағындағы Солтүстік Мұзды мұхит жақта өмір сүреді. Жабайылық жағынан оларға жер бетінде теңдесетін тірі жан жоқ... Оларда тіпті қамыспен жабылып бекітілген күрке де жоқ. Тау мен ормандарды кезіп, көшіп қоныстанады. Туған кезінен бастап, ыстық пен суыққа төзіп, шөлдемей жүруге үйретіледі. Олардың ешқайсысы егін екпейді, соқаның не екенін де білмейді. Нақты бір тұрғылықты жері жоқ, үйі жоқ, заңы да жоқ, белгілі бір салт дәстүрсіз-ақ көшіп қоныстанып жүре береді..."

Міне, білімді еуропалық оқымыстылар ата-бабаларымыздың салт дәстүрі мен өмір болмысын осылайша сипаттаған. Бірақ тағдырдың жазуына сәйкес, дәл осы халық жеңіске жетіп, ұлы империяны ыдыратып, күлін көкке ұшырды.

Б.з.д. 18-13 ғасырларда Кіші Азия аймағында (қазіргі Түркия) ұлы Хетт мемлекеті өмір сүрді. Бұл мемлекет бес жүз-алты жүз жылдай ғұмыр кешіп, ыдырап кетіп, басқа көшпенді халықтардың қоластына өтеді, осыдан кейін хеттердің бір бөлігі Қытайдың Солтүстік-Батыс бөлігіне өтсе, олармен бірге бұл елге әскери арбалар мен әскери тұлпарлар да бірге кетеді. Мұндай ғажайыпты Қытай мүлде білмейтін. Олар Батыс Чжоу мемлекстін құрады. Бұл құрылым көршілес мемлекеттердің бәрін бағындырып, Қытайды билеп төстейді. Ресейлік ғалым А.Абрашкин өзінің "Скифская Русь" (Москва, "Вече", 2008, 189 бет ) кітабында б.з.д XII-XI ғасырлар жайында былай деп жазады: "Скифтер хеттерді шығысқа қарай қуып, өздерінің ықпалын Солтүстік Қытайға дейін арттырды. Бәлкім қытайлықтарға осы елдің атауын Хеттер тартуы еткен шығар? Красноярск өлкесінде Енесай өзенінің орта және төменгі ағысы жанында кетелер деген халық тұрады. Оларды бұрын Енесайлық остяктар деп атайтын. Ал жай ғана остяктар болып ханттар табылатын. Дәлірек айтқанда, хетт патшаларының бірінің есімі –Хантелі болатын. Хеттердің ежелгі астанасы Неса қаласы еді. Сондықтан да Енесай өзенінің атауы оның есміне байланыстыболуы мүмкін. Хеттердің ірі қалаларының бірі –Тувана деп аталатын, тура сол Енесайдағы Тува республикасындағы тува халқы секілді..." Хеттер Кіші Азиядан келгенге дейін, Қытай аймағында Инь мемлекеті өмір сүретін. Бұл мемлекетті Шаң руынан шыққан Алтай көшпенділері құрған еді. Осы рудан тарайтынымды ерекше құрмет санап, ілтипатпен айтамын. Қазіргі кезеңде Шаң руынан шыққандар қазақтың Арғын және Найман рулары ішіне сіңіп кетті. Шыңғысхан империясы мен аталмыш: Чжоу және Инь мемлекеттері арасында үлкен тарихи сабақтастық тағылымы болғандығы аян. Өйткен сол хеттердің өзі қазіргі қазақ ішіндегі Кіші жүздің Әлімұлы руынан тарайтын Кете атты бұтағы болып табылады. Сонымен қоса, қытан-кете-қытан-қытайлар қазақтың ішіндегі Найман руы одағының қалыптасуына үлкен үлес қосты.

Академик Н.Марр және С.Толстов түркі тілдері мен хеттер тілінің арасында түбі тереңде жатқан байланыстар бар екендігін дәлелдеді.

Қытайда хеттер б.з.д. XI ғасырда Батыс Чжоу мемлекетін құрады, ал шамасымен б.з.д. 770 жылдары Қытайда Көктем мен Күз заманы басталған соң, хеттер Сібір мен Қазақстан арқылы Қара теңіз, Кавказ бен Еуропа және Балтық жағалауы елдеріне жетіп, гет-готтар деген атпен танымал болады. Хеттердің бір бөлігі Сібірде қалып қойды, бүгінгі таңда бұл халықтар: кет деп аталады, ал бұл тайпаның басқа бір бөлігі Батыс Қазақстанда кете деген атпен өмір сүреді. Қытайдың өзінде қалған хеттер б.з. X ғасырында қытандар деген атпен қайтадан билікке келді. Ляо әулетін құрып, Қытай мемлекеті осы тайпаның атымен атала бастайды.

Хеттердің басқа бір бөлігі шамасы, Оғыздардың Лидия қаласында қалған болса керек. Троян соғысынан кейін, кейбірі Аппенин түбегіне кетіп, сол жақта хетруск-этруск мемлекетін құрған. Лидияда қалған хеттер оны II ұлы Кир жаулап алған соң, астар деген атпен (ас, уз, ғуз, оғыз) Азов теңізі аймағына кетуге мәжбүр болған. Сонан кейін Скандинавия мен Балтық жағалауына жетіп, готтар-балттар деп атала бастаған. Лидия патшасы Крез скиф халқының шежіресін жақсы білетін оқымыстылардың бірі еді, бұл жайт Лидия халқы тұрғындарының құрамының түркілік этникалық құрамының қалыптасуы осыған байланысты екендігін білдіреді. Готтық тарихшы Иордан (YI ғ.) германдық гот тайпалары жайында сөз қозғағанда, олардың бұрынырақ гет деп аталғандығы туралы баян еткен.

Ол өзінің "О происхождениях и деяниях гетов" атты кітабында былай деп жазады: "...Дион, көне заманды егжейлі тегжейлі зерттейтін әйгілі тарихшы. Ол өз еңбегін "Гетика" деп атаған. (Ал, геттер жоғарыда аталып өткендей, готтардың тура өзі екендігі мәлім)..." Марцелиан (IY ғасыр.), Зосим (Y-YI ғ.), Траян (YIII ғ.) геттерді скифтер халқына жатқызатын.

Хеттердің шығу тегі жайында нақты түрде рим ғалымы және мемлекеттік қайраткері Үлкен Плиний (б.з.д. 23-79 жылдар) өзінің "Естественная история" кітабы арқылы былай деп баяндайды: "Истра өзенінің (Дунай – Қ.З.) арғы жағында, тек қана скифтер өмір сүреді. Бірақ жағалауын әртүрлі халықтар мекендейді: геттер - римдіктер оларды дак, немесе сарматтар деп атайды, сарматтар –грек тілінде –савроматтар деп айтылады... Скифтердің атауын үнемі сарматтар немесе германдықтар деп алмастырып қолданады..."

Осылайша римдіктер готтарды - дактар деп атаған. Бүгінгі күні Дактардың ұрпақтары болып Адай руы саналса, ал геттердің ұрпақтары - Кете руы деп тұжырымдаймын. Бұл қазақтың екі руы қазіргі кезде Батыс Қазақстанда көршілес аймақта тұрады.

Ресейлік зерттеуші Ю.Н.Дроздов "Тюркоязычный период европейской истории" (ООО ИПК "Литера", 2011г.) атты кітабында готтардың этникалық нәсілдік негіздегі шығу тегінің германдық тұжырымдамасы негізделетін әдеби ескерткіштерді нақты тұрғыда сараптай отырып, келесідей қорытындыға келеді: "аталмыш тарихи ескерткіштер –"Godex Argenteus", Y-YI ғасыр, Милан қаласының Амброзиандық кітапханасында "Codices Ambrosiani" деген атпен сақталған YII ғасыр мұрасы болып саналатын Godex Carolinus" жәдігерін готтардың мұрасы деп тануға болады және бұл халықты герман тілдес халықтың (Deutsch) қатарына қосамыз..." Бұл мәтінде герман тілді деген халық терминінің ұғымында қазіргі Германияның автохонды жергілікті халқы назарға алынып отыр. Этникалық тұрғыда қазіргі немістер – тас дәуіріндегі кезеңдерде өмір сүріп, ормандарды мекендеген тайпалар мен өркениеті әлдеқайда озық тұрған скифтік, түркілік тайпалардың араласуынан пайда болған симбиоз халық екендігі анықталды. Осы жаққа қоныс аударған халықтардың бірі – хет- гет- готтар еді. Неміс тілінің сөздігінде жабайы германдық орман тайпалары үшін қол жетпес Көк Тәңірі елінің Gott –Құдай сөзі пайда болғаны үшін, германдықтар хеттер-готтарға алғыс айтуы тиіс. Ал "хетт" этнонимі меніңше, түркінің "қатты" сөзінен туындаса керек. Яғни бұл тайпаның атауында қаттылық, мықтылық, күштілік ұғымы бар.

Б.з.д екінші мыңжылдықтың басында Кіші Азияға келген хеттер Хаттусу атты елордасын құрған өздеріне туыс хатт халқын кездестіреді. Түркі тілінен, қазақ тілінен аударғанда бұл қаланың атауы "хатты ел –сауатты ел" деген ұғымды білдірсе керек. Ш.Қуанғанов осы қаланың үйінділеріне археологтар қазба жұмыстарын жүргізген кезде, патшалық мұрағатты тапқандығын айтады. Бұл мұрағаттан 15000 қыштан ойылып жазылған кесте жазба табылды. Сондықтан да хет-хаттар атауы ұғымын –сауатты көзі ашық, хат оқитын халық деп түсіндіреміз. Бұл қыштан күйдіріліп жазылған жазба кестені Олжас Сүлейменов түркілік руна жазбаларымен байланыстырады.

Сөзімді жалғастыра келе айтарым, Ю.Н.Дроздовтың жазуына қарағанда, б.з. III ғасырында өмір сүрген Афанасий Публий Герснний Дексипп деген ғалым өз еңбектерінде готтардың шығу тегі скифтерден екендігі туралы атап өткен: "Готтар, деп аталатын скифтер" (өзім бөліп көрсеттім –Қ.З.) үлкен тайпасы Деция арқылы Истр өзенінен өтіп, римдіктрдің қоластындағы елдерді жаппай түрде тонауға ұшыратады..." Шығы тегі готтық болып табылатын тағы бір скифтердің атты әскері туралы мәліметтер әйгілі антика заман авторлары: Кесариялық Прокопий, Филосторгий, Юлий Капитолин, Иосиф Флавий және тағы басқа ғалымдардың еңбектерінде кездеседі.

Герман тайпаларының скифтік тегі жайында өткен заманның қайраткерлері көп естеліктер қалдырды. Мәселен б.з.д өмір сүрген көне грек философы және жағрафияшысы Страбон өзінің "География" атты еңбегінде былай деп жазады: "Рейннің арғы жағындағы шығысқа қарай ұласатын, кельттердің мемлекетінің шекарасынан кейін жатқан аймақтарды германдықтар тайпасы мекендейді. Олардың дене сымбаты және өмір сүру дәстүр салты жағынан кельт тайпасынан айырмашылығы шамалы... " Өмір сүру дәстүрі, өзім атап өткендей, кельттердің салт дәстүрлерінен өзгешелігі жоқ. Кейінірек біз кельттер жайында түркі тайпалары екендігін айтатын боламыз. Әрине ізінше германдықтар да түркі тектес болып шығады. Үлкен Плиний өзінің жоғарыда атап өтілген "Естественная история" еңбегінде Дунай өзенінің солтүстік жағалауында өмір сүретін тайпалар жайлы: олар скиф тайпалары деп жазып, германдық және сармат тайпаларын скиф тектес деп атайды.

Геттер алғаш рет тарихтың атасы –Геродоттың еңбектерінде аталып өтіледі: "Великая Скифия. История докиевской Руси" ("Алгоритм-книга") кітабында көне дәуір зерттеушісі В.Янович мынадай пікірді айтады: "яғни Алдыңғы Азиялық хеттер –геттердің арғы тегі болып табылады. Хеттер (астар) тайпасының бір бөлігі б.з.д. ҮІ ғасырда Алдыңғы Азиядан кетіп, Балтық жағалауында және Скандинавияда гот-балттар деп аталып кетіп, герман халқының негізін құрайды. "Гед-гет" этнонимі индоеуропалық ірі қара малдың атауымен байланысты. Ал қайғылы мағынадағы гетто сөзін еске салу арқылы аталмыш автор, геттер- бұлар қазіргі тілде "гетто"- деп аталатын қоршалған шарбақтарда малын бағып ұстайтын отырықшы, малшы халық деген көне ұғымды білдіретінін айтқысы келген.

## ҚАЗАҚТЫҢ АЛБАНДАРЫ МЕН СУАНДАРЫ. КАВКАЗДЫҚ АЛАНДАР МЕН СВАНДАР ИСА МӘСІХ (ХРИСТОС) ҚАЗАҚТЫҢ ҚАЙ РУЫНАН ШЫҚҚАН?

Ас-оғыздар әйгілі Троян соғысы біткен соң, Кіші Азиядан Қара теңіз жағалауына Армян таулары арқылы келеді, бұл жақты Урарту вандар – венет тайпаларының бір тобы мекендейді. Астардың қысымымен вандар Кавказға кетіп, кейінірек сол жақта қазіргі заманғы Сванетияны құрады. Вандар- меніңше, қазақтың Ұлы жүзінің ішіндегі қазіргі Суандар. Осы ойымды дәлелдеу үшін келесідей мысалдар келтірейін. Б.з.д. ІІ ғасырында түркілік Юечжи тайпасы Батыс Қытай аймағынан (Хэси аймағы) Модэ Матай Ғұндарының қысымымен басқа жаққа көшуге мәжбүр болады. Кейбір авторлар, дәлірек айтқанда Лайпанов пен Мезиев юечжи тайпасын қазақтың Қаңлы тайпасының ата бабасы деп санайды. М.Барманқұлов, жапон зерттеушісі К.Енокиге сілтеме жасай отырып, былай деп жазады: "Менің ойым бойынша, б.з.д. III ғасыр Юечжи тайпасы өзінің белгілі бір аймаққа орналасу көлемі және күш қуаттылығы жағынан алты-жетінші ғасырдағы көне түркі халықтарынан ерекшеленбейді."

Азияға келген юечжи тайпасы Грек-Бактрия патшалығы, қазіргі заманғы Орта Азия, Ауғанстан, Пәкістан мен Солтүстік Үндістан аймағында Тоқарыстан деп аталатын Кушан патшалығын құрады. Қазіргі кезеңде қазақтың Суан тайпасының ішінде жеке дербес ірі Тоқарыстан деп аталатын ру бар. Осы келтірілген дәлелге сүйене отырып, Армян тауларындағы Урарту вандарының құрамының ішіне көршілес Кушан патшалығының тоқарлары келіп қосылған. Ал қазіргі Сванетияның тұрғындары осы тоқарлардың ұрпақтары болып табылады. Тоқарлардың басқа бір бөлігі қазақтың Суан тайпасының құрамына енді. Сол себепті Солтүстік Кавказ свандары мен Қазақтың суан тайпасның шығу тегі бір болып табылады және олардың туыс халық екендігі айқын. Оның үстіне қазақтың Суан тайпасы қазақтың Албан тайпасына туыс болып келіп, әрқашан бірге көршілес өмір сүрген. Тарихтың аталмыш кезеңдерінде Албандар Каспий теңізінің батыс жағалауын мекендеген, ал Суан-свандар Қара теңіздің шығыс жағалауында оларға көршілес өмір сүрген. Ван-свандардың бір бөлігі хеттермен бірге Қытайға қарай бет алып, қазіргі кезеңде Найманның Қаракерей бұтағына еніп кеткен. Ізденімпаз оқырман осы ақпаратқа қол жеткізу үшін астар туралы көне исландиялық жыр-жинақтар: "Кіші Эдда" және "Үлкен Эдда" дастандарын зерделеп, мұқият зерттесін.

Алан-албандар Каспий және Қара теңіз жағалауы алқабына Ғұн тайпасы келген соң, Батысқа бет алып, Испания мен Англия жеріне қарай бет алады. Ұлыбританияны халық осы күнге дейін Тұманды Альбион деп атап келеді. Кейбір ғалымдардың деректеріне сәйкес, мысырлықтар мен ағылшындардың тіліне ортақ 3000-дай сөз бар екен. Бұл ортақ сөздер албан деген халықтың лексикалық қорынан енген сөздер. Олар сол кезеңде Мысырда гиксостар деген атпен өмір сүрген. Ү ғасырдағы Ұлы Шекспир елі атауының өзі, біздің бабаларымыз осы аралдарға келіп жеткенде, Ингленд деп аталатын. Бұл түркі тілінде "олжа болған ел"- деген ұғымды білдіреді. Түркілер осы шұрайлы жерлерді жаулап алғаннан кейін, осы жерде Кант және Кале шаһарларын тұрғызады. Бұл қазақ тілінде шаһар және қала деген мағынаны береді. Ал "сақ" этнонимі жергілікті диалектінің әсерінен сакс болып өзгерді. Бұл ұғым жаңа ағылшын ұлтының негізгі тірегіне айналды. Ал сақ-сакстарды Тұманды Альбион жеріне Италияның болашақ королі Одоакр ертіп келген болатын. Оның әкесі ғұн Эдико 448 жылы Константинопольге ұлы Аттілінің елшісі болып барған еді.

Осы мәтінде алан-албандар жайында түркі тектес, дәлірек айтқанда арғы тегі скифтік тайпалардан тарайтын туыс ру екендігі туралы ескеріп өттім. Қазіргі заманғы тарих ғылымында аландар – иран тілдес халық деген ұғым аксиома ретінде қабылданады.

Албандардың бір тобы қазіргі қазақтың бір бөлшегі болса, албандардың тағы бір бөлігі Балқанда өмір сүреді. Б.з. ІY ғасырында өмір сүретін Рим тарихшысы Аммиан Мерцелиан б.з.д. 60 жылдары Помпейдің Кавказ және Парсы еліне жасаған жорығы туралы жаза отырып, былайша баяндайды: "Албандар мен массагеттердің жерінен өтіп, қазір бұл тайпаны алан деп атап жүрміз, албандарға дүркірете шабуыл жасап, бұл тайпаны жеңіп, Каспий теңізін көреді... " (Аммиан Марцелиан. Римская история. СПб,1994г.)

Тек Рим тарихшысының массагеттерді ғана алан деп отыр ма, немесе аландарға ол албандарды қосып жазды ма? –белгісіз. Өйткені басқа бір жерде Шығыс Еуропа халықтарын сипаттай келе, Марцелиан былай деп жазады: Осы халыққа көршілес жерде массагет, алан және саргеттер, сондай-ақ бізге беймәлім көптеген халықтар өмір сүреді. Біз тіпті олардың дәстүрі ғана емес, аттарын да білмейміз. Яғни бұл мағынада аландар мен массагеттер әртүрлі тайпалар екендігі аян. Ғұндардың Каспий жағалауы аймағына жасаған жойқын шабуылдарын сипаттай отырып, көне римдік тарихшы былай дейді: "Бұл қанқұйлы тынымсыз жабайы халық соғыс пен шайқастарды арқалап, кісі қанын төгіп, тонаумен айналысып, ақыры аландар мен массагеттердің мекендеріне де келіп жетті..." Яғни, көне замандарда, Марцелиан бойынша, аландар массагеттер деп аталғаны ғой. Осыған сәйкес олардың тегі бір  скиф тайпаларынан тарайды. Осы ойымды дәлелдеу үшін аталмыш тарихшының тағы бір пікірін келтірейін: "олар бір-бірінен өте алыс аймақтарда номада ретінде көшіп қоныстанса да, бірақ уақыт өте келе, олар бірігіп, бір атауды иеленіп, салт-дәстүрі, жабайы өмір болмысы, қару жарағы ұқсас болғандықтан бәрі алан деп аталып кетті. Олардың күркелері жоқ, ешқайсысы егін екпейді, олар сүт ішіп, ет жейді. Ағаштан жасалған киіз үйлерде тұрады және бұл үйлерін шексіз далада көшіріп қоныстанғанда арбаға салып, бірге алып жүреді. Олардың қайсысы соғыста қаза тапса, сол бақытты саналады, ал қайсысы қария жасына жетіп, өз ажалымен өлсе, жұрттың күлкісіне қалады..."

Осы Аммиан Марцелиан естеліктерінен кейін, алан тайпасының тілі иран тілді емес болып табылмайтындығына басқа дәлелдің қажеті жоқ деп ойлаймын.

Аландардың иран тілдес емес, скиф тайпасына жататындығы туралы сондай-ақ Иосиф Флавий "О войне иудейской" (ВДИ, 1947, №4) атты шығармасында жазып кеткен. Б.з. 72 жылы аландардың Арменияға мен Мидияға жасаған қанқұйлы жорығы туралы хабарлай отырып, автор былай деп жазады: "Біз бұрын алан тайпалары скифтердің бір бөлігі деп түсіндіріп келдік" (автор бөліп көрсетті). Олар Танаис пен Меотиялық өзен маңын мекендейді деп есептейтінбіз. Б.з. ІІ ғасырында өмір сүрген көне грек жарафияшысы Клавдий Птоломей өзінің "География" атты кітабында былай деп жазады: "Сарматияны көптеген тайпалар мекендейді: барша Венед шығанағында венедтер,  Дакиядан жоғары жерде –певкиндер мен бастерндер, Меотиданың барша жағалауында –языга және роксоландар,, одан әрі бұл елдің түпкі шетінде –гамаксобия, скиф және аландар..." К.Птоломей мен А.Марцелианның еңбектеріне сүйеніп, "алан" этнотермині – бұл Солтүстік Кавказдың кең алқаптарында өмір сүрген көшпенді скифтердің жалпы атауы болып табылады. "Алан" сөзі қазақ тілінде ашық алаң деген ұғымды білдіреді. Өмір сүру дәстүріне сәйкес тайпаның атын қою ата баба салтына тән ұғым. Көне замандардағы Ұлы Даланы мекендеген қаңлы-қаңғылы тайпасын алайық. Бұл тікелей түрде қаңғыбас деген ұғымды білдіреді. Осы өмір сүру дәстүріне сәйкес алынған атау кейін этнотерминге айналып кетті. Аландардың да жайы осы.

Албандар мен тарихи аландардың туыстығын сөз етсек, ең алдымен қазіргі замандағы Дагестан аймағында көне замандарда өмір сүрген албандарға келейік. XXI ғасырдағы Балқан албандары Кавказ албандарына туыс болса керек. Кавказ албандарының Қазақ албандарына туыс болып келетіндігін грек тарихшысы Страбон дәлелдейді: Ол өзінің XI ғасырда жазған "Георгафия" еңбегінде былай дейді: "Албандар қой бағуға өте құмар. Әйтседе көшпенді өмір салтын ұстанады. Олар жабайы халық емес, сондықтан да жорықтар мен шайқастарға белгілі бір уақыт өте келе, кейде ғана аттанады. Қолына сойыл алып, садақ тартқан албандардың үстінде сауыттары бар, қолдарында қалқандары және бастарында аң терісінен жасалған дулығалары бар. Албандар егде тартқан адамдарды сыйлай біледі, олар тек өз ата-аналарын ғана емес, сондай-ақ өзге жұртты да құрметтейді... "

Албандар мсмлскстінің құдіреттілігі жөнінде рим тарихшысы Тацит "Анналы" еңбегінде жазады: "Оларға Германияда, Британия және Иллирияда Нерон өзіне қосып, жалдаған көптеген жауынгерлік бөлімдерді қосу керек. Албандармен соғысқа әзірленіп, бұл әскерлерді Каспий жағалауына аттандырды..."

Байқап отырғанымыздай римдіктердің барша әскери күш қуаты саны соншалықты көп емес, дегенмен, жауынгерлік рухы мықты албандардың ата-бабаларымен соғысуға бағытталған!

Жоғарыда аталған албан халқының барша қасиеттері қазіргі заманғы қазақтар- яғни бізге тән болып келетіндігін айтып өтуіміз керек. Б.з. Солтүстік Кавказға ғұндар келген соң, албандардың бір бөлігі өздерінің ата қонысы Қазақстан жеріне бет алады. Ол жақтан Кавказға бұл тайпа б.з.д. YII ғасырда келіп, қазақ нәсілінің қалыптасуына ықпал етті, ал бұл тайпаның басқа бір бөлігі Батыс Еуропаға қарай бет алып, Балқанға келіп тұрақтап, қазіргі заманғы Албанияның негізін құрады.

3-4 мың жыл бұрын белгілі бір рудың қалай аталғандығын бүгінгі таңда дәл тауып айту қиын. Б.з.д. YII ғасырда Эргунеконнан шығып кейінірек, түркі тайпаларының негізін салған рулардың ішінде әйгілі тарихшы тюрколог Рашид ад-Дин ("Сборник летописей" издательство АН СССР, 1952.) 16 рудың атын атайды. Осы рулардың ішінде қоңырат, қоралас, үйсін тапасы ғана қазіргі атауларына ие. Ал кейде жанама жол арқылы көне замандардағы атауды анықтаудың сәті түседі. Мәселен, Каспий теңізінің батыс жағалауындағы тауларды мекендеген қазақтың албандарын алайық. (Әзербайжан-сол кезеңдерде Кавказдық Албания деп аталған). Сол үшінші ғасырда Шығыстан ғұндар дүркіретіп жеткен кезде, албандардың бір бөлігі батысқа Испанияға аттанады, Нағыз таудың тұрғындары болғандықтан, албандар өздері үшін қасиетті жануар барысты киелі санап, әспеттеген еді. Сондықтан да өздерін барсила деп атайтын. Барсила- барыс елі деген ұғымды білдіреді. Кавказдағы ең биік тау нүктесі Эльбрустың атауы да қазақ сөздерінің этнониміне тікелей байланысты. Бұл тау о баста Елбарыс деп аталған болатын. Яғни қазақтың албан және беріш руларына арналып қойылған атау. Каталония сөзі түркі тілінен аударғанда, екінші Алания деген ұғымды білдіреді, ал оның астанасы Барселона – барыс халқының қаласы, яғни албан және беріш және қазақ руларының қаласы деген ұғымды білдіреді. Ал Испанияның Арагон қаласы қазақ руы Арғындарды еске салады. Өйткені арғындардың арғы тегі – ғұн тайпасы. Ал баскілердің астанасы- Бильбао ше? Белбеу – бұл қазақтардың беліне тағатын бұйымы. Ерлік пен батылдықтың бейнесі. Оны шешкен соң, бабамыз қой сияқты момын болып шыға келетін. Өте күрделі, адамзат тағдырына байланысты мәселелерді шешуге келгенде, тауға шығып, міндетті түрде белбеуін шешіп, Тәңірден жәрдем сұрап, ғибадат ететін Шыңғысханды еске алайық. Бүгінгі күннің өзінде әдебиетте кездесетін жұмбақ барсиларды табуға болады. Бірақ оларды әйгілі албан, дулат, немесе беріштермен салыстыру ешкімнің ойына да кіріп шықпайды. Л.Гумилев өзінің "Хазарияның ашылуы" (СПб., СЗКЭО "Кристалл", 2003) кітабында барсилалар Жайықпен Терек өзендерінің арасында көшіп қоныстанған деген пікірді айтады. Олар булгарлықтарға дейінгі тайпалар болған. Шынымен де, бүгінгі албандар мен дулаттар (волгалық булгарлардың негізі) бір қазақтың жүзіне кіріп, тамғалары да сәйкес келеді. Сонымен бірге дулаттар аландық тайпа одағына кірген, бұған Кавказда табылған X ғасыр мұрасы болып саналатын зеленчуг жазбасы дәлел болады.

Оның мәтіні мынадай: " Николайдың мұрагері Иса Мәсіхті (Христосты) Хобс үйі бірлестігінен (Дуло, Ботпай, Адван, Суван) адвант Бакатар бектің өзі сиыр жылы шақырып, әкесінің ордасынан аландарға (дала, алқаптар) бөлінуге тырысуда". (Лайпанов К., Мезиев И. "Түркі халықтарының шығу тегі жайында" "ПУЛ" баспасы, Черкесск, 1993 жыл. ) Осыған сәйкес Иса Мәсіхтің этникалық тегінің қазақтың төрт руы: дулат, ботбай, албан, суан одағына қатыстылығы жайында сөз қозғау заңдылығы туындайды. Сонымен бірге, осы тарихи құжатқа сәйкес, қазақтың дулат және ботпай рулары жеке дербес ру болып табылатын. Сондықтан да бүгінгі күндегі ботбай руының дулаттардың құрамына енетіндігінің тарихи негіздемесі жоқ.

Мұнда аландардың иран тілдестігі туралы мәселені тағы бір қозғауды жөн көрдім. Бұл болжам шамасы өздерін аландардың ұрпағы санайтын аландардың, иран тілдес болып келетініне байланысты туындауы ғажап емес.

Біріншіден, Т.Досанов өзінің "Руника құпиясы" атты еңбегінде көрсеткендей: 70 осетин тамғасының алтауын ғана алан тамғаларымен салыстырып қарауға мүмкіндік бар. Сол себепті аландардың түрк тілдес екендігі және қазақтардың ата-баларына тіелей қатысы бар екендігіне еш күмән жоқ.

Талқыланып отырған мәселенің скифтердің иран тілдес екендігіне тікелей қатысы бар. Ж.Байжумин мынадай пікірді айтады. Тарих ғылымында Геродоттың қате талқылауына байланысты скифтердің иран тілдес екендігі туралы жалған пікір қалыпатсты. Шамасы Геродот өз қортындыларында қателікке бой алдырса керек-деп санайды ол. Геродот айтқандай, Жайық өзенінің Қара теңіздегі скифтерден әрі, шығыс жағалауын мекендеген савроматтар, скифтердің тілінде сөйлейді. Ал енді иран тілдес осетиндерге келейік. Олар аландардың ұрпағы деп саналады, ал аландар - өз кезегінде савроматтардың ұрпағы. Яғни, егер, сарматтар мен савроматтар бір халық болса, онда скифтер иран тілдес халық болып шығады-деген қорытындыға келеді ғалымдар. Бірақ қарпайым логика заңдарына сәйкес, ақылға қонымды дәйектер бойынша, егер халықтың бір бөлігі басқа тілде сөйлесе, онда үлкен халықтың өзі тура сол тілде сөйлейді деген ұғым қалыптаспайды. КСРО-да бәрі орыс тілінде сөйледі. Бірақ оның он бес республикасының әрқайсысы өз тілінде сөйледі. Осыған сәйкес осетиндер -иран тілдес, аландардың ұрпағы болса да, аландардың өзі иран тілдес деген жалған ұғым қалыптаспауы тиіс.

Сондай-ақ, ең бастысы, Ж.Байжумин савроматтардың мүлде сарматтар емес екендігін дәлелдеп шықты. Савромат руының арғы тегі Сабыр немесе Сапар тайпасы. Олар қазіргі қазақтың Найман Және Қоңырат руларының ішіне енген. Ал Жапар атты ру Арғын мен Қыпшақтың құрамында бар, Забир руы, Керей мен Қыпшақтың ішіне енген. Ал Сарматтардың арғы тегі болып Сары немесе Сар тайпасы саналады. Олар қазіргі уақытта Оңтүстік Сібірде тұратын қазақ халқының көптеген руларының ішінде баршылық. Қырғыздың арасында да (Сару, Жору.), Хакастың ішінде де (Чоро) бар.

Сарматтар мен Савроматтардың түркі халықтарының әртүрлі тайпалары екендігі туралы Ю.Н.Дроздов жазады: ол " б.з.д. 90 жылдардағы жер сипаты" атты белгісі автордың еңбегіне сүйенеді. "Азия. Құрлықты скігс бөліп, Азияның шекарасы болып табылатын Танаисте, бір жағында 2000 дай стадия шақырымдай жерде – сарматтар тұрса, одан әрі жазушы Деметрийдің сөзі бойынша, язамат деп аталатын меотийлік тайпа өмір сүреді, ал Эфорға сәйкес, бұл тайпа савроматтар деп аталады..." (ВДИ,1947,№3)

Осыған сәйкес, аландардың түркі тілдес екендігі жөнінде мәлімдеуге толық негіз бар. Скифтер- иран тілдес деп қателескен бұрынғы заман ғалымдарының жалған пікірін түзетудің мүмкіндігі бар. Б.з.д. ҮІ-ІҮ ғасырларда сарматтар Тобыл мен Дон өзендерінің арасында өмір сүрген. Академик О.Исмагуловтың теориясы бойынша, олар- қазақтардың бабалары, яғни түркі тілдес халық болып табылады. Бір сөзбен айтқанда, сарматтар да, савроматтар да – түркі тілдес халықтар. Яғни, Геродот бойынша, скифтер де түркі тілдес халық болып шығады.

Тарих ғылымында аксиома ретінде бектілген скифтердің иран тілдестігі жайындағы тұжырым В.Абаевтың "Осетин тілі және фольклор" (М-Л.,1949 жыл.) еңбегінен бері келе жатыр. Бұл ғалым скифтік және осетин сөздері арасында кейбір ұқсастықтары тауып, осының негізінде асығыс түрде скифтердің иран тілдестігі туралы қате пікірді жариялаған. Бірақ басқа зерттеушілер скиф тілінен көптеген түркі сөздерін кездестірген. Сонымен бірге, ресейлік зерттеуші Ю.Н.Дроздов жазғандай, " Бүкіл заман тарихшыларына жақсы таныс антикалық заман мен орта ғасырлық тарихи мәліметтердің бай қоры осы кезеңде Еуропа аймағында көне парсылық мәдениет және этнонимиясы іспеттес тайпалар мен халықтардың тұрғандығы жайлы еш дерек келтірмейді..."

Профессор Барманқұлов басқа мәселе жөнінде әйгілі академик Гафуровпен пікір таластыра отырып, оның аты шулы "Тәжіктер" атты кітабына тоқтала келе, бұл академиктің пікірі бойынша, Орта Азияның байырғы тұрғындары болып иран тайпалары саналады, ал түркілер бұл аймаққа Солтүстік Қытайдан тек ҮІ ғасырда келген деген пікіріне қарсы наразылық танытып, былай деп жазады: "Яғни, сонда б.з.д. Орта Азияда Ү ғасырда пайда болған иран тілдес халықтар - байырғы жергілікті халық екен де, ал Үндістанда б.з.д. ІҮ мыңжылдықта (дравидтер халқы-Қ.З.), сондай-ақ Эламда – б.з. д. ІҮ мыңжылдықта, Хараппада – қазіргі Тәжікстан, Түрікменстан, Самарқан мен Хиуаның оазисті шұрайлы жерлерінде б.з.д. ІІ-ІІІ мыңжылдықта, б.з.д. ІІ мыңжылдықта-Қытайда, б.з. –Жапонияда дамып гүлденген түркі тілдес халықтардың тілі жергілікті, байырғы емес екендігі анықталды. Сонда олар Үндістаннан Қытай мен Жапонияға ұшақпен ұшып барған ба?

Скифтердің түркі тектес халыққа жататындығы туралы өзінің "Кодекс Куманикус" еңбегінде венгр түркологы Геза Куун (1880 жыл) дәлелдеген. Түркологтар К.Лайпанов пен И.Мезиев тура осындай пікірге келеді, ал 1523 жылы итальяндық Альберте Кампензенің ҮІІІ Папа Климентке жазған хатында былай делінеді: "Қазіргі кезде скифтер деп танылып жүрген татарлар", (өзім бөліп көрсеттім-Қ.З. ) көшпенді халық және көне замандардан бері өздерінің ержүрек батыл жауынгер мінезімен танымал" (Библиотека иностранных писателей о России, СПб.1836, I-том).

Аталмыш жайтты түсіндірудің қажеті шамалы.

# Троя, Каталауын алқабы: Түркілер түркілерге қарсы. Мұса пайғамбар 40 жыл бойы еврейлерді адам төзгісіз шөлдерде неге қаңғытты?

Өткен тарауларда адамзаттың барша мейірбандылық қарым-қатынас заңдарынан аттап өтіп, мұсылман әміршісіне бейбітшілік пен тату өмір туралы, Шыңғысхан Шығыстың әміршісі болып қала берсе, Хорезмшахқа Батыстың әміршісі болып қалу жөнінде ұсынысты жеткізген Шыңғысханның елшілігін қырып жойған, Хорезмшах Мұхаммедті әлемді дүр сілкіндірген Шыңғысханның қалай талқандағанын көзімен көрген, барша оқиғаға куә болған араб тарихшысы Ибн әл-Асирге сілтеме жасадық. Міне, осы кезде, қыпшақтарға қатысты айтылған моңғолдар сөзін келтірдім: "Сендер мен біздің шыққан тегіміз бір, Аландар сендерге жат халық, сондықтан оларға көмектесіп қайтесіңдер, сендердің дінің олардікінен бөлек. Сендерге шабуыл жасамаймыз, қалағандарыңша мал мүлік, сый-сыяпат тарту етуге уәде береміз. Сондықтан да бізді олармен жеке қалдырыңдар..." –дейді.

Осыған дейін аландардың иран тілді болып табылмайтындығына, скиф, түркі тайпалары құрамына енетіндігі туралы нақты айғақтар келтірдік. Онда Шыңғысхан неге аландарды түркілерге жат тайпа деп таныды? Егер, араб тарихшысының естеліктеріне күмәнсіз қарайтын болсақ, әрине. Өйткені б.з.д. III мыңжылдықтан бастап, түркілерге күш қуат, әлеует жағынан тең келетін халық жоқ болатын. Еуразияның шексіз алқаптарында жақсы өмір іздеген, жақсы қаруланған, батыл да, ожет көшпенділер керуені толқын-толқынымен ағылып, көбінесе өркениеттік дамуы жағынан бір саты төмен тұратын отырықшы халықтарды тізе бүктірді. Жаулап алған жерлерінде жаңа мемлекеттік құрылымдарды дүниеге әкелді. Мәселен Жұмажан Байжумин б.з.д. II мыңжылдықтың ортасында Пелопонеске арғы тегі қазақтың арғын, найман, қаңлы руынан тараған ахейліктер Еуразия алқабынан келгендігін анықтайды. Тек осыдан кейін ғана б.з.д XII ғасырда Пелопонеске көшпенді дорийлердің басқа толқыны келіп жетеді, олар көне германдық (көне түркілік десеңіз де болады) тәңір Торға табынып, Дон-Тана өзенін мекендегендіктен, өздерін донор немесе тана деп атайтын. Сондықтан да өмір сүруге қолайлы жерді иелену үшін көшпенді дорийлер көшпенді ахейліктермен соғысуға мәжбүр болған. Себебі, шұрайлы алқаптарды өздері тектес көшпенділер басып алса да, олардың өзара араласпағанына жүздеген жылдар өтті ғой!

Сондықтан да Шыңғысхан аландарды қыпшақтарға қатысты бөтен тайпа деп таныған. Өйткені қыпшақтардың тарихы Солтүстік Қытай мен қазіргі Моңғолияның аймағындағы Түркі қағанаттарынан басталады. Ал аландар болса, б.з.д Кавказда өмір сүріп келген түркі тайпасының басқа бір бұтағы. Осы аландардың өзге жұрт деп танылуына қатысты сәтті пайдаланып кейбір авторлар оларды иран тілдес халықтар қатарыша жатқызады. Оның үстіне XIII ғасырда аландардың бір бөлігі христиан дініне өтіп кеткен еді. Ал түркілер дәстүрлі түрде Тәңір дініне сиынатын. Шыңғысханның аландарға басқа діннің өкілдері ретіндегі наразылығы аталмыш оқиғаға байланысты туындады.

Ал енді Трояға келейік. Бұл қаланы түркілік фракий, дорий, ликий және тағы басқа тайпалар қорғады. Ал осы қалаға шабуыл жасаған тайпалар аргив (арғын) және ахей руынан шыққан түркі тайпалары болатын. Түркілер басқа халықтардан кез келген жерде басым түсті. Соғысатын жау қалмағандықтан, өзара шайқасып, күштерін сынады. Геродот "скифтердің келесідей тәңірлер -Гестия, содан кейін Зевс пен оның зайыбы Гея, олардан кейін Аполлон мен Афродита, Геракл және Ареске табынатындығы..." туралы жазды. Міне, Троя соғысының басты кейіпкерлері – Зевс тәңірдің тікелей ұрпақтары болып табылады. Өзара қарсыластар: Ахиллес пен Гектор, Одиссей мен Парис те –Зевстен тараған. Троя соғысы кейіпкерлерінің түрі болғандығы жайында, Трояның фракийліктер патшасы – Энейдің өз туыстарын жеті атасынан бастап, Зевстен Гекторға дейін түгендеп, атап шығатын сюжетінде Гомердің өзі жырлайды.

Жеті атасын міндетті түрде білу салты - тек түркілерге тән құбылыс.

Яғни осыған сәйкес, Троя аңызын одан сайын құлпырту үшін, Паристің Елена сұлуды ұрлағандығы жөнінде жалған аңыз сюжеттер ойдан құрастырылады. Ал келесі әскери шайқастар қарсылас жақтың кек алуы тұрғысында әдемі бейнеленеді. Мәселен, ресейлік зерттеуші А.Абрашкин өзінің "Скифская Русь" (80-бет) кітабында Троян соғысының мүлде басқа геосаяси себептерін келтіреді. Троя соғысы Мысырлықтар мен Семиттерге қолайлы еді, өйткені олар солтүстіктен келетін қауіп қатерді 30 жылға шегіндірді. Шамасы дәл осы уақыт аралығында еврейлер Палестинаға келіп орналасқан болуы керек. Мұса пайғамбар 40 жыл бойы еврейлерді адам төзгісіз шөлейттерде неге қаңғытты?- деген сұраққа айтар жауабымыз: "Ол Троя шайқасының басталуын күтті".

Ал енді Каталаун алқабындағы Аттілі мен Аэцийдің шайқасына тоқталайық. Батыс еуропалық тарихшылар келісіп алғандай, бірауыздан Каталаун алқабында Аттілінің ғұн тайпасы Аэций бастаған еуропалықтардың біріккен әскерінен жеңіліс тапты -деп шулайды. Шынымен осылай ма?

Гот тарихшысы Иордан өзінің "О происхождении и деянии готов" атты кітабында бұл аты аңызға айналған шайқасты былайша сипаттайды: "Оң қанатты везеготтарды бастаған Теодорид бастады. Сол жақта римдіктерді бастап Аэций тұрды, орта жаққа қолды бастап, Сангитан орналасты. Бұл жайында жоғарыда айтып өттік. Ол аландардың басшысы еді..." Мұнда соғыс алдындағы ғұндардың жауларының әскери тәртіпте орналасу хиқаясы туралы айтылып отыр.

Олардың қатарында тура сол аландар мен готтардың бар екендігін байқадық. Ал Аэций бастаған римдіктердің сол қанаты жайлы айтсақ, сол кезеңдерде рим әскерінің үштен бір бөлігі жалдамалы түркілерден құралғандығын ескерейік. Ал Аэцийдің шығу тегі - скиф-иллирийлік болатын.

Тағы да түркілердің түркілермен соғысы! Ғасырлар шеңберінде түркілердің шынайы лайықты қарсыласы түркілер болып келгендігін атап өтейік: түркілік қыпшақтар түркі хазарларды ойсырата жеңді, түркілік татарлар –түркі болгарлардан басым түсті. Самарқан билеушісі әмір Темірлан Алтын Орда ханы Тоқтамыс, Түркияның билеушісі I Баязидті жеңеді.

Ал Аттілінің жеңілісіне келсек, Еуропа ғалымдарының көзқарасы бойынша жеңілген ғұндар, тура сол 451 жылы баарша Италияны жаулап алып, ойран салып, тас талқан етеді.

# ТҮРКІЛІК ФРАКИЯ. АРИСТОТЕЛЬ, АЛЕКСАНДР МАКЕДОНСКИЙ МЕН СПАРТАК.

Троя соғысы аяқталған соң, ас-оғыздар Балқан түбегінің солтүстік-шығысындағы болашақ Фракия аймағына келіп орналасады (осыдан келіп, әйгілі фракийлік Спартак және ұлы Александр Македонскийдің тегі оғыз деген болжам жасауға болады, өйткені сол кездегі Македония көшпенділердің қоластында орналасып, Фракия мемлекетінің бір бөлігі ретінде саналды). Б.з. II-III ғасырында өмір сүрген Рим тарихшысы Марк Юниан Юстиниан қысқаша түрде біздің күнге жетпеген "Филипп тарихы" кітабына сүйеніп, IX ғасырда Помпей Трог былай деп жазады: "Сол кезеңдегі скиф патшасы Атей еді. Ол истриандармен соғысып, жағдайы қиындаған кезде, апполондықтар арқылы Филипптен (Александр Македонскийдің әкесі-Қ.З.) көмек сұрайды. Филиппті бала етіп асырап алып, кейінірек бүкіл скиф патшалығының тағына мұрагер ретінде таққа отырғызатындығын айтады..."

Сонда скифтік патша басқа тайпадан шыққан адамды мұрагер етіп сайлай ма?

ҮІ ғасырда өмір сүрген басқа остготтық тарихшы Иордан өзінің "О происхождениях и деяниях готов" атты кітабында былай деп жазады: "Ұлы Александрдың әкесі Филипп, готтармен достасып, Гудила патшаның қызы Медопаға үйленіп, осындай туыстық жол арқылы Македон патшалығын нығайтуды көздейді..."

Осылайша антикалық заман тарихшылары македондықтардың скиф және готтармен туыстығы жөнінде нақты баяндаған.

Александр Македонскийдің (Ескендір Зұлқарнайын) ұстазы, атақты данышпан философ Аристотель жайында бірер сөз. Ол да Фракияда туып өсті. Ал оның аты екі тіркестен құралады: арыс және тоты. Көпетеген шәкірттерді тәрбиелеп, философия мектебін ашқан Аристотельді оның замандастары мен ұрпақтары қадірлеп, бас трибунал немесе ұстаз деп атаған. Аристотельге дейін 200 жыл бұрын Көне Грекияның жеті данышпанының бірі Анарыс еді. Оны гректер Анахарсис деп атап кетеді. Шумерлерде Ан- аспан тәңірі, барша тәйрлердің әділ соты болатын. Анарыс сөзін "жер бетіндегі Аспан тәңірінің тірегі" деп аударуға болады. Анарыс шығу тегі жағынан скиф еді.

Геродот скифтер және олардың данышпан ұлы Анахарсис туралы сөз еткенде, былай деп жазады: "Понттың ар жағында (Қара теңіз-Қ.З.) өте ақылды скиф халқы мен даналығы әлемге жария Анахарсис патшадан басқа бір де бір халықты немесе данышпандарды біле бермейміз. Скиф халқының өмір сүру дәстүрі басқа халықтармен салыстырғанда анағұрлым жоғары. Олардың ойлап тапқандары да керемет. Осыдан кейін таңданудан да қалдым..."

Б.з. I ғасырында өмір сүрген грек философы Плутарх өзінің "Нравственные суждения" атты еңбегінің "Жеті данышпанның тойы" атты тарауында Анарысқа қатысты былай деп айтады: Осы әңгіме біткен соң, мен данышпандарға үйге кімді қонақ етіп шақыратындығымыз туралы ұсыныс жасадым, қала мен патшалықтарды басқаратындар аз ғой, ал ошақ пен үй әрқайсымызда бар. Эзоп оған күліп, былай деді: "Егер сен бәріміздің қатарымызға Анахарсисті қоссаң, онда айтайын: оның үйі жоқ, ол тіпті үйсіз-күйсіз арбаға мініп жүргенін мақтан тұтады. Күн де бұл сияқты арбасына мініп алып, аспанның ар жағына серуен жасағанды жақсы көреді".

"Сондықтан да, - деп тіл қатты Анахарсис, күн өз еркімен жүретін тәңірлердің бірі. Өз қалауынша жерді басқарып жүре береді. Бірақ өзі ешкімге бағынбайды, дегенмен, патшалық құрып, билік жүргізеді. Тек сен оның арбасының ұзындығы мен табиғатының қаншалықты сұлу және көркем екендігін ұмытып кеттің: әйтпесе оның арбасын біздің арбалармен салыстырмас едің"- деп, әзілмен жауап береді..."

Осылайша Анахарсис (Анарыс) – біздің ұлы бабамыз Көне Грекияның данышпандарының арасында тұрып, өз халқын мақтан етті. Яғни көшпенді халық - ғаламат күн секілді еркін ел. Бәрін басқарады, көшпендінің шаңырағы –киіз үйді күннің арбасымен салыстырды. Күннің мекеніндей барша жер көшпендінің мекен қонысы болып табылады.

Бір сөзбен айтқанда, Ежелгі Грекия өзінің атақты ұлдары ретінде біздің ата-бабаларымыздың есімдерін атаған. Бұл жайт қазіргі заманғы Түркияға да қатысты. Бұл мемлекет б.з.д. бірінші мыңжылдықтың ортасында Анатолия елі деп аталды. Ана төлі деген ұғым тікелей мағынасында ананың баласы, немесе Жер ананың жас өнімі деген мағынаны береді. Түркия мен Грекия аймақтары Еуразия алқаптарынан кеткен көшпенділер үшін жаңа Отанға айналғаны мәлім.

“Ан-Хан” лексикалық жұбына талдау жасау маңызды. Жоғарыда айтылғандай, Шумерлерде Ан –аспан тәңірі, барша тәңірлердің әділ соты. Ал Хан – түркілер мен рустарда жердегі билеші, патша ұғымын білідреді. Графикалық сұрыптау барысында шумерлік “Ан” сөзі қазақ тілінде қатаң түрдегі дауыссыз Х формантына ие болады. Сондай-ақ, “Ер-Герр” (Хер) лексикалық жұбы жайлы да осындай анықтама жасай аламыз. Қазақтың “Ер” сөзі –еркек деген ұғымды білдіреді. Ал неміс және орыс тілінде алынған формант дауыссыздар: ұяң Г және қатаң Х ер адамға қатысты және ер адамның жыныстық мүшесіне қатысты айтылатын сөзге айналды.

Балқан түбегіндегі Фракиялық мемлекет б.з.д I мыңжылдықта қалыптасты. Бұл мемлекеттің құрамына трер-турлардан басқа, Кеңестік энциклопедиялық сөздікке сәйкес, дах, одрис және гет тайпалары енді. Геттер- қазақтың кете-қытан тайпаларының ата-бабасы. Дак-дахтар қазіргі күні қазақтың адай руы ретінде жалғасын тапты. Одрис руының шыққан тегі қазіргі заманғы қазақтың Ыдырыс руының бабалары болып табылады. Геродот Фракиялықтар жайында былай деп мәлімдейді: “Олар жер игеруді жек көреді. Олар жауынгер мен қарақшының өмірін бақыт деп санайды. Бай фракиялықтарды жерлеу дәстүрі мынадай: Марқұмды үш күнге дейін жерлемей сақтайды. Құрбандыққа арналған әртүрлі малдарды сойып, жылап сықтап болған соң, марқұмға арнап ас береді. Кейін өлі адамның денесін жағып, немесе жерге көміп жерлейді. Марқұмның бейітіне қорған орнатып, әртүрлі сайыстар өткізеді. Сайыстың маңыздылығына қарай, жекпе жек үшін ең жоғары мәртебелі сыйлықтар тағайындалады. Бұл фракиялықтардың жерлеу дәстүрі...” Ж.Байжумин өзінің “История рождения, жизни и смерти пастуха Авеля. Арийский лексикон” (ТОО “Типография оперативной печати”, Алматы, 2009) атты кітабында Геродот сипаттаған фракиялықтардың жерлеу дәстүрінің көне түркілік және кейінгі заман қазақтарының жерлеу дәстүр салттарынан ерекшеленбейтінін дұрыс байқап, әділ бағасын берген.

Византия заманындағы Страбонның "Географиясындағы" мәліметтерге сүйене отырып, және Птоломейдің "Географиясынан" аздаған мәліметтерді пайдаланып жазылған "Хрестоматияның" жетінші кітабында былай делінеді: "Көне эллиндер Истр (қазіргі Дунай –Қ.З.) өзені жағалауын мекендеген готтар мен мисийликтерді фракийліктер деп атаған..." Геттердің түркі тектес халық екендігі туралы айтып өттік, яғни осыған сәйкес, фракиялықтар да түркі тектес және түркі тілдес халық болып шығады. Б.з.д. Y-IY ғасырда өмір сүрген көне грек философы және ақыны Платон (Платонның қазіргі аты -Арыстоқыл екенін атап өтейік. Оның шығу тегі скифтік деген болжам туындайды.) өзінің "Мемлекет" атты айтулы трактатында фракиялықтар туралы былай дейді: "Біздің бойымызда - мен баяндап отырмын, мемлекеттегідей рухани қасиеттер бар екенін амалсыз мойындауға тура келеді ғой. Әйтпесе бұл қасиеттер бізге қайдан қонсын? Рухтың ашуы сынды жеке мінез (Өзім бөліп көрсеттім –Қ.З.) кейбір мемлекеттерде осы себептің иегерлері осы мінезге душар болғандықтан, дами қойған жоқ: мұндай жағдайды Фракия, Скифия және барша солтүстік аймақтардың тұрғындары басынан кешіруде..."

Сондықтан да, Александар Македонский мен Спартактың тегі түркілік деген менің болжамым соншалықты қиял елес болып көрінбейді. Плутарх Спартак туралы жазғанда, жабайы варвардан гөрі ол білімді эллинге көбірек ұқсас деп айтады. Эллинбіз (еліні) -деп, өзін Еуразия алқабынан келген көшпенді жауынгерлер атайтын, олар б.з.д. екінші мыңжылдықтың ортасында Славяндық тәнір Пелеге табынатын және осыған байланысты пеласги деп аталып кеткен тұрғындары мекендеген Пелопонесті жаулайды. Кейінірек римдіктер эллиндерді гректер деп атай бастайды. Спартактың этникалық шығу тегі жайында сөз қозғап, Плутарх: "ол номадикон тайпасынан шыққан фракийлік" -деп тұжырымдайды. Осы арқылы Спартактың көшпенді халықтарға қатысы бар екендігі туралы айтады. "Фракия" этнонимі К.Бегалин "Кто вы и откуда, колесящие " атты кітабында (Алматы, 2004) "одақтас" (болгарлық пірақ) ден ұғымды білдіреді деп анықтайды. Шынымен де, олардың көршілері –туыстары, хеттер Фракия аймағында өздерінің сансыз үйір жылқыларын бағып өмір сүрген, оның үстіне фракиялықтар мысырлықтармен соғыста хеттердің сенімді одақтасы болатын. Көне заман тарихшысы Иосиф Флавий фракиялықтар туралы былай деп жазады: "Олардың руларының арғы тегі Яфеттің жетінші ұлы болып табылады. Белгілі мәліметтерге сәйкес, Яфетті Нұх пайғамбар Еділ (Волга) мен Орал өзендері жағалауына өмір сүруге аттандырады. Түркі халқы осы Яфеттен тарайды.

Осы кітапқа алғы сөз ретінде қазіргі заманғы Қазақстан аймағы мен Еуразия алқабынан атылған жанартаудай, көшпенділердің толқыны кезек-кезегімен ағылып, көшіп қоныстанып жүретіндігі туралы жазған едім. Олар кең жазира далаға сыймағандықтан, қысымның әсерінен көшуге мәжбүр болып, "Скифиялық қуғындалғандарға" айналып,

Таяу, Орта және Қиыр Шығыс пен Еуропа және Скандинавия халықтарын бағындырып, сол аймақтарда жаңа өркениеттердің негізін қалайды.

Көшпенділер толқыны ағылып, сан түрлі атаулармен әртүрлі тайпалар: киммерий, скиф, сармат, гот, ғұн, түркі, моңғолдар – біздің ата-бабамыз өздеріне жаңа мекен, қоныс тауып, сол аймақтарға орналасатын. Мәселен, Ж.Байжумин анықтағандай: көне исландиялық жырлар (сага), ежелгі заман скандинавиялық эпосы көне заман нормандары екі түрлі халық болғандығының айғақтайды: түлкі терісін жамылған, үлкен бөрік және қысқа кафтан кигендер, бұл киіну үлгісі олардың көшпенді екендігінің белгісі және тас дәуіріндегідей өмірді басынан кешіріп отырған жергілікті жұрт. Көшпенді жеңімпаздар дәулетті ақсүйектерге айналып, негізінен орманды мекендейтін халықтарды мал бағуға үйретті. Ал сәл кейінірек бұл көне германдықтардың бинарлық қоғамының жаңа этномәдени тайпалары өз ата мекендеріне қайтты. Ж.Байжумин жазғандай, көне герман тайпаларының көсемдері есімдерінің түркілік атауының болуы осыған байланысты. Мәселен: гутондар билеушісі - Берік, көне венгр көсемдері - Әлім, Кархан, Солтан, ғұндар патшасы-Баламбер және т.т.

Кейбір ғалымдардың пікірі бойынша, көшпенділер герман тайпаларының алғашқы қауымдық өмір салтына қола заманның жәдігерлері мен үлгілерін енгізді: скиф-сарматтық орнаменттер, өнердегі аң жануар стилі, жазу мәдениеті. Көрнекті еуропалық ғалым Ж.Ле.Гофф көшпенді жауынгерлер туралы былай деп жазады: "Олар өздерімен бірге металл темірлерді игерудің арнайы технологиясын, зергерлік өнер мен тігіншілік шеберлікті, сонымен бірге ұлы даланың таңқаларлық құбылысы - жануарлар бейнесі салынған бейнелеу үлгі өнерін ала келді".

Міне, сол кезеңдегі далалық жабайы варварлар мен оқымысты еуропалықтардың сипаттамасы осындай! Міне, сондықтан да көшпенді әлем, түркілер дүниесіне Аристотель, Александр Македонский және Спартакты заңды түрде жатқызуыма толық құқығым бар. Өйткені олар өз халықтарының ақсүйек әулетінен шыққан, ал бұл құрылымдар жаулаушы көшпенділер ішінен қалыптасатын.

# Ұлы Дала Гиксостары — Мысыр перғауындары

Ал енді қайтадан хеттерге келейік. Кіші Азияда хетт мемлекетінің құрылуына б.з.д. екінші мың жылдықтың басында Кіші Азияның солтүстігіндегі Қара теңіз жағалауында Миттания мемлекетінің пайда болуы ықпалын тигізеді. Бұл мемлекетті этникалық матайлар басқарып, кезінде Азов теңізіне өз атауларын бергендіктен, бұл теңіз Меотия (Матай) теңізі ретінде әйгіленді. Бұл мемлекет әлемге мысыр әулетінің бірнеше перғауындарын тарту етті.

Сондай-ақ б.з.д. ХYІІІ ғасырда пирамидалар елін жаулап алған, хеттердің алдында осы өлкеге Еуразия алқабынан көшіп келген гиксостар да Мысыр перғауындары атанды. Олар Гиксос перғауындарының ХY әулетінің негізін салды. Гиксостардың алғашқы патшасы болып, Хиян немесе Қиян жарияланды. Егер Шыңғысхан шыққан ірі тайпаның атын есіңізге түсірсеңіз, бұл тайпа Қият немесе Қиян деп аталды. Ал Әмудариядағы қазіргі заманғы Бируни қаласы бір кездері Қият деп аталатын. Олар өз астанасын Аварис (Абарис) деп атауына байланысты гиксостардың авар сынды тарихи халыққа тікелей қатысы бар деген жорамал жасаймыз.

Геродот та жанама түрде менің пікірімді растай түседі: Ол өзінің ІY "Тарих" кітабында әйгілі скиф тайпасынан солтүстік жаққа қарай өмір сүрген гипорберейлер туралы айта келе, былай деп жазады: "Гипорберейлер туралы сөз жеткілікті тұрғыда айтылды. Абарис туралы аңызды атап өткім келеді, ол да гипорберей болып, қолына садағын алып, барша жер жаһанды аралап, тамашалаған деседі..." Геродоттың еңбектеріне қазіргі заманда түсініктеме жасаушылар ("История Казахстана в произведениях античных авторов" "Фолиант", 1.т, Астана, 96-бет) еңбегін қараңыз. Олар Абарис сөзін этнонимі авар – Көне Алтайдың көшпенді тайпаларына қатысты талдайды. Шынымен-ақ гиксостар астанасының атауы бірінші түркі қағанаты құрылғанға дейінгі Солтүстік Қытай мен Моңғолия билеушілерінің этнонимін еске түсіреді, ҮІ ғасырда түркілердің қысымымен, атамекендерінен кетуге мәжбүрленіп, Еуропада өте күшті қуатты Авар қағанатының іргетасын көтереді. Шамасы "авар" этнонимі өте көне дәуірлер мұрасы сынды және б.з.д. ХYІІІ ғасырда гиксостар деп аталса, кейінірек, б.з.д. ХІІ ғасырда аварлар хеттармен бірге Қытай аймағына келіп, жужан деген атпен әлемге танымал болған.

Ұлы Константиннің замандасы, антикалық философ Ямблих өзінің "О жизни Пифагора" атты кітабында ("Скифы. Хрестоматия", Москва, "Высшая школа, 1992, 239 стр" еңбегін қараңыз) келесідей мәліметтерді келтіреді: "эллиндік мәдениетті біле бермейтін қария скиф Абарис гипорберейлер елінен Эллиндер жеріне келгенде, Пифагор оған біртіндеп осы елдің білім қайнарынан сусындатады. Оған аз уақыттың ішінде өзінің табиғат және басқа заттар, Жаратушы туралы еңбектерін түсіндіріп шығады..." Осылайша Геродот пен Ямблихтен гипорборейлік Абаристің тегі скиф екендігін білеміз. Осыған сәйкес, б.з.д. ХYІІІ ғасырда гиксостар (гректер Гипорборей деп атайтын) солтүстіктен Мысырға келіп, өздерінің жаңа Отандарының атын Абарис деп атаған. Яғни гиксостардың түп тамыры, ата тегі скиф екендігіне дау жоқ.

Еуропа аварлары өте қуатты баварларға айналады, олар хет-готтар, сақ-сақстар және тюрингтермен бірге қазіргі заманғы герман ұлтының негізін құрады. Осылайша, бізге әйгілі композиторлар: Бах пен Бетховен, ойшылдар: Ницше, Кант және Гегель, математик Ф.Гаус, ақын Г.Гейне, жазушы Бертольд Брехт және Ремарк ұрпақтарының түптегінде көне түркі және арийлердің қаны бар екендігі анық түрде айқындалады.

Кейінірек аталып өтілетіндей, қазақтардың ата-бабаларының келбеті б.з.д. көне дәуірлерде таза түрдегі еуропалық нәсіл тектес болып келетін, сол себепті аталмыш ұлы тұлғалардың есімдері түркі әлемінің өткені мен бүгінгісіне жақындатылып айтылғандығы ешбір дау тудырмаса керек.

Мысырды 150 жыл бойы билеген соң, Гиксостар Шам (Сирия) еліне бет алып, қазіргі Израиль мемлекетінің жерінде жаңа Иерусалим қаласының іргетасын тұрғызады. Бұл шаһар кейінірек Иудейлердің астанасына айналады. Израиль ұрпағы бүгінгі таңда киелі жердегі қалаға ие болғандығы үшін кімге алғыс айту қажет екендігін біле ме екен?

Егер біз, XIII ғасырда Мысырды қазақтың Беріш руынан шыққан Бейбарыс сұлтан билегенін, оның мөрінде барыс бейнеленгенін еске түсірсек, қазақтың беріш руы гиксостар құрамында болды деп жорамалдай аламыз. Өйткені барыс пен абарыс ұғымдары әуендес, ырғағы бір болып келеді. Яғни Бейбарыс ата-бабалары басқарған жердегі мемлекеттің билік басына келді. Көптеген зерттеушілер, "гиксос" этнониміне қатысты "гиксақ" этнонимін салыстырып қарастырады. Бұл этнонимді "патшалық сақтар" - деп түсіндіреді. Патшаның сақ-скифтері дәстүрлі түрде қазақтың Кіші жүзінің өкілдері мекендеген Жайық пен Днепр өзендері жағалауында өмір сүрген. Осының нәтижесінде келесідей қорытынды жасауға негіз туындады: гиксостар құрамында алшындар да (кете, адай, беріш, шеркеш және т.б.), сонымен қоса: матай, садыр, қаракрейлер болуы керек. Б.з.д. 1535 жылы гиксостар Мысырдан кетіп қалғаннан кейін, осы аталмыш қазақ рулары Месопотамия және Кіші Азияда Алше-Алзи ұлы хетт мемлекетін құрады. Өзімнің "Шыңғысханның түркілік ғұмырнамасы. Қазақтардың киелі шежіресі" атты кітабымда Гиксостардың Орта Азия және Каспий теңізі жағалауы алқаптарынан шыққандығы туралы болжам жасадым, бұлар басқа рулардан күш қуаты, әлеуеті басым түскен, Мәңгілік көк тәңірге сыйынған "көксесі"-рулары мен тайпалары.

Бір сөзбен айтқанда, патшалық скифтер. Қазақтың сес көрсетті ұғымы басқаларды қорқытты дегенді білдіреді. Оның үстіне қытайлардың қазақтарды хассақ деп айтатынын ескерсек, бұл қытай тілінен аударғанда, "шынайы сақ" деген ұғымды білдіреді.

Сол себепті, "гиксақ" (гиксос) және "хассақ" этнонимдері қазақ халқы атауының екі түрлі ұғымы деп қабылдасақ қателеспейміз. Жұмажан Байжумин өз зерттеулерінде "гиксос" этнонимінің шығуын қазіргі заманғы Арғын және Ысты тайпасы құрамындағы "Көкше" руымен байланыстырады. Бір кездері өте күшті Көкше руы Солтүстік Қазақстанның кең алқабында көшіп қоныстанып жүріп, өз атын жергілікті тауларға қойып, содан "Көкше тау" пайда болған деседі. Ал Қазақстанның Ақмола облысының қазіргі астанасының аты – Көкшетау.

Ғылымда дәстүрлі түрде тараған: "гиксостар Араб түбегінен шыққан тайпалардың арғы тегі" деген пікірлерге қарамастан, ат- тұлпарлардың – гиксостар әскерінің негізгі бөлігі болып табылатындығын, жылқылар бұл түбекте гиксостар басып кірген соң, тек екі мың жылдан соң, пайда болған деген ғалымның пікірі ақылға қонымды. Ал арабтар гиксостар дәуірінде тек түйелерді ғана асырап бақты. Жылқыларды б.з. басында ғана үйрете бастады. Страбон б.з.д. I ғасырда рим делегациясының құрамында араб жерін аралап, жылқыларды әскери мақсатта пайдалануды айтпағанда, осы аймақтан бірде-бір жылқы атаулысын көрмейді.

# Көне Алтай – Король Артурдың Және Шотланд Вискиінің Отаны.

## Түркілік Ұлыбритания

Англиядағы Король Артур туралы сан алуан кітаптарда жазылған аңыздардың танымалдылығы жөнінде Елизавета ханшайымның хатшысының (1568жыл.) айтқан сөздерінен біле аламыз: "Бұл кітаптар мәртебелі тақсырлардың бөлмелерінен ұдайы түрде Інжілді шеттетіп тынады..." Ағылшын ғалымдары тарихи Артур YI ғасырдың басында өмір сүрген және кельттік бриттер тайпасының көсемі болған-деген пкірді бірауыздан айтады. Кельттердің Орта Азиялық алқаптардан шыққандығы мәлім. Кельттердің Британ аралдарына алғашқы жорықтары б.з.д. екінші мыңжылдықтың басында орын алған, ал шабуылдың екінші толқыны б.з.д 750 жылдары, үшіншісі- б.з.д. I ғасырда жүзеге асырылады. 2001 жылдың мамыр айында Англияда маған Ковентри университетінің басшылығымен кездесудің қолайлы сәті түсті. –"Қазіргі ханшайым Елизаветаның шығу тегі қандай?" деген сұрағыма, туризм факультетінің деканы, профессор Джон Бич былай деп жауап берді: ханшайым кельттердің ұрпағы. Ал кельттер өз кезегінде Орта Азиядан шыққан халық! Академик Оразақ Исмагулов дәлелдегендей ("Қазақстанның этникалық антропологиясы", Алматы, 1982 жыл) сол кезеңдері Орта Азия мен Қазақстанды түркілік, қазақ тайпалары мекендеген. Жазба деректерге сәйкес, кельттердің тұратын аймағы орасан зор болатын: Германия мен Кіші Азияға дейін, Голландиядан Испания, Италияға дейін. Кіші Азия Түркия аймағында Анкара маңында кельттердің шағын ауылы бар. Бұл ескерткіш б.з.д. 270 жылдар болып саналады. Орта Азияда академик С.П.Толстов бастаған археологиялық экспедиция Арал аймағында неолиттік мәдениеттің қайнар көзін тапқан. Бұл ошақ Кельтеминар тұрғылықты мекенінде орналасқандықтан, кельт мәдени ошағы деп аталды. Кейінірек Орта Азияда құаңшылық орын алғандықтан, кельттер Днепр өзені маңына, Карпаты және Төменгі және Орта Дунай аймағына келіп орналасты. Жоғарыда айтылғандай, олар осы жақтан Британ аралдарына дүркін-дүркін жойқын жорықтарын бастаған. Зерттеуші Н.Кикешев "Мегаистория. Откуда мы родом? Мифы, гипотезы, факты" (Изд-о "Ниола-Пресс, 2010 ) кітабында былай деп жазады: көшпенділер тайпаларының толқын-толқын легі Еуропаға қарай б.з.д. IY-I мыңжылдықта бет алып, кельт, сақ, иллирий тайпаларының ата бабалары орман, таумен қоршалған, Тұранның алып өлкесінде дүркірей соғатын дүлей боран мен дауыл жетпейтін түбектерге жайғасып, қазіргі замандағы Еуропа әлемінің негізін қалайды".

Кейбір ғалымдар, "кельт тілінің Түркістандағы өлі тохар тілі мен хеттердің көне тіліне ұқсас бірқатар сипаты бар" - екендігі туралы айтқан. Бұның өзі хеттер мен кельттердің этникалық туыстығын дәлелдейді. Алдыңғы тарауларда хеттерді көне түрки тайпасы екендігі туралы айтып өттік, бұл тайпалардың ұрпағы ретінде Германиядағы гет-готтар мен Қазақстандағы кете руын атаймыз. Готтардың Тұран тайпасы екендігі туралы YI ғасырдың өзінде-ақ византиялықғалым Прокопий Кесарийский жазып кетеді: "Өткен дәуірлерде готтар, савроматтар деп аталған..." Византия тарихшысы Прииск Панийский ғұндар мен готтардың тілін байланыстыра қарстырады, ресей зерттеушілері Ю.Д.Петухов пен И.Н.Васильева былай деп жазады: "Римге басып кірген барша варварлар үшін ортақ болып табылатын гот тайпасының тілі қазіргі герман тобына еш қатысы жоқ. Гот савроматтардың тілі иран тектес халықтар тілінің тобына кірмейді: өйткені көшпенділер легі толқындай ағылған Еуропада ирандық және арийлік тайпаларының ізі қалған жоқ..." Бұл готтар ирандықтар болмаса, кім болғаны сонда? Жауабы бір –түркілер!

XYI ғасырда өмір сүрген Елизавета ханшайымның хатшысының сөзінс оралсақ, біз қазақтар - өзіміздің ұлы бабамыз –аты аңызға айналған король Артурға, алғашқы орта ғасырлық заман билеушілері өз бөлмелерінде Ұлы Даланың серісі Артурдың ерліктері жайында білгісі келіп, Інжілді кейінге қалдығандығы үшін құрмет білдіріп, рахметімізді айтуымыз қажет.

Біз Ұлыбритания кельттерінің тегі түрки екендігі туралы жеткілікті тұрғыда дәлелді дәйектер келтірдік деп ойлаймыз. Бұл кельттердің ұрпағы бриттер королі

Артур болып табылады. Плутархтың "Сравнительное жизнеописание" ("История Казахстана в произведениях античных авторов" Астана "Фолиант" 1-том, 2005 жыл, 289-бет) кітабын қараңыз.) еңбегінен кейбір мәліметтерді келтірейін: ол әйгілі Рим қолбасшысы Гай Марийге арнаған тарауында келесідей жайтты баяндайды: "Кейбіреулер Кельтика теңіздегі жерінің солтүстікке қарай көлемі мен ұзындығы жағынан шығысында Меотидаға бұрып, Понттық Скифияға барып ұштасады. Осы жақта халықтардың араласуы орын алған деседі. Ол жақтан бірте-бірте көтеріліп, қолайлы сәттерде алға жылжып, олар көптеген жылдар ішінде бүкіл құрлықтан өтеді. Сол себепті көптеген жеке атауларға қарамастан, олар өздерінің сан жетпес қолдарын кельт-скиф тайпалары деп атаған". (Өзім бөліп көрсеттім-Қ.З.)

Плутархтан көріп отырғанымыздай, кельттер өзін скифы халықтарының құрамындағы халық деп санаған.

Ал енді кельттік бритт тайпасының пайда болуы жөнінде егжей-тегжейлі баяндайық. Англо-саксондық хроникалық шежіре жазбаларда, Тұманды Альбионның алғашқы тұрғындары ретінде бритт тайпасы делінеді. IX ғасырда Геродот, сонан кейін Ненний жазып қалдырған британ тарихындағы Бриттердің ауыз әдебиетінде былай жырланады: "Ата- бабалардың өсиеті бойынша Британ аралы туралы білетінімді айтайын. Яфет әулетінен тарайтын Аланның ұлы Исиокон, оның ұлы Бриттонның құрметіне Британия аралына оның есімі беріледі..." (Ненний. История бриттонов// формы исторического сознания от поздней античности до эпохи Возрождения, Иваново, 2000) Біз Нұх пайғамбардың ұлы Яфеттен барша түркі руы тарайтынын білеміз, ал алан-албандар түркі әлемінің оғыз тайпаларынан тараған. Британия аралдарының алғашқы тұрғындары болып табылатын Скотт және Пикта тайпалары да түркі тілдес еді. Олар жайында Ненний былай деп жазады: "Жабайы варварлар, яғни скотт және Пикта тайпалары Бретон тайпасының мазасын ала бастаған кезде, римдіктерден көмек сұрайды". Сол кезеңдері жабайы варвар деп Еуразия алқабынан шыққан жауынгер тайпаларды атайтын. Ю.Н.Дроздов Британ аралдарында YІ ғасырдың аяғына таман құрылған жеті корольдіктің этнонимдерін сараптап, мынадай шешімге келеді: яғни төртеуінің атауы-Англия, Мерсия, Норт-Уимбрия және Кент этнонимдерінің түркілік тегі бар. Мәселен "Англия" деген елдің аты "англы" этнонимінен тарайды. Бұл сөз өз кезегінде "аңлы" - "ақылды, данышпан, зерек" сөзінің интерпретациясы болып шығады. Латын транскрипциясында түркілік үнді дауыссыз дыбыс /н/ /ng/ дифтонгі арқылы беріледі., ал жуан қысаң дауысты /ы/ жіңішке үлгідегі /i/ дыбысы болып ауысады.

Сонымен бірге деп дәлелдейді ғалым: британның құлағына жағымды естілетін көптеген ағылшын графтықтарының атауларына кіретін Шир аймағы мекенінің атауы-Стоунхедж, Йоркшир, Стаффордшир, Шропшир, Ноттингемшир атауларының да түркілік түп тамыры бар. Мұндай сөздердің қатарына: "лорд, парламент,кинг, барон, сквайр және т.б. енеді". Ю.Н.Дроздов зерттеу нәтижесінде "көне замандардан бері

Британияда түркі тектес тайпалар өмір сүрген"- деген пікірге келеді. Британдардың барлық есімдері этнонимдерінің түркілік тегі бар екендігі сөзсіз. Ал енді сәл кейін шегініп, біздің заманымыздың алғашқы жүз жылдығына келейік.

Сенімді дерек көздеріне сүйнетін болсақ, б.з. II ғасырының ортасында сарматтар мен языга тайпалары Дунайдан өтіп, рим империясына шабуыл жасап, Маркоман согысын басталуына жол ашады. Языгалармен бірге олардың жағында лангобардтар мен аландар шайқасты. Біз бұрын атағандай және кейін баяндайтынымыздай, олардың Қазақстанның кең алқаптарынан келген тайпа екендіктері туралы әлі айтамыз. Рим одақтастарымен бейбіт келісімге шартқа қол қоюға мәжбүрленеді. Осыған сәйкес языгалар рим иеліктерін күзету үшін жыл сайын сегіз мың атты жауынгер шығаруға тиісті болады. Осы жалдамалы языгалардың бір бөлігі римдіктердің бретондық легиондарында қызмет етті. Ж.Байжуминнің жазуына қарағанда, "осылайша Британия жерінде Сарматтық серілер пайда болды, зерттеушілер король Артур туралы аңыздардың пайда болуы осы мәдени ортаға тікелей байланысты деп шешті".

Еуропалық ғалым Х.Никель жазып кеткендей, "Артур аңыздары циклінің желісінде ұлы халықтар көші кезіндегі, Франция мен Англияға тап болып, римдіктер әскерінің қатарында қызмет еткен сарматтар мен аландар арасында феодалдық кезеңге дейін жырланған қаһармандық эпостың негізі бар..."

Король Артурдың шығу тегі сарматтық екендігі жайында тағы бір еуропалық ғалым Жорж Дюмезиль баяндайды:

Біз осылайша король Артурдың сарматтық языга тайпасынан шыққан тікелей ұрпағы Британ аралдарына тап болып, Сарматтар мен Рим арасындағы бейбіт келіссөзге сәйкес Рим империясының құрамында шайқасуға мәжбүрленеді. Бұған қосатыным: языгалардың арғы тегі қазіргі таңда Шығыс Қазақстанда өмір сүретін Қарауыл Жасақ руы болып табылады. Қазақтың "жасақ" сөзі –қол, әскер ұғымын білдіреді. Бірте-бірте сарматтық языга тайпасының аты ретінде трансформацияланып өзгерді. Ал Артур есімінің этимологиясы да оонің тегі түркі екендігін меңзейді.

Ар этнонимі - намыс, ар-ұждан, қасиетті деген мағыналарын білдіреді. Тур және Оғыз ұғымы түркілердің Оғыз атты көне ірі тайпасының атауы. Олар мәңгілік көк аспанның түнгі иесі –Айға табынады. Оғыз- қазақ тілінде бұқа деген ұғымды білдіреді. Яғни Артур есімі –Қасиетті бұқа деген мағынада түсіндірілуі мүмкін. Сонымен қоса языга-жасақтар түркі халқының Оғыз тобына жатады.

Страбонның "Географиясына" түсініктеме бере отыра, "История Казахстана в античных хрониках" академиялық басылымының редакциялық коллегиясы былайша баяндайды: сармат-языгалар - жаңа дәуірдің басында Меотия (Матай) көлі маңын мекендеген"- деген пікір айтады. Қазіргі қазақ руларының ішінде языга руы найман, тайпасының құрамына енген, ал бұл өз кезегінде - тарихи меоттар мен қазіргі заман матайлары бір халық болып табылатындығының тағы бір дәлелі.

Ал енді шотландиялық вискидің пайда болуы жайында бірер сөз.

Мен бұл жерде Мұрат Аджидің "Без вечного синего неба" (Москва, "Астрель", 2010) атты кітабынан жекелеген үзінділер келтіргім келеді.

Өзімізге қарапайым сұрақ қояйық: вискиді әзірлеуден басқа тағы қай шарада сұлы өнімі пайдаланылады? Бұл жылқылардың азығы деп жауап берсеңіз, онда жөн болғаны. Қазіргі кезеңде біз Оксфорд университетінің ғалымдарының анықтауы бойынша, б.з.д. IY ғасырда жабайы жылқы алғаш рет Қазақстан аймағында үйретілді, - деген айғақтарға ие болып отырмыз. Солтүстік Қазақстан аумағындағы Ботай елді мекенінде жүргізілген тарихи археологиялық қазба зерттеу жұмыстары нәтижесі осы айғаққа нақты дәлел болып отыр. Б.з.д. төрт мың жыл бұрын біздің бабаларымыз –қазақтар сұлы өсімдігін мәдени дақылға айналдыруды меңгере бастайды. Бұл үйретілген аттың негізгі қорегі. Оксфорд ғалымдары дәлелдегендей, қымыз ішуге арналған құмыра тостағандардың ішін зерделей сараптай отырып, дәл осы уақытта, көшпенді жауынгердің денесін масайрататын, рахатқа батыратын қымыз сусыны ойлап табылған. Біздің парасатты бабаларымыз қайнатылған биенің қымызында адамды мас ететін өнімнің жоғын, ал шикідей қымыз адамның жан рахаты екенін жақсы түсінген. Яғни ата-бабаларымыз барша мстық сезім бу арқылы шығып кететінін білді. Осыдан кейін алғашқы арақ жасайтын құралдар (самогон) пайда болды. Олар сонша қажетті түйіршіктерді бу ретінде жинап сақтап қалды. Тіпті осыған сәйкес атауын да қойды: "Көктің буын ал". Қымызды жылдың барша мезгілінде ішуге мүмкін болмайтындықтан, тек қана бие құлындаған кезде ғана ішу қымыз ішу мүмкіндігі болатындықтан, оның орнына басқа сусын ойлап табылды. Сұл ұнын жасап, одан брага арағын жасайтын. Ішімдік сусындары, Мұрат Аджи жазғандай, ішімдік сусындары Алтайлық бабаларымыздың темір, жүген, тері, кірпіш сынды заңды тұрғыдағы мәдени көрсеткішіміздің белгісі болып табылады.

Халықтардың ұлы көші орын алғанға дейін, жоғарыда атап өткенімдей, қазақ руы албандардың ата-бабалары б.з.д. YIII ғасырда Алтайдан Каспий теңізі жағасындағы алқаптарға келіп, Кавказдық Албанияны құрып, қоластындағы халықтарға Тәңір дінін уағыздады. Одан кейін тайпаның бір бөлігі Тигр мен Евфрат қос өзені жағалауына кетіп, Ахеменидтер әулеті бастаған ұлы Парсы мемлекетін құрды. Бұл патшалық әулетті құрған адамның аты Құрыш еді. Ол кейінірек Ұлы Кирге айналды. Құрыш қазақ тілінде –қатты, мықты мағынаны білдіреді. Қазақтың албан руланың ұлы ата-бабасы осындай мықты болатын. Барыс-парсы тотемі осы жаққа келген халықтың тамғасына айналады. Кавказдық Албанияны басқаша Арран деп те атап жүр. Түркі тілінен аударғанда "қасиетті" деген ұғымды білдіреді. Ұлы Парсы мемлекетін Алтайдан келген көшпенділер құрғанын ағылшын зерттеушісі Мэри Бойс та мойындайды. Ол өзінің "Зороастрийцы. Верования и обычаи" (Москва, 1987) атты кітабында: "Көне замандарда Жайық өзенінің шығыс жағалауында оңтүстік орыс алқаптарында мал бағып, тауда қару жарақ әзірлеген, Орта Азияда, әсіресе Алтайдың алқаптарында танымал болған протоирандықтар туралы жазады..." Онда бұған Шотландияның вискиінің не қатысы бар? –деп сұрағысы келетін шығар шыдамсыз оқырман. Яғни бар мәселе мынада: заманымыздың басында ғұндар Каспий жағалауы алқаптарына келген соң, қазақ албандарының бабалары Батысқа қарай жол тартады. Қазіргі Испанияда Барыс халқы Барселонаның (Барыс елі) негізін қалап, Ла Манш бұғазы арқылы өтіп, жаңа Отандарын Тұмандаы Альбион деп атайды. Сонымен бірге Мәңгілік көк аспан иесі Тәңір дініне сыйынатын келімсек дін өкілдері осы аралға жайғасқан соң, қазіргі Шотландия жерінде бұрынғы Каспий аймағында қалған өздерінің байырғы ата мекендерін еске алып, өз аралдарына Арран (Кавказдық Албания) деген ат қояды. Бұл ел осыдан кейін вискиді шығарған елге айналады. Қазіргі күннің өзінде археологтар Арран үңгірінің қабырғаларынан түркі руналары үлгісінде жазылған жазбаларды табуда. Сонымен бірге, алтайлық дәстүр үлгісі бойынша адамды жылқысымен бірге жерлеу рәсімі жасалған зираттары ұшырастыруда. Сонымен бірге басқа да көптеген дәйектер табылуда, Осы арқылы бұл аралдың шынайы иесі кім болғандығын болжай беріңіз.

Олардың бұрынғы қонысы Солтүстік Кавказда Арран деген мемлекет болғандығы жөнінде араб тарихшысы Ибн әл-Асир өзінің "Алтын Орда тарихына қатысты құжаттар жинағында" ("История Казахстана в арабских источниках" 1-том, Алматы, "Дайк Пресс", 2005) келтірген. Мәселен, монғолдардың 1221 жылдың жазында Мәуеннахрға жасаған шабуылын сипаттай отырып, былай деп жазады: Оны жөнге салып (Байлақан) барша жерді және оның маңын тонап, Ганджа қаласына жол тартты. Ал бұл - Арран өлкесінің негізгі қалаларының бірі. Бірақ олардың тұрғындар санының көптігін және олардың грузиндермен шайқастағы өжеттілігі мен батылдықтары туралы естіп, бұл қалаға баруға дәрмендері жетпеді, керісінше, тұрғындарына "ақша мен киім кешек беріңдер"-деген талап қойды..."

Егер кімде кім Англиядағы Шекспир мұражайын тамашаласа, онда тағы бір ерекше жәдігер –баланың бесігіне көз салған шығар. Тұманды Альбион аралдарына Бесіктің қалай барғандығы осы сұрақтарыма толық жауап береді деген ойдамын.

# Меотида, Митанни, Мидия.
## Матайдан келген Інжіл

Өзімнің "Шыңғысханның түркілік ғұмырнамасы. Қазіргі қазақтардың киелі шежіресі" атты кітабымда кейбір құжаттық деректерге сәйкес, "бұрынғы Меотия-қазіргі Азов теңізі жағалауында өмір сүрген көне меоттар қазіргі кезде қазақтың Матай руы ретінде жалғасын тапты" - деген батыл пікірімді білдірдім. Өзімнің болжамымды негіздей түсу үшін жаңа мәліметтер келтірейін. IV ғасырдағы антиктік философ тарихшы Евстафидің "Комментарий к "Землеописанию" Дионисия" ("Скифы", Москва, "Высшая школа", 1992) атты кітабында мынадай деректі кездестірдім: "Эвксиннен (Қара теңіз) солтүстік жақта Меотия көлі орналасқан. Скифтер осының маңын қоршаған. Жерлері осы аймақпен шектеледі,... Бірақ меоттар да скиф халқы болып есептеледі. Саны өте көп, күш қуаты жағынан басқа тайпалардан басым түседі, жер игеру мен және соғысумен айналысады. Меотиялық көлді олар Понттың (Қара теңіз-Қ.З.) анасы деп түсіндіреді. Яғни кейбірулердің пікірі бойынша, осыдан ол өзінің асыраушы деген - "mata" атауын иеленеді".

Осылайша Меотия көлінің сулары бұрын Киммерийлік Босфор деп аталған Керченск бұғазы арқылы өтіп, Қара теңізге келіп құяды. Сол себепті осы көл Меотия - яғни асыраушы деп аталып кеткен. Осыған сәйкес осы көлдің маңын мекендеген скиф халқы өздерін матай немесе меоттар деп атаған –"асыраушылар". Көне арийлердің айтуына қарағанда (Веда ілімінің санскриттік түсініктемесі): "Dyaur me Pita, Mata Prthivi iyam" – "Менің әкем –Аспан, менің анам – Жер". Мұнда "Mata" сөзі (грек транскрипциясында mata) асыраушы ана ұғымында қолданылады. Мысыр мифологиясында МААТ – ақиқат пен әділет тәңірі, күн тәңірі - Ра-ның қызы. Барша жер бетін асыраушы, қамқоршы тәңір. Кейбір деректерге сәйкес, о дүниеге кеткен адам Жер асты тәңірі - Осиристің қолына түскен соң, арнайы сынақтан өтеді, Осының нәтижесінде Осирис оны тозаққа немесе жұмаққа жіберітіндігін анықтайтын. Марқұмның жүрегі өлшеуіш таразыға салып өлшенетін, ал таразының екінші бөлігінде әділет тәңірі Мааттың бейнесі бейнелетін. Егер сыналушының жүрегі Маат тәңірінің бейнесінен жеңіл болса, онда ол жұмақтың қызығын көруге аттанатын. Осыған байланысты "таза жүрекпен өмір сүру" – рухани құлдырауға бой алдырмау –деген ұғым қалыптасқан.

Көріп отырғанымыздай, Евстафий меоттарды скифтік халықтар қатарына жатқызады. Б.з.д. I ғасырда өмір сүрген грек тарихшысы және жағрафияшысы өзінің "География" еңбегінің екінші кітабында былай деп жазады: Біріншіден, бұл жерлерде Гиркан теңізі мен Понт (Қара теңіз-Қ.З.) теңізі аралығында, Кавказға дейінгі жерлерді біріншіден, меоттар (савроматтар), сонан кейін ибер, албан, нақты айтқанда: савромат, скиф, ахейліктер тайпалары мекендейді...” Қазақтың меот-матай тайпасының арғы бабалары скиф немесе савроматтардың құрамына кірді ме, бұл біз үшін аса маңызды емес. Өйткені екі тайпа да қазақтың ата тегі болып табылады. Бірақ осы кезде мүлде басқа жағдай маңызды. Қазіргі заман тарихшыларының пікірі бойынша, ғайып болған скифтердің орнын савроматтар басқан. Бірақ сол заманда өмір сүріп, оқиғаларды көзімен көрген Страбон сөзі жалғастыруда: “Олардың оңтүстігінде, Меотиданың жоғарғы жағында шығыс скифтерінің тұрғылықты мекенінде савроматтар мен скиф тайпалары өмір сүреді...”

Қазақ матайларының өткен өмірі адамзат тарихындағы өркениеті әлдеқайда жоғары алғашқы Месопатамия мәдениетіне тығыз байланысты. Неміс ғалымдары ұжымы: Бригита Байер, Уве Бирнштайн, Беатрис Гельхофен, Эрнст Кристиан Шютт дайындаған “Адамзат тарихы” (ООО “Астрель” баспасы, 2002 жыл) еңбегінен қысқа мәліметтер келтірейін: Яғни, Орта Азиядан Месопотамияға көшпенді шумерлердің көшіп қоныстануы б.з.д. төртінші мыңжылдықта орын алған. Олар алғашқы қалаларды салып, жазу өнерін қалыптастырып, жоғары дәрежелі мәдениетті дамытты. Кейінірек б.з.д. 2340 жылға таман Орталық Азияда Аккад мемлекеті құрылады, бұл құрылымды 200 жылдан соң, көшпенді жауынгер халық куттея тайпасы жаулайды. Олар бұл аймақта 130 жылдай билік құрады.

Кейінірек бұл жерлерде Інжілде аморея деп аталатын эламит тайпасынан шыққан көшпенділер билік басына келеді.

Элам мемлекеті туралы айта келе, профессор Марат Барманқұлов өзінің “Тюркская вселенная” кітабында былай деп жазады: “б.з.д. үш мың жыл бұрын” осы аймақта әліпби қалыптасады. Осының негізінде табиғаты агглютинативті түркі тілдері пайда болады. Осы көне мемлекеттің тұрғындары түркі болмағанда кім болды екен сонда? Бүгінгі күндері эламиттердің ұрпақтары қазақ халқының Кіші жүз ішіндегі Әлімұлы тайпа одағы рулары арасында өмір сүреді”.

Б.з.д. 1531 жылы Месопотамияның оңтүстік бөлігі –Вавилон патшалығын хеттер жаулап алады, олар шамасымен б.з.д. 1900 жылы Кіші Азияға Каспий жағалауы маңы алқаптарынан келген. Хеттер Вавилонда ұзақ уақыт бойы билеп төстеген жоқ. Біраз уақыт өткен соң, саны олардан да көп, тарихта касситтер деген атпен белгілі көшпенділердің тағы да бір тайпасы “Дүниенің төрт бұрышы мемлекетін” 400 жылдай басқарады. Кейін Касситтер патшалығын көшпенділердің тағы бір легі – эламиттер өздеріне бағындырып алады. Хетте мемлекетінің құрылуымен қатар, Месопотамияда Миттани мемлекетінің іргетасы қаланады. Бұл мемлекет Таяу шығыста және Оңтүстік Шығыс Азияда өркениеттік даму тұрғысынан хеттердің нағыз бәсекелесіне айналды. Б.з.д. 1500-1000 жылдары Иран таулы қыратына көшпенділер бірінен соң бірі, леклегімен келіп жатты. Олар қазіргі Иран аймағы оның жанында жатқан елдерде Мидия мемлекетінің негізін салады. Осыдан кейін барып Парсы мемлекеті дүниеге келеді. Парсы мемлекетін шамасымен б.з.д. 550 жылдары ІІ ұлы Кир құрды.

Кейін б.з.д. 250 жылы Арсақ бастаған номада көшпенділердің бір тобы Иранда б.з.д. 224 жылға дейін үстемдік жүргізіп, биліп төстеген, Аршакидттер әулетінің негізін құрады. Б.з.д. ҮІІІ ғасырдаскифтер Қара теңіздің солтүстік жағалауынан өздеріне туыс болып келетін көшпенді тайпа –киммерийліктердің жерін тартып алғандықтан, бұл тайпаға басқа жаққа қоныс аударуға тура келеді. Киммерийліктер "Скифиядан қуғындалған" тайпаға айналып, Кіші Азиялық Лидия мемлекетінен пана тауып, Мидиямен одақтасып, Ассирияны талқандауға көмектеседі (б.з.д. 625 жыл).

Сілтеме жасалған дерек көзіне сүйне отырып, Еуразия алқабынан келген көшпенді тайпалардың Мысыр, Месопотамия, Парсы жерін жаулап алуы сынды мысалдарды әлі де келтіре беруге болады. Скифтердің жойқын шабуылынан туындаған ойран мен қан сойқан жайлы Иеремия пайғамбардың "Ветхий завет" атты кітабында келтіріледі: "Мен сендерге қарсы, өте күшті ежелгі халықтарды алып келемін. Олардың қорамсағынан өлімнің иісі шығады, бұл халықтар өте өжет, әрі батыл болып келеді. Егіндеріңді ойран етіп, нандарыңды асап жейді, ұлдарыңды-құл, қыздарыңды-күң етеді. Сиырларың мен қасқырларыңа дейін жеп қояды... Алынбастай берік қамалдарыңды қылыштарымен тас талқан етеді..."

Исмагулов-Байжумин теориясына сәйкес, осы екі мың жылдықтың ішінде өздерінен әлдеқайда күшті қуатты тайпалардың қысымымен Еуразиялық көшпенділер өздеріне көшіп қоныстанатын жайлы, нұрлы жер іздеп, Таяу Шығыс пен Оңтүстік-Шығыс Азия елдерінің отырықшы халықтарын өздеріне бағындырады. Кутей-хеттер қазіргі кезеңде қазақтың ішіндегі найман-алшын (қытай мен кете рулары), эламиттер - Кіші жүздегі Әлімұлы тайпалық бірлестігі ретінде жалғасын тапты. Касситтер - шамасы, ғалымдардың болжамы бойынша қазіргі қазақ халқына өзінің этникалық атын мұра ретінде қалдырып кеткен көне тайпа. Б.з.д. 1750 жылы түркі, қазақ тайпалары мекендейтін Еуразия алқаптарынан, Солтүстік Кавказ аймағынан өтіп, касситтер Месопотамия жеріне жетеді. Қандаша көсем бастаған касситтер Вавилонға басып кіреді. Қазақтың қасқыр мен мен ит сөзінің атауы –парсы тілінде "сақ" деп естіледі. Сол себепті "кассит" және "кассак" лексемалары бір мағынадағы семантикалық ұғымды білдіреді. Академик А.Бернштамның пікірі бойынша, ас-қас және сақ (бөрі халқы) тайпасының одағы нәтижесінде кассак сөзі - қазақ сөзіне трансформацияланады. Қазақ халқының атауы осы кезеңдерде пайда болады. Қытайлықтар қазақтардың ата-бабаларын "хассактар"-деп атағанын еске салайын. Кейінірек, қазақтардың аққу мен қасқырдан –қаз + сақ. пайда болғандығы жөніндегі аңызға тоқталғанда, бұл мәселеге әлі ораламын.

Ресей зерттеушісі А.Абрашкин "Скифтік Русь" атты кітабында митанниялықтар мен мидиялықтар меоттардың ұрпағы деген тұжырым тұжырым жасайды. Осы тайпалар қазіргі халқының ішінде Матай руы ретінде жалғасын тапты.

Мидияны сол кезеңдерде Түркі тайпалары мекендеген деген жанама пікірді б.з.д. екінші ғасырда өмір сүрген көне грек тарихшысы Полибий өзінің "Всеобщая история" ("История Казахстана в произведениях античных авторов", "Фолиант" баспасы, Астана, 1-том, 2005 жыл) атты кітабында келтіреді. Оныншы кітабында былай деп жазады: "...Мидия - Азиядағы таңғажайып мемлекет. Аймағы да кең, халқы да көп, мінетін жылқылары да асыл тұқымды-тұлпарлар. Мидия өз жылқыларымен барша Азияны қамтамасыз етіп отыр. Тіпті патшалардың үйір-үйір жылқылары да Мидиялықтарға сеніп тапсырылып, үндістандық шұрайлы жерлердегі оттықтарда семірту мақсатында бақтырылады... " Ұлы даланың көшпенділері –қазақтың ата-бабалары осындай керемет асыл тұқымды жылқыларды өсіріп бағу өнерімен барша әлемге әйгіленді.

Он томдық "Всемирная история" (Москва.1956, 1, 2 - том ) кітабында мидиялық тайпаның IX ғасырдан бері белгілі екендігін және Олардың Алдыңғы Азияға Солтүстік Кавказ бен Орта Азия аймағынан қоныс аударғандығы туралы" жазылады. Зерттеушілердің мәліметіне сәйкес, олар Меотия (Матай) көлі жағалауын мекендеген және сармат халқының негізгі бөлігін құраған. Кейінірек мидиялықтар өздеріне туыстас кутий және касситтерді қосып алып, қазіргі замандағы Иран, Армян тауы, Солтүстік Месопатамия және Кіші Азияның шығыс аймағын билеп, өте қуатты мемлекет құрады. Мидиялықтар парсылардың туыстары болатын, олардың ауызекі сөйлеу тілі бір, тіпті салт дәстүрлеріне дейін ұқсас еді. Кейінгі тарауларда Ұлы Парсы елінің негізіні салушылардың арғы тегі скифтер екендігіне дәйекті дәлелдер келтіреміз. Мидия мемлекетінің ішінде Экбатана (Көкбота) және Газак қалалары ерекше сұлулығымен көзге түсті.

Шумерлердің түбі түркі тектес екендігіне бұл кітапта бірнеше рет тоқталып өттім. Ал скифтердің киммериялықтарды қуып, оларды б.з.д УІІІ ғасырда Кіші Азия аймағында соңына түсуіне келсек, "Адамзат тарихының" авторлары бұл деректерді Геродоттан алған. Бірақ А.Абрашкин жазғандай кейде Геродоттың пікірлері бір-біріне қарама-қайшы болып келеді. Тарихтың атасы киммериялықтар Кіші Азияға Қара теңіз жағалауымен жол тартты десе, оларды қуғындаушы скифтер – Каспий теңізі жағалауымен ізіне түсті дейді. Бұл қашқандар мен олардың соңына түскен тайпалардың жүрген жол бағытына ұқсамайды. Ресейлік ғалым дұрыс қорытындыға келгендей, скифтер мен киммериялықтардың туыстас халықтары Месопотамия мен Кіші Азияға билік жүргізудің өзара ортақ міндеттерін шешуге күш салды. Б.з.д. XII ғасырда Кіші Азияға билік орнатқан хеттер, Батыс

Қытайға жол тартып, аспанасты елінде билік орнатуға өздеріне туыс болып келетін тайпаларға көмектесуге аттанады. Батыс Чжоу әулеті осылайша өмірге келген.

Көптеген қазақ рулары барысты өз тотемі деп санаған және бүгінгі таңда барыстың қазақ өркениетінің гүлденуі мен өркендеуінің символына айналуы кездейсоқ емес. Ал Қазақстанның оңтүстік астанасы –Алматы қаласы барысты өзінің таңбасы етіп белгіледі.

Ежелгі Миттани мемлекетіне келсек, кейбір зерттеушілердің деректеріне сәйкес, осы елді қазіргі күрдтердің арғы тегі хурритер мекендеген. Бірақ біздің зерттеуімізге сәйкес, Қытай, Парсы елі, Мысыр және еуропаның автохонды байырғы тұрғындарын көптеген ғасырлар бойы біздің ата-бабаларымыз басқарып келген. Сол себепті қазақтың арғы тегінің Миттанидегі курд-хурриттерді басқаруы ғажап емес. Әйтседе, көп ұлтты мемлекеттің негізгі құрамы Еуразия алқаптарынан шыққан арийлер – яғни, қазіргі қазақ руларының арғы тегінен қалыптасты. Оның үстіне Миттания патшаларының әскери гвардиясы марей-аморей тайпаларынан жасақталды. Тура осы марлар, кейін тоқталып өтеміз, түркі көшпенділердің ата-бабалары болып табылғандығы аян. Аморейлер – біз жоғарыда айтып өткендей, Інжілде эламит деген атпен кездеседі. Олардың ұрпақтары қазіргі кезеңде қазақтың Әлімұлы тайпасы құрамында өмір сүруде.

Қара теңіз жағалауы алқаптарында өмір сүрген меот-матайлардың атамекендерін кейінірек, б.з. 4-7 ғасырында оларға туыс болып келетін булгар тайпасы жайлап, Ұлы Булгария мемлекетін құрады. Булгар ханы Кубрат дүние салған соң, оның үш ұлы күш қуатына мінген түркі хазарларының ықпалымен үш жаққа кетеді: Аспарух Дунайға бет алып, Дунай маңындағы автохонды тұрғындарын бағындырып, қазіргі Болгарияның негізін салады, ортаншы ұлы Қотырақ Қама өзені бойында Волга бойы Булгария мемлекетінің іргетасын орнатады, ал кенже ұлы Ботбай Қазақстанның оңтүстігіне бет алып, қазақтың ірі тайпасының арғы атасы атанады. Булгар-ботбайлар Фанагория (қазіргі Тамань) деген астанасы бар мемлекетте Азов теңізі жағалауы алқаптары аймағында өмір сүрді. Булгар хандығының құрамында, қазақтың ботбайынан басқа, көптеген шағын қазақ рулары болды. Негізінде, Кіші жүздің Тама руы да енді, осы ру Таман түбегіне өзінің есімдерін қояды.

Болгар-булгарлар халқының атаулары қазақтың Балғалы руына байланысты аталып кетті, Бұл ру қазіргі кезеңде қазақ ішіндегі жалайыр тайпасының құрамына кіреді. Дәл осы ру Волга өзенінде өздерінің сансыз көп үйір-үйір жылқыларын бағып, бұл өзенге өзінің Балға-Волга деген есімін береді.

Қазақтың Ботпай руының ұлылығы туралы қазақ халқының мақалынан кездестіреміз: "Үйсін болсаң, Ботбай бол. Алшын болсаң - Адай бол, Арғын болсаң - Алтай бол, Найман болсаң - Матай бол" деген даналығы осы сөзімізге айқын дәлел.

Біздің қандасымыз, әйгілі, көрнекті академик, антрополог ғалым Оразақ Исмағұловтың ашқан жаңалығы мен үшін үлкен қолдау болып табылды. Ғалым б.з.д. екі мың жыл бұрын Қазақстан аумағында, Каспий және Қара теңіз жағалауы аймағын қосқанда, осы өлкелерді қазіргі таңда өмір сүретін тайпалар мен рулардың ата-бабалары мекендеген деген айқын пікірді дәлелдеп шығады. Шамасы осы жерде көне ықылым замандарда ата-бабаларымыз басқа этникалық атаулармен өмір сүрген шығар. Бірлестіктердің аттары өзгеріп, жаңа одақтар ыдырап, қайта құрылса да, қазақ рулары бөлінбейтін атом сынды өз жерінде көне замандардан бері өмір сүріп келеді. Тарихтың кейбір кезеңдерінде белгілі бір міндеттерді, саяси өзекті мәселелерді шешу мақсатында олар өзара одақ құрып, басқа да байланыстарға түсіп, тайпалық бірлестіктерге енді, бұл бірлестіктер мен одақтар тарихи тұрғыда ыдырағанмен, бірақ әр ру өз-өзін сақтап қала білді. Қазақтың рулары сақ, сармат, ғұн, түркі, моңғол одақтарын құрып, уақыт өте келе ғайып болатын, ал қазақ рулары әрқашан ғұмырын жалғастыра беретін. Қазіргі таңда, әлемдік энциклопедияларда Орталық Азияның көшпенділері мен Еуразиялық алқаптарынан келген басқа тайпалар белгілі бір кезеңде, мәселен, Мысыр, Парсы елі, Қытай аймағына келіп, нақты бір өркениеттердің негізін қалады, -деп жазса, онда олар міндетті түрде қазақтың арғы тегі болғандығы – академик Исмагулов теориясының негізгі мазмұны осында жатыр.

Тағы да бір рет атап өтейін, көне Алшындар қазіргі кезде қазақтың Кіші жүздегі руларының құрамына енген. Б.з.д. екінші мыңжылдықтың Орталық Азиядағы жоғарғы Месопотамия өлкесінде Алзи мемлекетінің негізін құрған еді – осыдан – алазон, қазақтың алшын және т.б. сөздері тараған. Б.з.д. екі мыңыншы жылдықтың ортасында өмір сүрген және "Авеста" кітабында аттары "дахи", Страбонда-даи деп айтылатын тайпа, Каспий теңізінің шығыс жағалауында және Түрікменстанның оңтүстігін мекендеген қазіргі Адай тайпасы екендігі сөзсіз. Мұрат Аджидің пікірі бойынша, ирандық ахеменид және аршакид тайпалар құрамына дахи-даи тайпалары да енген. "Всемирная энциклопедия": Энциклопедический словарь (Москва, изд-о "Эксмо" 2003) кітабында гет-готтар туралы дак-дайларға туыс болып келетін фракийлік тайпалардың солтүстік тобы делінеді. Олар б.з.д Ү ғасырда Румыния және Болгария аймағын мекендеген. Парсылық патша Дарий (б.з.д. 513 жыл) скифтерге қарсы жорыққа шыққанда, геттер мен дахтар скифтерге қолдау көрсетеді. Олар өзара одақтаса отырып, Александр Македонскийге де қарсы соғысады.

Біздің хеттерге оралайық. Бүгінгі таңда кете руы қытай руы деген құрылым ретінде Найман тайпасы одағының Төлегетай бірлестігіне енеді, ал оның шағын бөлігі

Кіші жүздің Әлімұлы құрамында жеке дербес ру ретінде өмір сүреді. Шамасы көне замандарда хет-кете-матайлар өзара жақын туыс болған. Мәселен б.з. 15 жылы түркі тектес герман тайпасының өкілі Германикті римдіктер өзіне әскери қызметке шақырғанда, германдық хатта тайпасымен шайқас нәтижесінде олардың Маттий қаласын қолына түсіреді (Бодо Харенбергтің "Адамзат хроникасында" Мәскеу, "Слово-Slovo" баспасы, 2000 жыл, осылай жазылады). Герман тайпасының негізін құраған Хатты-хетты-кете тайпасы астаналарын өздерінің халықтарының байырғы атауы – "Матай" атауымен атаған -деп, болжауға болады.

Інжілге сәйкес, Нұх пайғамбардың немересі, Яфеттің ұлы Мадай болатын. Кейбір финдік басылымдарда: "Евангелие от Матфея" –бұл тарихи шығарманы "Матайдан келген Евангелие "-деп атап жүр. Иосиф Флавий өзінің "Иудейские древности" еңбегінде: Яфеттің ұлы Мададан мадейлер тараған, оларды эллиндер "мидяндар" – деп атаған деп көрсетеді. Деректерге сәйкес, апостол Матвей – сәйкесті түрде Матай, аманат бойынша, Ыстық көл жағалауы маңында жерленген. Інжіл мен Әбілғазының "Родословная" ("Түркістан" баспасы, КФМУ, 1996) еңбегіне сәйкес, Мадайдың бауырлары Түрік, Хазар, Оғыз, Қимар, Рус, Чин және басқалары еді.

Рустан қазіргі заманғы орыстар тарады деп ойлаймын. Ал Қимардан –киммерийліктер, Чиннен-солтүстік қытайлар, оғыз, түркі және хазарлар да дәл осындай жолмен өсіп өнген. Найман тайпасы одағы руларының жеке дара тұрғандығын атап өтейік.

Түркі халықтарымен қатар бірге дүниеге келген көне заманғы Матай руынан басқа, бұл елдің қатарына маньчжурлар-жүржіндер (терістамғалы тайпалық одағы құрамындағы шүршіт руы), сонымен бірге, Солтүстік Қытайда Ляо әулетін орнатқан хетт-кете, көптеген қытандар да енді.

Жуырда өзімнің ДНК-тестімді (Матай руының ұрпағымын) өткіздім, американдық зертхана қолыма сертификат ұстатты: осыған сәйкес, менің анам жағынан ата-бабаларым Германия, Испания, Италия және Таяу шығыста өмір сүрген екен.

***

Байқап отырғанымыздай, қазақтың қазіргі матай және кете рулары көне замандарда бір-біріне ең жақын туыстық қарым қатынаста болып келуі мүмкін еді. Қазақтың арғын және найман руы туралы да осылай айтсақ, қателеспейміз. Ш.Қуанғанов өзінің "Арий-гунн сквозь века и пространство: свидетельства, топонимы" (ИКФ "Фолиант, Астана, 2001 жыл") еңбегінде б.з.д бірінші мыңжылдықта біздің ата-бабамыз Қара және Азов теңізі акваториясында құрған Боспор патшалығы туралы сөз қозғай келе, Синд кемежайы (қазіргі Анапа қаласы) синд тайпасын, Арғынның ірі Сүйіндік руымен байланыстырады. Боспор патшалығының барша билеушілері бүкіл Синд және Меоттардың архонт, басилевс атағын иеленгендігін атап өтейін. Мәселен, б.з.д. 349-344 жылдары билік жүргізген Левконның ұлы, II-Спарток, Боспор мен Феодосия архонты, барша Синд және Меоттардың басилевсі.

Сол кезеңдері Синдтер тайпасы Меоттар ( Матай) тайпасы одағына кіретін.

Тағы да бір Матай-Ботбай руларын қарастырайық. Алғашқысы қазақтың Орта жүзіне енсе, ал екіншісі – Ұлы жүздің құрамында. Бұл тайпалардың қазіргі мекендейтін аймақтары әртүрлі. Оның үстіне Матайлар Найман тайпасы одағы құрамында, ал Ботбайлар Дулаттардың ішінде. "Зеленуг жазбасына" сүйене отырып, Ботбайлардың Дулат тайпасы құрамына ену қолдан жасалған, жасандылұғ деп атап өттім. Ал іс жүзінде Матай мен Ботбай руларының өзара жақын туыс болғандығын дәлелдеуге күш саламын.

Қазақтар бөріні әртүрлі аттармен атайды: қасқыр, саққұлақ, көкжал, иткұс, бөрі,басқұрт және тағысын тағы. Осыған сәйкес матайлар мен садырлар өздері тұрған аймақтарға әртүрлі атаулар қойған.

Мәселен, Волга өзені, (Еділ) кезінде Итиль деп аталды – (Ит елі-бөрі халқы)  осы аймақтың жағалауын мекендеген   матай мен садыр руларының құрметіне орай осы атауға ие болған. Ал Днепр-Борисфен деп аталған. Мсніңше, бұл Борисфен сөзі - "бөрі өзен" ұғымын білдіреді. Яғни "Бөрі руының өзені". Мен өз кітабымда Волга (Итиль) өзені кейінірек осы өзен жағалауын мекендеген Жалайыр тайпасынан шыққан Балғалы руының құрметіне осы рудың атымен аталып кеткендігін нақты түрде дәйектедім. Яғни сөздік қор бірте-бірте: Балға-Болга-Волга болып ауысқан. Ал Балтық теңізі, өз атауын осы теңіздің жағалауында б.з.д. 5-6 ғасырларда өмір сүрген қазақтың ірі Балталы атты руынан алған. Менің бұл көзқарасымды ғалым Ю.Н.Дроздов қолдайды, ол өзінің жоғарыда бірнеше рет сілтеме жасалған кітабының 196-бетінде былай деп жазады: "Көне еуропа халықтары өз аймақтарын рельефтік ландшафтық белгілерге қарай емес, осы аймақты мекендеген тайпаның этнониміне сәйкес атаған (бірақ керісінше емес)..."

Қазақстанның Жамбыл облысы аймағы бойынша ағып өтетін Аспара өзенінің этимологиясы да қызықты. Қазақтың ірі жазушысы Қалихан Ысқақовтың пікірі бойынша, Дунайдағы болгар патшалығының негізін салған Аспарух ханның есімі мен осы өзеннің атауы іс жүзінде, "аш бөрі" ұғымын білдіретін ауыспалы тіркес.Яғни бұл контекстке сәйкес, Аспара - аш бөрінің өзені болса, ал болгар ханы –Аспархан – Аш Бөріхан деп түсіндіріледі. Яғни, қайтадан бөрі халқы мәселесіне келіп ораламыз. Сонда Кубраттың ұлдарының бірі, меот-матайлардың ата мекеніндегі Меотида жағалауында (Азов теңізі) Фанагория атты астанасы орналасқан ұлы Булгарияның ханы,  Аспарух ханның  туған бауыры Ботбайдың Матай атты тайпалық бірлестікке қатысы болғаны ғой. Қазіргі шежіреге сәйкес, Ботбай руы Дулат тайпасы одағы құрамына кіреді, X ғасырдағы "Зеленчуг жазбасына" сәйкес, ботбай және дулаттар –қазақ халқының жеке дербес және теңдес рулары болып табылады.

Сонымен бірге, мееот-матай мен волга булгарлары, жалпы айтқанда, ботбайлардың мекендеген жері-Азов жағалауы маңы осы тайпаларға ортақ, сол себепті, волга бойы булгарларының бөрі халқына, яғни – қазіргі матай және садырларға туыстық қатысы бар екендігі туралы болжам жасауға болады. Осының нәтижесінде, қазіргі шежіре бойынша, Матай мен Ботбай екі түрлі Жүзге жатса да, дегенмен олардың арасындағы байырғы туыстық қарым қатынас осылайша анықталады. Бұл жорамалды қазақтың Найман тайпасы арасында тараған көне аңыз да дәлелдейді. Осы аңыз бойынша, көптеген соғыстардың нәтижесінде Найман бабамыздың ерлер жағынан бірде мұрагері қалмайды. Оның келіні Дулат руынан шыққан ақылды әйел еді. Ол да Найман руына жоғалу қаупі төнгендігіне уайымдай бастайды. Бір күні таңертең ол еріксіз түрде қайын атасының кіші дәрет сындырғанын байқап қалады. Ақ көбік пен жердегі ойысты көріп, қайын атасының қартайған шағы -85 жасқа қарамастан, әлі бала сүю мүмкіндігі бар екендігін біледі. Өзінің төркіні-Дулаттарға жолығып, ақсақалдар кеңесінде, Найман руының жоғалып кетуге жақын екендігі туралы әңгімені айтады. Өз туыстарының көмегімен қайын атасы Найманға бөле сіңлісін айттырып, одан кейін екі ұл туады. Сүйінші және Сүгірші. Сүйінші 14 жасқа толған кезде, оған тұрмысқа шығып, дүниеге көп ұл әкеліп, осылайша Найман руын жоғалудан сақтап қалады. Сондай-ақ, Қалихан Ысқақов түркі жазбаларының орхон-енесайлық ескерткіштерінде жазылған тағы бір этнонимді талдап, анықтап шыққан: дәлірек айтқанда, Күлтегінге арналған тастағы түркі жауынгерлерін қытай қалаларын жаулап алған соң, нәпсіқұмарлыққа беріліп, рахатқа батудан сақтандыратын жазуға сәйкес, мынадай өсиет жазылыпты: "О, түркі халқы, егер де бұл жерге тұрақтасаңдар (Қытай жеріне-Қ.З.), құрдымға кетулерің мүмкін. Егер де сен Отүкен жерінде тұрып, салық жинап, сыйлықтар алу үшін керуен жіберсең, онда уайымның арта қалғаны. Өзіңнің мәңгілік мемлекетіңді сақтап ғұмыр кеше бер..."

Қазіргі кезеңде Қара қорым деп аталатын Отүкен жері түркі қағандарының ордасы болатын. Ал бұл сөздің этимологиясы-шығу төркіні мынадай: "Оты кең" – кең шаңырақ, туған жер, немесе ошақ деген ұғымды білдіреді. Меніңше, орыс тіліне аударғандағы "Отюкенская чернь" сөзі өте сәтсіз шыққан. Өйткені қазақтың қара сөзі бірнеше мағынада қолданылады. Бір ретте қара ұғымы болса, ал келесі мағынада-көпшілік, ұлы, күшті және қуатты дегенді білдіреді. Бұл сөзді "Отюкенская чернь" деп емес, "великий, могучий Оты кең"- күшті-қуатты туған шаңырақ деп аударған жөн болар еді.

# Этрускі, баскілер. Рим және Итеⅼⅰ.

## Жұмбақ болып келе жатқан этрускі халқы туралы не айта аламыз?

Олардың арғы тегі: тирсен, тавр, турлар (тигрсен –турдың балалары деген мағынада, тавр грек тілінде- тур дегенді білдіреді – бұлардың барлығы оғыздар) Кіші Азияға Каспий жағалауы маңы алқаптарынан шамасымен б.з.д II мыңжылдықта көшіп келіп, Лидия мемлекетінде өмір сүрген. О.Исмагуловтың ашқан жаңалығына сәйкес, олар біздің бабаларымыз болып табылады.

Ойымызды одан әрі жалғастырайық. Троя соғысы басталмас бұрын, (Троя Оғыз-Турдың қасиетті бұқаның қаласы дегенді білдіреді) Кіші Азия аймағынан Аппенин түбегіне Сицилияның билеушісі Итал (Итеⅼі) келіп қоныстанады.

Кейінірек оның аты осы Италия елінің этнониміне айналды. Троя соғысы біткен соң (б.з.д. 1260 жыл), Аппенин түбегіне Лидиядан тирсендер тайпасы көшіп келіп, қазіргі Италия аймағында Этрурия елінің негізін құрады. Шамасы олар жеті тайпа (оғыз бсн ссирлер) болған да шығар және олар өздерін Жетіру деп атайтын. 18 ғасыр тарихында тура осындай жағдай Қазақстанда да орын алған еді. Шыңғысханға туыс болып келетін саны жағынан аз жеті рудың басын қосып, оларды үлкен тайпа одағына біріктіріп, осы бірлестікті Тәуке хан Жетіру деп атайды.

Этрускі  этнонимінің басқаша болжамын А.Абрашкин өзінің "Скифтік Русь" кітабында келтіреді. Оның мәліметтеріне сәйкес, б.з.д. екі мың жыл бұрын Жерорта теңізінде арийлер құрған Русена мемлекеті өмір сүрген. Бұл ел Мысыр мен Ұлы Хетт мемлекетінің оратсында орналасты. Әйгілі, көрнекті тарихшылар: Н.Карамзин мен В.Татишевтің еңбектеріне сүйеніп, ғалым Русь тарихының Рюрик, Киевтік Русыⅼен емес, одан да көне дәуірлерде басталғандығы туралы пікірін айтады.

Трояндық соғис аяқталған соң, русен және хеттердің бір бөлігі Аппенин түбегіне хэтрус деген атпен жол тартады. Сондай-ақ "Ан-хан", "Ер-Хер" лексикалық жұп тіркесін талдағандай, "хэтрускілер" этнонимі бірте-бірте қазіргі заманғы Италия жерінде "Этрускі" этнонимі болып трансформациялынып, өзгеріске ұшыраған.

Этрускілердің пайда болуы жайында Ю.Н.Дроздов та осындай пікірді айтады. Ол этрускілердің жеке өзіндік атауы "расен" болған деп жазады. Ол сөздерді жеке түбірлерге бөлу әдістемесі арқылы, расендер этнонимі түркі тілінен аударғанда – "асс ерлерінің руы" деген ұғымды білдіреді деген пікірге келеді.

Римдіктер этрускілерді "тускілер" деп атаған. Тоскана провинциясы атының шығу тегі осындай. Бұл аймаққа о баста Кіші Азиядан келген хетрус-этрускілер келіп орналасады. Осы аймаққа қоныс аударғандар өздерінің қонақжайлы жаңа Отандарын "Апа-Ене" деп атап кетеді. Ш.Қуанғановтың жорамалы бойынша, Аппенин этнонимі осыдан туындаған.

Ойымызды жалғастырайық. Б.з.д. 8 ғасырда этрускілер Ұлы Римнің іргетасын қалап, Римнің негізін қалаған Ромул мен Рэмді асырап емізген қасиетті қасқырға арнап ескерткіш орнатады. Этрускілермен бірге Аппенин түбегінде галлдар тайпасы өмір сүрген. Олар да қазіргі Францияның жергілікті тұрғындарына айналады. Юлий Цезарь өзінің "Галл соғысы туралы жазбаларында" (СПб,1998 жыл) галлдарды –галл деп римдіктер атағанын, ал олоардың шынайы аты кельт болғандығы туралы жазады. Бұл тайпа, алдында аталып өткендей - тегі түркі халық.

"Италия" этнонимі – "Ителі" деген ұғымды білдіреді. Ал қазақтарда бөріден тараған рулар болып матай мен садыр ғана есептеледі. Қасқырдың (үйретілгенге дейінгі) о бастағы этнонимі "итқұс" еді. Қасқыр кең даланың падиша, қожайыны, ал барыс-таудың иесі. Сол себепті біздің ата-бабаларымыз - матай мен албандар бұл жануарларды өздерінің тотемі ретінде қастерлейді. Аппенин түбегіне біздің рулардың тікелей түрде келуіне қазақтың ірі жазушысы және ақыны Олжас Сүлейменовтың Голлини ғибдатханасындағы жазба ескерткішті анықтай алғандығы да себін тигізді, саркофагтан жоғары жаққа қарай жазылған фрескада арбаға жегілген жылқылардың бейнесі салынып, "zalt ad aidas" жазуы жазылған. Бұл қазақ тіліне аударғанда: "ат айдаушы жатыр" деген ұғымды білдіреді. Бұл жазба мұра б.з.д. YІІІ ғасырға жатқызылады. "Италия" топонимін Мұрат Аджи сәл басқаша түсіндіреді. Ол Аппенин түбегіндегі мемлекеттің атты Римнің соңғы императоры Ромул Августулмен тікелей байланысты деп санайды. Бұл император Аттілінің діни қызметшісінің ұлы болып табылады, оны Римнің тағынан, аты аталып өткен жаңа Италияның ғұн королі Одоакр тайдырады.

"Ытала" түркі тілінде – "бас тартқан" деген ұғым. Ұлы Рим империясының мұрагерлігінен бас тартқан елдің атауы ретінде қабылданды. Жаңа атауға байланысты байырғы атаулар: ромейлер мемлекеті, Гесперия және т.б. этнонимдері қолданыстан шықты.

Бұл бәрі халқының топонимiне қатысты басқа болжам.

Этрускілердің бір бөлігі Пиреней түбегіне жол тартып, қазіргі Испанияда астанасы Бильбао деп аталатын баскілер елінің негізін құрады. Кейбір ғалымдадың әділ түрдегі пікірі бойынша, егер Италия этрускілердің бесігінде өсіп-өнсе, Испания –

баскілердің бесігінде өсіп жетілді. Баскілер Францияның оңтүстік-батыс бөлігіндгі Гаскония аймағын мекендеген. Бәлкім, атақты гаскондық сері Д`Артаньян немесе оның прототипінің бойында қазақтың қаны бар шығар. Ғалымдар баскілердің тілі Мексикадағы атабаскілер тіліне ұқсайтындығы туралы пікір айтады. Өзімнің "Шыңғысханның түркілік ғұмырнамасы" кітабымда Солтүстік Америка мен түркілердіңұрпақтары- қазіргі қазақтардың арасындағы туыстық қарым қатынастарды нақты түрде талдап салыстырдым. Баскілер мен атабаскілер арасындағы ұқсастық та көп айғаққа меңзейді. Атабаскі- үлкен, негізгі ру, ал баскі- одан тараған бір бұтағы.

Қазіргі қоғамда римдіктер- Еуропаның ұстаздары деген тұжырым қалыптасты. Міне, осыған сәйкес, қазақтың арғы тегі – этрускілер – Римнің ұстаздары болған деген тұжырымды заңды түрде айта аламыз.

# АЛБАНДЫҚ ПАРСЫ ЕЛІ ЖӘНЕ АДАЙЛЫҚ ПАРФИЯ. КҮЛТЕГІН МЕН ТҰМАР ХАНШАЙЫМ (ТОМИРИС) ГЕРОДОТ СКИФТЕР ЖАЙЫНДА

Бүгінгі албан, матай, адай және тағы басқа қазақ рулары жайында тағы бір айтып өтер жайт бар. Бұл туралы өз кітаптарында әйгілі түрколог Мурат Аджи жазып өтеді: б.з.д. 550 жылы II Кирдің тұсында дүниеге келген Парсы елі өзінің күш қуаты мен құдіреттілігі үшін Иран жеріне б.з.д. 10-15 ғасырда Еуразия аймағынан келген көшпенді түркі тайпалары: парсы, дах, мидия және басқа көшпенді тайпаларға алғыс айтуы керек деген пікір білдіреді.

Парсылар – ғалымдардың пікірі бойынша барыс этнонимін білдіреді, жоғарыда атап өткеніміздей, қазіргі заманғы беріш, албан және қазақтың басқа рулары. Дахтар – қазақтың адай руы екендігі сөзсіз, оларды Страбон біздің заманымызға дейінгі бірінші ғасырда скиф тайпасы деп атап көрсетеді. Мидийліктер, олар жайлы алдыңғы тарауларда сөз қозғадық, скифтік меот-майталардың ұрпақтары екені мәлім. Белгілі жайттарға сәйкес, б.з.д. 612 жылы Мидияны тегі Матай скифтік патша Мадийдің жауынгерлері кезекті түрде жаулап алады. Кейінірек Мидияның бір бөлігі Әзербайжанның құрамына өтеді, Мидиялықтардың арғы тегі түркілік оғыздар болып табылады. Олардың арасында қазіргі қазақ халқының өкілдері, соның ішінде Матайлар да бар.

Б.з.д. Y-IY ғасырда өмір сүрген грек грек тарихшысы Ксенофант өзінің "Кирдің тәрбиесі" атты кітабында былай деп жазады: "Кир мұрагерлік бойынша немесе басқа жолмен таққа келген патшалардан парасат жағынан әлдеқайда асып түсетін, дегенмен скиф ретінде, (өзім бөліп көрсеттім-Қ.З.) скифтер көп болса да, бірде бір тайпаны бағындыра алмай, өзінің тайпасымен ғана шектелер еді, ал Кир болса, керісінше барша тайпаларға үстемдік жүргізер еді".

Ксенофанттың осы еңбегінің үзіндісінен біз II Кирдің шыққан тегі скифтік деп тікелей түрде жариялай алмаймыз. Бірақ жанама дәлелдер мен айғақтар баршылық. II Ұлы Кирдің шығу тегі скифтік екендігі жөнінде I ғасырдағы римдік тарихшы Квинт Курций Руф баяндайды: ол өзінің "История Александра Великого Македонского" ("История Казахстана в произведениях античных авторов" 2-том, "Фолиант" баспасы, 2006 жыл еңбегін қараңыз)  атты кітапта Александр Македонскийдің бұйрығы бойынша, Кирдің зиратын қопарып, мәйітін қазып алуға бұйрық беріледі, бұл зиратта, Кирдің тат басып кеткен қалқаны мен екі скифтік садақ пен акинактан (қылыш) басқа ештеңе табылмайды. Парсылар патшасы II Ұлы Кирдің этникалық шығу тегі жайында Аммиан Марцелиан өзінің "Римская история" шығармасында атап өтеді. Оның сөздерін келтірейін: "Сол себепті парсылардың арғы тегі –скифтік болып табылады..." ("История Казахстана в произведениях античных авторов" 2-том, "Фолиант" баспасы, 2006 жыл, 242 бет.).

Бодо Харенбергтің "Дүниежүзілік энциклопедиясына" сәйкес, б.з.д. 224 жылы Арсақ патша Парфияның негізін салады, түрки тілінен аударғанда: патшаның есімі - "ары мен намысы бар сақ" деген ұғымды білдіреді. Ахеминид (II Кир) және Аршакидтердің шығу тегі түрки-қазақ екендігі туралы Иранның мемлекеттік мұражайында сақталатын парсылардың мөрі айғақтайды, бұл мөрде түрки руланаларына негізделген түрки руналары мен жазбасы бейнеленген.

ҮІ ғасырдағы остготтық тарихшы Иордан өзінің "О происхождениях и деяниях готов" атты шығармасында, король Танауизис бастаған геттердің Мысыр патшасы Весозиске қарсы шайқасын сипаттай келе, геттердің бұл шайқаста жеңіске жетіп, мысырлықтарды Нілге дейін қуығындағаны туралы айтып, былай деп тұжырымдайды: "Помпей Трогтың айтуына қарағанда олардың атаулары мен руларынан (готтардың-Қ.З.) кейіні парфийліктердің ұрпақтары тараған. Сол себепті оларды осы күнге дейін скиф тілінде "қашқындар немесе парфяндықтар" -деп атайды..." Ғалымның келтірген пікірі ақылға қонымды. Еуразия алқаптарынан өздерінен әлдеқайда күшті тайпалардың ықпалымен кезекті түрде "Скифиядан қуғындалғандар" легі қазіргі замандағы Иран аймағын қоныстанып, жаңа Отандарын "Парфия" деп атайды.

Кебір деректерге сәйкес, Аршахидтер әулетінің негізін салған I Аршак қазақ руы адайлардың арғы тегі - дах тайпасының көсемі болатын. Бұл ойымды көне римдік тарихшы Тациттің пікірі растайды. Ол өзінің "Анналы" кітабында  ("История

Казахстана в произведениях античных авторов" 2-том, "Фолиант" баспасы, 2006 жыл-кітабын қараңыз) былай деп жазады: "Олар тегі Арсакидтік, дахтардың арасында өскен Артабанды шақырды. Ол бастапқы шайқаста жеңіліс тапса да, жаңа күш жинап, Парфия патшалығын жаулап алады..." Шығармасының басқа жерінде былай деп келтіреді: "Скифияда жауыз болып өскен Артабанды қарғап сілегендер үшін бұл қуанышты жағдай еді... Скифтерді көмекке шақыру үшін қажетінше кідіріс жасай білді..." Помпей Трогтың өзі "Филипповские истории" атты еңбегінде Юстиннің қысқартуы бойынша, скифтер туралы айта келе, былай деп жазады: "Олардың өзі Парфия және Бактрия патшалықтарын құрды, парфийліктер мен бактриялықтардың ата-бабалары болып табылады..." ("Скифы", Хрестоматия, Москва "Высшая школа" баспасы, 1992 жыл, 249,251 бет).

Біз қазақтардың ата-бабалары Алдыңғы Азиядағы мемлекеттер: Парсы елі – қазақтың албан, Мидия-қазақтың матай, Парфияны- қазақтың адай руы құрып және басқарып-билегендігіне қатысты тікелей түрде дәйекті дәлелдерді жеткілікті тұрғыда келтірдік деп ойлаймын. Біз қазақтар Парсы патшасы ІІ Ұлы Кир, Мидия патшасы Киаксар, Парфия патшасы Арсакты өзіміздің ата-бабамыз деп атауға толық құқығымыз бар.

Риммен терезесі тең тұрған, Парфиялықтар мемлекетінің құдіреттілігі жөнінде көне грек философы Плутарх "Сравнительное жизнеописание" шығармасында атап өтеді, ол римдік қолбасшы және трибун Помпейге арнаған тарауында былай деп жазады: "Басқаларға жағыну үшін, Помпей парфян патшасына жазған жауап хатында сөзді басын басқалар айтатындай, оны патшалардың патшасы деп атауға нист стеді..."

Ал енді басқа мәселеге келейік.

Әйгілі аңыз бойынша түркі руларына тамғаларды Оғыз хан тарататын. Т.Досанов "Руниканың құпиялары" (Алматы, "Өлке" баспасы, 2009 жыл) шығармасында өзінің ашқан түркі руларының бүкіл тамғалары мен түркі әліпбиінің барша руналарын қамтыған тамғалар кестесінде Оғыз ханның тамғасы болуы керек деп дұрыс тұжырымдап, нәтижесінде ханның тамғасын да анықтаған.

Көк аспанды білдіретін    тамғасын ол "Көк" - "оғыз" – қалқаланған өзен ("уг"-көне түркі тілінде –қалқаланған, "уг"-өзен ұғымын білдіреді).  Бірақ – иероглифі – бұл қазақ халқының ішіндегі қазіргі адай руының тамғасы болып саналады. Адай мен Оғыз ханның дүниеге келуі жөнінде аңыздарды сараптай отырып, Т.Досанов Оғыз бен Адай бір адам деген ұғымға келеді. Білуімізше, Оғыз- Яфеттің ұлы.  Сол себепті де оның ұрпағы көп. Мәселен түркі қағанаттары дәуірінде көк түркілердің Аде, Адьйе тайпалары Баегу- Байұлы бірлестіктерімен бірге Екінші түркі қағанаты құлаған соң, Ұйғыр қағанатын құрған тоғыз-оғыздардың құрамына енген. Қазіргі ұйғырлардың Ұйғыр қағанатына еш қатысы жоқ, - деп есептейді Т.Досанов, өйткені олар руға бөлінбейді, сонымен бірге рулық тамғалары да жоқ. Т.Досановтан бұрын осы тұжырымды жасап кеткен профессор М.Барманқұлов жоғары аталып кеткен кітабында, көне ұйғыр тілі қазіргі заманғы ұйғыр тілінің негізі болып табылмайтындығын дәлелдейді. Сондықтан да қазіргі заман ұйғырларының Екінші түркі қағанатын басқарған, қытайлықтар хойху немесе хуйхэ деп атаған халыққа еш қатысы жоқ екендігі анықталды. Мұндай халықтарды қазақ халқы жеккөрінішті түрде сарт деп атайды, егер де көне түркілер қасқырдың ұрығынан тараса, сарттар қасқырдың сідігінен пайда болған-деген аңыз бар. Көне түркі қағандары Күлтегін мен Могилянның тегі Адай болып табылады, -деп Досанов, Н.Я.Бичурин еңбектеріне сілтеме жасайды. Әйгілі шығыстанушы ғалым В.В.Струве 1968 жылы жарық көрген "Этюды по истории Северного Причерномья, Кавказа и Средней Азии" атты еңбегінде дахи, даи, массагет, каспии және алан мен адай тайпаларының тегі бір екендігі туралы айтады, көне Вавилондық дін қызметкері Мардук Бероса жазбаларына сүйене отырып, парсылық патша II Ұлы Кир даи алқабында мәңгілік сапарға аттанып, келмеске кеткені туралы баяндайды. Яғни, осыған сәйкес, - деп ойын жалғастырады Т.Досанов, - "II Кирді талқандаған сақ массагеттер патшайымы Тұмар (Томирис) адай руының өкілі болып шығады". Ханшайымның ерлігі ұлы парсы патшасы I Дарийдің бұйрығы қазіргі Иран қаласы Хамадан жанындағы Бехистун қабырғасына бейнеленген. Адайлар негізінде Каспий теңізінің шығыс жағалауын мекендеген, аттары да әртүрлі: даи, парфи, алан және каспиилер.

Өзара ішкі қырғын тартыстардың салдарынан, осы халықтың бір бөлігі алан деген атпен Батысқа бет алса, тағы бір бөлігі- оңтүстікке Иран тауларына қарай жол тартты. Бұл жайында айтып өткенмін, Парфиялықтар мемлекетінің негізін салады. Даилар Балқанға аттанып, Ұлы Рим империясымен бәсекелеске түскен Дакия патшалығын құрады. Түркменстанға кетіп қалғандарды оғыздар деп атайды, ал Қазақстан аймағында қалып қойған тайпалар өздерінің этникалық тұрғыдағы Адай аттарын сақтап қалады.

Тарихтың атасы Геродот ата бабаларымыздың болмысы мен табиғатына сәйкес мінез сипаттамаларды анық, дәл бере білген. Ол өзінің "Тарих" кітабының IY томында былай деп жазады: "Бізге әйгілі халықтардың ішінде скифтер адамзат өміріндегі өте маңызды өнерге ие. Олар өз елдеріне шабуыл жасаған бірде-бір жаудың аман қалуына жол бермейді. Егер де абайсызда өздері қолға түсіп қалмаса, скифтерді ешкім соңынан қуып, жет алмайды. Скифтердің қалалары мен бекіністері жоқ қой. Өз үйлерін арбаға салып көшіп жүре береді. Олардың бәрі атқа қонған көкжал мерген садақшылар. Жер игерумен айналыспайды, тек мал бағады, киіз үйлерде тұрады. Мұндай халық жеңімпаз болмағанда қайтсін?"

Б.з.д. Ү ғасырда Ежелгі Грекияда өмір сүрген, осы елдің ұлы азаматы, тарихтың - атасы Геродот осындай қаһармандық мадақ жырын қазақ халқының бабаларына арнаған. Көп уақыт өткен соң, ғасырлар ширегінде (б.з.д I ғасыр –б.з. I ғасыры) римдік тарихшы Помпей Трог Ұлы Дала көшпенділері скифтердің мінез қасиеттері туралы былай дейді: "Әділеттілік ұғымын олар заңмен емес, ақыл санасымен түсінеді, Ұрлық-қарлық олардағы ең қатал қылмыстардың бірі болып саналады. Өз мүліктерін қорғамайтын, ірі қара және ұсақ малдарды бағатын халық ішінде ұрлыққа жол берілсе, онда олардың ормандарында не қалар еді? Жер бетіндегі басқа пенделер секілді алтын мен күміс көрсе, олар тура жолдан таймайды... Мұндай қанағатшылдық олардың бойында ар-абырой, яғни өзгенің мүлкіне қызғана қарамау сынды адамгершілік қасиеттерді қалыптастырды... Жер бетіндегі пенделердің бәрі біреудің мүлкіне қол сұқпайтын болса ғой! Таңқалатыны: гректер өз философтары және данышпандары, ғылым-білім арқылы ұзақ сонар жолмен, аталмыш руханиятқа қол жеткізе алмай тұрғанда, табиғаттың өзі көшпенділердің бойына жоғары дәрежелі адамгершілік қасиеттерді ұялатқан. Қараңғы жабайы варварлық әлем салыстыра келгенде, ең жоғары дәрежелі білімді ұстанымдардан асып түседі: алғашқыларына нәпсіқұмарлық кері пиғылдан аулақ жүру қаншалықты қажет болса, кейінгілеріне жақсылық пен адамгершілік әрекеттерді білуінің қажеті соншалықты шамалы..."

Скифтердің жауынгерлік рухы мен ерліктерін Помпей Трог былайша сипаттайды: "Скифтер Азияны үш мәрте жаулап алды, ал өздеріне ұдайы тұрғыда ешкім тиіспейтін және оларды соғыста ешкім жеңе алмайтын. Парсылық патша Дарийді олар масқара етіп, Скифиядан қуып шықты. Кир және оның жауынгерлерінің басын шапты, Александр Македонскийдің (Ескендір Зұлқарнайын) қолбасшысы Зопирионды барша әскерімен бірге тас талқан етті. Ал өздері Парфия және Бактрия патшалықтарын өмірге әкелді..." ("Скифы. Хрестоматия" Мәскеу, "Высшая школа" баспасы, 1992 жыл, 250,251-бет).

Осы кітаптың авторына Қазақстан мен Түрікменстан арасындағы шекара аймағын бөліп реттестірудегі делегимитизация туралы келісімінде орын алған жағдай жақсы белгілі. Бүкіл қажетті шаралар шаралар жүзеге асырылып болған соң, марқұм Түрікменбашы біздің Елбасымызга былай деді: "оғыздың байырғы атамекенін қазақ халқына беріп жатырмыз". Президентіміз оған былай деп жауап берді: "Қазақ адайларының ата-бабаларының ержүрек батыл рухы арқасында елдеріміз арасындағы шекара қазіргі сипатта көрініс тапты, тіпті Ашхабадтың оңтүстік жағына да орналасуы мүмкін еді". Ал өз басым, осыған қосып айтарым: егер халқымыздың ішінде ержүрек адайлар болмағанда, онда қазақ халқының береке көзі, күш қуаты –ертеңгі болашағы – Каспий мұнайының да болуы екіталай еді.

Әйтседе айтарым: бұл оқиғада ұтылған жақ болмады. Қазіргі Қазақстанның Маңғыстау облысы аймағынан шеттетілген түркі оғыздар, XI ғасырда Парсы елінің үлкен бөлігін, Әзербайжан, Күрдістан, Ирак, Армения, Грузия, Кіші Азияны жаулап алып, патшалық билік құрған Селжүктер мемлекетінің негізін құрады. Біраз уақыт өткен соң, олардың ұрпақтары Азия мен Еуропаның көптеген елдеріне ықпалын тигізген Осман мемлекетін дүниеге әкеледі.

## АРҒЫНДАР МЕН АРГЕНТИНА.
## ФРАНЦИЯНЫҢ ҚАЛЫПТАСУЫНЫҢ ҚАЙ НАР БАСТАУЫНДА КІМ ТҰРДЫ?

Қазақтың Орта жүзіндегі Ергенекті Наймандардан тарайтын Бура туралы бірер сөз. Мурат Аджи өзінің "Тюрки и мир. Сокровенная история" (Мәскеу, "Хранитель" баспасы, 2004 жыл) атты еңбегіндегі жазуына қарағанда, рим әскерін басқаратын, болшақ рим императоры - Дунай қыпшағы Констанций, 411 жылы Алтайлық бургундарды өзіне жақын тартып, қазіргі Франция аймағын мекендеуге рұқсат етті. Франциялық Бургундия этнонимі ғұндық "Бура" руына байланысты пайда болды деп ойлаймын. Бура руы қазіргі қазақтың ішіндегі ергенекті найман тайпасының құрамына енеді. Ресейлік ғалым Н.Кикешев аса көрнекті кеңес ғалым археологы А.П.Окладниковтың еңбектеріне сүйеніп, бур түбіріне байланысты этнонимедер интерпретациясы үлгілерін келтіреді. Шумер тілінен "бур" сөзі су, су қоймасы деп аударылады. Алтай мен Сібірде Бурей, Бурунда, Буркала өзендеріі маңында орналасқан Бур, Бурухан, Бурхан, Бурхал, Буран т.б. елді мекендері бар. Евфрат өзенінің көне атауы Буратта болатын. Македон әулетінен шыққан X ғасырдағы Византия императоры Константин Багрянародный дунайлық булгарларды-бургар деп атаған. Ал Болгария королі II Симеон сак-бурготтық королі дәрежесін иеленген.

Осыған сәйкес, мынадай нәтиже туындайды: Бургундар Алтайдан келсе, онда бургундар – бұрынғы кезеңдерде қазіргі Ертіс, Обь, Енесай өзендері жағалауы маңында өмір сүрген ғұндар болып шығады, ал бурготтар да бағзы замандарда көлді-өзенді аймақтарды мекендеген гот тайпалары екендігі сөзсіз. Бір сөзбен айтқанда, ықылым замандарда француздық Бургундияда біздің бабаларымыз өмір сүріп, өз атымен жергілікті мекендерді атаған.

Скифтік бургундар тайпасы Ұлы Дала тарихында айқын іздер қалдырып кеткенін ескеріп өтейік. Қазақ халқының "Алаңқай батыр" эпосында б.з.д. Солтсүтік

Кавказдағы оқиғалар туралы жырланып, келесідей деректер кездеседі: "Айдаһардай алыпты аттан құлатты. Бургундтарды шегіндіріп, атын босатты. Азов теңізінде батыр жауынгерлер аттарын суарды..." Аттілі о дүниелік болған соң, бургундар тайпасы қазіргі Франция аймағына орналасса, ал бір бөлігі Алтайдағы туған жеріне қайтып оралды.

Жасырып қайтеміз, Аргентина туралы айтқанда жұрт мырс етіп күледі, бұл сөзді барша халық қазақтың әйгілі Арғын руымен байланыстырады. Француздық бургундарға қатысты келтірген пікір біздің санамызға басқа ойды қалыптастырады: Қазіргі кезеңде біз оңтүстік америка халықтарының тілі түркі тілдеріне ұқсастығына қатысты (О.Рериг, Ә.Ахметов, А.Каримуллин т.б. зерттеушілердің еңбектерін қараңыз.) зерттеліп жасалған бірқатар еңбектермен таныспыз. Бәлкім, сонау алыс Аргентинада, қазақтың арғын руы өзінің іздерін қалдырып кеткенін кім білсін? Б.з.д. көне грек философ ойшылы Ксенофокт Эгей теңізінде Аргинууз аралдары бар екендігі туралы жазып кеткен. Б.з.д бірінші мыңжылдықта ғұндардың Еуропаға келуімен қатар, ескі құрлықта арген, аргим, аргентин этнонимдері пайда болады. Ү ғасырда Аттілі дәуірінде өздерінен кейін "Кодекс Аргентиус" атты туындыны мұра етіп қалдырған түркілік тайпа лангобардтар өз кемеліне жетеді. Осыған сәйкес Солтүстік Италиядағы Милан атты астанасы бар Ломбардия провинциясын қазақ руы арғындардың ата бабалары мекендеген. Милан ғұндық патша Аттілінің елордасы болған. Бұл рудың топонимдері барша аймақтардан кездеседі: Қиыр Шығыстағы Аргун өзенінен бастап, Тынық мұхиты жағалауындағы Арагон мен Пиреней алқаптары - Еуразияның батыс аймағына дейін ұшырасады. Б.з.д 22000 жыл бұрын Беринг бұғазы, Панама каналының өмірде болмағанын айта кетуге тиспіз. Түркі көшпенділері Еуразия алқаптарында емін еркін көшіп қоныстанып жүріп, Солтүстік және Оңтүстік Америкаға дейін емін еркін жететін.

2010 жылдың ақпан айында Қазақтың спорт және туризм академиясының бір топ мамандары жер бетінің батыс жағында орналасқан таулардың Аконкагуа атты ең биік нүктесін бағындырды. Бізге қазақтарға осы ел тұрғындарыны етке құмар екендігін жаңалық ретінде ашу қуанышқа ұласты. Жергілікті тұрғындар мәлімдегендей, Аргентинадағы мал шаруашылығының ежелгі дәстүрі бар және бұл салт дәстүрді Колумбқа дейін бағзы замандарда Еуразия аймағынан Оңтүстік Америка құрлығына келген жергілікті тұрғындардың ұрпағы берік ұстанады.

Біздегі мәліметтерге сәйкес, түркілік лангобард тайпасы Еуропаға ғұндармен бірге келген, ал олардың құрамында тек арғындар ғана емес, сонымен бірге қазақтың басқа рулары да болған. Олардың рәміз - туларында барыс желбірегендігі мәлім, сондықтан қазақтың беріш, албан этностарын барысқа қатысты байланыстыра қарастырамыз. Сонымен бірге, лангобардтар, По өзені аймағын мекендейтін герман тобы тайпаларына жатқызылады. Олар ұлы Римді дамып, гүлденіп тұрған кезінде талай рет қоршап, қыспаққа алған еді. Ал герман тайпалары, бірінші кезекте, гот-гет-кете рулары болып табылады, яғни лангобард тайпасының құрамына қазіргі Найман тайпасының рулары мен Әлімұлы тайпасының рулары да енген. Лангобардтар итальяндықтарға айналған соң, Италияның байырғы тұрғындарын өздерінің құлдары санап, жек көргендіктерін атап өту керек. Бұл оқиға олардың 643 жылғы Заңдар жинағында көрініс тапқан. Бұл жайында мәселен, Мұрат Аджи да жазады. Лангобардтың өте күшті тайпа болғандығын келесі айғақ дәйектейді. 774 жылы Францияның негізін салушы Ұлы Карл лангобардтардың тәжін киіп, таққа мінеді. Тіпті, король сөзінің өзі, Карл есіміне байланысты қолданысқа енген. "О тюркских племенах и народах Азии и Европы" атты еңбегінің авторы К.Томпиев Мұрат Аджиге сілтеме жасай отырып, мынадай қорытынды жсайды: Франция королі түркілік балттар руынан шыққан. Оның өмірдегі шынайы аты Шарламақ еді. Түркі тілінен аударғанда - жер аралауды жақсы көретін адам деген ұғымды білдіреді. Сол кезеңдері герцог Бургундскийдің де есімі Темір деп аталатын. Ал кейінірек оны ел сері "Батыл Карл" деп атап кетеді. Бүгінгі таңда балттар-Найманның ішіндегі Балталы руының құрамында және олар лангобардтар тайпасының құрамына енуі мүмкін. Ж.Байжуминнің айтуынша, орыстың әйгілі ғалымы, Батыс Еуропа жазбаларының кермет білгір маманы, академик А.Шахматов Ұлы Карлдың түркі-болгар көшпенділерінің арасынан шыққандығы туралы мәлімдеген. Осыған сәйкес оның немерелері Франция, Италия, Германияны билеген алғашқы корольдер еді. Яғни келтірілген тұжырымға сәйкес, қазақтың ботбай руынан тарайтын Каролингтер әулетін құрған Ұлы Карлдың шығу тегі жайында тағы бір болжамды негіздейміз. Ботбай қазіргі Болгарияның негізін салған Аспарух ханның туған бауыры еді, Байжумин-Томпиев-Аджи пікірлерінің дұрыстығын ресейлік зерттеуші Сергей Баймухаметов растайды. Ол өзінің "Призраки истории" (Мәскеу, АСТ: Олимп баспасы, 2008 жыл) кітабында былай деп жазады: ҮІІІ ғасырда түркі мұсылмандардың қоластында өмір сүрген Испанияның мавритандық (мұсылмандық) әмірлерінің бірі Сарагоса әмірімен шайқасып, Каролингтер әулетінің негізін салған, франктер королі Ұлы Карлды көмекке шақырады.

Туыстық қарым қатынас болмаса, Францияның императоры Испаниядағы провинцияның түркі билеушісіне қол ұшын созып қайтсін? Яғни, осылайша ҮІІІ ғасырда тек Француздық Бургундия ғана емес, барша Францияда біздің ата-бабаларымыз билік жүргізген. Иезуиттердің астыртын әрекеттерінен кейін Ұлы Карлдың бұл жорығы Христос діні үшін дінсіз кәпірлермен киелі соғыс деп аталып кетті.

# Қос мүйізді Ескендір және Алтай.
# Артур мен Аттілінің қылышы.
# Пір Бекеттің киелі аса таяғы
# Гиперборей мен Аполлонның скифтік тегі туралы

Барша жұртқа мәлім деректерге сәйкес, Колумбтың аузынан шыққан бір ауыз сөзден кейін, күллі дүние Солтүстік Америка тұрғындарын үндістер деп атап кетті. Бұл әйгілі теңіз саяхатшысының үлкен қателігі болып табылады, өйткені Колумб өмірінің аяғына дейін жаңа құрлық аштым деп емес, Үндістанға жүзіп келдім деп санаған. Тағы да бір ұлы қайраткер, атақты қолбасшы Александр Македонскийдің үлкен қателігін біз сілтеме жасаған кітапта Н.Кикешев келтіреді. Қос мүйізді Александр (Ескендір) дүниеден өткеніне 500 жылдан соң, "Александр жорығы" атты кітапты жазған Арианға сүйене отырып, сонымен бірге Эратосфеннің шығармасын пайдаланып, Александрдың Үндістанда болмағандығы туралы сенсациялық жаңалық ашады. Ескендір Зұлқарнайын Қазақстан аймағы арқылы Ертіске келіп, кейін Обь өзені арқылы Орталық Қазақстан аймағы арқылы туған жеріне оралады.

Осы ұлы адаммен байланысты Қазақстан жерінде қанша киелі есте қаларлық жер бар десеңізші! Нағыз туристік Мекке!

Б.з. I ғасырында өмір сүрген және "Александр Македонскийдің тарихы" шығармасын жазған Квинт Курций Руф, ұлы қолбасшының Үндістанға жорығын сипаттап, Ескендірдің жауынгерлеріне арналған сөздеріне қатысты келесідей мәліметтерді баяндайды: "О,жауынгерлерім, Үндістан тұрғындары сендерді үрейлендіретін әңгімелерді көп айтқанын жақсы білемін. Бірақ жалған өтіріктің арты белгілі. Дәл осылай парсылар бізге Киликия, Месопотамия мен Тигр және Евфрат қос өзендері кеңістігінде осындай қорқынышты үрейлерді айтып, сан түрлі әрекет жасайды... Сендер неден көбірек қорқасыңдар? Жаулардан ба, әлде жануарлардан ба? Пілдерге келер болсақ, онда мысал дайын: олар өз адамдарын бізге қарағанда көбірк таптап жаншыды. Біз өз жорықтарымыздың шарықтау шегіне жетіп қалдық. Жақында жорық аяқталады. Біз жақында күншығысқа жетіп, үлкен мұхитқа шығамыз. Балалықты қойыңдар. Ол жақта, әлемнің шетін жаулап, Отанымызға жеңімпаз ретінде оралaмыз... Менің қолымнан жеңісті жұлып алып, менің Геркулес немесе Либер әкейге теңелуі мүмкіндігіме кедергі жасамаңдар... Кімге айтып тұрмын? нені талап етемін? Сендердің атақ-даңқтарыңды құтқарып келгім келеді. Өзінің жаралы патшасын жерден көтеріп алуға асыққан менің ержүрек батыр сарбаздарымды көрдім. Өзіммен бірге баратындарды табамын, сендер менен кеткенмен, менімен бірге скифтер және бактриялықтар аттанады. (Өзім бөліп көрсеттім-Қ.З.) Әмірші қолбасшының сұраншақ болғанша, өлгені артық... Үйге қайтыңдар! Патшаларыңнан кетіп, той жасаңдар! Ал мен мұнда сендер сенбейтін жеңістерге жететін боламын, немесе жауынгер ретінде соғыс алқабында жер жастанамын!"

Қолбасшының жаны қиналған, әлсіреген жауынгерлермен әңгімесі Ауғанстанның солтүстігіндегі Бактрияда, қазіріг заманғы Балх қаласының маңында орын алды. Үндістанға дейін әлі алыс еді...

Рим тарихшысы жауынгерлердің өз патшасын тыңдаған немесе, тыңдамағаны жайында хабарламайды. Бірақ Арриандікі дұрыс – Александр Үндістанға жете алмай қалды.

Қазақстанның көрнекті қайраткері Өмірбек Байгелді маған аспаннан түскен қылыш жайындаға аңызды айтып берген болатын. Жартаушы бұл қылышты Аттілінің үлесіне белгілейді. Еуропа ғалымдары мен жазушылары "Құдайдың қылышы" - деп атаған тұлға кім өзі? Византиялық тарихшы Понтиялық Прийск Аттілі туралы айта келе, былай деп жазады: "Римдіктер оның кез келген талабын орындауға дайын тұрды, Оның кез келген сөзін өз әміршілерінің бұйрығындай қабылдады".

Оқиға былай басталған еді. Ү ғасырдың басында Аттілі шамасымен қазіргі Шығыс Қазақстан облысы аймағындағы Самарское ауылы жанында ағып жатқан Ертіс жағалауында тұрған кезде, Ертістің оң жақ жағалауына жетіп, Вэй әулеті тұсындағы қытайды салық төлемегені үшін жазалауға атттанған кезде, аспаннан үлкен қылыш жарқ ете түсіп, жерге қадалады. Аттілі жауынгерелерінің жерден қылышты жұлып алу әрекеті нәтижесін берген жоқ. Бұл қылышты жерден тек ғұндар патшасы ғана суырып шықты. Ал қылыштың жарқыраған жүзінде "Ескіні ендір" - деген жазу бар екен. Бұл яғни жер бетіндегі патшалардың ұмытып кеткен байырғы салт дәстүрлері, тәртіп пен жақсы өмірді қалпына келтіру ұғымын білдіреді. Бір сөзбен айтқанда, ғұндар патшасы күнә мен кінәға белшесінен батқан Рим еліндегі адамның рухани ұстанымдарын қалпына келтіру үшін Жаратушының өзінен әмір алады. Ол ойға шомып, қолындағы аспаннан түскен аманатқа зер салып тұрған кезде, жол шатқалынан Қытайдың елшілері көрінді. Олар бағынбағандары үшін, сыйлық, тарту таралғыны молынан алып, кешірім сұрауға келіпті. Қолбасшы Аттілі еркін тыныстады, енді артыңа қарамасаң да болады. Жау ту сыртыңнан келіп, соққы жасай қоймас, бірден Батысқа жол тартып, Жаратушының бұйрығын орындайды.

Ескендір-Александр есімі этимологиясын "Ескіні ендір" тіркесімен байланыстырып жүр. Міне, енді Александр Македонскийдің Ертіс жағалауына барып қайтуына байланысты, Шығыс Қазақстандағы Александр шатқалының Аттілі немесе Александр Македонский есімінің қайсысымен байланысты екендігін түсіне алмай қаласың.

Аспаннан түскен қылыш туралы аңыздар, немесе қылыштың қатысуымен болған басқа сюжеттер көптеген халықтардың фольклорында айтылып жүр. Бірақ әйтседе бұл аңыздар көне түркілердің тағдыры мен өміріне тікелей байланысты. Егер король Артурға келсек, бұл аңыздың бсқа түрі былайша баяндалады: Британия королі Утер Пендрагон Тинтагель қамалындағы кәрі герцогтің Игрейна атты сұлу әйеліне ғашық болып қалады. Ол сиқыршы Мерлинге Игрейнамен көңіл көтеру үшін өзін уақытша герцогтің кейпіне айналдыруын сұрайды. Сиқыршы корольдің айтқан сөзін орындайды. Бірақ туған баланы өзіне беруін талап етеді. Біраз уақыттан соң король көз жұмады. Мемлекеттің тағына мұрагер жоқ болғандықтан, ел арасында өзара қырқысу шайқастары басталады. Артур 20 жасқа толған кезде, Кентербериялық епископ пен сиқыршы Мерлин Лондон қаласында жиналған серілерге "тасқа қадалған қылышты суырып алыңдар!" деген талап қояды.

Сайысты жеңген адамға корольдің тағы бұйыратын болып белгіленді. Бұл қылышты суыру тек Артурдың ғана қолынан келді. Міне, дәл осы жерде сиқыршы Мерлин жиналған серілерге Артурдың өмірге келу құпиясын жариялап, оны бүкіл Англияның королі етіп жариялайды. Кейінірек, бұл қылыш, Аттіліне Жаратушы тарту еткен қылыштай, қолдау көрсетіп, оның жеңімпаз атандырады. Бірақ серілердің арасында Артурды өз королі деп танымағандар да болды. Үлкен соғыс басталып кетті, тек Еуропа құрлығындағы сармат тайпасындағы туыстары ғана Артурға Британия тағына отыруға көмектеседі. Қазіргі заманда Жаратушы тарапынан аспаннан түскен қылышқа ие болу жайындағы бұл аңыз бірте-бірте Аса таяқ туралы аңыз ретінде трансформацияланып өзгерді, аса таяқ әлем мен адамдарды рухани тұрғыда басқаруға мүмкіндік береді. Сопылық әлемнің рухани жетекшілерінің бірі - Пір Бекет, Қазақстанның Маңғыстау облысында оған арналып мемориалды кешен орнатылды. Ол Көк Аса таяқтың иесі. Осының нәтижесінде суфийлер ағымының орденіне ие болып, аса таяқтың құдіретімен адамдарға өз әмірін жүргізе білді. Аңыз бойынша, аса таяқты Жаратушы таңдаулы адамға арнады. Тек Алланың мейірімі түскен адам ғана оны жерден тауып, немесе тастан суырып алып, өзінің рухани ізденістеріне пайдаланды. Өзінің өмірінің соңында осы аса таяқтың иесі оны аспанға қайта лақтырады, тек қана лайықты шәкірті ғана аса таяқты тауып, жаңа рухани көшбасшыға айналатын. Пір Бекеттен кейін Көк Аса таяқтың қожайыны болып Шекті бай деген біреу шығады, қазіргі оның немене ұрпағы Тұрсынғали Нәкеш Ақтөбе облысындағы Хобды ауданында Қобыланды батырға арналған мемориалды кешеннің директоры осы аспаннан түскен тарту сый- қылышқа иелік етуде. Кезінде өзінің суырып салма ақындығы үшін Ауқын (Ақын) деген атқа ие болған зайыбым Мәрзияның атасы Ілияс та қолында аталмыш аса таяқты ұстаған. Бірақ осы аса таяқты иеленетін адамға ауыр жауапкершілік жүктелетінін біліп, өзінің қалауы бойынша қасиетті жәдігерді басқа бір адамға тарту етеді, ал қасиетті аса таяқ иеленушісінің ұрпағы Маңғыстау облысының әкімі Қырымбек Көшербаевтың шақыртуымен Ақтау қаласына тұруға жол тартты. Бүгінгі таңда, мұнай саласына қатысты бұл аймақтың әлеуметтік-экономикалық тұрғыда мол табыстарға қол жеткізуі Жаратушының мейірімі түсу арқылы жүзеге асты деп те айтсақ қателеспейміз.

Қазақ халқы және мұсылман әлемі үшін Үстірт тауларындағы қасиетті Бекет ата жатқан Огланды шатқалы бүкіл ғаламшардағы ислам діні өкілдерінің табынатын жері болып табылады. Бұл пікірді келесідей өлең жолдары дәлелдейді: Мекке-Мәдинеде-Мұхаммед (с.ғ.с.), Түркістанда-Хожа Ахмет, Маңғыстауда –пір Бекет. Әр кезде адам тағдырдың тәлкегіне ұшырған сәтте, Адай руы қазақтары әруақтарды көмекке шақырып, Пір Бекет деп ұрандап, жауға ұмтылған, қазіргі кезеңде шешімі қиын сәттер туындаған кездері, Бірінші Аллаға, сонан кейін Пір Бекетке сыйынып, "Бекет ата қолдай гөр!" деп ұрандап, мақсаттарына жетеді. Мұсылмандар арасында бұл адам жайында көптеген аңыздар тараған. Ол Иса пайғамбар сынды адамдардың дертін жазып, әділет орнатып, кедей жұтаңдарға болысқан. Осы оқиғалардың біріне тоқталып өткім келеді. Ол Үргеніш қаласындағы медреседе оқып жүрген кезде, бірге оқитын жігіттер қалжыңдап, оны сынап көрмек болады. Біреуі үстіне марқұмның киімін киіп алып, өлген сыңай танытып жата қалады. Басқалары Бекетті шақырып алып, қайтыс болған адамға Құран аяттарын оқып, жаназа шығаруын сұрайды. Айтқандарын орындап, жас Бекет аят оқып, "Алла Тағала оны алып кетті деп айтады". Ойын шынға айналып кетті. Бұл қалжыңның салдарынан медресе шәкірті шынымен-ақ тіл қатпай кетті.

Солтүстік Америка үндістеріне оралар болсақ, өзімінің "Шыңғысханның түркілік ғұмырнамасы" атты кітабымда Солтүстік Америка үндістері мен қазақтардың туыс болып келетіндігі туралы пікірді дәйектеп негіздедім. Жердің астероидпен соқтығысу нәтижесінде орын алған топан судан кейін Гиперборея тұрғындары өз мекенінен біржола кетіп қалады. Бір бөлігі жердің шығыс бөлігіне жол тартса, бұл халықтың басқа бөлігі қазіргі Америка Құрама Штаттары аймағы орналасқан жердің батыс аймағына аттанады. Біртұтас халық екі жаққа бөлініп, ыдырап кетеді.

Осы болжамымды Юкатан аралы майя тайпасының сөздіктері растай түседі. Татар лингвист тілші ғалымы Арибжанов, 1562 жылы Мексикалық майя тайпасын көріп қайтқан Диего де Ланданың қолжазбаларымен танысып, түркі халықтары мен майя тайпасының арасындағы генетикалық тұрғыдағы туыстық туралы жорамал жасайды. Әйгілі ғалым Әділ Ахметовтың зерттеулері де осы тұрғыда. Юкатандық майя тайпасының сөздік қорындағы сөздер мен сөз тіркестерінің бірнешеуін келтірейік. Ал жақша ішінде олардың қазақ тіліндегі эквивалент балама үлгілері жазылады: Таш (тас), Яш чилан (жас жылан), туле (толы), цибенче (шыбын), калак мул ( қалақ мол), ак (ақ), чамо (шама), ич (іш), ики (екі), бакалар (бақалар), тун (түн) және т.т. Юкатан аралында осы күнге дейін келесідей топонимдер сақталып қалды: цилан (жылан), ячил (жасыл), сойыл (сойыл), залив бакалар (бақалар бұғазы) т.б. Майяның ірі Қалақмұла қаласының билеушісі Хан деп аталғаны мәлім.

Үндістердің майя тайпасы құрып кеткен өркениет таңдануға әбден лайықты. Бұрынырақ майялардың санаудың 19 жолдық үлгісінің негізін салғанын айтқан болатынмын. Бұл санау үлгісін кейін YII ғасырда араб түбегіндегі құрайыш тайпасы Құранды жазу барысында пайдаланады. Ондық еселеп санау үлгісі жүйесінің логикасы баршамызға түсінікті. Қолымызда он саусақ. Бірақ 19 саны Солтүстік Америкадағы біздің ата-бабаларымыз майя үндістері үшін неге соншалықты қасиетті сан болып табылады? Олардың ақыл ойын қандай тылсым күштер басқарды? Бұның жауабын Николай Кикешевтің кітабынан таптым. Оның жазуына қарағанда, Гипорбореяда дүниеге келген күн тәңірі Апполон, өзінің алыста қалған мекеніне әрбір 19 жыл сайын барып тұрған, өйткені дәл осы уақытта аспандағы жұлдыздар, аспанды айналу жолын тоқтатып, бұрынғы орындарына қайта оралады. Ал ай және күнге арналған күнтізбелер сәйкесті тұрғыда орналасып, бір жүйеге келгендіктен, күн тұтылуының мерзімі мен орнын анықтау мүмкіндігі туындайды.

Біздің заманымызға дейін ата-бабаларымыздың білімі осындай ғаламат, керемет болған! Құранннның 19 сандық үлгі негізінде жазылғандығы (мәселен: оның жазылу жылы: 568 жыл: 5+6+8=19, Құран мәтіні 114 сүре және 634 аяттан құралады, осы сандардың бәрі 19 санына бөлінеді. Рахман және Рахим сөзін қайталау санының өзі 19-ға бөлінеді және т.б.) Бұл тағы да бір рет мұсылмандардың киелі кітабы "Құранды" біздің ата-бабаларымыздың тікелей тұрғыда қатысуымен жазылғандығын айғақтай түседі. Бұл жайында кейінгі зерттеулерімізде әлі айтатын боламыз.

Тағы бір аса маңызды жайтқа тоқтала кетейік. Көне гректер мифологиялық Гиперборея скиф және сарматтардың атамкені деп таныған, яғни осыған сәйкес, Гипорбореяда дүниге келген Аполлон (бұл пікірді б.з.д.YI ғасырда өмір сүрген ақын Пиндар да растайды) шығу тегі жағына скиф еді. Оған галл-кельттер сыйынатын. Ал қазіргі заман зерттеушілері Апполонға сыйыну дәстүрі көне Грекиядағы Еуразия аймағынан келген шығу тегі дорий болып табылатын тайпалары арасында қалыптасты деп санайды. Жоғарыда атап өткеніміздей, Көне Грекияны бұрынғы дәуірлерде Еуразиялық көшпенділер: пеласги, ахей, дории, ионий және тағы басқалары кезек-кезек билейді. Олар кейін грекиялық деп танылып кеткен, аңыз-әпсаналарды өмірге әкелген.

Профессор М.Барманқұлов "Тюркская Вселенная" (Алматы, "Білім" баспасы, 1996, 158-бет) кітабында былай деп жазады: Александр Македонский дәуірінде Орта Азияда Аполлон мен Артемида, Афродита мен Геракл, Зевс және Посейдонға арналған теңгелерді шығарған. Бірақ бұл баяғы заманда орын алған тәңірлер (көне грек тәңірлері-Қ.З.) христиандық емес, кәпірлік болғанда (Түркілік-деп санай беріңіз-Қ.З.) шыққан.

# АЛМАТЫЛЫҚ АДАМ АТА МЕН ХАУА АНА.
# ЖАРАТУШЫ ҚАЙ ТІЛДЕ СӨЙЛЕДІ?

Ал енді дүниенің пайда болуының қайнар көздеріне тоқталайық. Бұл жерде біз таңқаларлық кездейсоқтықтарды кездестіреміз. Олардың кездейсоқ болуы да екіталай дүние. Мәселен қазақ тіліндегі "адам" сөзінің бір-ұғымы болса, ал алма - сөзінің екі ұғымы бар: тиіспе және алма синонимі (етістік) мағынасында. Ал енді Жаратушы Алла Тағала Адам ата мен Хауа ананы жұмақтағы тыйым салынған алмаға тиіспеу туралы ескерткендігі жөнінде Інжілдегі сюжетті еске алайық. "Алма" өсімдігінің – "алма" сөзі болып қолданылуы кездейсоқ па?

Британ ғалымдары Қазақстанның Оңтүстік астанасы –Алматы қаласы орналасқан жер алманың атамекені екендігін дәлелдеп шықты. Осыған сәйкес, адамзаттың бабасы Адам ата мен Хауа ананы жұмақтан қуып шығу сюжеті Алматы қаласының маңына байланысты деген жорамал туындайды. Мұндай жағдайда біздің ғажайып қаламызға ғасырлар бойы аталып келген Алма-Ата атты бұрынғы атауын қайтарудың уақыты келген жоқ па? Осы айтылған ойға байланысты "Кенгуру" сөзінің шығу тегін есіме түсті.

Отарлаушылар Австралия жеріне келіп, бұл таңғажайып жануарды алғаш рет көрген соң, бұл не деген жануар және оның аты қандай?-деп сұрайды. Олар жауап ретінде –кенгуру! деген сөзді естиді. Жергілікті тілде бұл сөз – білмеймін, яғни тіліңізді білмегендіктен, айтып тұрғаныңызды түсінбеймін деген мағынаны білдірсе керек.  Ал келімсектер "кенгуру" сөзін осы жануардың аты деп қабылдап, осылайша кенгуру- кенгуру болып шыға келеді.

Ал алма сөзі қандай өзгерістерге ұшырады, ал Хауа ананың серігі Адам ата қазақ тілінде адамның кісі екендігін білдіретін ұғымға айналды.  Ал Ева сөзі қазақ тіліндегі Ана, ене сөздерінен трансформациялану нәтижесінде пайда болды. Егер қазақтар ана тілінде, алғашқы адамның атын адамзат ұғымын білдіру үшін сақтап қалса, сонымен бірге жұрттың бәрі жақс ы көретін жемістің де аты алма болып қалыптасты. Жаратушы алғаш рет "алма" - деп бұйырғанда, бұл оның қазақ тілінде сөйлегендігінің белгісі. Інжілдегі деректерге сәйкес, әлем жеті күнде жаралды, егер ғалымдар алманың Отаны – Қазақстан болып табылады деп анықтаса, онда алғашқы алмалардың қазақ жерінде өскені ғой. Осы жұмақтағы ағаштардың жанында серуендеп жүрген алғашқы адамдар- Адам ата мен Хауа алмалар пайда болған аптада, осы аймақта дүниеге келген. Қарапайым тұрғыда логика заңдары бойынша, біздің - қазақ жері алғашқы адамның атамекені болып табылады. Осыған сәйкес, Жаратушының тілі қазақ тілі болғандығы айқын.

# Тәңір дінінің тірегі —оғыздар мен сеирлер.

Барша түркі әлемін шартты түрде екіге бөліп қарауға болады: Күнге табынатындар – сеир-сирлер, Тәңірліктер кейін тарихта елеулі орын алатын қыпшақ тайпасы болып аталып кетті және ғарыштың түнгі иесі айға табынатындар – оғыздар. Осыған қатысты қазіргі кезде мынадай: қазақтың рулары осы екі тайпаның қайсысына енеді? - деген жекелеген мәселені шешу үшін, ойланып көруге тура келеді.

Мәселен оғыз тайпаларының рулық белгілері жүйесінде жарты айдың белгісі бар және бұл тайпаға: ергенекті найман, шапырашты, алаша рулары кіреді – деп, нақты тұрғыда айта аламыз. Сонымен бірге, оғыздарға: матай, садыр, қаракерей, төртұлы рулары қатысты болып келеді. Өйткені олар, б.з.д. XII ғасырда хеттердің құрамында Кіші Азия аймағынан Қытайға, содан кейін б.з.д. YIII ғасырда Қазақстан аймағына, ал б.з.д. III ғасырда Қара теңіз жағалауы мен Батыс Еуропаға оғыз тайпасынан шыққан языга, роксолан және алан деген атпен келіп жетеді. Сарматтық языга тайпасы туралы жоғарыда айтып өттік, қазіргі қазақ халқы ішіндегі найман тайпасы одағы құрамындағы қарауыл жасақ руы олардың жалғасы болып табылады. Ал аландар туралы сөз қозғасақ, жоғарыдағы тарауларды толықтыру мақсатында мынадай мәселеге тоқталайық: Хань әулеті тұсындағы (б.з. 1206 жылы) қытай деректерінде осы жылдары асы оғыздардың атауы - а-лан-а, яғни, алан болып өзгергені туралы жазылады.

Менің мәліметтеріме сәйкес, қазақтың албаны мен адайлары осы аландарға туыс екендігі аян. Ал роксоландарға келер болсақ, бұл этноним неміс тілінен – "патшалық аландар"-деп аударылады. Еуропаға тұрақты тұрғыда жайғасып алған соң, олар герман тайпаларының негізін құрайды. Қазіргі заман түрік, түрікмен, әзербайжан және т.б. елдер оғыздар құрамына кіреді. Мәселен қырғыздар – бұлар –қырыққазы (ас, уз, гуз, оғыз), яғни, оғыздың қырық одағы тайпасының бірлестігі болып табылады, ал қазіргі заман ұйғырлары – бұлар тек оғыздар: оғыздың тоғыз тайпасы одағы құрамынан тарайды. Оғыздың сегіз руы қазақ наймандарының негізін қалыптастырды. Қолымдағы деректерге сәйкес, исламның жасыл белгісіндегі жарты ай тек оғыздардың ықпалымен пайда болды десек қателеспейміз, олар екі мыңыншы жылдықтың басында мұсылман әлемінің орталығы Бағдат қаласына басып кіреді. Сонымен бірге ислам дінінің пайда болғаны үшін де ислам әлеміне түркілердің сіңірген еңбегі өте зор. Сеирлерге тамғалары күн белгісі болып саналатын қазақ руларының басым бөлігі енеді: арғын, қаңлы, сиқым, жаныс, ботбay, шымыр, ысық, адай, байбақты т.т. Тұрғындарының негізін сеирлер құрайтын Бірінші Түркі қағанаты құлаған соң, олар өз халқының атын өзгертіп, Қыпшақ деп аталып кетті, Дунайдан бастап, Ертіске дейінгі ұласатын ұлан асыр аймақ – Дешті Қыпшақ – қыпшақтардың далалық көшпенді мемлекеті деп аталатын. Қазақтар сеир-сирлердің сыйынған қасиетті жануары сиырға ерекше қарайды. Олар сиырлардың пірін –Зеңгі Баба, ал жылқылардың пірі- Қамбар ата, қойлардың пірі- Шопан ата - деп атаған. Әйтседе баба мен ата сөздері синонимдес болғанмен, дегенмен екеуінің негізінде әртүрлі семантикалық реңк бар екендігі даусыз. Сеирлердің құрметіне ғаламның солтүстік бөлігіндегі жұлдыздар шоғыры Сеирші деп аталып кетті.

Айға табынушыларды оғыздар деп атағандығының нақты бір логикалық түсінігі бар: өйткені жарты айды бұқаның мүйіздерімен салыстырып қарастыруға болады (бұқа қазақ тілінде-оғыз деген ұғымды білдіреді). Сонымен қоса, көне шумерліктер ай тәңірін – Ас деп атайтын, ал осыдан барып, ас, ус - оғыз атаулары шыққан. Түркілер неге күнге табынатындарды сеирлер деп атаған? Шумерлердегі күн тәңірі – Гор, ал оның әйелі Хаттор деген есімге ие болып, сиыр бейнесінде бейнеленген. Міне, нағыз байланыс осында жатыр! Мифологияға сәйкес, күн мен ай Гор тәңірдің көздері болған. Яғни осы аңыз бойынша, түркілер: оғыз және сеирлер Көк аспанның жер бетіндегі жанары екен. Бір сөзбен айтқанда – қараушылар!

Б.з.д. ҮІІ ғасырдың басында Түркі қағнаты құлағаннан кейін, сеирлер қыпшақтар болып өзгерді. Осы мерзімге дейін барша әлем оларды кун- немесе ғұн (қазақша-күн) деп атап жүрді. Мәселен қазақтың ішіндегі ОО сынды шеңбер тәріздес тамғаны иеленетін Арғын руының этимологиясы- шығу төркіні ғұн тайпасы атауының негізінде өмірге келген. Өйткені "ар" сөзі – ұят, абырой, ұждан деген мағынада қолданылады.

# Ресейлік Самара, қазақтың Самары және месопотамиялық Самарра Алтай – Шумерлердің ежелгі атамекені.

Тарих ғылымы сеирлер деген бір халықты кейде маралар деп атап келді. Осы ұғымға қатысты мәселен, қазақ тілінде марал деген жануар бар. Марал - бұғының ұрғашысы. Месопотамияда ежелгі өркениеттің негізін салған шумерлер халқы, меніңше шумар халқы –мар жұрты Тигр мен Евфрат қос өзен жағалауына Қазақстанның оңтүстігі мен Қырғызстан аумағында ағатын Шу өзені алқабынан келген. Мысалы, ғылыми ортада аты кеңінен мәлім, чех ғалымы Б.Грозныйдың пікірі бойынша, шумерлер Месопотамияға қазақ даласындағы Ертіс өзені бойынан келген, белгілі бір уақыт ішінде Шу алқабында өмір сүріп, кейін Каспий теңізінің оңтүстік жағалауы арқылы көшіп-қоныстанып, Тигр мен Евфрат атты қос өзен жағалауына келеді. Көне шумерлердің бұл ежелгі этнонимі Шығыс Қазақстанда сақталып қалғандығын ескерейік. Осы облыстың Самар ауданында тұратын жерлестерім: "XX ғасырдың басындағы Столыпин реформалары кезеңінде, осы аймақты Ресейдің Самар губерниясынап шыққапдар құрған"-деп қателікке бой алдырады. Іс жүзінде "Самар" этнонимі - өте көне сөз екендігі сөзсіз. Бірақ, ең өкініштісі, әдеттегі аймақтық-әкімшілік бөлінісу барысында осы ауданның атауы республика картасынан алынып, ғайып болды. Өзінің тұп тамыры, ата тегін, шынайы тарихын білмеу бұл тек шенеуніктерге ғана қатысты емес, ал осы уақиға орын алған кезде, ғалымдардың ай қарап жүргені ме сонда? Олардың пікірін сұраған бір адам болды ма? Дж.Кантеллидің көне картасында (1683) Самар жері РСФСР-дың қазіргі Алтай өлкесі мен Шығыс Қазақстан аймағын алып жатыр. Месопотамияда Самарра қаласы б.з.д. 4 мың жыл бұрын Тигр өзені жағалауы бойында орпаласты. Ғалымдар Месопотамиядағы бұл қала атауының шығу төркіні Алтайлық атауына қарағанда, "екінші" болып табылатындығын айтады. Сондай-ақ шумерлер Қос өзен аралығына қалыптасқан мәдениеті және жазуын ала келді. Шумерлердің қыш жазуы мен түркілердің руналары бір-біріне жақын. Византиялық император Юстиниан антикалық тарихшы Помпей Трогқа сүйене отырып, қыш жазуды тұрандықтар Урарту патшалығына (Месопотамияның солтүстік бөлігі) келгенге дейін ойлап тапқандығы туралы баяндайды. "Шумер" этнониімінің фонетикалық эквиваленті (баламасы) – сумер, шумар, сувар, сабир жәна т.б. болып табылады.

Сеир –марлар туралы тағы бірер сөз.

Б.з.д. XY ғасырда және б.з. YII ғасырда Шығыс Еуропа мен Қара теңіз жағалауының солтүстік аймағы мен Днепр жағалауын мекендеген тарихқа аты мәлім киммериялықтар халқының шығу тегіне келейік, Б.з.д. XYI ғасырда гиксостар Мысырдан кетіп қалған кезде, олардың негізгі бөлігі атамекендеріне оралып, киммериялықтар деген атты иеленеді. Менің қолымда бұл этнонимнің бірнеше этимологиялық болжамдық үлгілері бар. Днепр, Дунай өзендері жағалауын мекендеп, керемет өзеншілер ретінде танылып, қайықты жүргізген кезде олар қия атты ескектерді пайдаланған. Қимарлар – мар және қиялар деген осыдан келіп туындайды. Ал басқа бір үлгісі –" киелі" сөзі - яғни, мейірімді қолдаушы жебеп жүрген қасиетті адам ұғымы. Осыған сәйкес, қимар сөзі – киелі тәңірдің қолдауындағы мар, киелімар этнонимі ретінде түсіндіріледі. Қимар этнонимінің талдауына индоеуропалық Ки тәңірі сөзінен шыққан "кимер" этнонимінің этимологиясы да жақын, Ки тәңірі ұлы құдіретті- яғни кимер халқы – тәңірдің өзінен тараған күшті, қуатты маралар дегенге меңзейді. Сақтардың тайпалық одағы құрамына кіретін сақмар – яғни, мара тайпасы этнонимін де осылай талдай аламыз. Бұл жайында өзінің "Зеңгі Баба" (Алматы, "Алаш" баспасы, 2000 жыл.) атты кітабында Сарқытбек Шора жазады. Марлардың кейбір ұрпақтары қазіргі кезде мәселен, Ресей Федерациясында өмір сүреді. Бұл мари халқы –черемистер немесе мордвиндер екендігі аян. Бұл халықтардың барлығы түркі тілдес финн-угор тайпалары құрамына енеді.

Оғыздардың да тарихи сеирлер тағдыры іспеттес. Оғыздар халқын кейде тарихи хроникалық жылнамаларда "тур "-деп атап көрсетеді. Тарихи оқу құралдарында Шығыс Иранның көшпенді тайпалары "тур" деп белгіленеді. Бұл түбірден: Тұран, Түркістан, Түркия елі, Турку, Турино, Туруханск қаласы және т.б. ұғымдары тарайды. Бүгінгі кездері "оғыз" этнонимі түркі халықтарының этникалық шығу тегіне қатысты, мәселен түрікмен халқының шығу тегіне қатысты бұқа лексемасына қатысты тікелей түрде пайдаланылады.

## Сир, сэр және қазақ даласының серісі-Ер Сері

"Сир-сеир" этнонимінің тағдыры басқаша өрбіді. Жоғарыда атап өткенімдей, Бірінші Түркі қағанаты тұрғындарының негізгі бөлігін құрайтын сеирлер, бұл қағанат құлаған соң, қыпшақтар этнонимін қабылдайды, бірақ көптеген халықтардың тілінде сир-сеир айналымы сақталып қалып, жаңа фонетикалық және лексикалық мәндер мен реңктерге ие болды. Мәселен, мен еуропалық сербтер, түркі сеирлердің тікелей мұрагерлері деп санаймын. Б.з.д. II ғасырда өмір сүрген грек астраномы және жағрафияшысы Клавдий Птоломей өзінің "География" атты еңбегінде Волга (Еділ) өзенінің батыс жағалауында өмір сүрген сербтер: "Кераван тауы мен Ра өзені аралығында көшіп қоныстанған – ориней, вал және сербтер" жөнінде жазады. Антикалық заман тарихшысы Плиний сербтерді меотиялық тайпалар құрамындағы Sernis атты тайпа деп атап көрсетеді. Бірінші Түркі қағанатының басында меот-матайлардың ғана тұрғандығын жақсы білеміз, ал төрт түркі қағанының кеңесшісі Тоныкөкке арналған орхон-енесай жазба ескерткіштерінде түркілік сир халықтары туралы бірнеше рет баяндалады.

Кавказдың түбінен шыққан, ғұндардың қысымымен, батысқа бет алып, Каталонияның іргетасын көтерген алан-албандар сынды Кавказдық сербтер Еуропада кейін Сербия мемлекетін құрады.

Жоғарыда айтылғандай, түркілер Еуропа халықтарының ішінде және оның тілінде ұмытылмастай, үлкен із қалдырғандығы анық. Француздың "сир"- және ағылшындық –сэр сөзі корольдің мәртебесін, екіншіден- жоғары дәрежелі әулеттен шыққан ақсүйектердің атақ-дәрежесін белгілеу мақсатында қолданылады.

Жоғарыда аталып өткендей, түркілер Еуропа халықтарының мәдениетінде өшпестей үлкен іздерін қалдырған. Бұл лексема негізінде түркілік сир-сеир түбірі бар.

Бірнеше транскрипциялу трансформациялық өзгерісі барысында бұл сөз мәселен Ресейде- "царь, (патша) Италияда- "кесарь", Германияда – "кайзер" сөзіне айналды. Қазіргі кезіңде қазақ тілінде "ерсері" атты ер адамға арналған рухты сөз бар. Бұл сері ұғымы - ерекше дарынға ие, үлкен тобырлардың табынатын жұлдызына айналған, сәндене киіне білген ер адам -рыцарь-серіге қатысты қолданылады.

Осылайша ана тіліміз ата-бабаларымыздың адамзат тарихындағы алатын саяси және тарихи салмағын нақты айғақтады. Сеирлер Бірінші Түркі қағанатын құрған соң, Барша Азия мен Батыс Еуропа, Каспий және Қара теңіз жағалауы алқаптарына өзінің ықпалын сақтап қалды.

Түркі халқының атауын білдіретін "түркі" сөзінің тағдыры да сан қилы болғанын айта кетуге тиіспіз. Уақыт өте келе бұл сөз түрленіп, Еуропа елдерінің билеушілері (сир, кесарь, кайзер, царь) мен ақсүйек шонжарларының аристократиялық топтарының (ағылшындық-сэр) атақ дәрежесін білдіру үшін қолданылды.

Сонымен қоса, бұл лексема сир-сеирлерге тән рухани өжеттілік мағынасын жоғалтпай, Ұлы даланың серісі деген ең жоғары атаққа негізделетін еуропалық әскерлердің ең күшті және ең басты болып табылатын Серілік дәрежелерін белгіледі, осы атақты өз кезегінде мыңнан бір, немесе ең лайықты деп танылған ержүрек жауынгерлер ғана иеленді.

Қазақ Даласының көптеген руларының қаһарман ұлдары өжеттілігімен аталып, оларға лайық батыр атағы болып танылды, дегенмен де, бұл атақ ең жоғары қасиеттер және дәрежелерге бөленген сері атағына қарағанда, бір саты төмен тұрды. Менің ойым бойынша, республикамызда қазақ мемлекетінің өсіп гүлденуіне үлес қосып жүрген мемлекеттік қайраткерлерді қазақтың Ер Серісі – қазақ ұлтының Ер-Серісі деген атақпен марапаттайтын қоғамдық беделді топтан жасақталған арнайы орган құрған жөн.

Серінің тек соғыста ғана емесе, сонымен бірге тұрмыс тіршілікте де үлгі бола білгенін айта кетуге тиіспіз. Серіліктің нағыз үлгісі, француз маршал де Бусико, "сен көшеде қателесіп кетіп, екі жезөкшеге бас идің" деген наразылыққа былай деп жауап береді: әйел затына лайықты нәзік жандыларға көңіл бөлмегенше, одан да тәнін саудалайтын он әйелге бас игенім дұрыс. Тек ер серілердің арқасында ғана, түркілердегі Ұмай анананың қадірі мен құрметіне сәйкес, әр әйел қоғамда өзінің лайықты орнына қол жеткізді.

Осы кітапты жазу барысында қалыптасқан заңдылықтар мен көзқарастарды тас талқан еткен көптеген пікірлерді келтірдім, олар қаншалықты ерекше өзгеше тұжырымдық болжамдар болып келгенімен, бірақ осы пікірлерім – жаңа зерттеулер нәтижесінің жемісі. Тарихшылардың ортақ пікіріне сәйкес, әлемде орын алған барлық оқиғалар: шумерлер өркениетінен бастап, темір дәуіріне дейінгі оқиғаларды сипаттау үшін қажетті дерек көздерінің жоқтығына байланысты бірбеткей тұжырым жасай салу жүзеге аспайды. Біз тек болжамдап, сараптап, өз жорамалдарымызды ғана айта аламыз. Бұл жорамалдарды құптап немесе жоққа шығару әсте мүмкін емес. Мәселен Меккеде Аллаға ғибадат етіп, қажылық жасаушыларға Алла Тағала тарапынан жасаған күнәлары үшін жұмақтан жер бетіне қуып жерген Адам ата мен Хауа ана кездесетін жер -деп , бір қара тасты көрсетеді. Бұл ақпарат қайдан алынды? Айғақтар қайда? Мұсылмандар бұған жай сене салуы керек, ал осы жайтты ғылыми түрде айғақтауға жол жоқ) Бірақ бұның арты неге апарып соқтыратынын кім білсін? Ұлы Гетенің "көзді тарс жұма салып, соқыр сеннімен дінге мойынұсына беру дінннің бастамасы емес, кез келген даналықтың соңы" деген қанатты сөзі бар. Бұл әрине керемет сөз, осы мәселеге байланысты өз ойын орыстың ұлы ақыны және дипломат елшісі Федор Тютчев былай деп келтіреді: "Ресейді ақылмен түсініп болмассың, ортақ аршынға салып өлшей алмассың. Бұның ерекше ғана қасиеті: Ресейге тек сенуге болады". Поппер шарты бойынша, ең алдымен теория пайда болады, ал сонан кейін айғақтардың көмегімен оны жоққа шығару әрекеттері жасалады. Ал енді өз басым кезінде Қытай, Үндістан, Месопотамия, Мысыр және Еуразия ата мекенінде үлкен өркениеттердің негізін салған ата-бабаларымыздың ұлылығы туралы пікірімді айғақтардың көмегімен теріс деп жоққа шығарғысы келетін маман ғалымдарды пікірталасқа шақырамын. Пікірталас барысында әрине әркім өз пікірін растау үшін жаңа теорияларды келтіруі тиіс. Мәселен, қазақ албандарына испан каталондықтарымен туыстығын дәлелдеу үшін өздерінің ДНК-анықтау мақсатында қандарын салыстырса, жетіп жатыр.

Арафат тауы - "Эдем" жұмағынан қуылғаннан кейінгі Адам ата мен Хауа ананың жер бетіндегі қайтадан қауышқан орны. Эдем - қазақ тілінде "Әдемі" деген ұғымды білдіреді.

# Түркілер – көне өркениетердің негізін қалағандар

## - Шумер, Эллада, Элам...
## Алғы сөздің орнына. Түркілік этнонимдер:
### оларДЫҢ қалыптасу ерекшеліктері.

Ресейлік зерттеуші Ю.Н.Дроздов өзінің "Тюркоязычный период европейской истории" (Мәскеу, ООО ИПК "Литера" баспасы, 2011 жыл) кітабында былай деп келтіреді: "жекелеген бір халықтың (тайпаның) көне немесе қазіргі замандағы тілдік ерекшеліктері ежелгі замандардағы атауына қатысты сенімді тұрғыда анықталуы мүмкін". Бар мәселе мынада: байырғы замандарда өмір сүрген халықтардың автоэтнонимдік атаулары қазіргі кезеңдерге қандай күйде жетті? Осы мәселеге сәйкес, біз түркі халықтары еуропалық халықтармен салыстырғанда, жағдайымыз әлдеқайда тәуір. Еуропа халықтарының тілдерін әлдекімдер, белгісіз бір себептерге байланысты индоеуропалық тілдер деп атап кеткен. Осы Ю.Дроздовтың жазуына қарағанда, қазіргі замандағы Үндістандық үндістердің ата бабаларының Еуропа аймағына келіп кеткендігі жөнінде айғақты антикалық заман тарихшыларының бірде бірі келтірмеген.

Осыған сәйкес ғылымда әлемдік тілдердің нақты түрдегі екі құрамды классификациялық бөліну жігі бар: флективті және аглюнативті. Флективті тілдерде, олардың көптеген ғасырлар бойы дамуы барысында сөздің құрамы көптеген өзгерістерге ұшырап, уақыт өте келе, флективті тілдердегі сөздер мүлде өзге фонетикалық құрылымға ауысады. Сол себепті флективті тілдердің этникалық түп тамырын зерттеуде үлкен қиындықтар кездесуде. Еуропаның көптеген елдерінің тілі флективті тілдер тобына жатады.

Түркі тілдес халықтардың тілдері туралы әңгіме бөлек. Олар агглютинативті тілдер тобына енеді. Тілдердің бұл тобындағы сөздердің түп тамыры мыңдаған жылдар өтсе де байырғы қалпын сақтап, фонетикалық өзгерістерге ұшырамайды. Осылайша, қазіргі замандағы агглютинативтік тілдер тобындағы этнонимдер мен сөздердің фонетикалық құрылымын көне замандардағы жазба деректерден де кездестіруге болады. В.Н.Буданова өзінің "Этнонимия племен Западной Европы: рубеж античности и средневековья" (Мәскеу, 1991 жыл) атты еңбегінде атап өткендей: "Этнонимдер, атаулар сынды үлкен консервативтілік пен өміршеңдікке ие болып келеді. Бұл ұғымдарды сәйкесті тұрғыдағы этникалық қауымдастық топ өкілдері сақтап келіп, атадан балаға мұра етіп қалдырып отырған…" Осы қорытынды түркі тілдес халықтардың этпонимдеріне апықтама болып табылады. Барша келтірілген мәліметтер Ю.Н.Дроздовтың келесідей қорытынды шығаруына мүмкіндік береді: "Түркі тілдес лексикалық бірліктердің фонетикалық тұрақтылығы ерекше құбылыс екендігі сөзсіз, көне замандардағы жекелеген лексемаларға қарап отырып, этнонимдерге сараптама жүргізу арқылы жекелеген бір халықтар мен тайпалардың этникалық болмысын анықтау мүмкіндігі туды…"

Ірі тюрколог ғалым М.З.Закиевтің "Происхождение тюрков и татар" (Москва, 2003 жыл ) зерттеуіне сүйене отырып, түркі тілдеріндегі этнонимдердің қалыптасу ережелеріне тоқталады. Бұл ережелер келесідей грамматикалық схемалар тізбегіне қатысты: жай сөздердің күрделі сөздерге және жекелеген сөздердң этноқұрылымдық аффикстерге жалғануы арқылы қалыптасады. Ол былай деп жазады: "Бірінші жағдайда, күрделі сөздің бастапқы түбірлік негізі келесі сөздің қызметінің анықталуын белгілеп, бұл ұғым анықталатын сөзге айналады…. Анықтау мақсатында сөз таптарының бірнеше түрі пайдаланылады – сын есім, сан есім, етістіктердің түбірлік құрамдары. Әдетте зат есімдер анықталатын сөз болып табылады. Этнонимдердің үлкен тобы бар, мұнда анықталатын сөз ретінде анықталуы жағынан әркелкі болып келетін бірнеше немесе жекелеген сөздер тобы қолданылады. Бұл типтік анықталатын сөздер тізбегі түркі тілдес этнонимдердің сенімді тұрғыдағы этникалық негізі болып табылады. Мұндай сөздер қатарына әдетте келесі лексемалар енеді: ир(ер), ер адамның фонтикалық үлгілері –ар, эр, ур, ор; мин-мен - фонетикалық үлгілері –мен, ман, бан; бай-фонетикалық үлгілері – би, бей, май, пи, бик, бэк; ас-фонтетикалық үлгілері – ас, аз, уз, ус. Кейде анықталатын сөз бастапқы түбір негіздің орнын алуы мүмкін".

Бұл ережелерді ұйғырлардың көне атауына сәйкес мысал ретінде көрсетейік – тоғыз оғыздар, яғни оғыздың тоғыз тайпасының одағы немесе қазақ халқының ішіндегі найман тайпасы одағындағы қаракерей, сондай-ақ қоңырат, албан тайпасының ішіндегі қоңыр бөрік және қызыл бөрік тайпалары. Мұнда қара, қоңыр, қызыл сөздері қолданылып отыр. Осы тізімге қазақ руларының келесідей этнонимдерін: беснайза, сары жомарт, төртқара, жетіру сынды ру атауларын қамтуға болады.

Біз алдыңғы тарауларда "Эллин", "Италия", "Барселона", "Тұманды Альбион" т.б. этнонимдеріне талдау жасадық, кейінгі тарауларда да бұл мәселеге кеңінен тоқталатын боламыз.

Ю.Дроздовты өзі б.з. алғашқы мыңжылдықтың басындағы рустардың аймақ ету мекенін – Осили аралы немесе Балтық теңізіндегі Эзель аралы деп көрсетеді. Бұл сөзді ол АсИль немесе АсЕль – "ас халықтарының елі" деп түсіндіреді. Бұл тайпалардың тегі түркі екендігі мәлім. Басқа бір жағдайда, "Каталония" сөзін таладауға қатысты арнайы әдістемені пайдалана отырып, былай деп жазады: осы лексеманың негізгі түп тамыры "кат" бөлігі көне түрі тілінен "қатты" - деген мағынада аударылады, ал екінші алон- бөлігі, бұл алан сөзінің біртіндеп интерпретацияланған түрі, ал үшінші бөлігі –ия –шаруашлық, аймақ, ел деген ұғымды білдіреді. Яғни Каталония этно аймағының атауының толық мағынасы – "күшті аландардың елі" ұғымы болып табылады.

Қазақ тілінде ие (қожайын, еге) деген сөздің бар екенін ескерейік. Ал қазақтың "ұя" атты басқа бір сөзі – шаңырақ, отау, туған мекен деген мағынаны береді. Сол себепті Каталония атауын қазақ тілінде талдағанда: "күшті аландардың үйі" деген мағынада қолдануға болады.

Ал енді этноқұраушы аффикстердің көмегімен түркі этнонимдерінің құрылу мәселесіне келсек, онда бұлардың ішінде көптеген фонетикалық үлгілері бар - лы аффиксі лы/ды немесе лық/лік, олардың инварианттары:

" -лек, люк, лок; -дік, дық, дек, тық, тек; -нек; -лі, ны, ды, зы, т, ты".

Мәселен, осы аталмыш этноқұраушы аффикстер арқылы жасалған қазақ руларының этнонимдерін келтіруге болады: тобықты, шапырашты, ошақты; қаңлы, балғалы, балталы, бағаналы, қанжығалы, шанышқылы; шекті; сіргелі, қуандық, сүйіндік, бегендік, сондай-ақ сырманақ, шуманақ; молдыстық, желдіыстық; байұлы, әлімұлы және т.т.

\*\*\*

Ғылыми әдебиетте "Еңбектің ұлы бөлінісі" аты түсінік қалыптасқан. Бұл кезең шамасымен әртүрлі пікірлерге сәйкес б.з.д. IY-III мыңжылдықтарға қатысты екендігі белгілі. Бұл кезеңде қоғам екіге қарама қайшы топқа бөлінді: бірі-отырықшы жер игерушілер, екіншісі – көшпенді малшылар. Олардың антогонистік қарама қайшылығы жөнінде қазіргі заманда көрнекті ғалым Арнольд Тойнби айтып кеткен еді. Ол қарама қайшылықтың негізгі түп тамыры осы топтардың рухани құндылғына байланысты екендігін анықтады. XIX ғасырда Германияның тарихшылары арасында бірқатар даңқты көрнекті ғалымдардың жұлдыздық шоғыры шықты. Олар: Оппенгеймер, Ратцель, Прийак, Гумпловиц және т.б. Осы ғалымдар мемлекет, таптық қоғам және өркениеттердің пайда болуының "жаулаушылық тұжырмын" негіздеді. Олар бұл үрдістердің Еуразия алқабынан шыққан мал шаруашылығымен айналысатын тайпаларға қатысты екендігін айқын көрсетті.

Қазақтың дарынды жас ғалымы Ж.Байжумин өзінің "История рождения, жизни и смерти пастуха Авеля. Арийский лексикон" атты тамаша еңбегінде нақты тұрғыдағы түркілік және қазақ руларын мысалға ала отырып, мыңдаған жылдар ішінде өзінен әлдеқайда басым, күш қуатты тайпалардың ықпалымен Еуразиялық алқаптардан кетуге мәжбүрленген түркі рулары Қытай, Үндістан, Месопотамия, Түркия, Мысыр, Шығыс және Батыс Еуропа отырықшы халықтарының жерін жаулап алып, олардың аймағында жаңа мемлекеттік құрылым, қала және өркениеттерді құрғандығы туралы мәлімдейді. Мал шаруашылқ топтарындағы экстенсивтік шаруашылық жүргізу амалдары өсіп өніп келе жатқан малдар үшін жаңа жайылымдық жерлер қажеттілігін тудырды, осылайша, қазақтың күш қуатты түркілік тайпалары әлсіз руларды антикалық тарихшы Помпей Трогтың айтуына қарағанда, "Скифтік қуғындалғандарға" айналдырып отырған. Олар өз кезегінде Еуразия алқабынан кетсе де, жер игерумен айналысатын отырықшы халықтардың жерлерін жаулауға көшті. Басқа жерлерге көшіп келген көшпенділерді (олардың саны аз) өмірдің өзі бір жерде ортақтаса өмір сүруге мәжбүрлеген. Яғни осыған сәйкес, қала, мемлекет, өркениеттердің пайда болуының алғышарттары қалыптасты. Өйткені жаулап алған халықтарды билеп төстеу үшін мәжбүрлеу институттары: полиция, салық органы, соттар т.б. қажет еді. Жоғарыда айтып өткенімдей, Каспий теңізі жағалауынан өзінен әлдеқайда басым түскен тайпалардың ықпалымен көшуге мәжбүрленген оғыздар XI ғасырдың басында Армения, Грузия, Ирак, Парсы елі, Кіші Азия мемлекеттерінің жер игерушілік өркениеттерін жаулап алып, осының негізінде сельджуктер мемлекетінің негізін қалыптастырады.

XIX ғасырдың аяғында –XX ғасырдың басында өмір сүрген неміс ғалым Альфред Вебер анықтағандай:  "Әлемдік тарих көшпенділердің сансыз топырлаған тұлпарларының тұяғы дүбірінің аккомпаненменті арқылы жасалынды..." б.з.д. IY мыңжылдықта Месопотамияда осындай оқиға орын алады: Тигр мен Евфрат атты қос өзеннің жағалауына келіп, біздің бабаларымыз көне Шумер мемлекетінің негізін құрады, көрнекті ғалым Алтай Аманжолов, ірі ақын, ойшыл Олжас Сүлеймонов т.б ғалымдардың  айтуына қарағанда, осы мемлекет тұрғындары көне түркі тілінде сөйлеген.

Біз қазіргі кезде ұлы Шумер мемлекеті жайлы не білеміз? Шамасы олар Тәңір дініне (Тигр өзені – Денгри Тенгри өзені) сыйынған болса керек. Кейінірек біз шумерлердің таңғажайып жаңалықтардың авторлары екендігі туралы білдік. Жазу, дөңгелек, секунд, минут, градусқа бөлудің алпыс еселік жүйесі, темірді өңдеу құпиясы және тағы басқасы – осы жаңалықтарсыз XXI ғасырды елестету мүмін емес.

Ағылшын зерттеушісі Л.Вулли ("Малая история искусств", Мәскеу, "Искусство" баспасы, 1981 жыл) былай деп жазады: "Біз өнер атаулысының басында Грекия тұрды деп саналатын кезеңде өмірге келдік. Грекия Афина Паллада секілді Зевстің басынан жаралды-деп санадық. Бірақ бізге Грекияның өзі барша күш қуатын лидия, хет,финикия мәдениеті, Крит аралдарынан алғанына көз жеткізудің мүмкіндігі туындады. Осы мемлекеттердің мәденистінен күш сарқығандықтан, мысырлықтар өсіп гүлдене түсті, оның түп тамыры көне замандарға қарай жетелейді. Осы халықтардың негізінде шумерлердің ізі бар. Ш.Қуанғановтың ойы бойынша, шумерлік "Урук" атты қала мемлекетте (түрі тілінен аударғанда ұрық – ауыспалы мағынада бастамалардың бастауы деген мағынаны білдіреді) үш тәңірге: жеміс беруші және махаббат тәңірі Инанну (түркі, қазақ тілінде илану), Ана тәңірі мен оның бауыры күн тәңірі - Утуға (Уту-қазақ тілінде от мағынасын білдіреді) сыйынып табынған. Олжас Сүлейменов өз еңбектерінде Месопотамияның алғашқы тұрғындары мифтік прототүрктер емес, қалыптасқан оғыз, қыпшақ, болгар диалектісінде сөйлеген тайпалардың өкілдері болғандығын айтып өтеді. Мәселен, шумер және түркі тілдерінде "йер" сөзі жер ұғымын білдіреді, ал "ұш" үш - үш саны, Денгри- Тенгри- Құдай мағынасында қолданылады.

Месопотамияның көне жерінде бір көшпенді тайпаларды келесі бір көшпенді тайпалардың толқыны ауыстырып жатты. Ь.з.д. XYII ғасырда касситтер тайпасының көсемі Қандаш Вавилонияны басып алып, әлемнің төрт бұрышының патшасы атанады. Жоғарыда айтқанымдай, бұл тайпаның Касситтер деген этнонимі кейінірек қазақтардың атауы ретінде өзгеріске ұшырайды, бұл тайпа Вавилонды төрт жүз жылдай билейді.

Б.з.д. II мыңжылдықтың ортасынан бері Үндістан аймағына еуразия даласынан шыққан көне арийлік көшпенді тайпалардың көш толқыны басталды. Ал б.з.д. I мыңжылдықта бұл ежелгі елді сақтардың шығыс скифтік тайпалары өзіне толық бағындырып алады. Олардың келуімен бұл аймақта жаңа буддизм діні пайда болды, ал оның негізін салушы Шакья Муни кейбір деректер бойынша, Шақа руынан шыққан. Бұл рудың ұрпақтары қазіргі кезеңде қазақтың ішіндегі Арғын және Найман тайпаларының ішінде ғұмыр кешуде. Олар сондай-ақ қазіргі заманғы қазақтың Адай, Жалайыр, Суан, Уақ, Қыпшақ тайпалары арасында да бар.

Жапонның ірі тарихшы ғалымы Эгами Намионың айтуына қарағанда, б.з.д. III ғасырда жапон аралдарындағы алғашқы мемлекеттік құрылымды Алтайдан көшіп келген Ямото атты көшпенділер құрған, олар ең алдымен Шығыс Маньчжурия мен Кореяны жаулап алып кейін Жапон аралдарына бет алады. Алғашқы жапон императорының Мейман есімінің шығу тегі түркілік еді. Ал қола дәуірде прототиптері қырғыздың Саяқ тайпасы арасында қалған Саэк тайпасы қазақтың қазіргі Жайық, Шапырашты, Адай, Шуақ, Сауық руларының ішінде кездеседі. Қазіргі заманғы Тама мен Жалайыр руларының арғы тегі Жапонияда Яён атты қола мәдениеттің негізін салды.

Ал, Кореяға келсек, осы мемлекет атауының шығу төркіні б.з.д. бірінші мыңжылдықтың басында корей аралдарына келіп, осында Пэкче, Когурё және Силла мемлекеттерінің негізін қалаған көне түркілік руынан шыққан жаулаушы Қараның есіміне тікелей байланысты. Бүгінгі таңда Қара руының ұрпақтары қазақтың Арғын, Найман, Қоңырат, Дулат, Ысты, Байбақты жән Уақтар арасында да өмір сүреді. Осы рудың өкілдері түрікмен тайпалары арасында да ұшырасады. Осы тұрғыда Корея Президентінің Қазақстанның Елбасын қабылдау салтанатын ерекше атап өтуге болады. Кездесу барысында Қазақстан Президентіне Корей жерінде жүргізілген археологиялық қазба зерттеу жұмыстары нәтижесінде табылған қылыш тарту етілді, бұл қылышты б.з.д. ғасырлардың басында қазақтың зергер қолөнерлері жасаған екен.

2011 жылы Шығыс Қазақстанның Өскемен қаласында өткен "Алтай-түркі әлемінің алтын бесігі" атты ғылыми форумда Жапониядан келген тарих профессоры Марико Харада былай деп мәлімдеді: "Жапония мен Кореяның этнолог ғалымдары осы халықтардың Алтай аймағынан шыққандығы туралы пікірді қолдайды". Осыған сәйкес, аталмыш елдердің тілі түркі алтай тілдер тобы қатарына жатады.

Келтірілген пікірлердің көпшілігін Жұмажан Байжуминнің жоғарыда айтылған еңбегінен табуға болады. Мәселен, б.з.д. XIII ғасырда аты аңызға айналған Трояны жеңген грек-ахейлік - Ақай руы қазақтың Арғын Және Найман тайпасы және Қаңлы тайпасының ішінде Ағай руы ретінде жалғасын тапты. Ал осы оқиғалардан бұрын бұл көшпенділер Пелопонесс түбіне Еуразия алқаптарынан келген болатын. Гректер өздерін эллин деп атайтынын ескеру маңызды. "Эллин" сөзі – "еліні" (құрлықтық негізгі тайпаның інілері) мағынасын білдіреді. Яғни Еуразия алқабынан Пелопонесске бет алып, осы жақта орныққан көшпенділер өзін Еуразияда қалып қойған көшпенді түркі тайпаларының "інілеріміз" –деп санаған.

Көп уақыт өткен соң, XX ғасыр ғалымдары сол кезеңнің оқиғаларын мүлде басқаша түсіндіруде. Мәселен Ж.Байжумин ғылымдағы көр соқырлықтың классикалық үлгісін келтіреді. Ол кеңестік академик Д.А.Авдусиннің "фракиялық тайпалардың салт дәстүріне қатысты Буга өзенінің жоғарғы жағындағы "белогрудов мәдениетінде" кенеттен орын алған өзгерістеріне" жасаған түсініктемесі туралы баяндайды.. Аталмыш академик былай деп жазады: "Б.з.д. YIII ғасырда"-деп жалғастырады ойын ғалым, бұл тайпаның негізгі шаруашылығы жер игеру болып табылды, онымен қоса, мал шаруашылығымен де айналысты... Олардың бағатын малының ішінде шошқа көп. Бұл сипаттама көшпенді мәдениетке сәйкес емес. Осылайша бұл мәдениет негіздерінің скифтік мәдениетке еш қатысы жоқ..." Академик ойын былайша негіздейді: "Б.з.д. YIII ғасырдан бастап, белогрудов-чернолесс тайпалары аяқастынан соғыспен айналысатын жауынгер тайпаларға айналды. Олардың қару жарағы зираттардан табылып, скифтік қару жараққа ұқсай бастайды..." Академик көшпенді болып табылмайтын егіншілер мен жер өңдеуші тайпалардың қалайша аяқастынан соғыспен айналысатын жауынгер тайпаға айналғандығына? - аң таң болып, қайран қалады. Өркениеттердің қалыптасуының "Жаулаушылық теориясы" осы феномендік оқиғаларды оңай түсіндіріп, бәрін қалпына келтіреді. Б.з.д. YIII ғасырда Еуропаның оңтүстігіндегі егіншілікпен айналысатын тайпаларын көшпенді скиф тайпалары жаулап алады, олар отырықшы халықтың өміріне көшпенді малшылардың дәстүрлерін енгізеді. Дәлірек айтсақ, фракиялық, иллириялық тайпалар деп аталып кеткен тайпалар еуразиялық алқаптардан келді, бұл тайпаларға өз кезегінде бздің арғы тегіміз болып табылатын, осы тайпалардан әлдеқайда күшті, қуатты тайпалар қысым жасап, ата қоныстарынан кетуге мәжбүр етеді. Жоғарыда келтірілген фракиялық және иллириялықтардың тайпаларының құрамы, гректің дорий, ахей, ионий тайпалары сынды жергілікті жер игерушілер мен Еуразия алқаптарынан келген көшпенді малшылардан жасақталды. Римдіктер гректерді осылай атайтын, олар болса, "өздерін эллин немесе данайлықпыз", -деп мақтан тұтты. Яғни олар өздерінің Дон-Тана өзендері жағалуынан келгенін меңзейді, ал бұл аймақта қазақтардың эллиндерге аттас тайпа өмір сүрді. Жоғарыда атап өткенімдей, Эллин –Еліні ұғымын білдіреді, осы атау арқылы эллиндердің құрлықтық жаулаушы халыққа туыс болып келетіндігі аңғарылады.

А.И.Тойнби және А.Вебер өз зерттеулерінде отырықшы немесе егіншілік мәдениеттердің олардың консервативтілігіне сәйкес өркениеттік қоғамдарға жеке дербес түрде келуі мүмкін еместігі туралы жазады. Сонымен бірге, тәңір дініндегі салт дәстүр заңдылықтарына сәйкес, аспан – ер адам ұғымы, жер-әйелдің бейнесін белгілейді. Алғашқысымен - көшпендінің қоғамдық өмірі тығыз байланыста болса, екіншісінің тағдыры – жер игеруге қатысты болып келеді. Тек "ұрықтандыру" немесе көшпенділердің отырықшы халықтарды жаулау нәтижесінде жаңа өмір немесе өркениет туындайтын.

Көшпенділер өміріндегі әдет ғұрып салттар негізіндегі шаруашылықты жүргізудің экстенсивті тәсілі экономикалық жағдайлардың дамуына жағдай тудырды, Осыған сәйкес, баайлықтың негізгі көзі - малдың санын одан сайын арттыра түсу үшін жекелеген тайпалар өздерінен әлсіз тайпаларға шабыл жасап, күш көрсету арқылы жерлерін тартып алатын. Кейінгілері тұрақты мекендерінен кетіп, "Скифиядан қуғындалғандарға" айналып, жер игерумен айналысатын отырықшы халықтарды бағындырып, жаңа жерлер кеңістігінде жаңа мемлекеттік құрылымдардың негізін құратын. Бұл мемлекеттерді осы аймаққа көшіп келген тайпалар басқарып, билеуші шонжарлар ретінде билеп төстеумен айналысатын. Ал байырғы жергілікті халықтар қызметші, құл ретінде оларға қызмет атқарып, екінші санаттағы адамдар болып табылатын. Бірақ жоғары білімді бинарлық қоғамдар уақыт өте келе өзара тығыз араласу нәтижесінде ортақ этникалық кейіпке енетін. Жүздеген жылдар өтіп, атамекендері – Еуразия алқаптарына оралған соң, осы аймақты мекендейтін байырғы нәсілдерге жаңа этникалық түр сипаттарды ала келетін. Ұлы Дала тұрғындары этникалық түр түсінің сан алуан, әркелкі болып келуі осылайша түсіндіріледі. Мәселен, қазіргі заманғы қазақ қыпшақтары келесідей руларға бөлінеді: құба қыпшақ және торы қыпшақ т.т.

Ал енді өзімізге мынандай сұрақ қояйық – көшпенділердің отырықшы халықтардан басым түсуінің себебі қайда жатыр?

Иә, біз номад-көшпенділер адамзат тарихында бірінші болып жылқыны қолға үйретіп, коммуникациялық байланыстың дамуына үлес қостық. Көшпенділер-ата бабаларымыз өз аймағында жер тарихында тұңғыш рет қола құюды қолға алып, темір игеруді жолға қойдық. Осының нәтижесінде қару жарақ жағынан басқалардан басым түстік. Ал бірақ рух жағынан өзге халықтармен салыстырғанда, номадалар неге әлдеқайда жоғары, биік тұрады? Адам төзбес шыдамдылық пен ержүрек өжеттілік, жанкешті батырлыққа ата-бабаларымыздың қолы қалай жетті? Бұған жауаптарды ата-бабаларымыз ұстанған діннен іздеу керек және Ұлы Даланың адам төзгісіз, қатігез ауа райы жағдайында өміршеңдігі басым түсіп, осы аймаққа сұрыптала білудің де өзіндік ықпалы бар. Тәңір діні – бүкіл әлем діндерінің түп негізі – адамның өмірге қайта жаралатындығын уағыздайды, сол себепті көшпенді бабаларымыз бұл жалғанға философиялық тұрғыдағы көзқарспен қараған. Өлім –ол үшін өмірдің ақыры болып есептелмейтін, өлім –жаңа өмір бастауы. Ал Ұлы Даладағы жауынгер көшпендінің рухына ықпалын ерекше тигізген қатігез ауа райы мәселесіне келсек, бұл өз кезегінде көшпенді малшылардың полигамдық отбасыларға айналуының басты себебі болып табылды.

# Көп ӘЙЕЛ АЛУ – ҚАЗАҚТАРДЫҢ АТА-БАБА САЛТЫНЫҢ ҚҰДІРЕТТІЛІК НЕГІЗІ.

Қазақтар сан ғасырлар ширегінде туысқандыққа негізделген дәстүр-салтқа сәйкес, отбасыларды қауымдастық күйінде құратын. Осыған сәйкес көп әйел алу дәстүрін жаңғыртуға мәжбүр болатын. Кейде маусымдық ауа райы көрсеткіштері 80° сынап бағанасы көрсеткіші, -40 °-тан +40 ° сынап бағанасы көрсеткішіне жеткен жағдайда сұрыптала білу, тірі қалу қиямет қайым дүние. Игерілетін жерлер жоқтың қасы, кейде жұт басталып, осының нәтижесінде мал саны азаятын. Үнемі бір жайылымнан келесі бір жайылымға көшу, мал шаруашылығына қатысты құралдарды игеру мақсатында көптеген мөлшердегі жұмыс қолдарының қажеттілігі, өз малдарын жабайы аңдар мен көзі тоймас барымташылардан қорғау мәселелерін тек отағасы мен әйелі, бес-алты баладан құралатын дәстүрлі отбасы шеше алмай қалды. Ал туыстық шарттарға негізделген полигамдық отбасы алға қойылған мақсатқа жету үшін бір бағытта сапалы және жемісті тұрғыда қызмет атқарды. Бұл үлкен отбасының нақты бір белгіленген тәртіп бойынша жүруі, кішілердің үлкендерді сыйлап құрметтеуі, ата-аналар мен қарияларды сыйлауы, "жеті ата" салты бойынша генетикалық тазалықты сақтауы сынды отбасылық "ойын тәртібі" белгіленді. Жеті ата заңы бойынша, жеті атадан кейін қыз алысып, туыстық қан араласпай, жаңартылып отыруы нәтижесінде, ата-бабаларымыздың табиғи болмысы тазалыққа негізделді, осы шаралар арқылы ата тегіміз қатал ауа райы жағдайларын да игеріп, үйреніп алды. Тауарлы өндірісті қалыптастырып, киім тігу үшін шикізат өңдеумен айналысты, азық түлік әзірлеп,үйір-үйір жылқылар мен қора-қора мал бақты, металлургиялық өнімдер: ең алдымен – қоладан, сонан кейін темірден бұйым, әшекей-заттарды әзірлеуді игерді. Осының нәтижесінде Ұлы Далаға көпестер әлемнің түкпір-түкпірінен ағылды. Өйткені Ұлы Жібек Жолы салынып, өркендеу жолына түсті. Бірақ көп әйел алу тағы бір мәселені тудырды: егер бұл мәселе нәтижслі тұрғыда шешімін тапқан жағдайда, онда ата-бабларымыздың рухы одан сайын артып, Ұлы Даладағы демографиялық ахуал да жақсаратын, ата-бабаларымыз Дунай мен Хуанхэ өзендері аймағын толығымен мекендей түсетін еді. Қазіргі Қазақстан жайлы осылай айтудың өзі қиын, елімізде "қытай мәселесін" төтенше тұрғыда көтеру қажеттілігі туындады. Көп әйел алу арқылы сапалы тұрғыда өмір сүру дәстүрін жақсарту нәтижесінде қоғамда күрделі гендерлік ахуалдар орын алды. Егер жеті ағайындылардың бірі өзіне жеті әйел алса, ал қалған алтауы қосағын таппай, өздерінің қарапайым табиғи қажеттіліктерін өтей алмай, жалғыз қалып қойды. Бірақ олардың болмысы генетикалық тұрғыда мөлдір таза болғандықтан, табиғаты таза жерде өсіп жетілгендіктен, күш қуаттары артып. бойға сыймай тұрғандықтан, олар көбейіп, жүйелі тұрғыда ұрпақ таратуды аңсады. Осы мәселеде де сан ғасырдан бері келе жатқан ата баба салты көмекке келді. Барша ағайындылар, кенже баланы (шаңырақ иесі) әке-шешелерімен бірге қалдырып, басқа аймақтарға бет алатын. Өзінің маңдайына жазылған жарын табу үшін, атқа қонған, қолында қылышын ұстаған, иығына садағын ілген, ержүрек жас жігіт қай жаққа бет алды - деп ойлайсыз? Қазақтың көршілес басқа руларында да осындай ахуал орын алғандықтан, бәрі бірігіп, қол жасақталып, көшпенділердің әскерлері Қытай, Үндістан, Парсы, Мысыр және Еуропаға аттанып, өздеріне қажетті бірнеше кербез сұлуларды табатын, олар көшпенділердің әйелдеріне айналып, мал бағып, ет әзірлеп, жүн-мата тоқуға көмектесетін.

Келесідей маңызды сұрақ тыңғылықты зерттеуді қажет етеді: ата-бабаларымыздың өзге туыс болып табылмайтын халықтардың жеріне белсенді түрде аттануына соншалықты тұрғыда не себеп болды? Алғашқысы – экономикалық мәселе – мал басын арттыру үшін жайылымдық жерлер жетіспеді, осыған сәйкес, жерге ие болу мақсатында, көршілес туыс тайпалар мекендеп жатқан жерлерінен қуылды, олар өз кезегінде "Скифиядан қуғындалғандарға" айналып, басқа отырықшы халықтардың жерлерін басып алып, оларды өздерінің қоластындағы халықтарға айналдыратын. Бәлкім, барша себеп ұрпақ жалғастырып, бала сүюде де болуы мүмкін. Бұл Зигмунд Фрейд зерттеген "таза түрдегі "физиологиялық себеп" болуы ықтимал. Өз басым екінші себепке көбірек сүйенемін.

\*\*\*

Ата-бабаларымыздың осыған іспеттес өмір салты туралы қазақ әдебиетінің классик жазушылары сан мәрте қалам тербеген еді, бұл тақырып қазіргі заманғы қазақстандықтарды да алаңдатуда. Олардың ішінде металлургиялық құрал инженері Нұрқасым Абуев маған тікелей түрде хат жолдапты, бұл хаттың негізгі мазмұнына байланысты мәселелерді осы кітабымда тоқталып өттім.

Сонымен бірге "осьтік уақыт" деп аталатын ерекше бір феномендік құбылысқа тоқтала кетейік: жағрафиялық тұрғыда бір-бірінен алшақ жатқан Қытай, Үндістан, Месопотамия, Мысыр, Грекия сынды аймақтарда бүкіл әлемдік діндердің ошақтары мен көне заман ойшылдарының рухани туындылары да бір уақытта дүниеге келіп жатты. Альфред Вебердің мұндай осы феномен құбылыстың пайда болуын зерттеудегі басты себептері ерекше тұрғыдағы теориямен тығыз байланысты: бірінші кезекте, Еуразия көшпенді халықтарының бір уақытта отырықшы жер игерушілердің аймақтарына басып кіріп, шабуыл жасау айғақтарына тығыз байланысты болып табылады. Бұл сонау ежелгі алмағайып тарихи замандарда көшпенді бабаларымыздың мерейі үстем және басым түскендігінің белгісі емес пе?

## Пассионарлық теориясы Л.Гумилевтікі дұрыс па?

Ұлы еуразиялық ғалым "пассионарлық ұғымы" – деп, адам немесе біртұтас халықтың биохимиялық күш қуатының шектен тыс артып көтерілуі деп түсінген. Осыған сәйкес осы күш қуатқа ие халық өркениетті жаратуға немесе мемлекеттерді қиратып, талқандауға құмарлығы артады.

Ал осы күш қуат көзінің шектен тыс артықшылығы күн шуағының белсенділігі немесе жаңа жұлдыздардың жарқырау кезеңдеріне байланысты өрбитін, ғарыштан келетін пассионарлық ықпалынан кейін орын алады. Белгілі бір уақыт және белгілі бір кеңістік ішінде белгілі бір этнос өзінің пассионарлық әрекеттерінің жемісін жинаған соң, әлемдік сахнаға шығып, өзі туралы кеңінен жариялай бастайды. Осы құбылыс арқылы Лев Гумилев Ұлы Римнің іс әрекеттері мен араб халифатының жаулаушылық жорықтары және моңғол билеушілерінің үстемдігі туралы сөз қозғайды. Ал іс жүзінде осылай ма? Әрине, бұл әдемі теория Лев Гумилевті "ұлы еуразиялыққа" айналдырды. Бұл болжамдық теория көптеген тарихи құбылыстардың себептерін түсіндіруге көмектеседі. Бірақ, менің ойым бойынша, жаңа заманға дейінгі екінші мыңжылдықтан бастау алатын Еуразиядан шыққан көшпенділердің рухани серпілісіне Л.Гумилев болжамының еш қатысы жоқ деп санаймын.

Бұның себептері тағы да – айқын және қарапайым тұрғыдағы тарихи айғақтарға негізделеді.

Осы кітапта келтірілген дәйектермен айғақтарды қорытындылай, жинақтай келе, келесідей пікірге келеміз: ата-бабамыз адамзат тарихында бірінші болып жабайы жылқыны қолға үйретті, жер бетінде бірінші болып металлургиялық өндірістің қыр-сырын меңгерді. Осының нәтижесінде ол жауынгер ретінде жеңілмейтін жеңімпазға айналды. Ұлы Даладағы қатаң тұрғыдағы ауарайы жағдайы оның мінезін шыңдады, ал көшпенді малшылыққа негізделген Ұлы Дала экономикасы "Скифиядан қуғындалғандардың" пайда болуының алғышарттарын негіздеді, олар өз кезегінде жаңа жерлерге көшіп, жергілікті егіншілер мен орманшыларды бағындырып, жаулап алған жерлерінде жаңа мемлекеттер мен өркениеттерді орнатты.

# ДҮНИЕЖҮЛІК ТОПАН СУ ЖӘНЕ БӨРІ ХАЛҚЫНЫҢ АЛЫСТАҒЫ АТАМЕКЕНІ

Өз кітабымда мен қазақтардың арий атты арғы бабаларының қазіргі қоныстану аймағына солтүстіктен-Гипорбореядан келгенін атап өттім, бұл мемлекет шамасымен жиырма мың жыл бұл бұрын өркендеп гүлдене бастаған еді. Ата-бабаларымыздың туған мекенінен кетуіне не себеп болды? Бүгінгі таңда ғалымдар 22000 жыл бұрын Камчатка аймағында Жер бетіне үлкен астероидтың бөлшегі келіп түседі, осы қақтығыс нәтижесінде о баста Батыс Еуропа арқылы өтетін жер өсі 23.5° ауысып, қазіргі Солтүстік полюске қарай ауытқыды. Н.Кикешевтің "Метаистория. Откуда мы родом? Мифы, гипотезы, факты" кітабында келтірілген көптеген айғақтар жердің қазіргі солтүстік аймағының соқтығыс нәтижесінде жедел түрде ерекше суық ауа райы бедері болып ұласқандығына меңзейді. Бұған 2001 жылы Таймырда француздардың жақсы сақталған мамонт денесін аршып алғандығы дәлел. 22000 жыл бұрын, ғалымдардың деректері бойынша, Сібірге мәңгілік суық ауа райы орнаған еді. Сонымен бірге, гляцилог мамандардың деректеріне қарағанда, Батыс еуропа мәңгілік суық құрсауынан тек 9000 жыл бұрын ғана босаған, ал Балтық жағалауы аймағында алғашқы адам б.з.д. 5000 жыл бұрын пайда болған.

Жүз қырық елдің аңыздарында дүниежүзілік топан су туралы айтылады. Інжіл бұл құбылысты адамдардың жасаған күнәлары үшін Жаратушының жазасы - деп түсіндіреді. Ғылым бұл ерекше оқиғаны жердің астероидпен қақтығысуы нәтижесінде орын алған деп баяндайды. Соқтығыс нәтижесінде, жердің түбі ойылып, тынық мұхит сулары Беринг бұғазын қалыптастырып, қазіргі Солтүстік полюске қарай жүйтки жөнеліп, Солтүстік мұзды мұхитты өмірге әкелді. Әрине, осы аймақты мекендеген халықтар шұрайлы жерлерден кетуге мәжбүр болады, олардың арасында ата-бабаларымыз да бар еді. Н.Кикешев Қиыр Шығыс аудандарының топоним, гидронимдері және сол замандағы тұрғындардың қазіргі мекендеген жер атауларын мұқият түрде салыстырып, таңқаларлық нәтижелерге қол жеткізеді. Мәселен, ол Ресей Федерациясының Архангельск және Вологда облыстарының гидронимдері 90°- пайызға дейін Иран, Ауғанстан, Үндістан мен Пәкістан гидронимдеріне ұқсас болып келетіндігін анықтаған. Бұны түсіндіру оңай, өйткені адамдар басқа жақтарға көшіп қоныстанған соң, жаңа өзендер мен көлдерді өздерінің ата қоныстарынң әдеттегі үйреншікті атауларымен атайтын.

Дәл осындай жағдай Қазақстан аймағында да орын алып отыр. Мәселен Байұлы атты тайпалық бірлестікте "Тана" атты ру бар. Бұл ру байырғы кезеңдерде Дон өзенінің басейні бойындағы оңтүстік орыс алқаптарында өмір сүрген. Осы өзеннің қазіргі атауы Тана руының атына байланысты трансформацияланып өзгеріске ұшыраған. Мәселен, Баренц теңізінде Тана-фьорд бұғазы бар, оның сулары Тана-Эльв өзеніне келіп құяды. Анар-Йокка осы өзеннің ағыс болып саналады, бұл ағыстың жағалауында Ишкурс қаласы орналасқан. Қазақтардың арғы тегі шумерлерде найзағай тәңірі Ишкур деп аталатын. Ал қазақтарда Анар есімі – көкөністің атауы болып табылатындығы аян. Осыншама ауыр апаттан кейін бабаларымыз Гипербореядан кетіп, жаңа жерлерге келіп қоныстанып, осы жерлердегі көл- өзен, тау, өлкелерді өздерінің бұрынғы үйреншікті, дәстүрлі атауларымен атайтын.

Түркілердің ата-бабалары шамасымен жиырма мың жыл бұрын қазіргі Америка Құрама Штаттарының аймағында өмір сүргендігі туралы пікірді доктор Теодор Шур бастаған америкалық ғалымдардың ғылыми тобы айғақтады. Олар 1982 жылы әйгілі Лепск тіреуіштерінен 40 шақырымдай жерде орналасқан, кейінгі неолит дәуірі мұрасы болып саналатын геологтар тапқан "диринг-юряхский" жәдігерлерін сараптау барысында, америкалық ирокез және могикандардың арғы тектері көне түркілердің байырғы атамекені таулы Алтай мекенінен шыққан-деген шешімге келеді. ("Комсомольская правда" www.kp.ru. 2-9 ақпан, 2012 жыл)

Антикалық заман тарихшысы Клавдий Птоломей арийлердің көне Отандарын былай сипататайды: "Сармат" (Балтық –Қ.З.) бұғазының ар жағында үлкен арал бар, оны Скандия немссс Эритий деп атайды. Бұл жер аты аңызға айналған бабаларымыз гиперборейлердің ата қонысы. Халықтардың шыққан жері, адамзаттың қалыптасып, кемелденген шеберханасы. Ритей тауларынан сол жақта үлкен өзендер ағады, олардың жағалауында көлінде балық ойнаған, тоғайында құлан шулаған, сансыз малдар жайылған орасан зор алқап жайылымдары бар. Үлкен ормандардың арасында өнімді құнарлы жерлер жатыр. Басқа жерлердің әрқайсысында дәл осындағыдай мол егін шықпайды. Осыған байланысты жерді игеру және темірді балқыту ұғымы қалыптасты.

Қазақтардың алыстағы ата қонысы дегеніміз- осы!

Бүкіләлемдік топан судан кейін біздің ата-бабаларымыз өздерінің қазіргі мекендейтін аймақтарына тұрақты орналасып алды деп санаймын. Жоғарыда айтылғандай, осы өлкеден неолит дәуірінде Қытай, Жапония, Мысыр, Иран, Үндістанның шұрайлы алқаптары орналасқан аймақтарын игеруге аттанған.

Түрі тілінен аударғанда, "Гиперборея" сөзі- "үлкен бөрі" –деген ұғымды білдіруі мүмкін. Т.Досанов өзінің "Тайны руники" кітабындағы Жаратушы Тәңірге негізделген руна тұжырымдамасына сәйкес келесідей қорытынды жасайды: Үлкен аю мен Кіші аю жұлдыздар шоғырының контур кескіндемесі – екі бөрінің бейнесі болып табылады. Ал Арийлерді Гипорборейлер осы жұлдыздардан ұшып келгендер деп санаған. Бәрі жөнімен, арийлердің ұрпақтары- түркілер- бәріні өзінің ата тегі деп санайды. Ал қазақ этнонимін Т.Досанов "қазсақ" деп талдап, қаз бен бөрінің қазақ халқының арғы тегі екендігін айқындап көрсетеді. Ал "қазсақ" сөзінің екінші тіркесі: сақ бөлігі – қасқыр атауының бір түрі ретінде қолданылады. Мәселен, осы дала жануарына халқымыз "саққұлақ" деген атау берген. Қазіргі заман қазақтарының арғы тегі қасқыр мен қаз болғандығына ғалым М.Тынышпаевтың Жетісу өлкесіндегі Қаратал ауылы маңындағы ашқан жаңалығы дәлел болады.

Табылған сурет тасқа салынған, басы қаз және денесі қасқыр болып табылатын жануарды бейнелейді. Бір сөзбен айтқанда, итқұс. Қазақтардағы қасқыр атауы. Оның үстіне қазақтың Матай руының дәстүрлі тамғасы да мойны аққудың мойнындай иірілген қасқыр кейпін сақтаған, бірақ басы құстан аймайтын бейне ретінде белгіленеді. Аңызға сәйкес, о баста барша түркі елі – бөрі елі  болып саналған, ал кейінірек барша Еуразия аймағының Хуанхэден Дунайға дейінгі аймақты мекендейтін түркілік тұрғындары сынды   Қыпшақ этнонимі тек Орта жүздің ішіндегі жекелеген руы ретінде жалғасын тапты. Яғни осылайша, түркі халықтарының ішіндегі қазақтың қазіргі Матай және Садыр рулары ғана көк бөрінің ұрпағы ретінде танылу құрметіне ие болды.

Британиялық мұражайда б.з.д. ҮІ-ІІІ ғасыр мұрасы болып саналатын, қола шәйнек күйіндегі қымбатты жәдігер сақталуда.   Т.Досанов өзінің сілтеме жасаған кітабында Аманқос Мектептігінің ерекше қызық болып келетін болжамын келтіреді. Ол осы композицияға талдау жасай отырып, шәйнектің тұтқасы қасқырдың бейнесі іспеттес, бөрі азуының төменгі жағымен металл теміргe жабысқан. Бұл көрініс халық арасында Темірқазық деп аталатын жұлдыздың бейнесі болып табылады. Ал шәйнектің тұтқасының өзі Үлкен аю жұлдыз шоғырын бейнелейді. Шәйнектің мұрнында қазақтың арғы тегі- Аққу ананың бейнесі көрініс тапқан, ал шәйнектің қақпағының жанында Кіші аю шоқ жұлдызы бейнесіндегі бөлтіріктің суреті салынған. Осы бейне қазақ халқының ұлдары – Қасқыр мен Аққуды бейнелеген. Егер солтүстік жақта орналасқан Сиыршы, Үлкен аю Кіші аю шоқ жұлдыздарын еске алсақ, онда Аманқос Мектептегі болжамының негізі бар.

Осыған орай И.М.Крафтың "Сборник узакононенений о киргизах степных областей" атты кітабында қазақтардың пайда боулы туралы аңыз келтіріледі. Ол былай деп жазады: Ғажайып оқиға орын алды! Суы жоқ шөлде жан тәсілім етуге жақын Қалча Қадырдың дұғасын естігендей көк аспан айқара ашылып, аққу бейнесіндегі аяулы хор қызы көктен түсіп, қанатында шөлді қандыратын су әкеліп, жас жігітті ажалдың аузынан арашалап алып қалады... Олар үйленіп, ұрпақтары қазақ немесе қайсақ деп аталып кетеді".

Кейде туған халқымыздың түп тамырын іздеймін деп осындай ғаламдық шырғалаңдарға да тап болуыңыз ғажап емес!

# Скифтер патшасы Мәди мен ғұндардың шаньюй билеушісі Модэ немесе қазақ рулары қалай қалыптасты

Қазақтар неге жеті атасын танып білуге тиіс және осы жеті атадан тыс некелерге неге тыйым салынды?- деген мәселелер жайында ойланып толғанып көрдім. Себебі, қазақтың жеке дербес руы жеті атадан тарайтын. Қарапайым тұрғыдағы математикалық есептеулер бойынша, қолайлы жағдайлар туындай қалғанда (соғыс, апат, індет-обалардың болмауы) осы жеті атадан тарайтын тұрғындар саны жүздеген мың адамға дейін еркін жететін. Бұл адамдар тобы жеке ру болып қалыптасып, аталмыш ру өзінің бастапқы атасының атымен аталып, жеке дербес түрде өмір сүретін. Жеті атадан кейін әрбір ұрпақ өзінің руын қалыптастыра алатын. Сол себепті рулардың атаулары тым көп болғандықтан сан ғасырлар ширегінде жоғалып кетті. Өздерінің руластарынан бір саты басым түсетін ерекше адамдар құрған күшті қуатты рулардың ғана аттары сақталып қалды. Сіздер, неге осындай жағдайлар орын алған?-деп сұрайсыздар. Өйткені руда өз руына атын берген күшті тұлға болса, онда жеті атадан кейінгі рулар өз ұрпақтарына сол рудың атын шығарған ерекше тұлғаның есімін беріп, әйгілі тұлғаның атын ұмыттырмауға тырысатын.

Мәселен, б.з.д. 209 жылы ғұн халқын билеген Модэ Матайды тарихшылар айтулы тұлға деп таныды, ол хандық Қытайға теңдес мемлекетттің негізін құрады. Бірақ ғұндар мемлекеті патшасының есімі б.з.д. YII ғасырда Алдыңғы Азияны жаулап алып, Вавилонда 28 жыл бойы билік құрған скифтер көсемі Мадий-Матай аты ретінде жалғасын тапты. Скифтік патшасы Мәдидің басқа бір есімі Ишпақай болатын. Ол сақ массагеттердің атақты патшайымы Тұмар ханшайымның арғы атасы еді. Тарихта Наймандардың құрамындағы Матай аты сақталып қалды, өйткені бұл рудың қайнар бастау құрамында ғұндар патшасы Модэ және скифтер патшасы Мадий сыпды айтулы, қайталанбас тұлғалар өмір сүрген. Алғашқы Матайдың ұрпақтары жеті атадан кейін, өз атауларын өзгерткен жоқ, өйткені өз бабаларының есімдерін пір тұтып, қадірлейтін.

Модэ Матайдың таққа келуі және патша ретінде әйгілену тарихын өзі қызығушылық тудырады. Онрың әкесі ғұндардардың шаньюй көсемі Тұман өзінің сюзерен - одақтасы Қытай императорының әмірін орындап, хандықтар билеушісінің сұлу қызын өзіне әйелдікке алады. Қытайлардың жоспары бойынша, ғұндар патшасы тағының мұрагерлігіне аспанасты елі императорының немере жиені келуі тиіс. Ал оның жиені ағасымен билікті теңдей етіп бөлісе алмайды. Соның салдарынан ғұндар еш соғыссыз-ақ ханьдықтардың құлына айналады. Осы мақсатта қытай тарапының талап етуі бойынша өзінің үлкен ұлы Матайды аманат ретінде, одақтастық туралы келісімге келген юечжи тайпасы императорының ордасына аттандырады. Келісім бұзыла қалған жағдайда ұлының қытайлықтардың қолынан қаза табатынын білсе де, ол юечжи халқына қасақана тұрғыда шабуыл жасайды. Бірақ оның ұлы таңғажайып ерлік көрсетіп, тұтқыннан құтылып кетеді. Әкесі оны он мың әскердің қолбасшысы етіп тағайындайды. Өзінің қоластындағы адамдардың сенімділігіне Матай ерекше амал тәсілдері арқылы қол жеткізе білді. Ол өзінің істерін ештеңе сұрамастан қайталауды талап етті. Ол өзінің сүйікті тұлпарына садақтың жебесін жіберген кезде, осы істі жасамағандардың бәрін өлім жазасына кесті. Өзінің сүйікті кәнизагын де о дүниеге аттандырған кезде, дәл осындай жағдай орын алды. Аң аулап жүрген кезде ұлы өз әкесін нысана ретінде көздеген кезде, жауынгерлер жебесінің бірде бірі мүлт кеткен жоқ. Кейінірек ғұндардың жас билеушісін ханьдықтар патшасы "мінезінің қаншалықты тұрақты, шымдамды" екендігін тексеруге ниеттенеді. Ол өзінің үйіріндегі ең күшті, таңдаулы арғымақты беруге келіседі, өйткені көршіні сұрағанын беріп, сыйлай білу керек. Сондай-ақ қоластындағы кеңесшілері наразылық білдірсе де, қытай билеушісіне өзінің сүйікті кәнизагын тарту етеді. Бірақ араны ашылған, нәпсіқұмарлыққа әбден берілген қытай императоры жас шаньюй әрқашан оның айтқанын орындайды деп ойлап, өзіне бос жатқан жерлерді тарту етуін талап етеді. Бұл талапқа жас шаньюй былай деп жауап береді: "Ұлы Тәңірдің әміріне сәйкес жер халықтікі болып табылады, жер болса, тұрғындары жақсы өмір сүретін, дамып, гүлденген ел болады. Ал иелігінде жері жоқ халық еріксіз түрде қорлық пен сорақылық көріп, жер бетінен жойылып кетеді". Қысқа уақыт ішінде үлкен әскер жинап, Қытай императорын жеңіп, оның елін өзіне салық төлететін мемлекетке айналдырады.

Айтып айтпай не керек, үлгі аларлық, таңқаларлық, қызықты оқиға!

Менің жетінші атамның аты Шаң еді. Ал Қытай тарихында б.з.д. екі мыңыншы жылдықтың ортасында алғашқы Инь әулетіне Шаң тайпасынан шыққан көшпенділер билік жүргізген болатын. Ұлы Қытайды сан ғасырлар ширегінде көшпенді түркілер құрған әулеттер билегендіктен, менің бабаларым әрбір жетінші атадан кейін Аспанасты империясын басқарған ұлы бабаларының есімін ұмыттырмас үшін, келесі ұрпақтарға оның есімімен атап отырған,-деуіме негіз бар. Шаң есіміне ғұндар мемлекетінің ең жоғары дәрежелі билеушісі –шаньюй атағы сәйкес келетінін айта кетейік. Осы лексеманы түркі тілінен сөзбе сөз аударғанда, "Аспан үйі немесе аспан мемлекеті" деп тәржімаланады. Өйткені "Шаң" этнонимімен ауа, көк аспан, шаң сөздерінің ұғымы байланысты болып келеді.

Қазақ тілінде "шаң тимес" деген қанатты тіркес бар. Бұл ұғым зымырап жүйткитін тұлпарға қатысты айтылады. Тұлпарыңыз жер бетінде жүгірмей, көк аспанмен ұшады. Біздің бабаларымыз туралы ("Татары. История возникновения вольного народа") айтарлықтай тамаша еңбек жазған ағылшын зерттеушісі Э.Паркердің ойы бойынша, шаньюй атағы – "Көктің ұлы" деген ұғымды білдіреді екен. Оның ойы ақиқат ауылынан алыс емес, өйткені түркілер мемлекетіне әрқашан мәңгілік көк аспан қолдау көрсететін.

# ЕУРОПАЛЫҚ ОТБАСЫДАН АЗИЯЛЫҚ ӘУЛЕТТЕРГЕ НЕМЕСЕ ҚАЗАҚТАР ӨЗДЕРІНІҢ ЕУРОПАЛЫҚ КЕСКІН КЕЛБЕТІН ҚАЛАЙ ӨЗГЕРТІП АЛДЫ?

Қазақтардың кескін келбеттерінің антропологиялық ерекшеліктері туралы мәсслен, академик Оразақ Исмагуловтың кітабы мен басқа авторлардың "Этническая дерматоглифика казахов" (Алматы, 2007 жыл) еңбектерінен таңғажайып мәліметтер кездестіре аламыз. Соңғы ашылған ірі жаңалықтарға сәйкес, соңғы қырық жылдық ғасыр ішінде Қазақстан аймағында қазіргі кезде тұратын рулардың ата-бабалары өмір сүрген. Олар андронов мәдениетін құрған еді. Антропологиялық тұрғыда бұл тайпалардың физиологиялық кескін келбеттері еуропалық нәсіл тектес болып келген. Яғни, Қазақстанның байырғы жергілікті ұлты таза түрдегі еуропа тектес ұлт болып табылған. Осыдан кейін келесідей оқиғалар орын алды: б.з.д. 4000 жыл бұрын біздің бабаларымыз әлем тарихында б.з.д. 4000 жыл бұрын алғаш рет жылқыны қолға үйретті.Осылайша бабаларымыз өздеріне жылдам жүруге мүмкіндік беретін көлікке қол жеткізді. Сәл кейінірек адамзат тарихында бірінші болып, қола мен темірден қару жарақ әзірлеуді меңгеріп алды. Рухы жағынан дала жауынгерлері көршілес және алыс жатқа елдерге жорықтар жасап, Араб түбегі, Мысыр, Ганг және Хуанхэ өзендерінің жағалауына дейін жеткен болатын. Палеоантропологиялық зерттеулердің нәтижелеріне сәйкес, краниалогиялық мәліметтер көрсеткіші бойынша, академик Исмагулов әріптестерімен бірге б.з.д. Ү ғасырда моңғол тәріздес кескін келбет Қазақстан тұрғындарының нәсілдік табиғи болмысына ене бастап, бұл сан 10 пайыздық көрсеткішті құрған. Бұған не себеп болды? Жоғарыда айтқанымыздай, осы кезеңдерге дейін ата-бабаларымыз Кіші Азияда өмір сүріп үлгерген, кейін хет-кете тайпалары Қытайға аттанып, тек б.з.д. YІІІ ғасырында ғана туған жерге оралған. Бірақ осы жолы сары тектес нәсілдердің кескін келбетін, бет ажарын әбден өздеріне сіңдіріп алады. Кіші Азиядан қайтқан осы тайпалар және басқа руларымыз Қазақстанға моңғол тектес кескін келбеттің 10 % ала келді.

Үйсін кезеңінде (б.з.д, III және б.з. IY ғасыр) халқымыздың ішіндегі моңғол тектес кескін келбет 25 % жетті. Шынымен-ақ, осы кезеңде ата-бабаларымыздың үлкен бөлігі (үйсін қаңлы) ғұндардың ықпалымен Моңғолия мен Қытай жерінен кетіп, Қазақстан аймағына бет алғаны туралы білеміз. Бірақ моңғол тектес қытайлар арасында ұзақ уақыт бойы өмір сүру нәтижесінде, еуропалық кескін келбетке аздаған өзгерістер енгізіп, халқымыздың ішіндегі 25 % сары нәсілдік кескін келбеттің пайда болуы осыдан өрбіді. Одан кейін моңғолдар шабуылдары басталғанға дейінгі кезең (б.з. Y-XIII ғасырлары) басталды. Осы кезеңде Моңғолия мен Солтүстік Қытай аймағында түркі қағанаттары бірде тарап, бірде құрылып, бірінің орнына бірі келіп билік құрады. Қытайлықтардың қысымымен түркілер Батысқа-Қазақстанға бет алып, оның үстіне күшіне еніп, гүлденіп келе жатқан ислам дінінің ықпалымен Алдыңғы Азияда тұратын біздің басқа бабаларымыз атамекеніне оралады. Яғни олар біздің байырғы, жергілікті еуропа тектес ұлтымызға моңғол тектес бет пішіннің тағы да 25% реңкін ала келеді. Б.з. XY ғасырында Қазақстан аймағындағы метисациялық үрдіс толық аяқталып, осыған байланысты тұрғындардың қазіргі кескін келбеті біржола толық қалыптасып, моңғол тектес- 70 % және еуропа тектес -30% деңгейдегі кескін келбет, нәсілдік реңк анықталады. Бұл жағдай қазіргі XXI ғасырда да жалғасын тауып келеді. Осыған қосымша моңғол тектес 20 % үлестің қосылуын Шыңғысханмен бірге өздерінң атамекен қоныстарына найман, керей, қоңырат, жалайыр және тағы басқа қазақ руларының оралуымен байланыстырамын. Олар ұзақ уақыт бойы қытайлық және тунгус-маньчжур тайпаларымен көршілес өмір сүргендіктен, айқын түрдегі моңғол тектес бет пішінге ие болған. Бүгінгі таңдағы қазақстандықтардың нәсілдік тегі қазақстандық тектес тұраноид нәсілділер қатарына енеді. Ал тұраноид нәсілінің өзі үш түрге бөлінеді: қазақстандық, тяньшаньдық, алтай-саяндық. Қазақтар - біріншісіне, қырғыздар- екіншісіне, хакастар- үшінші түрге жатады. Олар өздерінің еуропа тәріздес кескін келбетінің ерекшелігімен өзгешеленеді. Қазақтарда еуропа тектес кескін келбет айқын көрініс тапса, сонан кейін-қырғыздар, ал олардан соң –хакастар келе жатыр. Сонымен қоса, метисациялық үрдістердің тек Қазақстан аймағында ғана орын алғанын айта кетуге тиіспіз. Қазақстанда көршілес елдер тайпалары жаппай түрде келіп шоғырлануы орын алған жоқ. Біздің халықты ешкім ешқашан жаулаған емес. Жалпы айтқанда, біз қазақтар - өзіміз көршілес елдердің жерлерін жаулап алып, моңғол тектес халықтарды бағындырып, еуропалық кескін келбетімізді аздап өзгертіп алдық, ал жаулап алынған елдерде ұзақ уақыт бойы өмір сүру нәтижесінде ата-бабаларымыздың табиғи кескін келбеті өзгеріске ұшырады. Өйткені бабаларымыз осы елдерде өмір сүрген кездерінде ұрпақ таратқан болатын. Алдыңғы тарауларда бұл жайлы егжей-тегжейлі тұрғыда әңгімелегенбіз.

# Кресті таңбасымен

## Наймандар мен Керейлердің христиандығы жайында. Мешітте неге қазақтың сөзі естілмейді?

Қазақстанның байырғы тұрғындары негізінде ислам дінін ұстанады. Бүгінгі таңда ислам дінінің қалай дамып келе жатқанын барша жұрт жақсы біледі. Сүнниттік және шеиттік ағымдар арасындағы қайшылықтар осы діннің іргетасын шайқалтуда, оның үстіне уахавиттік ағымдар да күшіне еніп келеді. Біздің ұлы отандасымыз Шоқан Уәлиханов қазақтар ресейдің қоластына өткенге дейін, тек қағаз жүзінде ғана мұсылман болғанын, ал мұсылман дінінің ұстанымдары мен әдет ғұрыптарын ресей мемлекеті бағынбаған халықты бағындыру мақсатындағы ықпал ету құралы ретінде пайдаланған.

Қазақстан аймағында ислам діні XIII ғасырдың ортасынан бері жаңа белестерге көтерілуде. Бірақ қазақ халқында бұл діннің түп тамыры терең емес екендігін айта кетуге тиіспіз. Өйткені тұрғындар Жаратушымен өзіне түсінікті ана тілінде сөйлеу мүмкіндігіне қол жеткізе алмау- деп ойлаймын. Адамдар шынайы түп мағынасын түсінбесе де, мұсылман дәстүріне ғибадат етуді жалғастыруда. Жаратушымен өзге тілде (араб тілі) арқылы араласқан соң, дінге бас ұрған пенде өзінің күәналарына шынайы тұрғыда арылуға мүмкіндігі жоқ.. Бір сөзбен айтқанда дінге сену арқылы қажетті тұрғыдағы тыныштық пен тепе теңдікке қол жеткізе алмай келеді, өйткені оған дін сөзі түсініксіз.

Оның үстіне қазақтар қазақ тілінде сөйлеуі үшін қаншама іс шараларды жүзеге асыруда, толағай қыруар шаруаларды тындырып келеміз. Егер де біздің мұсылман жамағатының Діни Басқармасы Жаратушымен қазақ тілінде сөйлесу құқығына қол жеткізсе, онда барша қазақтардың өз ана тілінде сөйлейтіндігіне сенімдімін, өйткені әрбір жұмыр басты пенде Жаратушымен ана тілінде сөйлескісі келеді! Ал Жаратушының қазақ тілін білетіндігі туралы сенімділік, қазақ тілін одан сайын жетік меңгеруге әкеледі. Ислам апологеттері, уағыздаушылары жергілікті халықтың тілінде Аллаға сыйынуға тыйым салады. Өйткені, олардың айтуына қарағанда, Құранның мәтінін жер бетіне Жаратушы араб тілінде жолдаған. Шынымен осылай ма? Бұл жайында кейінірек. Бірақ әлбетте бұлай емес.

Соңғы уақытта Алтын Орданы қиратуда біздің ата-бабаларымыздың арасында ислам дінінің күштеп ендірілуі үлкен ықпалын тигізді деген пікір тарауда. Меніңше, мұндай көзқарастың негізі бар. Біріншіден, тәңір діні әлемнің ең көне діндерінің бірі болып табылады. Бұл дін біздің көшпенді бабаларымыздың арасында кеңінен тарап, түп тамырын жайған еді. Басқа елдерді жаулай отырып, мейірбанды түрде өз діндерін автохонды жергілікті халықтар арасында уағыздайтын. Парсы еліндегі зороастризм жайлы айтып өттім, Заратуштра пайғамбар (Қазақстанның Уральск қаласынан шыққан) Парсы елінің жергілікті тұрғындары арасында Тәңір дінін енгізуге қолы жетіп, осының нәтижесінде Парсылық арамейлер арсында зороастризм атты жаңа дін пайда болды. Дәл осылай Батысты христиан дінімен, осы аймаққа тек басқа атаумен келген ата-бабаларымыз таныстырды. IY ғасырда бұл дінді Шығыс пен Батыс та қабылдады. Бір Құдайға сенуді батыс әлемі көшпенді түркілерден үйренді. Y ғасырда көшпенділер тас талқан еткен ежелгі Рим Иисус Христостың ілімін білмей-ақ өтті. Римдіктер Марс, Юпитер және басқа тәңірлерге сыйынып, Иисус Христостың кім екенін де білмеді. Христос бұл жерге кейін келді. Бірте-бірте батыс діліне негізделген Тәңір дінін, Рим әкейінің иезуиттері еуропалықтардың санасынан шығаруға барынша күш салды. Жаңа діннің түп тегі түркілік екендігі жөнінде халық ұмытып кетті. Мұрат Аджи христиан дінінің шығу тегі жайлы ойлану қажеттілігі туралы айтады: ал егер иудаизмде болмаса ше? Палестина христиан дінінің отаны болып табыла ма? Осыған байланысты Шыңғысхан дәуіріндегі наймандар мен керейлердің христиандығы туралы сөз қозғағым келеді. Біріншіден, біздің бабаларымыз несториандық бағыттағы христиан дініне сыйынған. Константинополь архиепископы, Византия империясының дінбасы Несторий, Иисус Христос Құдай емес, бар жоғы пайғамбар деген ілімді ұстанған діни ағымның өкілі еді, бұл жайт тәңір дінінің әдет ғұрыптарына қайшы келмейді. Парсы елінде несториандық ілімнің сан алуан түрлері парсы халқының ішіндегі Тәңір діннің ағымы ретінде б.з.д. YI ғасырда ахеменидтер дәуірінде пайда болды. Несторий ілімін 431 жылы Эфес соборы жоққа шығарып, бұл қағида атам заманнан бері Солтүстік Қытай мен Моңғолия аймағында өмір сүріп келе жатқан қазақ рулары арасында өз жақтастарын тапты. Алғашқы даму сатысындағы христиан дінін біздің бабаларымыз өздерінің ілімі ретінде қабылдады. Сол себепті Шыңғысхан дәуіріндегі христиан дінін ұстанған найман немесе керей, іс жүзінде Тәңір дініне ғибадат етушілер болып табылады. Христиандықтың символ белгісі – крест, Тәңірдің белгісі, көптеген қазақ руларының, дәлірек айтқанда керейлердің тамғасы болып табылды, Мұрат Аджидің пікіріне қарғанда, барлық жағы тепе тең крест – Тәңірдің белгісі – бұл екі тізбектің қиылысы емес, Алтай тауларында шамасымен үш төрт мың жыл бұрын пайда болған крестінің мағынасы мынада: орталығынан әлемнің төрт бұрышына күннің төрт шуағы тарап, Тәңір жаратқан барша тірі жан иелерін өзінің нұрлы шұрайлы шуағымен жылуға бөлейді.

# Тәңірдің белгісі.
# Қазақтың киіз үйі және Ресейдің туы.

Бұрыштары тепе теңе крестің мағынасын өзімше тұжырымдау ойым бар. Шаңырағы бар қазақтың киіз үйінің тарихы көшпенділердің тек тұрмыстық қана емес, сонымен бірге рухани өмірінің негізіне байланысты болып келеді. Киіз үйдің үстіндегі киелі шаңырақ ғарыштағы әлемнің көрінісін дәл қайталайды, шаңырақта Шығыстан Батысқа қарай жол тартқан күннің жолы бейнеленген. Бұл ілімді көшпенділер өзінің рухани тұрғыдағы Тәңір діні іліміне теңеп, салыстырып отырған. Мыңжылдықтар ішінде күн ата-бабаларымыздың көш керуендер легінің Шығыстан Батысқа, Батыстан Шығысқа қарай жолын белгілеп көрсетіп отырған.

Солтүстіктен Оңтүстікке қарай ұласатын Құс жолы, Тәңірдің аспандағы мекенінің тұрғындары –құстардың басқа жаққа қоныс аударып, ұшу жолын белгіледі. Осы құс жолына қарап, бұған көшпенділер өздерінің тәуелсіздігі мен еркіндігін балап, салыстыратын.

Осының нәтижесінде Тәңірдің қасиетті символ белгісіне айналған крестінің нақты сипаты келіп туындайды.

Аталмыш жайттарға байланысты келесідей анықтамаға назар аударамыз. Бабаларымыздың ежелгі діні екі бастама негізге сүйенді: ер адам бейнесі-Көк аспан (рух, жан), әйел бейнесі – жер (махаббат). Жер және құнарлылық тәңірі Ұмай ана өмірдегі махаббат бастамасы болып табылды.

Осының нәтижесінде Тәңір белгілеген, Ұмай ана қолдаған көшпенді номадалардың Шығыстан Батысқа қарай жылжу бағыттары, құстардың солтүстіктен оңтүстікке қарай ұшу бағытымен қиылысып, бұл көрініс, табиғаттың түп негізі, алғашқы бастауы – Тәңір сызып берген жер бетіндегі өмірдің пайда болу заңдылықтарын айқындады. Осылайша крест – басты символы және барша болмысымыздың мәнін көрсетті. Сондықтан да христиан дінінде де крестіні - Жаратушы қасиетті крест деп атауы кездейсоқтық емес.

Осы жайтты баян ете келе, Шыңғысхан империясындағы ордалардың шығу тегіне де мән беру өте маңызды. Батыс Сібір мен Шығыс Қазақстан жерін қамтыған Шығыс бөлігі - Көк Орда, Орталық бөлігі (Сарыарқа алқаптары) –Ақ орда, ал Батыс бөлігі- Алтын Орда деп аталды. Мұндай атаулардың ұқсастығы айқын. Күн өзінің қозғалысын Шығыстан бастайды, ең алдымен аспанды көк түске бояйды, кейін көкке көтерілгенде – ақ түске, ұясына батып бара жатып – алтын, қызыл түске бояйды. Ресейдің мемлекеттік туы-триколорды еске алайық. Бәлкім мұнда көне түркілік мәдениеттің ықпалы бар шығар. Триколор Ұлы Русьтің түп тамыры түркілік екендігінің айқын белгісі емес пе?

Мен тек тарихи тұрғыдағы туыстық белгілері ғана емес, сонымен бірге түрілер мен славяндардың тілдік деңгейде және әсірсе, лексикалық тұрғыдағы туыстық қарым қатынастары бар екендігі туралы сан мәрте рет жазуыма тура келді.

Бұл жағдайда ең алдымен, мемлекеттік рәміздердің ерекшелігін белгілеген рулық жады негізіндегі осы екі этнос- орыс және қазақтарды біріктіретін ортақ болмыс белгілері жайында мәсел қозғалып отыр.

Кезінде тарих бізді ұзақ ғұмырларға дейін бір-бірімізден алшақтатып тастады. Жылқыны қолға үйретіп, кеңістікті игерген қазақтар өздерінің ықпалын көптеген ірі аймақтарға тигізіп, сол елдердің байырғы тұрғындарын сіңіріп қана қоймай, өздері де осы жерлердің тұрғындарының ішіне еніп, сіңіріліп кетті. Осының нәтижесінде халықтың бет әлпеті, кескін келбеті де өзгеріп шыға келді.

Еуропа мен Азия ұлт генотипі қазіргі кездері крест тәріздес ретінде бір-біріне қосылды. Номада көшпенділердің бет әлпетіндегі және кескін келбетіндегі үлкен айырмашылықтар осыдан келіп туындайды.

Қазақтың киіз үйі туралы бірер сөз. Оның оң жақ бөлігі әйелдікі - деп аталатыны мәлім. Ол жақта ыдыс аяқ сақталып, тамақ жасалады және т.б. Ал сол жағы – ерлердікі. Киіз үйдің бұл бөлігінде аң аулау құралдары мен қару жарақтар орналасады. Киіз үйдің орта бөлгі –төр. Өз басым көп уақыттан бері Қытай, Ресей, Қазақстан аймағы арқылы ағатын туған өзенім Ертістің этнонимін таба алмай, аздап қиналғаным бар. Бірақ жуырда қазақ халық ауыз әдебиеті үлілері мен нұсқаларының маманы, салт-дәстүрлерінің білгірі Нұрберген Балғымбаев мынадай жайтты баян етті: "Егер түркілердің атамекені - Алтай тауынан –солтүстікке зер салсаң – орталық жағына қарай, Обь өзені, сол жағында – Ертіс, оң жағында – Енесай өзені ағып жатыр. Яғни ойға салынып, қазақ киіз үйінің аспан тәріздес шаңырағын Ертістен Енесайдың батысына дейінгі жерді жапса, онда қазақы киіз үйдің құрылымдық тәртібі бойынша, ортасындағы өсінде Обь өзені (алтай халықтарының тілінде Обь - ось), Обьтен сол жаққа қарай – Ертіс (Ер тұс) бұл жағдайда- ерлер бөлігі, ал Обьтен оң жақта Енесай өзені, (яғни – киіз үйдің оң жақ бөлігі) ағады. Қазақтарда тұрмыс құрмай, отырып қалған қызға қатысты, "оң жақта отырып қалды" –деген сөз бар".

Бұрын мен Тәңірдің белгісі - крест және киіз үйдің шаңырағы арасында тығыз байланыс бар екендігі туралы жаздым. Көшпендінің киіз үйіне көне түркілердің тағы бір символы –сегіз бұрышты жұлдыз тікелей байланысты. Киіз үйдің босағасы оңтүстік-шығысқа қарай орналасатыны мәлім. Сол жақтан жазғы шуақты күндердегі күннің шығыстан шуақ шашып, жарқырай шығуы басталады. Түркі күнтізбесіне сәйкес, шығыс деп 90 градустық мөлшердегі, ал солтүстіктен-шығысқа және оңтүстіктен-шығысқа қарай аспан бөлігі алынады. Ал оңтүстік-шығыстан солтүстік-батысқа қарай созылатын екі тізбек – киіз үйдің босағасынан төрге дейінгі жерден оңтүстік-батыстан солтүстік-шғысқа қарай ұласатын тізбек киіз үйдің шаңырағына салынып, сегіз қырлы жұлдыздың нақты сипатын белгілейді. Біздің дәстүр бойынша, киіз үйде адам басын солтүстік - батысқа, қарай бұрыш ұйықтайтын. Ал марқұмның басын солтүстік-шығысқа, жүзін шығысқа қарай бұрып жатқызатын. Оңтүстіктен шығысқа қарай жол арқылы марқұм аруақтардың жаны ұшып кетеді, - деп саналған. Орыс жазбаларында оңтүстіктен солтүстікке қарай ұласатын Құс жолын Батый жолы деп атайтын. Шамасы бұл жол өмірді соңын білдірсе керек. Бұл жағдайда көк аспан шығыстан батысқа қарай- кресті өмір жолының қиылысын білдіреді, ал, солтүстіктен оңтүстікке қарай –аруақтар жолы.

Мәңгіліктің аталмыш белгілері қазақтың шаңырақ күйінде бейнеленген крестіде бейнесін тапқан.

Ал 45 градусқа қарай сәл ауытқыған басқа крест оңтүстік-шығыстан солтүстік батысты меңзейді. Жердегі болмыстың уақытша және өмірдің жалған екендігін білдіреді, босыған сәйкес қазақтың киіз үйінің тәртібі бойынша өмір мен өлім жолдары қиылысады.

Осы екі белгілер- көк аспан кресті және жер кресті мен  бір-біріне салынуы нәтижесінде сегіз бұрышты жұлдыз пайда болады. Бұл жұлдыз - Екі бастама: Тәңір мен Ұмай – еркек пен әйел, аспан мен жер, өмір мен өлім қосындысының белгісі.

Тәңір діні  философиясы туралы тағы бір айта кетерлік жайт. Көне түркілерде Тәңір мен Көк Аспан материалды және иделды болмыстардың бірлігі ретінде қарастырылды. Тәңір барша әлемді, соның ішінде аспанды да жаратады. Өз кезегінде, көк аспан тәңір дінінде –Жоғарғы әлем, адамдар мекендейтін жер – орталық әлем, төмснгі әлсм-аруақтар әлемі емес, Жоғарғы және төменгі әлемдердің мағынасы мүлде басқаша түсіндіріледі. Егер адам адал өмір сүріп, жер бетінде өте пайдалы, игілікті амалдар жасап, тұлға атанса, өлген соң, оның жаны –жоғарғы әлемге Тәңірдің қасына баратын, қазақтар оны аруақ деп атайды. Аруақ тайпаластары қиын жағдайға душар болған кезде, орталық әлемге түсіп, көмекке келетін. Ал күнәһар адамның жаны Ерлік бсқаратын төменгі әлемге бет алатын. Кейде Ерлік осы адамдардың жанын адамдарды жаман істерге азғырту үшін Орталық әлемге аттандыратын. Жоғарғы әлемнің адамдары мойнына өзіндік орамал (галчстук) тақса,

Орталық әлемнің адамдары –белбеу тағып, Төменгі әлем адамдарының аяғында тұсау болатын –олар өз тағдырларының иесі болып табылмайтын. Өмірде де осылай: мойнына галстук таққан адам қоғамда – зиялы, дербес адам болса, ал еш қайрат, жігері жоқ адам туралы "бос белбеу екен" деп айтады.

# КҰРАН ЖАЙЫНДА. ҰЛЫ НИЗАМИ МҰХАММЕД (С.Ғ.С.) ПАЙҒАМБАР МЕН АЛЕКСАНДР МАКЕДОНСКИЙДІҢ (ЕСКЕНДІР ЗҰЛҚАРНАЙЫН) ТЕГІ ТҮРКІЛІК ЕКЕНДІГІ ЖӨНІНДЕ

Ал енді исламның қайнар көздеріне келейік. Біздің замнымыздың басында араб түбегінің негізгі бөлігі ата-бабаларымыз құрып кеткен Парфян патшалығының құрамына енген. Бұл түбекте олар кейінгі замандарда да өмір сүре берген. Өзімнің "Шыңғысханның түркілік ғұмырнамасы. Қазақтардың киелі шежіресі" атты кітабымда Мұхаммед пайғамбар (с.ғ.с.) заманында ата-бабаларымыз жеке дербес құрама деген ру болып бірігіп, жаңа ислам дінінің негізін салуға қатысқандығына тоқталып өттім. Олар тәңір дінін Х ғасырда араб деп атала бастаған жергілікті халықтардың діліне байланысты бейімдеп ендіреді.

Ал пайғамбардың өзін Низами былай деп жырлайды: "Сені мадақтаймыз о түркі! Жеті тайпаның басқардың, балықтан бастап айдың да шапағатына бөлендің". Мұхаммед пайғамбар (с.ғ.с) дүние салған соң, оның күйеу баласы Әли мен және исламның шииттік ағымның негізін салушы -ізбасар сахабалары тәңір дінінің көптеген дәстүрлерінен бас тартады, оларға дейін еврей, грек, мысырлықтар осындай әрекеттерге барып, христиан дініне тәңірлік діннен мүлде бөлек жаңа мән берген еді. Жаңа ислам дінін Орта Азия жән Қазақстан жеріне араб түбегінен шыққан этникалық түркілер – құрайыштар алып келді. Құрайыш – қойдың терісінен тігілген бас киім- дегенді білдіреді. Олар өздерін қожа деп атайды. Бұл әбден ойластырылған қадам еді, өйткен Тәңір дінінің қазақ даласындағы табынушылары өзге жат халықтардың уағыздауымен жаңа дінді қабылдамас еді ғой. Қазақстан аймағына ислам дінінің ендірілу кезеңі араб түбегінде Құрайыш тайпасы Аббасидтер әулетінен шыққан билеушілердің басқару кезеңінен сәйкес келеді. Бұл тайпа екі жүз жыл бойы 750-945 жылдар аралығында исламның даму жолдарына бақылау жасаған. Бүгінгі таңда араб түбегінің байырғы тұрғындары бәдәуилер деп аталады. Ал олардың арғы тегін ақмар- шашы ақ түсті марлар деп атаған. Ал марлар, жоғарыда атап өткеніміздей, түркі-сеирлер болып табылады.

Исламның түп тамыры жайында Мурат Аджи өзінің "Тюрки и мир. Сокровенная история" атты көлемді еңбегінде нақты тұрғыда тоқталып өтеді. Ол көне заманғы Құран (б.з.д.III ғасыр-б.з.III ғасыр) Парсы еліндегі тегі түркілік Аршахидтер әулеті тұсында қолданылған тілде жазылған. Мұхаммед пайғамбар (с.ғ.с) дәуіріндегі ислам тілі араб тілі емес, түркілік болып табылған, ғалымның айтуына қарағанда, Эрмитаж мұражайында X ғасырда түркі жазуымсн жазылған Құранның мәтіні сақтаулы. Араб тіліне ислам діні б.з. X ғасырда Әбу Мансұр Мұхаммад ибн-ад-Азхар әл-Азхаридің "Түзетулер кітабы" шықаннан кейін ғана біржола көшті. Осы кезеңде түркі тілінде жазылған Құранның жасы үш жылдан асып кеткен!

XXI ғасырдың атақты, көрнекті тюркологі былай деп жазады: "кеңестік тарихшылар, араб мәдениетін қалыптастыруға көптеген халықтардың, ең алдымен түркілердің қатысқандығын жақсы біледі... "

Академик А.Е.Крымскийдің зерттеулері бойынша, араб тілінде жазылды деп саналып келген түпнұсқалардың көпшілігі іс жүзінде түрік тілінен аудармалар болып шыққандығын айта кету артық болмас. Әйгілі "Мың бір түн" еретігісінің де халі осындай күйге ұшырды. Ең өкініштісі Құран да бұл шырмаудың тұзағына ілінді. Мұрат Аджидің айтуына қарағанда, шынайы Құранның мәтінінде Жаратушының тарапына айтылған мынадай сөздер кездеседі: "Менің түркілер атты әскерім бар. Оларды Шығысқа орналастырдым. Бір халыққа ашуланған кезімде, өз әскеріме осы халықты билетіп қоямын!"

Осы өмірден ерте кеткен ірі ғалым, профессор М.Барманқұлов өзінің "Тюркская Вселенная" ("Білім" баспасы, Алматы, 1996) кітабында былай деп жазады: XII ғасырда өмір сүрген парсы ақыны және философы Низами түркінің бойынан тек ұлттық нышандарды ғана емес, сонымен бірге, жақсылық, мейірбандылық, әділеттіліктің белгілерін байқаған. Біз бұрын Александр Македонскийдің тегі скифтік екендігі туралы атап өттік, М.Барманқұлов Низамидің ұлы қолбасшы жайлы айтқан сөздерін келтіреді: "румийлік өлкенің тегі түркі қолбасшысы Үндістанның тағы мен Қытайдың тәжін қалай иеленді?"

Мені сыншылар көптеген тарихи оқиғалардан "қазақы іздерді" іздеумен жиі айналысатыным туралы айтып, жазғырады. Ал Низамидің тегі түркі емес пе? Өйткені біз Парсы, Парфия, Иран сынды алып мемлекеттердің ұлы ұрпағы саналатын Низамидің отанынан түркілердің түп-тамырын, іздерін таптық қой.

# "Бер Тәңір, қолда Тәңір"
## Орыс православиесінің қайнар көздері
## Тәңір діні: өлімнен кейінгі өмір жайлы

Тағы бір рет қайталап өтейін, қазақтардың ата-бабалары мыңдаған жылдар бойы тәңір дініне сыйынған, ата бабалырымыздың арасында қылыштың жүзімен, қорқытып үркітумен ислам дінін күштеп ендірсе де, олар тәңір дініне сенімін сақтап қалды. Бұл таңғажайып айғақ!

Қазақ тілінде таң және іңір деген ұғымдар бар. Бірте-бірте Тәңір сөзі таңнан іңірге дейінгі мәңгілік көк аспан иесі ұғымына айналды.

Он төрт ғасыр бойы бабаларымыз жүрегі мен жандарында Тәңірге деген сенімдерін сақтап келді. Менің марқұм ата-анам үнемі қайталап отыратын: "Бер Тәңір, қолда Тәңір!" Яғни әлі де болса кеш емес, қазақ халқына байырғы дінін қайтаруға болады.

Осыған байланысты мынадай сұрақ туындайды: бұл мәселге ислам қандай көзқараста? Мен тіпті Мекке мен Мәдине емес, біздің Діни басқарма мен мұсылман жамағаты жайында айтып отырмын.

Қазіргі кезеңде барша діндердің ойы бір жерден шығатыны бар: Құдай бір және Құдай жалғыз. Мен үшін мәселен Аллаһ- Тәңір болып табылады. Мұнда ешқандай қайшылық жоқ. Бар жоғы бір құбылыстың әртүрлі тарихи атаулары. Бірақ осыған сәйкес келесідей сұрақ туындайды: онда қазақтың ішкі дүниетанымы, көзқарасы, болмысы арабқа ұқсас болуы керек? Аллаһ барша халықтарды әртүрлі етіп жаратты емес пе? Мұхаммед пайғамбардың (с.ғ.с) сахабалары өздерінің ұрпақтарын бір рухани заңдылықтар бойынша өмір сүруге үйретті, бірақ біз қазақтар – араб емеспіз ғой. Сол себепті Құдай бізде біреу, ал пайғамбарлар түр-түрлі болып келуі мүмкін, бұл қалыпты құбылыс. "Өз Отанында пайғамбар жоқ" деген сөз бар. Бұл пайғамбарлар бізде баршылық – Қорқыт ата, Бекет ата, Бұқар жырау, Абай, Мұстафа Шоқай, Әлихан Бөкейханов және еліміздің көптеген даңқты азаматтары. Мәселен, мен осылардың қатарына Ходжа Ахмет Яссауиді енгіземаймын. Бұл ерекше дарынды адам Тәңір діні мен исламның өзара біргіп, одақтасуының жолдарын іздеп, суфизмді ойлап тапты. Осының нәтижесінде біз өзіміздің жеке дербестігіміз бен ұлттық ойлау жүйеміз, өркениетімізден айрылдық. Өйткені кез келген өркениет үш негізге келіп сүйенеді: дін, жазу және тіл. Дәлірек айтқанда біздің тіліміз ғана қалды. Осыған байланысты қазақтар ұлт ретінде сақталып, ұлттық мүдделерін қалпына келтіру үшін жеке шаралар қабылдау қажет.

Әйгілі ағылшын тарихшысы Эдуард Гиббон Шыңғысханның діні көзқарасы тұрғысында былай деп жазады: "Шыңғысханның діні біздің тарапымыздан таңдануымызды және мақтан тұтуды қажет етеді. Еуропада католиктер өздерінің шатпақтарын қорғу мақсатында ең қатігездік әрекеттерге барса, оларды осы жабайы варвардың әрекеті ұялтуы тиіс. Ол философияға сәйкес, таза деизм заңдарын орнатып және басқа діндерге сабыр етушіліктің негізін қалады Оның жалғыз да, әрі сенімді ұстанымы Құдай еді. Құдай өзінің құдірті арқылы жаратылған аспан мен жерді жақсылыққа толтырады." (Өзім бөліп көрсеттім-Қ.З.). Шыңғысханның Ясы заңдарында былай деп жазылған: "Барлығыңа аспан мен жерді жаратқан, байлық пен кедейлікті тарту ететін, өмір мен өлімнің иесі, барша затқа немесе құбылысқа күші жететін бір Құдайға сыйынуларыңа бұйырамын".

Басқа сөзбен айтқанда, Шыңғысхан қоластындағы адамдарға Тәңір дінін уағыздаған, ал қай пайғамбарға сыйынатындығын туыралы мәселені діндардың өзіне қалдырған . Мәселен ол Будда, Иисус, Мұхаммсд (с.ғ.с) Мәңгілік жалғыз Тәңірдің көптеген пайғамбарларының бірі деп есептеген. Қаһарлы Иоанның мысалын келтірсем артық болмас, ол өзінің көріпкелдігі арқылы, 1551 жылы ол Мәскеулік Русьтің ресми тұрғыдағы діні арқылы "Стоглавый соборында" Тәңірлік дінін ресми деп жариялап, Мәскеуді бұрынғы Алтын Орда мемлекетінің рухани өмірінің негізгі ошағына айналдырып, өзін Шыңғсханның ұрпағымын деп жариялады. Осы болашақты көздеген дарынды әрекеті арқылы Ресей империясының болашақ құдіреттілігінің негізін салып кетті, қоластындағы бүкіл Дешті Қыпшақ тұрғындарынан өзін мойындауды талап стті. Ойткені Алтын Орда құлағаннан кейін Қазақ, Қазан, Қырым, Астрахан хандықтары және Мәскеу князьдықтарында қалған біздің бабаларымыз, көшпенділердің Тәңір дінінің орны басқан, осы елдің мемлекеттік дініне айналған исламмен келіспеді.

1667 жылғы "Стоглавый" соборының шешімі құпия болып жарияланып, оларға бір жола тыйым салынды, барша күллі Ресейдің патриархы Никон бұл шешімді дінге қарсы, кәпірлер шешімі деп жариялайды, осыған байланысты бұл құжат XIX ғасырға дейін мұрағатта сақталып келген. Мұндай жағдай неліктен орын алғандығы да түсінікті. Себебі, Борис Годуновтың патшалық құрған кездерінен бастап, Русьтегі мемлекеттік дін ретінде түп тамыры гректік болып табылатын христиандық дін жарияланады. Русь X ғасырда христиан дініне өткен жоқ, осы мерзімнен кейін 600 жыл өткен соң, іс жүзінде христиан дінін қабылдады. Ал бұл мерзім ресми тұрғыда Русьтің шоқынған мерзімі болып есептеледі. 1586 жылы Борис Годунов Мәскеуге Антиохийлық патриарх Иоакимді шақырады, бұл кездесуде Русьте Грек шіркеуінің филиалын ашу мәселесін талқылау шаралары көзделеді. Бір жыл өткен соң, Мәскеуге грек патриархы Иеремияның өзі де келіп жетеді. Орыстың православиелік шіркеуі осылай қалыптасқан! Русьте христиан дінін қабылдаған кезден бастап, қазіргі заманғы орыс ұлтының қалыптаса бастағанын айтып өту өте маңызды. Мәселен Новгородта өз тілінде сөйлесе де, варяг-скандинав, венед, вепса, финн, карел халықтары орыс ұлтының құрамына еніп кетеді. Финн-угор халықтары: коми, мариймен мордвиндер де орысқа айналады. Мери, кривич және муровичтер, саны көп түркі халықтарын айтпағанның өзінде, бәрі орыс ұлтының құрамына сіңіп, бастапқы тегінен айрылды. Бұл таңқаларлық жайт емес. Өйткені осыдан 500 жыл бұрын ислам дінінің негізі салынған соң, араб ұлты да дәл осылай қалыптасқан еді. Мысыр, Сирия, Ливан және Түркі тұрғындарының бәрі өз тілінде сөйлесе де, өзіндік жеке дара мәдениеті болса да, араб халықының құрамына енді.

Халықтар мен ұлттарды дін осылайша қалыптастырды. Түркілер ата тайпаның аты алғаш рет б.з.Ү ғасырында айтылатыны туралы және олардың тарихи қауымдастық ретінде б.з.д. бағзы замандарда қалыптасқаны, түркі тайпасының қалыптасу негізіне тәңір дінінің кеңінен ықпал еткендігі туралы батыл пікірімді білдірігім келеді. Түркі этнонимінің пайда болуының көптеген жорамалдық үлгілері бар, бірақ Тәңір және түркі сөздерінің фонетикалық тұрғыда бір-біріне ұқсас болып келетіндігіне де назар аударуымыз қажет. Қазіргі заманғы орыстар мен қазақтар туралы сөз қозғасақ, менің ойымша этникалық тұрғыда тегі бір екі халықты дін бөліп жіберген. Бүгінгі таңда барша жұрт экология қасіретін айтып, дабыл қағуда, ал тәңір дінінің өзі жан, сана және тән тазалығы (экологиясы) емес пе? Адам кей жағдайда өлімнен қорыққан соң, Құдайға сыйынады. Әлемде қолдарында билігі барлар адамдардың әрекеттеріне баға бере отырып, өлген соң, тозаққа барасың, - деп қорқытады. Ал Тәңір діні ілімінің негіздері адам-табиғат перзенті. Бір жылдық мерзімге сәйкес, ағаштан жапырақтар түссе, көктем келе салысымен, әлемнің бәрі қайтадан құлпырып шыға келеді. Адамның өмірі де осы кезеңдік көрсеткішке ұқсайды. О дүниеге кеткен соң, әруақтар әлемінің тұрғынына айналады, ал белгілі бір мерзім өткеннен кейін (мен Қайрат Закирьянов болып) ол жер бетінде қайтадан адам кейіпінде жаралады. Басқа діндерде жұмақ пен тамұқ, нирвана тұрғындары жер бетінде өрмекші, жылан, жылқы ретінде жаралады деген ұстаным бар. Реинкарнация – қайта жаралу мәселелері қазіргі заманғы ғалымдарды қызықтырып отыр. Бұл көбінесе алғаш рет француз психологы Эмиль Буарак сипаттаған дежавю әсеріне (француз тілінен аударған – бұрын көріп қойған) тікелей қатысты. Адамзаттың 90% орын алып жатқан оқиғаны бұрынғы заманда да бір рет көргендей сезімді басынан кешіреді, бірақ жады мен сана мұндай жағдайдың болуы мүмкін еместігін меңзейді. Лев Толстой өзінің аңға шыққан кездегі мынадай бір оқиғасын баян етеді: жазушы атының тұяғы шұңқырға түсіп кеткен сәтте, ат үстінен жерге құлайды. Басын қатты соғады, дәл осы кезде тура 200 жыл бұрын дәл осындай оқиғаны басынан кешіргенін есіне түсіреді. Дежавю феноменін көптеген ғалымдар зерттеп жүр. Мәселен бұл құбылысты қазіргі заманғы кванттық психология арқылы түсіндіруге талпынған. Ал ғалымдардың басқа бір тобы Нобель сыйлығының лауреты Судзума Тонегаваның бастамасымен дежавю құбылысы үшін жауапты адам басындағы ми бөлігін табады. Мамандардың пікіріне қарағанда, дежавю құбылысы өткен өмір туралы генетикалық тұрғыдағы жады болып табылады. Веда ілімі психологиясы бұл құбылысты былайша түсіндіреді: адамның алған әсерлері (санскрит тілінде самарлық деп аталады) адамның жіңішке рухына жазылып, сезімге байланады. Адам қайтыс болған кезде, оның жіңішке рухы физикалық денеден бөлініп, белгілі бір уақыт өткен соң, басқа бір денеге еніп, қайта жаралады (санскритте бұл құбылыс – самсқара деп аталады). Сол кезде адам бұрынғы өмірі өткен жерге немесе бұрынғы өмірінде болған оқиғаларды басынан өткізсе, арнайы бір самсқаралар жіңішке рухтан белгі бере бстайды. Сол кезде адамда мұндай жағдайдың орын алмағандығына нақты тұрғыда сенім болса да баяғыда тура осындай оқиғаны басынан кешіргендігі туралы сезім оның санасына ықпал етеді. Өткен өмірдің шынайы белестері мен елестері –дегеніміз осы!

Тәңір діні – табиғаттың басқа қайта жаралатын құбылыстары тәрізді, адамның қайтадан өмірге келетіндігін түсіндіретін ілім. Яғни өлім де жоқ, қорқыныш та жоқ, онда бұл өмірде өзіңді дамытып, таныта түсу үшін ерінбестен еңбек ет. Ал егер үлгере алмай қалсаң, келесі бір өміріңде жасайсың. Оның кезегі міндетті түрде келеді. Туған туыстардан айрылған кездегі қасіреттер де, өз мәнін жоғалтып, философиялық тұрғыда қабылданады. Өйткені біз олармен о дүниеде қайта қауышатын боламыз.

Яғни осы сенімнің күштілігіне байланысты он төрт ғасыр бойы ата-бабаларымыздың бойындағы Мәңгілік көк аспан Тәңіріне деген сенімді арылта алмады.

Шыңғысханмен байланысты тағы бір оқиғаны келтірейін. Шыңғысхан Бұқараны бағындырған соң, мешітке келіп, иммамдармен кездеседі. Олар ұлы қағанға ислам дінінің негіздерін түсіндіреді, Оларды тыңдап болған соң, "ислам діні – бейбіт дін, адамзат баласына жақын, мақтауға лайық" - дейді. Бірақ ол былай деп сұрайды: "Сендер неге барша мүминдерді, ислам жолындағыларды тек Мұхаммед пайғамбардың (с.ғ.с) Отанына ғана бас иіп, тағзым етуге мәжбүрлейсіңдер? (бұл мұсылманның негізгі қағидасы)" Шынымен де, күніне бес намазын үзбей оқитын мүмин мұсылман мынадай сөздерді жиі қайталайды: "Мұхаммед пайғамбар (с.ғ.с) және оның әулетіне игілік пен құрмет болсын!" Ал енді кешіріңіздер, Жаратушыдан өз отбасы, Отан, туған жерің үшін берекені кім сұрамақ сонда? Орыс православиелік шіркеуіне Құдаймен орыс тілінде сөйлесу жайында Византиямен келісім жасаудың мүмкіндігі жүзеге асырылды. Мұндай жағдайда Қазақстан Мұсылмандар Діни басқармамызға неге дәл осындай батыл қадамға бармасқа? Мұндай әрекеттен кейін ислам діні көптеген мұсылмандарға одан сайын жақын бола түседі. Жоғарыда атап өткенімідей, бастапқыда Құран мәтіні түркі түлінде жазылды және ислам дінін ұстанғандар оз қызметін түркі тілінде жүргізді.

Бұқараның имамдарын тыңдап болған соң, біздің ұлы бабамыз былай деді: "нәрестенің кіндігі кесіліп, алғашқы қаны тамған жер адам үшін ерекше қасиетті". Тәңір дініндегі негізгі шарт: өз жеріңді, туған мекеніңді сүйіп, адал қызмет ету.

Түркілер діндерін көздің қарашығындай сақтайтын. 711 жылы түркілік төрт қағанның кеңесшісі данышпан Тоныкөк ислам дінін түркі жеріне ендірмеу үшін Солтүстік Қытайдан Қара теңізге дейін жедел аттанады. Сондықтан да Шыңғысханның дінге деген сенімділігі туралы ойды қозғамастан бұрын, бір шешімді айқын және тұрақты тұрғыда ұстануды қажет еткен жағдайлардың да орын алғанын айта кетуге тиіспіз. Сондықтан да ислам діні түркі халықтарына толық таралып кетпеуі мақсатында Батысқа жорыққа шығу туралы шешімге келеді. Осы кезеңде Хорезмшах Мұхаммед Бағдат халифінің "уәзірілік өкілі атанған соң, Азияның көптеген халықтарын басып алып, оларды ислам елдеріне айналдырады. Осыдан бұрын Геродот "скифтердің Скилла патшаны ата-баба дінін сатып кеткені үшін өлім жазасына кескендігі туралы" жазған еді.

# Русь және Қазақ даласының ұлы трагедиясы.<br>Қыпшақтар – орыс дворяндар әулетінің түп тамыры

Дүниеден өтіп, бақилық болған ірі ғалым және жазушы Ақселеу Сейдімбек: "арабтар қылыштың жүзімен сойқан салып, ислам дінін Қазақстанның оңтүстігінде енгізген кезде миллиондаған адамдардың құрбан болғандығын" айтып кетті. YII ғасырдағы бұл оқиғалар Алтын Орда тағы үшін орын алған талас тартыс ретінде күрес ретінде жалғасын тапты. Осы кезеңде тақтан дәмелі үміткерлер бай араб көпестерінің ақшасынан да бас тартқан жоқ. 1312 жылы Өзбек хан арабтардан алған несиені қайтару мақсатында исламды Алтын Орданың діні етіп жариялағанын еске түсірейік. Ол өз ордасына Шыңғысханның ең атақты ұрпақтарын шақырып, оларды арам ниетпен қырып жояды, өйткені олар Шыңғысханның "Яссы" заңдарын қолдап, түркілердің көне дінінің исламға алмасқанын қаламады. Осының салдарынан Ұлы Даладағы көзқарас ұстанымдар екіге бөлінеді: ең танымал билеушілер және тектілер ордадан кетіп, Мәскеу князьдығына аттанып, орыс дворяндар әулетінің негізгі түп тамырына айналады. ХY ғасырдың басына таман орыстың ең әйгілі отбасылық әулеттерінің 95% Ордадан шыққан Шыңғысханның тікелей ұрпақтары құрады. Н.Баскаков "Русские фамилии дворянского происхождения" (Мәскеу, 1979 жыл) атты кітабында тегі түркі келесідей фамилияларлы келтіреді: Сабуров, Мансуров, Годунов, Глинский, Куракин, Ермолов, Черкасский, Ушаков, Суворов, Апраксин,

Юсупов, Аракчеев, Урусов, Аксаков, Мусин-Пушкин, Голенищев-Кутузов, Ахаматов, Бердяев, Тургенев, Корнилов, Шереметьев және т.б. Сонымен бірге тегі түркі тағы да бір атақты есімдерді атайды: Л.Гумилев, Алябьев, Арсеньев, Бабичев, Балашов, Баранов, Басманов, Батурин, Бекетов, Бибиков, Бильбасов, Бичурин, Боборыкин, Булгаков, Бунин, Бурцев, Бутурлин, Бухарин, Вельяминов, Гоголь, Горчаков, Горшков, Державин, Епанчин, Ермоолов, Измаилов, Кантемиров, Карамазов, Карамзин, Киреевский, Корсаков, Кочубей, Кропоткин, Курбатов, Милюков, Мичурин, Рахаманинов, Салтыков, Строганов, Таганцев, Талызин, Танеев, Татищев, Тимашев, Тимирязев, Третьяков, Турчанинов, Тютчев, Уваров, Ханыков, Чаадаев, Шаховский, Шишковтар.

Әділеттілік үшін айта кетейік: католик дінін енгізу арқылы, мәселен орта ғасырларда Балтық теңізінен Қара теңізге дейін созылған, негізгі тұрғындарының құрамы түркілерден құралған литвалық князьдығында да Тәңір дінін жақтаушылар Мәскеу князьдығына қарай ағылды. Кейінірек Қаһарлы Иоанн кезінде түркі руларының ордалық және литвалық ұрпақтары алғашқы орыс патшасын Тәңір дінін Мәскеу князьдығынының мемлекеттік діні ретінде жариялануына ықпалын тигізеді. Жүз жылдан соң, патриарх Никон тұсында Русь Тәңір дінінен бас тартып, гректің христиандық дінін қабылдаған кезде, шіркеу мен мемлекеттің тағы бір рет бөлінуі орын алды. Көне заманғы дәстүрлі ілімге сыйыну пайда болды. Орыс қоғамындағы осыншама кескілескен қатігез түрдегі қайшылықтың мәні менінше, екі немесе үш саусақпен шоқынуда емес, ата-бабаның тәңір діні мен өзге жұрттық христиан дінін таңдауда екендігі айқын.

Жоғарыда еңбегіне сілтеме жасалған С.Баймұхамедов саясаткер Сая Фрумкиннің еңбегіне сүйене отырып, келесідей қорытынды жасайды: 1,4 млрд мұсылмандар арасында ғылыми жетістіктері үшін бар жоғы үш Нобель сыйлығының иегері бар. Бұл жайтты түсіндірудің өзі шамалы.

Маған Қазандық әйгілі ғалым Рафаэль Безертинов мәлім еткендей: Татарстанда 2000 мешіт салынды, осы амалдары үшін Саудовиялық Аравия бұл республикаға миллиард доллар қаражат бөлген. Бірақ Араб түбегіне келген татар мырзалары өздеріне лайықты сый көрсетілмей, немқұрайлық танытылғанда, қайран қалады, оларға: "сендер мұсылман емессіңдер, аруақтарға сыйынып, бабаларыңа сыйынасыңдар. Исламға сәйкес емес шірік әрекеттер жасайсыңдар"-деп жарияланған.

Сондықтан да, қазақ-мұсылмандар, өзіміздің болмысымызды жоғалтпайық. Бұрынғыдай үлкенді сыйлап, қасиеттерімізді қастерлейік. Өздеріміздің баба аруақтарымыздан көмек пен кеңес сұрап, өзіміздің кіндігіміз тамған жер - киелі атамекенімізді сақтайық.

# СКИФТІК РУСЬ. БАСТЫСЫ ҚАЙСЫ: ҚАЗАҚТЫҢ ОРЫСЫ НЕМЕСЕ СЛАВЯНДЫҚ РУС ПА?

*Ресей тек Еуропада емес, сонымен бірге Азияда,*
*өйткені орыс тек Еуропалық қана емес,*
*сондай-ақ азиалық. Еуропаға қарағанда,*
*Азиядан үмітіміз көп. Бәлкім сан*
*қилы тағдырымыздың түпкіріндегі Азия басты*
*мәселенің шешімі болуы мүмкін.*

*Ф. М. Достоевский.*

Қолымыздағы көптеген деректер қазақтар мен орыстардың тарихы және қаны бір туыстас халықтар және қазіргі заманғы орыс халқының шығу тегі скифтік екендігін екендігін айғақтайды. Соңғы жылдары осы мәселені зерттеушілердің бірнеше мәрте қозғағанын айта кетейік. Қазақ және орыс ғалымдары: К.Томпиев ("О тюркских племенах и народах Азии и Европы", Алматы "Қазақпарат", 2009 жыл-328 бет), А. Мырзаболатов пен Қ.Данияров ("Аманат", 2005, №5,121-146 бет), В.Демин, Е.Лазарев, Н.Слатин (Древнее древности.-М.:ООО "АИФ Принт", 2004 жыл, -542 бет. Иллюст. бірге). ("Русь многоликая" сериясы). А.Абрашкиннің ("Скифская Русь", М. "Вече", 2009 жыл) және басқалардың еңбектерінде тереңінен дәйекті тұрғыдағы дәлелдер бар.

Осыған байланысты Геродот заманынан бастау алатын, қазіргі заман ғалымдары, соның ішінде ресейліктер зерттеп жүрген Гипорборей теориясы жайында бірер сөз қозғағым келеді.

Осы тұжырымға сәйкес, сондай-ақ менің "Шыңғысханның түркілік ғұмырнамасы" атты кітабымда негізделіп келтірілгендей, шамасымен кемінде б.з.д. 30 мың жыл бұрын қазіргі Солтүстік мұзды мұхиттың толқындары шулап жатқан үлкен аймақта гипорборейлердің өркениеті дамып-гүлденіп, өркендеу жолына бет бұрған еді.

Жердің астероидпен соқтығысы орын алған деген болжамнан соң және жер өсі өзергеннен кейін шамамен 22000 жыл бұрын дүниежүзілік топан су басталып, бұл өркениет оңтүстік аймақтарға ауыса бастады. Осының нәтижесінде оның бір бөлігі солтүстік америка құрлығына барып ауысса, ал басқа бір бөлігі еуразиялық құрлыққа келіп тұрақтады. Қазіргі заман ғалымдары анықтаған солтүстік американдық үндістер мен алтай түркілерінің (соның ішінде қазақтардың) генетикалық тұрғыда ұқсастығы осы болжамды растайды.

Шамамен б.з.д. 5-6 мың жыл бұрын гиперборейлердің ұрпақтары Еуразия аймағына көшіп, Рейн, Одер, Висла, Дунай, Еділ (Волга), Орал, Ертіс сынды үлкен өзендердің жағалауын мекендеп, арийлер деген атпен өмір сүре бастайды.

Қазіргі заманауи ғылыми мәліметтер дүниежүзілік топан судан кейін қазіргі Қара, Каспий, Арал теңіздерін қамтыған ортақ табиғи су құрылымы болғандығын және жердегі құрғақшылық нәтижесінде бұл аймақтың қазіргі бедері және Еділ (Волга) өзенінің ағысы қалыптасқандығын айқындайды, осылайша кейінірек гиперборей атанған Еуразия арийлері батыс және шығыс жағалауда қалып, екіге бөлінді. Дәл осы кезден бастап шығу тегі ортақ халық қазақ және орыс болып бөлінеді. Жоғарыда атап өткеніміздей, арийлер Кіші Азия, Месопотамия және Таяу Шығыс аймақтарына орналаса бастайды. Тарихшылар б.з.д. 4-3 мың жылдықтарда құрылған Русена (Арзава), Митанни, Хатти (Хаттар мемлекеті), Шумер, Аккад мемлекеттері жайлы мәлімдейді.

Б.з.д. екі мыңыншы жылдықта Троян соғысы аяқталған соң, арийлердің өз атамекеніне жаппай түрде оралуы басталады. Академик-антрополог ғалым Оразақ Исмагуловтың еңбектеріне сүйенсек, меніңше, б.з.д V ғасырдағы қазақтар мен қазіргі орыс адамдарының арғы тегі бір этникалық құрылымды құраған. Қазіргі рустардың ата-бабалары негізінде Еділ өзенінің батыс жағалауында қалып қойды, өздеріне ұқсас славян халықтарымен араласып кетіп, өздерінің еуропалық келбет кескіндерін сақтап қалды. Ал қазақтардың бабалары б.з.д. бірінші мыңжылдықтың аяғынан бастап б.з. 2 мыңжылдығының ортасына дейін сары нәсілділердің өкілдері: қазіргі иран, үндіс, қытай, моңғол және т.б. халықтармен тығыз түрде араласып, ассимиляцияға түсті.

Сондықтан да бір кездері ортақ этнос басқа халықтар және өркениеттермен көптеген байланыс және қарым қатынастар негізінде қазіргі уақытта әртүрлі келбет кескінге ие болды. Қазіргі заманғы орыстар – сан ғасырлар бұрын қазіргі Ресей аймағына келген рус, түркі тілдес, финн-угор және славян халықтарының арасынан шыққан халық, ал қазақтардың нәсілдік тегінде 30% еуропалық келбет кескін сақталып, ал 70 % реңк моңғол тектес нәсілдерден алынды.

Ресей зерттеушісі А.Абрашкин өзінің "Скифтік Русь" еңбегінде мынадай мәселеге ден қояды: "орыс" және "славяндық" атаулары X ғасырдан кейін синоним ретінде қолданыла бастағанын нақты түрде аңғару керек". Бұрын бұл екі түрлі этностың арасында өзара өзгешіліктер болған. Бұл түсінікті жайт. Өйткені славяндар - орыс алқабына басқа жақтан келген халық, ал орыс жұрты - осы өлкенің байырғы, жергілікті тұрғындары".

Әйгілі ғалым, академик Б.А.Рыбаков өзінің "Мир истории" ("Молодая гвардия" баспасы, Мәскеу, 1984) атты елеулі еңбегінде Константин Багрянародный жазбаларына сүйеніп, былай деп жазады: "Осы рустардың қияңқы қыстағы өмірінің сипаты мынадай. Қазан айы басталғанда, олардың князьдары барша рустармен бірге Киевтен шығып, рустарға салық төлейтін славян жерлерінде шоғырланған: варвиан, джругувид, криветеин, северий тайпаларының қоныстарына аттанады..." Бұл жерде түсініктеме берудің қажеті шамалы...

Белгілі мәліметтерге сәйкес, 852 жылы Болгарияда билік басына кейінірек Борис деп аталып кеткен, Бағара хан келеді. Ол өз кезегінде қазақтың арғы тегі Ботбайдың (оның ұрпақтары қазіргі қазақтың Дулат тайпасының құрамында өмір сүруде) ағасы Аспарух ханның ұрпағы болып табылатын. Ол гректердің ықпалы нәтижесінде, болгар хандығына өзгерістер әкеліп, қоластындағы барша халықтарды славяндар деген ортақ атаумен атап теңестірді. Ғұн түркілік хандықтан христиандық славян мемлекеті қалыптасты. Көршілес тайпалар: серб, босниялық, богемдік, моравтық, хорват, чех, поляк және басқалары болгар халықтарының ішіне еніп, славян халықтары деп атала бастады. Тайпааралық қарым қатынас ретіндегі славян тілі пайда болғанға дейін, қарым қатынас құралы ретінде түркі тілі пайдаланылды. Бориске дейін славяндар атты бірлестіктер бұрын соңды болған емес.

Алғаш рет "славе" (құл) ұғымын антикалық тарихшы Иордан қолданады. О баста "славе" атауы Орталық Еуропаны мекендейтін венедтер тайпасына қойылады, олар орманшы-аңшылар еді, норманндар оларды үнемі құлдыққа сату үшін қолға түсіретін. Құлдардан славяндар қауымы басталды. Славяндық сөзінің этнос ұғымына еш қатысы болмады. Осындай іспеттес мәмлүктер басқарған мемлекетті, мәселен қазақтың Беріш руынан шыққан Мысыр сұлтаны Бейбарыс құрған еді. 852 жылдан бастап, Болгарияның халықтарының біріккен ортақ бірлестігі тарихи тұрғыда славян халықтары деп атала бастады. 864-65 жылдары Бағара хан өз қоластындағы тұрғындарды христиан дініне үгіттей бастады. Оларды шоқындырудың нәтижесінде славян тайпалары, соның ішінде славянға айналған түркі тайпаларын еркін түрде билеп төстеудің мүмкіндігі туды. Ал менің славян бауырларға деген құрметті ілтипат көзқарасымды орыс ақыны М.Волошин жақсы анықтаған: "Славяндықтарда лаулаған құпия оттың ұлы мақсатын түсінуге тырыс: мұнда ертеңгі күннің даңқы бар, крест бүкіләлемдік құлшылық. Оның екі түрлі тағдыры бар: есімі оның екі мәнді: SCLAVUS-құл, бірақ Славия, слава –құлдың басына киген тәж бен атақ қой".

Одан кейін тарих сахнасына варягтар келді. Жылнамашы Нестор былай деп жазады: "Біздің жылнамамызда варягтар атты ержүрек жаулаушылар Балтық теңізінің ар жағынан келіп, Чуд өзені бойы халықтары – славян тайпаларына келіп; ильмен, кривич, мерю тайпаларына салық салды". Өзара ішкі тартыстардан әбден қалжыраған славяндар 862 жылы (?) рустардың варяг тайпасынан шыққан үш ағайындыны өзіне шақырады. Олар Русь деп аталып кеткен атамекеніміздегі алғашқы билеушілер болып табылды. Жоғарыда сілтеме жасалған кітабымда, келімсек-варягтардың қазақтарға тікелей қатысы бар екендігі туралы айтып өттім. Варягтар келген жер Готландия деп аталған. Яғни, гот-балттардың елі. Жорамалдардың біріне қарағанда, Рюриктің тегі датчандық, ал Данияны Дон жағалауынан келген дан тайпалары құрған. Олар сол кезеңдерде қазақтың Тана руы деп аталып, осы өзен жағалауында көшіп қоныстанатын.

Орыс жылнамашылары, нақты айтқанда Нестор, варягтарды "рус" халқына ұқсастатын. А.П.Новосельцев "Восточные источники о Восточных славянах и руси YI-IX в.в"("Древнерусское государство и его международное значение" Мәскеу, 1965 жыл) атты еңбегінде араб тарихшысы Әл-Ханифидің деректерін келтіреді: "Рус халықтарының сипаты. Олар түркілер арасындағы үлкен халық. Олардың елі славяндармен шекаралас жатыр. Бұл жердің халқының түсі ақ, сары шашты, еңсегейлі бойлы Олар Алла Тағаланың жаратқан пенделерінің ішіндегі мінезі ең нашар халық және олардың тілі белгісіз". Осылайша біз славян жеріне қоныс аударған варягтардың түрі тілдес екендігі туралы тағы айғаққа ие боламыз. Бертин аналлдарында рустардың билеушісінің атағы қаған еді, ал бұл атақ тек түркі тілдес билеушілерге берілетін,-деп тұжырымдалған. Мәселенің түбі көрінді деген осы! Басқа бір араб жағрафияшысы Әл-Гарнати, өзінің славян жеріне жасаған саяхатын сипатта келе, былай деп жазды: "түрі жағынан түркілерге ұқсас, түркі тілінде сөйлейтін және садақ жебелерін дәл көздейтін түркі тектес мыңдаған магрибиндіктер..." (Путешествие абу Хамида ал-Гарнати В Восточную и И Центральную европу, 1131-1153г.г."М,1971). Араб тарихшысының алған әсері түсінікті жайт. Киевтің толық тұрғыда Түрклік Русь елі деп атауынан кейін, ол жақта әрине, түркі тілі – қарым қатынас құралы ретінде пайдаланылды. К.Томпиев өзінң "Очевидное и вероятное" (Алматы, 2011) кітабында келесідей мәліметтерді келтіреді: Зальцбург (Австрия) қаласындағы таста мынадай жазу қашалып жазылыпты: "Жаратушы жаратқан 447 жаз мезгілі. гепид, гот, унгар, мен герул, Русиндер патшасы Одоакр (өзім болып көрсеттім Қ.З.) Құдайдың шіркеуіне қарсы жабайы тағылық танытып, үңгірді паналап, бой тасалаған киелі Максимді елу жолдасымен бірге ұстанған діндері үшін биік жартастан жерге құлатты." Яғни рус-русиндердің ғұндар әскерінің құрамында болғаны ғой. Бұл таңданатын құбылыс емес. Өйткені ғұндар Еуропаға шығыстан келді, ал Махмұт Қашқари "Собрание тюркских наречий" атты кітабында былай деп жазады: Көне рустар этносы Алтайда өмір сүрген. Рустар ғұн әскерінің құрамында Еуропаға келіп, кейін оның шығыс аймағында Ұлы Русьті құрды.

Н.В.Кюнер "Китайские известия о народах Южной Сибири, Центральной Азии и Дальнего Востока" (Мәскеу, 1961) кітабында былай деп жазады: "Орыстар Усунь тайпасынан шыққан келімсек көшпенділер. Бұл нақты тұрғыда дәлелденеді". Усунь мемлекетінің Дуньхуань мен Цилянь арасында орналасқан, ал олардың тұрғындары олостар деп аталған. Қытайдың жуан дауыссызы сөздің ортасында жіңішкеге айналдырады, осының нәтижесінде орос-орыс сөзі олос этнонимінe айналған.

Тарих ғылымдарының докторы, профессор Б.Ирмаханов "Усунь и этногенез казахского народа" (Алматы, "Наш мир"2006) атты еңбегінде деректердің бай қайнар көзін зерделей келе, келесідей пікірге келеді: "усунь тайпасының шығу тегі еуропа тектес нәсіл..." Орыс халқының этногенезіне қатысты мәселені қорытындылай келе, рустардың арғы тегі б.з.д. дәуірдің аяғында (шамасымен б.з.д.120 жыл) Қытай аймағынан Жетісу өлкесіне келіп, сонан кейін заманымыздың басында ғұндармен бірге Еуропаға аттанады, бір бөлігі Скандинавияға (Балтық теңізіндегі Осилия аралы) жол тартады. Міне, осы жақтан варягтар деген атпен орыс мемлекетін құруға қатысады.

Еуропада рустарды скифтер деп те атаған. 1042 жылғы грузиндік деректер көзінде 626 жылғы Константинопольдың қоршауға алынуы жөнінде былай делінеді: "Рус болып табылатын скифтердің қасиетті қала Константинопольді қоршауға алып, шабуыл жасауы жөнінде..."

9 ғасырда "еуропалық славяндар" атты түркі тілдес лексикасы мен диалектілері бар халық пайда болды. Олардың көне замандағы этникалық түп тамыры анықталмады. Хронологиялық деректер бойынша, б.з.д. көне дәуірлерден бастап, Еуропада түркі тайпалары: киммерийлік, скиф, сармат, алан, ғұн, авар, оларға туыстас: рус, гет, гот, германдықтар және тағы басқалары өмір сүріп, билік құрғандығы мәлім. Қара теңіз жағалауын поляндар (анттар), печенег (қазақтың қаңлы тайпасы), косогтар (қазақтың шеркештері) және басқа да түркі тайпалары мекендеген. Тегі түркі рус-варягтар 882 жылы Киевтік Русьті құрады. Бұл мемлекетті құрған славяндар емес. Днепр аймағында, яғни Киевтік Русь жерінде ықылым замандардан бері киммерийлік, скиф, сармат, рус тайпалары және 8-9 ғасырдан бастап олардың ұрпақтары өмір сүріп келеді. Скандинавия варягтары осы тайпаларға туыс болып табылады, олардың бір бөлігі біздің деректер бойынша, алғашқы 1 мыңыншы жылдықтың басында Еуропаның солтүстігіне келіп орналасып, үстемдік жүргізгендіктен, Сондықтан да қазіргі орыстар мен қазақтардың бабаларын билік құрып, князь тағына отыруға шақырады.

Рус варягтар 882-944 жылдар аралығында 60 жыл бойы үстемдік жүргізді. Олардың ұрпақтары осы кезеңнен кейін де, көптеген ғасырлар бойы билікті уысынан шығармады. Көне орыс жазбаларында рустар варягтардың досы, славяндардың жауы және хазарлардың вассалдары ретінде танылған деген деректер келтіріледі. Яғни рустар түркі тайпаларына жақын туыс болып келген. 10 ғасырда рустар мен славяндар арасында тығыз түрдегі метисация үрдісі жүріп, аралас шығыс славян этносы, славян халқы қалыптасады. Рустар Тәңір ілімін сенімін сақтап қалды. Олардың хохол атануы да сондықтан шығар (Хохол сөзі түрі тілінен аударғанда – көктің ұлы, көкұл).

16 ғасырда Русь христиан дініне өткен соң, Борис Годуновтың патшалық құрған кезінде, олар түркі, финн-угор, вятич, муром және тағы басқа тайпалардың бірігуі нәтижесінде қазіргі орыс адамына тән кескін келбетті иеленді.

Моңғол тектес реңкке ие болған қазіргі қазақтардың бабалары шығыс арийлерінің шығу тегі мәселесіне жоғары жақта тоқталып өттім.

Ал мәдениеттің консервативтік бөлшегі болып табылатын  тіл мәселесіне келсек, егер қазақ тілінен парсы, араб, қытай және маньчжур-тунгустық кірме сөздерді алып тастасақ, ал орыс тілінен батыс еуропалық тілдерден енген кірме сөздерді алсақ, онда қазақ тілі мен орыс тілі бір-біріне ұқсас тіл болып шыға келеді. Осылайша, рулық жадының басты сақтаушысы – тіл осы екі ағайынды халықтың туыстық белгілерін сақтап қалды. К.Томпиев Мұрта Аджиге сілтеме жасай отырып, Рубруквистің 1253 жылы келесідей мәліметтерді баяндағанын келтіреді:

"Русин, поляк, богем (чех) славяндардың тілі" – жабайы вандал-түркілердің тіліне ұқсас болып келеді..." Рустардың католик дінін қабылдауы туралы мәселені зерттеуге Руське аттандырылған қасиетті папа- әулие әкей легаты, әулие әкейге Русьтің тұрғындары түркі тілінің славяндық диалектісінде сөйлейтінін баян етті.

Қазақ КСР Ғылымдар академиясы әзірлеген төрт жүз беттен тұратын "орыс тіліндегі тюркизмдер сөздігіне" сәйкес, славяндардың құлағына жағымды әдеттегі келесідей сөздердің шығу тегі түркі екендігі анықталды: стакан, слово, сын, товар, карман, карандаш, диван, деньги, влага, боярин, князь, богатырь, Бог, Господь, амбар, нефть, кочерга. Немесе келесідей жақы есімдердің тегі түркі екендігі айқын: Матвей, Александр, Ермолай, Арсений, Глеб, Борис, Даша-Дарья және т.б. Бұл тізімге Мұрат Аджи түбірі түркі тілдес келесідей топоним және гидронимдерді жатқызады: Дон, Волга, Ока, Урал, Иртыш, Обь, Енисей, Амур, Орел, Тула, Тамбов, Саратов, Челябинск тағы басқасы. Киім-кешек бұйымдары: штаны, карманы, шапка, колпак, кафтан, башмак, сапог, каблук, шуба, тулуп. т.т.

Рус, орыс сөзі этнонимінің шығу тегі туралы мәселе әлі ашылмай отыр. Бұрынғы КСРО-ның халықтары рустарды (русский) орыстар деп атаған. Мүмкін урыс этнонимі орыс сөзінің пайда боулына тікелей қатысы бар шығар? Ш.Қуанғанов өзінің "Арий-гун. Сквозь века и пространство: свидетельства и топонимы" (ИКП "Фолиант", 2001) кітабында келесідей қорытындыға келеді: Поляндар рус тайпаларының негізгі бөлігін құрағанын білеміз. Б.Рыбаков жоғарыда келтірілген кітабында, жылнамалық жазбаны келтіреді: "Поляндар – қазіргі Русь халқы. Поляндар этноним емес, дала, сахараны мекендейтін скиф халықтарын осылай атайтын, қазақ тілінде "өріс" деген сөз бар. Сондықтан да осы даланың тұрғылықты мекендейтін тайпалардың мекенінің атауы рус-русский деп аталып кетті. Сол кезеңдерде итальяндық Палермода өмір сүрген араб жағрафияшысы және саяхатшысы Әл-Идриси өз еңбектерінде рустардың тегі түркі тайпа екендігін және олардың этнонимі түркінің "орыс" сөзінен тарайтындығын баяндаған. Жалпы айтқанда, Інжілдегі Яфеттің ұлдары Рус пен Түрік, Нұх пайғамбардың немерелері болғандығы туралы пікірдің шындық екендігін растаймыз.

## ТҮРКІ-ОРЫС ЗИЯЛЫЛАРЫ ӘУЛЕТІНІҢ ТАМҒАСЫ

Жоғарыда, тоқталып өткеніміздей, қазіргі заманғы Ресей және Қазақстан аймағында б.з.д 5 ғасырларға дейін тегі ортақ, бірақ аттары әртүрлі этностар: киммерийлік, скиф, сармат, гот, балт, ғұн, түркі тайпалары және тағы басқалары өмір сүріп келді. Тек б.з.д 5 ғасырдан бастап қана қазақтардың еуропа тектес этникалық келбет-кескініне сары нәсілдестердің моңғолоидтық реңктері ене бастаған. Бірте-бірте ежелден бері біріккен ортақ этнос қазіргі заманғы қазақтар мен орыстардың кескін келбетіне ие болады. Ұлы далада қауырт өзгерістер 1312 жылы орын алды, осы кезде Өзбек хан тәңір дінінен шығып, қарудың көмегімен Алтын Ордаға исламды мемлекеттік дін ретінде енгізеді. Түркі билеуші шонжарларының ең беделді және ең танымал өкілдері Мәскеу князьдығына кетіп, қазіргі заманғы орыс дворяндар әулетінің негізін қалыптастырады.

Скифтік Русьтен біржола кетіп, бірте-бірте қазіргі Ресейге айналу үрдісі XVII ғасырда, дүрбелең заман аяқталып, билікке Романовтар келген кезде жүзеге асты. Мұрат Аджи "Без вечного синего неба" (Мәскеу, "Астрель" баспасы) кітабында былай деп жазады: Иезуит орденінің мүшесі Лаврентий Зизанияның қалам тартуы нәтижесінде, түркі тілінің славян тілдес диалектісі пайда болған, кейінірек, 1618 жылғы иеузит орденінің тағы бір мүшесі Мелетий Смотрицкийдің бекітілген "Грамматика" оқу құралы арқылы тағы да өзгерістерге ұшырайды. Кремльде боярларды дворяндар әулеті ауыстырып, Русьтің түркілік түп тамыры жойыла бастады. Онымен қоса ойдан шығарылған славяндық аңыздар арқылы жаңа идеология іске қосылды. Скифтік русьте қазақтар мен орыстардың ата-бабалары бір халық, бір этникалық қауымдастық болып табылғандығын тағы бір рет қайталап өтейік. Ресей тарихшылары: В.Татищев, М.Ломоносов, А.Чертков славяндық рустар мен б.з.д. 4-2-мыңжылдықтарда Жерорта теңізін мекендеген пеласг, Балқан түбегіндегі фракиялық және Аппенин түбегіндегі этрускілік тайпалар арасында этномәдени туыстық бар екендігін нақты айқындаған. Олар шамасы аталмыш халықтардың Ұлы Даладағы бұрын Ресей патшалығы қырғыз-қайсақтар деп атайтын халыққа тікелей тұрғыда қатысы бар екендігі ойларына да кіріп шықпаған болар. Біз фракиялықтардың тегі түркі екендігі жайында бастапқы тарауларда жетерліктей дәлел келтірдік, онда шамасымен Көне Грекияның байырғы жергілікті автохондары саналатын пеласгтер жөнінде пікір білдірейік. Б.з.д. 5 ғасырда өмір сүрген ежелгі Элладаның ең беделді тарихшыларының бірі Фукидид пеласг тайпасы туралы: "Пелопонессті б.з.д үшінші мыңжылдықта жаулап алған және оған өз атауын қойған азиялық тайпа"-деп жазады. Біз олардан кейін Балқан түбегінде кезек-кезегімен ахей, дорий, ионий тайпалары мекендегінін айтып өттік, олар да Еуразиялық алқаптан келген еді. Көріп отырғанымыздай, бұрынғы замандары қазіргі орыстар мен қазақтардың ата-бабалары осы құрлықтың шұрайлы жерлерін бірігіп, игере бастаған.

Көне Русь пен Половец алқабы мәселесіне оралайық. Тегі түркі көптеген орыс князьдарының арасында даңқты қолбасшылар аз болмаған. В.Кожиновтың мәліметтеріне сәйкес, князь Игорь үштен төрт бөлігі, немесе жартылай половецтік болған. Онымен бірге әйгілі орыс билеушісі половец ханы Күншуақтың (Кончак) қызына үйленген еді. Игорь мен Күншуақтың достығы шынайы, Игорьдің әжесі, атасы Олег Святославовичтің әйелі половец ханы Асылуықтың (Осулук) жары. Яғни Игорьдің бойында, сол кездегі орыс князьдарындағыдай половецтердің қаны ағатын. Ал Аип (Аеп) ханның қызы оның әкесі Святослав Олеговичтің әйелі болатын. Сондықтан да Игорь половецтік нағашыларымен достық қарым қатынасты берік ұстанатын.

Түркі-орыс зиялы әулетінің тағы бір өкілі князь Андрей Юрьевич еді. Ол Мәскеудің негізін қалаған Юрий Долгорукий мен половецтік Айып ханның ұлы. 20 ғасырда антрополог және мүсінші М.Герасимов Андрей Юрьевичтің бет әлпетін қайтадан қалпына келтіреді. Андрей Юрьевичтің мүсіндік портретінде айқын түрдегі қазақы половецтік үлгідегі бет әлпет көзге түседі. Князь Александр Юрьевич тарихта өшпестей із қалдырып кетті, ал православиелік шіркеу оны әулиелердің қатарына қосты.

Әулие князь Андрей Юрьевичтің бөле інісі әйгілі Всеволод Большое Гнездо болатын. Андрей Юрьевич сынды ол да жартылай половецтік және Аип ханның жиені еді. Ол көптеген атақты князьдар әулетінің негізін салушы: Суздаль, Владимир, Стародуб,

Ярослав, Ростов, Тверь және Нижегород князьдықтары әулеті, сонымен бірге Мәскеулік Рюриктер патшалары әулеті өз бастауын Всеволод Большое Гнездо князьдан алады.

Всеволод ұрпақтарының бірі князь Александр Ярославович еді. Жас князь Невада шведтерді тас талқан етіп, жеңімпаздығымен күллі әлемге танылады. Осы ерлігі үшін халық оны Александр Невский деп атап кетеді. Кейінірек тағы да бір ірі жеңісті – тевтондық орденнің талқандалуын да князьдың атына жазады. Әулие князь Александр Невский ¼ ретінде жартылай түркі половец тегінен тараған. Александр Невскийдің түркілік тегі оның Хан Батыйдың ұлы Сартақпен достығына септігін тигізеді. Сартақ ханзада мен князь Александр Невский бір-біріне анда - бауыр атанады. Жалпы айтқанда, Алтын Орда заңдары бойынша, орыс князьдарына өзінің әскери құрылымдарына ие болуға тыйым салынған еді, сондықтан да Александр Невскийдің айтулы жеңістері іс жүзінде Сартақ түмендерінің жеңісі болып табылды.

Сартақ пен Александр Невскийдің достығы орта ғасырдағы ең қуатты империя Алтын Орданың әскери-саяси әлеуетінің негізгі тірегіне айналды. Түркілік Алтын Ордамен одақтасу нәтижесінде Русь мемлекеті оның мұрагері атанып, кейінірек әлемдік озық мемлекетке айналды.

Кейінгі дәуірлерде Алтын орда хандары мен орыс билеушілері арасындағы қыз алысу қыз берісу дәстүрі жалғасын тапты. Бүкіл Ресейдің патшасы III Иван өзінің қызы Евдокияны Қазандық ханзада Құдайқұлға береді.

Урусов әулеті князьдары анасының шығу тегі жағынан Алтын Ордадағы Орыс Ханның ұрпақтары болғандықтан, олар Ресейдің билік құрушы әулетімен туыстық қарым қатынас құрады. Орыс, Урус және Рус этнонимдеріне зер салыңызшы! Князь Петр Урусов Шуйский әулетінен тарайтын бояр Василий Шуйскийдің қызына үйленеді. Князь Семен Урусов алғашқы орыс патшасы Михаил Федорович Романовтың бөле қарындасымен некесін қиса, олардың балалары бірінші орыс императоры Петр біріншінің әкесі – Алексей Михайловичтің бөлелері еді. Түркілік ақсүйектер мен орыс шонжарларының өзара қыз алысып, қыз берісуі нәтижесінде түркі-орыстық зиялы қауым пайда болды. Бұл қауым еуропалық дворяндардың бетке ұстары болып табылып, Ресейдің атын күллі әлемге паш етті.

Ресей империясының негізін қалаушы Қаһарлы Иоанның да тегі түркілік. Ол әкесі және шешесі жағынан да түркілерден тарайды. Әкесі жағынан Қаһарлы Иоанн половец ханы Айып ханның 13 ұрпағы болып саналады. Герасимов қайта жаңғыртқан түркілік текке тән кескін келбет Иван Васильевичтің де болмысынан да көрініс тапты. Қаһарлы Иоанн мен Андрей Юрьевичтің портреттерінде солтүстік қазақтарға тән түрілік-половецтік кескін келбет аңғарылады.

Ұлы мәртебелінің тегі түркі екендігі оның татар әулетімен қарым қатынасынан баяқалатын. Қаһарлы Иоанн өзінің үлкен ұлы Федорды Ирина Годуноваға үйлендіреді. Годуновтардың аксүейек дворяндық әулеті татар мырзасы Шетадан тарайтын. Сабуровтар дворяндар әулеті де Шета мырзаның ұрпақтары еді. Қаһарлы Иоанның түркілік тегі оның ұлдарының татарлардың қызына үйленуіне ықпал етті. Ксйбір дерсктер бойынша Шста татар руы мсн Кіші Жүз құрамындағы Шекті руының шығу тегінің түп тамыры бір болып саналады. Шета руынан тарайтын Ирина Федоровнаның туған бауыры Борис Годунов сарай билігінде үлкен ықпалаға ие болып, Земской соборының шешімі бойынша, таққа мініп, халық үшін көп игілік жасап, шығыс пен оңтүстіктің отарлануына жағдай жасайды. Бористің тұсында Саратов, Самара, Царицын, Воронеж, Белгород, Оскол, Тюмень, Тобольск, Сургут, Нарым қалалары бой көтеріп, сонымен бірге Ям, Орешек және Иван шаһары қалпына келтіріледі.

Борис Федорович дүние салған соң, "ауытқымалы дүрбслсң ксзсң" басталады. Романовтар әулетінің билікке келуі осы кезеңнің аяқталуына септігін тигізеді. Осы әулеттің екінші өкілі Алексей Михаилович патша Наталья Кирилловна Нарышкинаға үйленген еді. Нарышкиндердің дворяндық әулеті түркілік мырза Нарыштың ұрпағы болып есептелетін. Наталья Кирилловна мен Алексей Михаиловичтің ұлы Бірінші Петр патша атанады.

Император Бірінші Петр әлемдік тарих желісіне ықпалын кеңінен тигізді. Ұлы Петр Біріншінің атқарған жемісті істері мен нәтижелі еңбектері Ресейдің алтын ғасырына айналды. Петрдің ұйымдастырушылық қабілеті қолбасшылық дарынымен ұштасып, Русьті озық алдыңғы дамыған елдердің қатарына қосты. Императордың соғыстарда жеткен ірі жеңістері Русьті Алтын Орда мемлекетінің мұрагері, Еуропаға үстемдік жүргізуші мемлекетке айналдырды. Ресей әлемнің ең озық басты мемлекетіне айналды, осының барлығы Ұлы Петрдің тегі түркі екендігіне толығымен байланысты.

Петрдің түркілік тегі оның түрі зиялыларымен достығынан көрінетін. Императордың ақылшысы және кеңесші досы Федор Апраксин еді, оның графтық әулеті түркілік мырза Салихмирден бастау алады.

Мәртебелі Петр Алексеевич өзіне туыс татар тегіне өте жақын болатын. Ол Еуропаны аралауға аттанған кезде, Ресейді басқару ісін нағашысы Лев Кириллович Нарышкинге сеніп тапсыратын. Байқап отырғанымыздай, орыс мемлекетінің негізін салған, Ресейдің күш қуатын арттырған үш патшаның шығу тегі түркі екендігі анықталды. Ресей империясының негізін салушы – Қаһарлы Иоанн – әйгілі Куликов шайқасына қатысушы әмір Мамай мен половец ханы Айыптың ұрпағы. Бірінші Петр – Нарыш мырза мен Абатур мырзаның ұрпағы. Орыстың үш ұлы патшасы сан ғасырлар шеңберіндегі қазақ және орыс халқының мызғымас достығы іспеттес. Бұл мәселені егжей-тегжейлі тұрғыда өзімнің "Шыңғысханның түркілік ғұмырнамасы. Қазақтардың киелі шежіресі " атты кітабымда қарастырғанымды айта кетейін. Яғни этникалық шығу тегі жағынан Қазан, Қырым, Астарахан және Литва татарлары негізінде қазіргі қазақтардың руларынан құралады. Шындыққа келсек, қазіргі заманғы орыс қоғамы барша жан-тәнімен еуропалық өмірге бет бұруда. Бірақ Еуропа Ресейді еуропалық мемлекет ретінде қабылдайтын емес. Оның бұл атаққа лайықты болмағандығынан емес, керісінше Ресейдің өзіндік, ерекше алатын орны бар. Тютчев Ресей жайлы айтқандай: "Бұл ерекше жеке дара ел. Ресейге тек үміт артуға болады". Ресей – азиялық ел. Сондықтан да оның тарихы да өте көне болып табылады. Түркі азиялықтар мен орыстардың әлемдік өркениеттің сарқылмас қайнар көзіне қосқан үлесі, әлемнің басқа халықтарымен салыстырғанда, әлдеқайда орасан зор.

# Біздің ұлттық идеямыз

## Жабайы жылқы – көшпендің күш қуат негізі.

Осы кітапты жазу барысында Мысыр, Месопотамия, Парсы, Қытай, Еуропа елдерінің әлемдік өркениетінің жетістіктеріне қатысты ата-бабаларымыздың қосқан үлесінің орасан зор, елеулі екенін айтып жеткіздім. Көшпенді номадалардың ғаламдық білім қазынасына қосқан таудай үлес құбылыс-феноменін зерттейтін ғылыми зерттеу еңбектер де өте көп. Қазақтардың жеке дербестігі, ұлы бабамыздың құдіреттілігінің сыр құпиясы туралы айта келе, әлемдік деңгейде дөңгелектің ойлап табылуы сынды дәрежеге ие болатын бір құбылыс жайлы айтқым келеді. Әлемде жеңімпаз жауынгерлерді ат үстінде бейнелейтін ескерткіштер жетерлік. Бірақ Алматы, Астана немесе тағы басқа тарихи орындарда басты маңызды ескерткіш жетіспейді, яғни тіз қатар тізілген мүсіндер ансамблі арасында бабаларымызды ұлылық дәрежесіне жеткізген жабайы жылқының да ескерткіші тұруы тиіс. Ежелгі Грекия аңыздарында кентаврлардың пайда болуы кездейсоқ емес қой. Олар біздің ата-бабаларымыздан қалған сарқыт ретіндегі, ат үстіне біржола байланып қалғандай, өзінің сенімді тұлпарының тұяғы тие қалған жерді иеленіп, билік құрған ата-бабамыздың мұрасы. Б.з.д. 4000 жыл бұрын атамекенде жабайы жылқыны үйретіп (Солтүстік Қазақстандағы Ботай қалашығына қазба зерттеу жұмыстары жүргізілді), ата-бабамыз ең тиімді қозғалыс құралын ойлап тапты. Алтай, Жезқазғаан, Арқайымда бірінші болып қола, сонан кейін темір балқытып үйренген бабамыз б.з.д. төртінші мыңжылдықта Тигр мен Евфргат жағалауына, б.з.д. екі мыңыншы жылдықта Араб түбегі мен Ніл өзеніне дейін, сәл кейінірек Сары өзен (Хуанхэ) мен Ганг өзеніне дейін, Тұманды Альбион жері мен Баскілер жұртының жеріне дейін сан мәрте рет жеңімпаз жорықтарын жасаған. Сонымен бірге жабайы қойларды үйрету жағынан да бабаларымыз бәрінен басым түсті. Маңғыстау облысында осы күнге дейін қазақтың еділбай тұқымдас қойларының арғы тегі жабайы муфлондар жайылады.

Грекияда б.з.д. бірінші мыңжылдықтың 499 жылы гректердің парсыларды жеңгендігі туралы афиндіктерге ұзақ күткен хабарды жеткізген марафондық жауынгерге естелік ретінде ескертіш орнатылған. Егер сол кездерде гректер әскери амалдардарды жүргізу мақсатында жылқыны пайдаланса, онда бұл қуанышты хабарды атқа мінген шабарман арқылы жеткізген оңай еді ғой. Ол үшін адамның өмірін қиюдың не керегі бар? Марафоншыға ескерткішті қайнаған ыстық күнге қарамастан 42 шақырым жерді тоқтамастан жүгіріп өтіп, жерлестерін ұлан асыр жеңіспен құттықтап, тіл тартпай кеткендігі үшін қойылды.

# Интеллектуалды зиялы қауым – болашақ Қазақстан құдіреттілігінің бренді және түп қайнар негізі

Арий, сеир, оғыз, немесе мар, шумар, қимар, самар, тур, таврлар, сонан кейін барып, скиф, сақ, ғұн, сармат, түркі, моңғолдар қазіргі біздің иелігіміздегі өркениеттің негізін қалап кетті. Әлемдік тарихтың біздің ата-бабаларымыздың жасампаз ерліктері ақиқаты жайына қатысты үнсіздік танытып отырғаны өте өкінішті. Біздің Елбасымыз тағайындаған таңғажайып "Болашақ" бағдарламасының қаншама түлегі бар?! Олар неге үнсіз? Бәлкім оларды басқа ілімге үйреткен шығар, әлде олар өздерінің кіндік қаны тамған, анасының ақ сүтін ішіп, өсіп жетілген туған Отанын ұмытқан шығар.

XXI ғасырдағы қазақтардың ұлттық идеясына келсек, бұл күрделі мәселе Отанымыздың тағдырына немқұрайлы қарамайтын адамдардың басты назарында. Ресейдің Президенті Борис Ельцин алғашқы қаулыларының бірін Ресейдің ғылымдар Академиясына халық және Ресей мемлекеті алдында тұрған ұлттық идея міндеттерін дәл анықтап шығуға жария етті. Бірақ білуімше, бұл мақсат әлі шешімін таппай келе жатыр.

Америкада мәселен, Ұлы дағдарыстан кейінгі Ф.Рузвельттің әрбір американдық азаматты басқа мемлекеттердің адамдарынан әлдеқайда ауқатты ету жөніндегі алға қойған мақсатына ерекше ден қойылып, барша жұрттың назарын өзіне аударды. Екінші дүниежүзілік соғыстан кейін запа шегіп, қасірет тартқан Жапония өз жеріндегі тауарлардың сапасын арттыру және бәсекеге қабілетті етудің арқасында қайтадан жанданып, дамып шыға келді. Сондай-ақ Жапония фирманың мақсатын отбасы мен мемлекет мүдделерінен жоғары қою нәтижесінде үлкен табыстарға қол жеткізді. Ал Қазақстанға келер болсақ, Елбасымыз Н.Ә.Назарбаев бұл тақырыпқа қатысты талай рет ойын айтқан болатын. Ұлттық идея ретінде әр қазақстандықтың берекелі өмірге қол жеткізуін, қазақстандық қоғамның бірлігі және т.б. мәселелер жайында ойын ашық білдірді. Кез келген мемлекетті дамыту үшін осы аталмыш шарттардың бәрі керек. Меніңше, Президентіміздің қоғамды біріктіріп, әлемдік көшбасшыға айналдыру мәселесіне қатысты ұлттық идеяны тыңғылықты тұрғыда іздеуі өз жемісін берді.

Өзінің ұлттық, интеллектуалды зиялы қауымын дайындау –біздің мемлекетіміз үшін ең биік және өзекті мақсаттардың бірі!

Ата-бабаларымыз мыңдаған жылдар бойы көптеген мемлекеттерді жаулап, оларды өзіне сіңіріп, кейінгі ұрпақтары үшін өте қуатты генетикалық тұрғыдағы әлеуетті мұра ретінде қалдырды. Бүгінгі таңда, жастарымыз спортта әлем чемпионы және Олимпиада чемпионы атағына қол жеткізіп қана қоймай, сонымен бірге халықаралық математикалық олимпиадаларда бірінші орынға ие болып, халықаралық бүкіл фестиваль және байқауларда Гран-при иегері атанып келеді, Президентіміздің "Болашақ" бағдарламасының түлектері шетелдегі көптеген озық фирмаларында жетекші маман ретінде қызмет атқарады.

Өзінің атын қалалар мен ауылды мекендерге арнап қоюға қатысты көптеген ұсыныстардан бас тартып, Президентіміз назарбаев мектептері мен университетері, назарбаев орталықтарының ашылуы және олардың өнімді тұрғыда жұмыс істеуіне келісімін берді. Егер әрбір қазақстандық олигарх, немесе бай ауқатты кәсіпкер немесе компания-олардың саны бізде он мыңнан астам, өзінің табысынан бір пайызын бөліп, қазақстанның түкпір-түкпірінде жүрген математика, өнер, жаратылыстану ғылымдары, спортқа икемі бар, дарынды бір ғана баланы іздеп тауып, оның дарынын дамытса, онда әлемде бізге жетер ел болмайды! Біз сол кезде күш-қуатты ұлтқа айналып, қаруымыздың күшімен емес, ақыл парасатымыз арқылы әлемді бағындырамыз!

Міне, барша қазақстандықтар үшін ұлттық идея дегеніміз - осы!

Ұлттық идеяның жүзеге асырылуы Қазақстанның брендтік өнімінің шығарылуы арқылы толықтырылып отыруы тиіс. Назарбаев университеттері осы брендтің қайнар бұлағына айналмақ. Осы оқу орындарының түлектері арасынан Қазақстандық Нобель иегерлері міндетті түрде шығуы тиіс. Иә, Нобель сыйлығының иегері – мақтанышымыз бен намысымыз. Тіпті, олар өзін өсіріп жеткізген елдің бренді дей беріңіздер. Мәселен Парсы шығанағы елдерінде сәби дүниеге келе салысымен, сол елдің кішкентай азаматының есепшотына белгілі бір көлемдегі ақша аударылып отырады. Осының нәтижесінде оның білім алуға ықыласы жоқ, өйткені олар даярға маяр болуда. Маған Араб Әмірліктерінен шыққан лауреат немесе Олимпиада чемпионының есімін атаңызшы. Ондайлар жоқ! Ал Қазақстандық мұнайға бай өлкеде өзінің Эйнштейндері мен Шеспирлері болуы тиіс. Олардың есімі аталған кезде, Сарыарқаның кең алқаптары мен Маңғыстаудың каньон шатқалдары немессАлтай таулары еске түсіп, елестеуі тиіс. Балқан түбегіндегі Македония сынды шағын мемлекетті кім білсін? Бірақ барша әлем осы жердің жасампаз ұлы –Александр-Ескендірді жақсы біледі.  Ұрпақтары оны құрметтеп, Македонский деген ат береді! Өндірістік кәсіпорындардағы  өнім беру көлемі тұрғысынан бәлкім, Англия, Ресей, Қытайға жете қоймаспыз, бірақ Қазақстанда өзінің Ньютондары, Пушкиндері, Рокфеллері және Конфуцийлері өмір сүріп, жаңалықтар ашуы тиіс. Көп ұлтты Қазақстан үшін ұлттық идея жайындағы мәселені осылайша ұсынар едім.

**\* \* \***

Осы кітап, жарық көру үшін баспаға тапсырылған соң, Франциядан жеделхат жарияланды ("Аргументы недели" Мәскеу, 2012 жылдың 22-29 ақпаны.), бұл ақпаратта Шарль Наполеон –әйгілі қолбасшының туған інісінің ұрпағының ДНК үлгісіне сараптама жасау барысының нәтижелері, Наполеон Бонапарттың шығу тегі Кавказдық екендігі туралы айтылады. Бұрынырақ оның бір уыс шашына зертету жүргізу нәтижелері, оның таяу шығыстан шыққандығын меңзеген. Бірақ осы кітаптың баяндалуының сюжеттік желісі барысында Таяу шығыс пен Кавказ аймағында түркі, скиф руларының мекен еткендігі туралы жеткілікті тұрғыдағы айғақтар мен дәлелдерді келтірдік. Мәселені анықтап, бұл жайттың анық-қанығынап жету үшін француз генетиктері Наполеонның денесіне сараптама жүргізу үшін рұқсат алуға ниет білдіріп отыр.

Өз басым әлемді дүр сілкіндірген ұлы қағанның шығу тегін анықтау мақсатында Шыңғысханның үлкен ұлы Жошы ханның мәйітіне зерттеу жүргізу қажеттілігі туралы талай рет мәселе көтердім. Осының барлығы келешекте жаңа зерттеулеріміздің тақырыбына айналады, - деген сенімдемін.

Ғасырлар бойына тыныштық сақтап келген біздің ата-бабамыздың ежелгі Жері соңғы онжылдықта терең ұйқыдан «тірілгендей», біздің жүрегіміз бен ақыл-есімізді үсті-үстіне еліктіре бастаған түріктер әлемінің шексіз бай, таңқаларлық жұмбақ оқиғаларының тарихи деректерін ұсынып отыр.

Қасиетті Құранда былай делінген: «Сендер бір-біріңді танып-білу үшін мен сендерді әртүрлі етіп жараттым, әртүрлі нәсілдерге бөлдім, әртүрлі тілдер бердім. Жаратқанның ғажап даналығы осы сөздерде бекітілген. Барлық адамзат баласы бір тілде сөйлеп, бір нәсілді болса, бір-бірімізді танып-білу оңайырақ болады деп көрінер еді. Дегенмен де, бұл өте зеріктіріп жіберер еді!

Қазірде бар адамзаттың өткір қызығушылығын тудыратын тарихы мол «Жер жүзін дүрілдеткен» ұлы империяны, бірегей өркениетті құрушылар кімдер деген сұрақтың соңына түсетін кез келді.

Не шек, не шалғайлық, не өлім дегенді білмеген ержүрек жауынгерлер, көшпенді түркілердің әлемі ғажап. Талапты зерттеуші Қайрат Закирьяновтың «Шыңғыс ханның түркі сағасы», «Көкжал белгісімен. Түркі рапсодиясы» кітаптарын оқи отырып, от түтінінің иісін сезінесің, жауынгерлік аттардың кісінеуі мен тұяқтарының гүілін, жасақ саймандарының зыңылын, түркілердің көмейден шығып сөйлеген дыбыстарын естисің, түркі ордаларының шатырлары мен ақ киіз үйлерді көресің.

Олар – біздің сонау заманғы арғы аталарымыз, өліммен ойнай отырып, өзге әлемдерді жаулап алып, қашықтықтарды игере отырып, бөгде жерлерде өздерінің өшпес іздерін қалдырып кеткен.

Автордың пікірі — бұл бос қиял жемісі немесе ұлттық өзімшілдіктің арзан сезімдері емес, ол әрдайымғы ізденіс пен терең еңбек нәтижесі, әлемге әйгілі тарихшылар еңбектерінен құжатты айғақтармен растатылған өз түп-тамырын танып-білуге деген қанбалатын құмарлық. Түрік империясының құдыретінің күштілігі сондай, тіпті автордың келтірілген дәйектері басқа оқырмандар үшін ойдан шығарылған сөздер секілді көрінеді. Бірақ, жеке халыққа тиімді тарихты әлсін-әлі көшіре адамзат зердесінен, ең алдымен сол түркілердің өздерінен, түркілер әлемінің парақтарын сызып тастау үшін қай уақыттан бері, қандай күш жұмсалғанын, тіпті, көз алдымызға елестету қиын. Жалған ілім жақтаушыларының "дәлелдемелері" бойынша буддизмнің іргесін қалаушылар, және, тіпті, қытай иероглифінің негізін салушылар славяндар болған екен. Біздің заманымызда жалған-ғалымдар Атилланың алғашқы орыс князі болғанын, көшпенділердің құрылым тарихы болған емес, тіпті, болуы да мүмкін емес, ғұндар - олар славяндар, яғни, орыстар деген "дәйектемелерді ойлап табудан" жалықпайды. Қуанышымызға орай, бүгінгі күнде осы "ғылым" зұлматына қарсы қоюға болатын әлемге әйгілі тарихшылардың көптеген дәлелді зерттеулері бар.

"Қорғаныс - қорқақтықтың белгісі. Кім соққы берсе, сол батыр. Кек алу – табиғаттың берген ұлы сыйы. Жеңіске қарай жүргендерге оқ тимейді. Ұлы жауынгер Атилла: - «Кім тыныштықта болса, ол әлдеқашан жерленген» деген.

Түркілер Атилла бастаған жасақпен Византияны екі рет бағындырған. Гректер өз жеңілісін мойындап, Солтүстік Балқаннан кеткен. Дешті-Қыпшақ шекарасы Жерорта теңізі мен Константинопольге жақындаған. Халықтардың Ұлы қоныс аударуының бар тарихы кезеңінде түркілер бірде-бір жерді, не елді бағындыра алмаған. Олар тек жаңа жерлерге ел қоныстандырып, сол жерлерде өз қалаларын тұрғызған.

Құрамына еуразиялық дала тарихында маңызды рөл ойнаған көптеген тайпалар мен ұлыстар кіретін қазақ халқы Еуразиядағы ең ежелгі халықтардың бірі болып саналады. Орталық Азия Солтүстік пен Оңтүстікті, Шығыс пен Батысты байланыстырып тұратын «жіп» міндетін атқарған. Ол – христиандық, ислам және буддизм діндерінің түйіскен жері болды. Ол континентаралық маңызы бар сауда маршруттары үшін және көшпенділердің басып кірулері үшін өтпелі аймақ болды. Қазақстан және Орталық Азия жерінен бастап көшпенділер әлемнің бар бұрыштарына жаулап алу жорықтарын жасаған. Бұл аймақтың этномәдени үдерісі басқа барлық аумақтың, көптеген Еуразияның ежелгі, орта және жаңа ғасыр халықтарының этногенездік үдерісінде аса маңызды рөл атқарған. Түркілердің ғажайып әлеміне деген қызығушылық, ең алдымен, Еуропалық елдерде туған. Бір кездері Францияда пайда болған "Turguere" қозғалысы түркі елінің мәдениетіне үлкен қызығушылық көрсеткен. Түркі елдері шеберлерінің тамаша туындылары жеке топтамалары үшін иеленіп, қолдан жасалған шығармалардың бүкіләлемдік көрмелеріне қойылған.

Ежелгі түркілер, ғұндар, моңғолдар туралы Еуропа елдері зерттеушілерінің археологиялық қазбалары, тарихи зерттемелері түркілердің ежелгі халық екенін, олар өте үлкен кеңістікті алғанын, ұлы хандықтар құрғанын, және де әр тарихи кезеңдерде әлемдік тарихтың дамуына зор әсерін тигізгенін дәлелдеді. Осылай «Түркітану» деген ғылым туған. Тарихи зерденің қайта оралуы, тілдің, діни құндылықтардың қайта өркендеуі, олай болса, мәдениет пен халықтардың қарқынды араласу заманында халықтың рухтандырушылығын сақтап қалу материалды әлем шынайы құндылықтардан үстем болуы қазіргі заманның мұрағатты аса маңызды тапсырмасы болып келеді.

Әлем халықтары бір-біріне өздерінің қайталанбастығымен, бірегей ерекшелігімен, халық пен тұқымның, тілдер мен мәдениеттің, діндер мен сенімдердің алуан-түрлілігімен қызықты.

Бір кездері қазақ бабаларымыз жүріп өткен жолды танып-білу біздің рухымызды көтеріп болашаққа сеніммен қарауға, ұйып қалған қанға дем беріп, мәдениеттің ұлттық ерекшеліктерін сақтап қалуға шақырады.

Ырықсыз уақыт бәрін өз шеңберіне қайта шегеріп отыр. Халықтың бетке ұстар ұлдары мен қыздарын жойқындаған советтік идеологияның механизмі туралы естеліктері осы күнге дейін естен шықпаған, күні кеше ғана, сол естеліктер бізге құлдық сана-сезімін туғызып еді. Кейбір елдердің өзімшілдік алға ұмтылу батылсынуы әлі де болса сақталған. Ал біз болсақ, әлем картинасының бүлінбеген, бояусыз және асырамасыз ақиқатын қайта жандандыруға тырысамыз. Талассыз дарынды және түркі әлемінің шыншыл зерттеушісі Қайрат Қайруллиновичтің кітаптарын оқи отырып, бар адамзат тарихын құруда үлкен рөл ойнаған кең де жарқын түркілер ғаламына өзіңнің де қатысың бар екенін сезінесің. Бұл сезімдерден тынысың тарылады!

Адамзаттың ақиқатты тарихын қайта өркендету үшін бүкіл әлемнің тарихшы-зерттеушілеріне бас қосып, жиналуы қажет. Бұл уақыт әлі келмеді, бірақ ол кез де қарқынды түрде жақындап келеді.

Қайрат Закирьяновтың бұл ісі – ерлік дер едім. Дешті-Қыпшақ тарихына құштар, әділ зерттеуші ерлігі. Жер ғаламшары азаматының және Дешті-Қыпшақтың шынайы ұлының ерлігі.

Жалған отансүйгіштік емес, ол тарихи естеліктермен қайтарылған Отан және Тарих алдындағы шынайы азаматтылық жауапкершілік сезімі АДАМ деген биік атқа лайықты өмір сүру үшін жасалатын үмітті ақтай алатын қадамдарға кез-келгеніміздің барарымыз анық.

**Роллан Сейсенбаев**
**Жазушы**
**Абай Халықаралық**
**Клубы Президенті**

**Қайрат Закирьяновтың «Көкжал белгісімен. Түркі рапсодиясы» кітабы туралы (Алматы, 2012 ж. – 212 б.)**

Еуразияның тарихи дамуында өз дәуірінде ғана емес, сонымен қатар, келешек ұрпақтың да этномәдени пеманенттік дамуында тағдыршешті рөл ойнаған алдыңғы қатарлы үздік тұлғалар аз болған жоқ. Әсіресе, Шыңғысханның үздік тарихи рөлі бұл тұрғыда ерекше көрінеді, Еуразияның бытыраңқы және жігерсіз ортағасырлық шарттарында алғаш рет сол заманда мүлде ешкімге белгісіз зор әлеуметтік-экономикалық өзгеріс және мемлекеттік жаңашыл қызметті енгізді. Тура осы және де басқа айбынды және келешегі бар жаңалықтары, тіпті, 800 жыл өтсе де, заманауи әлем үшін әлі күнге дейін өз өркениеттік мәнін жоғалтпаған.

Сол үшін, ең кеңпрофильді зерттеушілер – математиктерден әдебиетшілерге дейін Шыңғыс хан феноменіне көпжоспарлы және нағыз қызығушылық танытуы кездейсоқтық емес. Оның мысалы ретінде ғылым докторы, математика профессоры және Қазақтың спорт және туризм академиясының басшысы Қайрат Закирьяновтың көпжылдық еңбегі 2012 жылы Алматы қаласында жарық көрген «Көкжал белгісімен. Түркі рапсодиясы» атты кітабы қызмет көрсете алады.

Автор көпшілігі алғаш рет таңдап алынған тақырып бойынша тартылып отырған тарихи-әдебиеттік бастаулардың біркелкі топтары кең түрде қолданған. Сонымен қатар, автор Шыңғыс хан қызметімен байланысты негізгі тарихи жерлер бойынша жеке зерттеулер қатарын жүргізген. Соның нәтижесінде, кітапта халықтардың кең тарихи өрісте этникалық, лингвистикалық және діни қарым-қатынастары, түркі әлемінің көнелігі туралы жеке көрінісі, және генезисі, сондай-ақ, Шыңғыс ханның этникалық құрамы мен тарихи фоны жөніндегі тым қызық түсіндірмелер келтірілген. Расында, біздің ойымызша, осы тақырып бойынша автордың барлық айтылғандары дау туғызбайды емес. Солай болса да, қазақ халқы мәдени бастауының көнелігімен байланысты автордың тұжырымдамасы Қазақстан тарихнамасында өмір сүруіне құқы бар.

Ауқымды оқушылар шеңберіне арналған бұл кітаптың негізгі ақпараттық құндылығы, ең алдымен, философиялық көзқарас пен ерекше тарихи пайымдамалар, және де, Шыңғыс хан феноменімен байланысты көркем картиналар жасау бойынша жеке идеялары ұсынылған, олар, әдеттегідей, жай тарихи іздеулерде не белгіленбейді, не бақыланбайды. Кітапта Шыңғыс ханның айрықша қызметі сол кездері әлемнің екі бөлігі де: Шығысы мен Батысы, ортағасырлардағы сылбыр даму шарттарыпда болған кезде іске асқанына заңды түрде назар салынған.

Сондықтан да қазіргі заманның зиялы әлемін оқырмандарының үшін осы кітапты енгізу Шыңғыс ханның, асып кеткенде, заманауи жаһандастырумен салыстырыла алатын реформаторлық идеологиясын, әсіресе, елдердің келе-келе тығыз және жалпыәлемдік үдерістермен байланысы артып келе жатқан алуан түрлі жақтарынан жаңаша қарастыруға мүмкіндік береді.

Жалпы кітапта келтірілген тарихи оқиғалар, этникалық құрылымдардың өзара қарым-қатынасы, Шыңғыс ханның ортағасыр дәуіріндегі қоғамдық-мемлекеттік қызметінің рөлі оның Еуразия масштабындағы шынайы этникалық түбірлерін танып-білуі үшін белгілі қызығушылық тудырады. Антропологиялық зерттеулер нәтижелерінің кейбір батылталдамаларына қарамастан, кітаптың даусыз құндылығын атап өту қажет: ол жеңіл әрі қолжетімді тілмен жазылған, сезімдер мен елес-қиялдарды дүрліктіреді, бірақ ең бастысы – оқырманды терең ойлануға, терең әрі кең көруге, іргелі білімнің академиялық шеңберінен шығатын және әрдайым бірмәнді емес болса да, басқа көзқарастардан тарихи ақиқатқа қазбаланып жетуге тырысуға мәжбүрлейді.

Шыңғыс хан феноменін зерттеу үшін Қ. Закирьянов жеке «Тюркская сага Чингисхана, Сокровенное сказание казахов» кітабын арнағанын атап кету қажет. Өзінің жаңа «Көкжал белгісімен. Түркі рапсодиясы» кітабында көшпелі мал өсірушілердің (ол негізінен түркілер мен қазақтар тайпалары) Орта Азия мен басқа да елдердің отырықшы және жартылай отырықшы тұрғындарын бағындырғаннан кейін ғана еуразиялық және шығыс елдері ұлы өркениеті пайда болды деген «жаулап алу тұжырымдамасын» негіздеуші XIX ғасырдағы неміс философиялық мектебінің атақты өкілдері еңбектеріне сүйене отырып, автор ежелгі әлемнің тарихи тұжырымдамасын құрады.

Нәтижесінде, келімсек көшпенділер басым ұстанымда болған осы елдерде өз сипаты бойынша бинарлы этикалық қоғамдар пайда бола бастады, ал бұрыннан мекендеп келе жатқан жергілікті тұрғындар болса олардың беделінің астында қала берген, және осыған сәйкес, біз бұл өркениеттің атақты қайраткерлері тобы Орта Азиядан келген мигранттар ұрпағына жатуы мүмкін деп болжауымызға толықтай құқымыз бар.

Қазіргі заманғы әдістеме ғылымына сәйкес, көне авторлардың еңбектеріне көңіл бөле отырып, Қайрат Закирьяновтың Шыңғыс хан, Екінші Ұлы Кир және тағы да басқа өткен ғұлама қайраткерлердің түркілер түбірлерінен шыққан деп қорытындылауының толықтай себебі бар.

Жалпы, Қайрат Закирьянов жан-жақты мәліметтерді бірыңғай жүйеге біріктірген тұжырымдама жасады, осылайша, түркілердің, яғни, көшпенділердің Еуразия көлеміндегі көптеген өркениет элементтерін тудыру рөлі анықталады.

Егер XIX ғасырдың атақты неміс ғалымы Альфред Вебердің сөзімен айтатын болсақ, «...Дүниежүзілік тарих көшпенділердің стратегиялық атты әскерінің көптеген зор дүбірін сүйемелдеуімен жасалған...», және Қайрат Закирьянов өзінің зерттеу еңбектерінде осы процесстің терең тарихи бастауларын үнемі сендіре дәлелдейді.

Қайрат Закирьяновтың «Көкжал белгісімен. Түркі рапсодиясы» кітабы көптеген түркілердің әлеуметтік-мәдени тарихын, сонымен қатар, қазіргі өркениетті әлемде екінші мыңжылдықтың жаңа дәуір Адамы болып мойындаған Шыңғыс хан феноменін тануға құштар тілектес оқырмандар және адамдардың кең тобы ішінен ізет тұтушыларын табады деп ойлаймын.

**Қазақстан Республикасының**
**Білім және ғылым Министрлігі**
**Этнология және тарих Институты**
**антропология және этнология бөлімінің**
**бас ғылыми қызметкері,**
**Қазақстан Республикасы**
**Ұлттық ғылым Академиясының академигі,**
**Болон ғылыми Академиясының тілші-мүшесі,**
**Тарих ғылымдарының докторы, профессор**
**Оразақ Исмагулов**

Тамаша математик және еліміздің ең ірі педагогикалық академиялары бірінің басшысы Қайрат Қайруллинович соңғы күндері өз елінің тарихына арналған кітаптардың авторы ретінде де белгілі болып жүр. Қазақ оқымыстысының ұлттық тарих тақырыбындағы нақты зерттеулер аясындағы кәсіби зерттеулермен байланысты болған әуелгі ғылыми қызметінің үндеуін толықтай заңды деп мойындауымыз керек. Өз ата-бабасының тарихына деген қызығушылығы таяудағы еуразиялық дала көшпенділерінің ұрпағында өте терең тектік дәрежеде қаланған. Корея түбегіндегі ежелгі Бозцы мемлекетінің негізін қалаушы дала тұрандары туралы ерте қытайлық жазбалардың бірінде былай жазылған: «... Атпен садақтан оқ ату және ежелгі тарихпен айналысқанды жақсы көреді...».

Сонымен бірге, Қазақстанның жақында ғана қол жеткізген мемлекеттік тәуелсіздігі оның зиятқерлік элитасының алдында және идеологиялық қасиеттердің бірқатар мәселелерінің өз шешімін талап ететін өте күрделі мәселелерін қойды. Ең алдымен, Кеңестік және Ресейлік империялардың өте терең саяси мүдделері және батыс еуропалық орталықшыл белгілі көзқарастарға әуелгі пікір, ең алдымен, ұлттық тарихты түбегейлі қайта ойлауға еріксіз мәжбүрлейді. Өз халқының шынайы тарихын жаңғырту қазақ мемлекеттігінің алдағы табысты дамуының идеологиялық қажетті және маңызды шарты болып табылады.

Ескерте кету керек, соңғы жылдары айтарлықтай нақты ерекше бір беталыс байқалады. Гуманитарлы-тарихтық сипаттағы жалпыұлттық мәселелерді шешуде нақты бір ғылым өкілдері келе-келе белсене қатысуда. Анығырақ айтсақ, солардың ішінде математиктер мен физиктерге тән аналитикалық ақыл-ой жүйесі өз халқына деген сүйіспеншілігімен, ежелгі тарихына деген терең қызығушылығымен сәтті түрде үйлескендер.

Солардың қатарына өзіміздің бұрынғы жерлесіміз және Ресейдің заманауи жетекші ғалым-атомшыларының бірі, физико-математика ғылымдарының докторы Дмитрий Мадигожинді («Богатырская сверхцивилизация»), физико-ядролық қару шығарушы, «Логика небесного закона Кок Торе» атты зерттеу жұмысын Мадигожинмен авторласып шығарған Сматай Аязбаевты, махмұны жағынан өте қызық басылымдар қатарының авторы математик Самат Набиевты айтуға болады.

Әсерлі мысал ретінде осы бағытта сәтті қызмет жасаған жақында ғана басылып шыққан іргелі тарихи-лингвистикалық зерттеу жұмысының авторы, Мәскеулік техникалық ғылымдарының кандидаты Юрий Дроздовты айтуға болады. Бұл заманауи және ежелгі түркі тілдерінің аумақты дәйектерін меңгерген дарынды ғалым әлемдік тарихи ғылым әлі күнге дейін жақындай алмаған іргелі қорытындыларға келген. Ерте ортағасырлардағы және көне замандағы Еуропаның этникалық атауларының терең нәтижелеріне сүйене отырып, ол құрлықтағы байырғы даму Орталық Еуразия даласынан шыққан мал бағушы таптардың қозғалысымен анықталды, және сол таптар түркітілдес халықтар болған деп тұжырым жасаған.

Осы келтірілген зерттеушілер тобында Қ.Қ. Закирьянов өзінің еуразиялық этнонимдердің лингвисикалық қорытындысына маңызды орын бере отырып көңіл бөлген және де түркілер тарихындағы басты мәселелердің бірі – Шыңғыс хан «моңғолдарының» қалыптасуы жайлы мәліметтерімен ерекше орын алады. Бұл мәселе ортағасырлар мен көне замандағы құрлықтың аму тарихының сипаттамасын мәнмәтінінде ерекше маңызды. Сонымен қатар, Шыңғыс хан және оның ұрпақтары – Шығыс Еуразия мен Азияның көптеген елдерінің көпжылдық тарихымен берік байланысы бар барлық ортағасырда аса кең және әйгілі хандық құрушылар.

Аталған тақырыпқа деген терең қызығушылық, байқауымызша, Қ. Закирьяновтың қазақ наймандарынан шыққандығы да шартталған. Бастапқы кезде Шыңғыс ханның басты қарсыласары ретінде шыққан ұлы ортаазиялық көшпенді наймандар, кейінірек хан құрған жасақтың маңызды стратегиялық элементіне айналды.

Шыңғыс хан империясының білімдегі тек-тайпалық одақтың осы өкілдерінің үлкен рөлі туралы ежелгі далалық тарихы айғақтайды. Оған сәйкес, Жәр әлемді Дүрілдеткішті жерлеу кезінде оның ақ боз атының оң жағында наймандардың құла аты тұрды. Наймандар мұсылмандық Шығыстағы құдыретті Ілхандар мемлекетінің Шыңғыс хандықтармен құрылған басты әскери тірегі және Алтын Орда құрамына кіретін көне орыс кназдықтарын жаулап алуға қатысқан көшпенділердің төртрулық топтарының бірі болған.

Монғолия өз аймағына ғылыми экспедиция жасауымен және жетекші монғол тарихшыларымен кездесуімен байланысты Шыңғыс хан "моңғолдарына" этникалық тиістілігі туралы мәселенің Қ. Закирьяновтың көп жылдық зерттемесі бұл оқымыстының ортағасырдағы ұлы империяны құрушылардың түркітұқымдастардан шыққаны жайлы берік шешімге келтірді. Қ.Қ. Закирьяновтың зерттеу бағытындағы қызметін маңыздым ойындатуы оны Ұлан-Батордағы Халықаралық Шыңғыс хан академиясының академигі етіп сайлауы болды.

Қ. Закирьяновтың өзге қызмет бағыты - ол белгілі тәңірге табынушылық секілді дала тұрандықтарының ежелгі монотеистік сенімдерінің тарихи орны жайлы сұрақты зерттеу. Мұрад Аджимен және де басқа зерттеушілермен қатар, Қ. Закирьянов көлемді дәлелді базасына сүйене отырып, мынандай қорытындыға келді: сол тәңірге табынушылықтың өзі ең ежелгі сахаралық түпдерек, немесе иудаизм, христиандық және ислам секілді таяу шығыстан шыққан ірі діндердің бастапқы тарихи-мәдени ядросы болды.

Профессор Қ.Закирьяновтың гуманитарлық білімдер аясындағы аса маңызды зерттеу қызметінің нәтижесі ретінде оның Қазақстан мен Ресейден шыққан өз пікірлестерінің, әлі де болса, саны аз тобымен ежелгі және ортағасырлық уақытта континенттегі дамудың басты заңдылықтарын түсіне алды. Аталған процесстегі біздің ата-бабаларымыздың іргелі, өзекті рөлі туралы нәтиже өз ғылыми-тарихи маңыздылығы бойынша негізін қалайды...

**Жұмажан Байжумин**
**Тарихшы, «История рождения, жизни и смерти пастуха Авеля. Арийский лексикон» кітабының авторы.**

Тек «қарақшылық үшін» өмір сүретін және мүлдем өркениеттілік бастамалардан хабары аз далалық халық «дүрілдетуші» мен «қиратушы» рөлін ойнауға тура келген жерлерде жақын уақытқа дейін жалпыға ортақ тарихқа еуропаорталықтық көзқарас басым болды. Олардың өз жазба мәдениеті, философиясы және мүлдем бір нәрсені тудыруға қабілеттіліктері болмаған деп саналған. Өкінішке орай, бұндай көзқарасты ұстаушылар өз арамызда да бар. Дегенмен, соңғы археологиялық табыстар мен тарихи ашылымдар отандық тарихи ғылымда осындай тұжырымдаманың мүлдем қателік екенін сендіруге мүмкіндік береді. Голландық ғалымдар Шілікті қорғанынан шыққан сақ хандары геномалық сараптамасынан жасалған нәтижелер негізінде алтайлық сақтар Еуразияның көптеген халықтарының ата-бабалары деп тұжырымдайды.

Бұл тұрғыдан алғанда, Қайрат Закирьяновтың ұсынып отырған «Көкжал белгісімен. Түркі рапсодиясы» еңбегі орынды қызығушылық туғызады. әр алуан бастауларға сүйене отырып автор скифтардың, ғұндардың және түркілердің жетекші рөлін ерекше атап өтіп, еуразиялық кеңістіктегі этникалық, әлеуметтік-саяси түсіндірмелер мен бағаларын, өзінің тарихиқа деген көрінісін ұсынады.

Ұлы дала тарихы тек халық аңыздары, ертегілері және Шығыс пен Батыстың ежелгі жазба бастауларының қаһармандық дәстүрімен ғана бай емес. Ең әуелі бұл мәдениет, дүниетаным, философияның араласу тарихы. Орта Азияның далалық тайпалары үш мыңжылдық бойына Батысқа және Шығысқа үздіксіз жүріп отырды. Автордың өзіне ғана тән қозғалып отырған тарихи үдеріске деген көзқарасы оқырманды жоғарыда аталған тарихи ғылымдағы бекітіліп қалған тұжырымдама жайлы ойлануға еріксіз итермелейді. Атты қолға үйретуден және оны ерлеуді үйрену кезінен бастап Ұлы Дала барлық іргелес мемлекеттер мен халықтарға үлкен әсерін тигізді және бүкіл Еуразияның мәдени және этникалық тарихында өшпес ізін қалдырды. Салт атпен жүруді меңгерудің арқасында еуразиялық дала жайылымдары қысқа мерзімде өзінің құндылықты нысанасын барлық жерде құрған Адаммен игерілген.

Көне дүниеде алғашқы салт атты көшпенділер ежелгі грек мифологиясында Кентавр бейнесінде суреттелген. Мүмкін, бұл бейне ең алғашқы салт атты көшпенділерді көргендегі қатты толғаныстан туған болуы керек. Кентаврлар көне мифологияның болашақ хандары мен батырларының білім берушілері мен тәлімгерлері болғаны өте қызықты жайт. Осы кезден бастап, алғашқы грек сурет өнерінде күйіктаста сақ-скифтік жауынгерлерінің бейнесі, ал көне бастауларда скиф философтары мен патшалары, олардың өмір салты мен дәстүрлері жайлы мәліметтер пайда бола бастады. Күнделікті өмірдің далалық белгілері және көшпенділердің әскери ісі көрші халықтарға еліктеп, үлгі ала бастайды, мысалы, дөңгелек үстелдің пайда болуы – Артур патша сарайының кезіндегі «далалық демократияның» нышаны. Сол үшін де, олардың көбінде дәстүрлері мен әдет-ғұрпында исламға дейінгі сенім-нанымның далалық жұрнағының қалуы кездейсоқтық емес. Мұндай түйінді Қайрат Қайруллинович дәлелсіз айтпайды. Автор жазба бастауларынан өз пайымдауларын растайтын салмақты дәлелдер, топонимикалар келтіріп, логикалық қорытындылармен нығайтады.

Түркілердің, сақтардың және ғұндардың дала тайпалары үздік әскери істерінен басқа, әлемге өз дүниетанымын – Тәңірге бас иушілікті, монотеизм идеясын – біртұтас жаратушыны берді! Далалық тайпалардың тіршілік ету әрекеті үлкен радиуста таралып келеді, кейде бірнеше мың километрге жетеді. Сахаралық құрғақ аймақтар, орманды массивтер, биік тау алқабындағы көгалдар мен ойпаттар...

осының барлығы Тәңір деген жалғыз қасиетті көк астында жалғыз шаруашылық кезеңде кездеседі. Кітаптың тағы бір есте қаларлық бөлігі – ода бұрында дала тайпаларымен түйіскен халықтар мен мемлекеттер туралы ой анық бақыланып отырады, өз дамуында келесі жоғарырақ даму дәрежесіне ауыса бастайды. Көпшілікке бұл тұжырымдар тарихтың «мифологизациясы» болып көрінуі мүмкін. Дегенмен де, ұқыпты сараптау кезінде тура ғұндар келгеннен бастап құл иеленушілік құрылым құлағанын және Еуропада жаңа феодалды қатынастар мен мемлекеттер пайда бола бастағанын байқауға болады. Рейн мен Балқанның арғы бетіндегі және оңтүстік орыс далаларындағы славяндық тайпалардың қызметтен түсуі басталады. Алтын Ордадан кейін біз бытыраңқы феодалды емес, бірыңғай орталықтандырылған Русьті көреміз. Бүгінгі күні әлем тарихы сақтарсыз, ғұндар мен түркілерсіз толық болмас еді деген түсінік пайда болады. Далалық тайпалардың рөлі мен мәні туралы ежелгі қолжазбалар және шежірелер парақтарына түскен сөздер мен ойлар айтады. Уильям Черчиль айтқандай: «Тарих жазылып жатқанда, ақиқат әйтеуір бір тармақ арасында қалып отырады». Бұл тұрғыда, Қайрат Қайруллинович сол ақиқатты тауып және қайтаруға, оған ғалым тарихшылардың және де, тарихтағы «ақ дақтарды» жоюмен айналысатындардың назарын аударуға тырысады.

«Көкжал белгісімен. Түркі рапсодиясы» кітабындағы Қайрат Закирьяновтың тұжырымдамалары дұрыс мағынаға қарсы кследі қана қоймай, сонымен қатар тарих ғылымы үшін тарихқа жаңа көзқарас орнықтырып және «өткен буын ескерткішін» береді отырып, нақты қызығушылықты тудырады.

Әлдекімдерге автор дала тайпалары мен мемлекеттердің рөлін асыралайтындай болып көрінуі, тексерілмеген мәліметтермен асыра сілтеді және тағы да басқадай ойлар тууы мүмкін. Алайда, оны қатал кінараттауға асықпаңыздар. Осы кезде Англия, Германия және басқа да еуропалық елдердің тарихшылары өз назарларын Шығысқа бұрып, Қазақстан мен Орта Азия ежелгі тарихына көп көңіл аудара бастады. Бұл кездейсоқтық емес, олар сопау көне кездегі Ұлы дала жазығында өз ата-бабаларынан қалған мұраларды тапқысы келетін болуы керек.

Кітап тек тарихшыларға ғана емес, сонымен қатар, ең алдымен әділетті тарихты қалпына келтірумен айналысатындарға арналған.

**Жәкен Таймағамбетов**
**әл-Фараби атындағы Қазақ Ұлттың университетінің**
**тарих, археология және этнология факультетінің деканы,**
**Шоқан Уәлиханов атындағы сыйлықтың иегері,**
**Тарих ғылымдарының докторы, профессор**

## Birds of Uzbekistan

### by Boris Nedosekov

This is a superb collection of full-colour photographs provided by the members of Uzbekistan Society for the Protection of Birds, with text in both English and in Russian.

Since the collapse of the Soviet Union and Uzbekistan's declaration of independence in 1991, unlike in other Central Asian states there have been no such illustrated books published about the birds of this country's rich and diverse wildlife.

There are more than 500 species of birds in Uzbekistan, with 32 included in the International Red Data Book. After independence, Uzbekistan began to attract the attention of foreign tourist companies, and particularly those specialising in ornithological tourism and birdwatching. Birds of Uzbekistan is therefore a much-needed and tim ely portrait of this element of the country's remarkable wildlife.

## When The Edelweiss Flowers Flourish

### by Begenas Sartov

The author frequently explored the tension between Soviet technological progress, the political and social climates and Kyrgyz traditions in his work, and When The Edelweiss Flowers Flourish depicts an uneasy relationship between two worlds. Using the science fiction genre, the novel's main character is Melis – derived from Marx, Engels, Lenin and Stalin – who has his counter in Silem, an alien being sent to earth to remove Edelweiss plants to help save his own planet from a deadly virus.

The essence of the story was attributed by Begenas to a childhood experience when a village elder helped him recuperate from breaking his arm, using a herbal mixture of seven grasses. These grasses – Edelweiss, Ermen, Ak kadol, Shyraajyn, Oo koroshyn, Kokomirin and Shybak – are still found in the high Kyrgyz mountains today, and are still widely used for their medicinal properties.

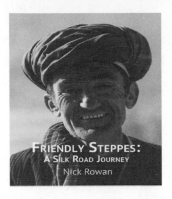

**Friendly Steppes: A Silk Road Journey**

**by Nick Rowan**

This is the chronicle of an extraordinary adventure that led Nick Rowan to some of the world's most incredible and hidden places. Intertwined with the magic of 2,000 years of Silk Road history, he recounts his experiences coupled with a remarkable realisation of just what an impact this trade route has had on our society as we know it today. Containing colourful stories, beautiful photography and vivid characters, and wrapped in the local myths and legends told by the people Nick met and who live along the route, this is both a travelogue and an education of a part of the world that has remained hidden for hundreds of years.

Friendly Steppes: A Silk Road Journey reveals just how rich the region was both culturally and economically and uncovers countless new friends as Nick travels from Venice through Eastern Europe, Iran, the ancient and modern Central Asia of places like Samarkand, Bishkek and Turkmenbashi, and on to China, along the Silk Roads of today.

**Chants of the Dark Fire**

**by Zhulduz Baizakova**

The author, a former press attaché at the Embassy of the Republic of Kazakhstan, in London, offers with Chants of the Dark Fire a fascinating portrait of, and insight into, life both past and present within this largest of all of the Central Asian states.

The short but colourful career of her grandfather Isa, who dedicated his entire existence to art, provides an ideal tableau for an infectious enthusiasm for the culture of Kazakhstan and Central Asia as a whole.

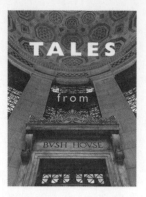

### Igor Savitsky:
### Artist, Collector, Museum Founder

### by Marinika Babanazarova

This is the biography of the astonishing life of Igor Savitsky, who rescued thousands of dissident artworks from Stalinist repression that survive today in the Karakalpakstan Museum, in Nukus, Uzbekistan; a collection of Soviet avant-garde art rivalled only by the Russian Museum in St Petersburg.

The remoteness of the area, and its proximity to chemical weapons testing sites nearby, helped Savitsky keep his collection secret while, tragically, some of the Russian and Uzbek artists involved were either imprisoned or executed.

The author is the director of the museum, a post she has held since the death in 1984 of Savitsky, who was a regular visitor to her family. Savitsky's life is vividly narrated through detail from correspondence, official records, and family documents that have become available only recently, as well as the recollections of so many of those who knew this remarkable man.

### Tales from Bush House

### collected and edited by Hamid Ismailov, Marie Gillespie, and Anna Aslanyan

This is a collection of short narratives about working lives, mostly real and comic, sometimes poignant or apocryphal, gifted to the editors by former and current BBC World Service employees. They are tales from inside Bush House - the home of the World Service since 1941 - escaping through its marble-clad walls at a time when its staff members began their departure to new premises in Portland Place.

In its collective authorship, it documents the cultural diversity of the World Service, showing how the extraordinary people who worked there, and the magnificent, chaotic building they shared, shaped one another. We use the word tales to signal that this is a book that mixes genres - ethnographic and folkloric stories, oral histories and jokes. Recounting tales involves an intricate relationship between talking and telling - as in the working life of a broadcaster.